Java™:
A Beginner's Guide

Fourth Edition

Java™:
A Beginner's Guide

Fourth Edition

Herbert Schildt

New York Chicago San Francisco
Lisbon London Madrid Mexico City
Milan New Delhi San Juan
Seoul Singapore Sydney Toronto

McGraw-Hill books are available at special quantity discounts to use as premiums and sales promotions, or for use in corporate training programs. For more information, please write to the Director of Special Sales, Professional Publishing, McGraw-Hill, Two Penn Plaza, New York, NY 10121-2298. Or contact your local bookstore.

Java™: A Beginner's Guide, Fourth Edition

7 8 9 0 DOC DOC 1 5 4 3 2 1

ISBN-13: 978-0-07-226384-8
ISBN-10:   0-07-226384-9

Sponsoring Editor   Wendy Rinaldi
Editorial Supervisor   Patty Mon
Project Editor   Laura Stone
Acquisitions Coordinator   Mandy Canales
Copy Editor   Robert Campbell
Proofreader   Madhu Prasher
Indexer   Sheryl Schildt
Production Supervisor   James Kussow
Composition   Apollo Publishing Services
Art Director, Cover   Jeff Weeks
Cover Designer   Jeff Weeks

About the Author

Top-selling author **Herbert Schildt** is an authority on the C, C++, Java, and C# languages, and is a master Windows programmer. His programming books have sold more that 3.5 million copies worldwide and have been translated into all major foreign languages. He is the author of numerous bestsellers, including *Java: The Complete Reference, Swing: A Beginner's Guide, C++: The Complete Reference*, and *C#: The Complete Reference*, and the co-author of *The Art of Java*. Schildt holds both graduate and undergraduate degrees from the University of Illinois. He can be reached at his consulting office at (217) 586-4683. His Web site is **www.HerbSchildt.com**.

Contents at a Glance

Contents

Preface

Java is the preeminent language of the Internet. Moreover, it is the universal language of Web programmers around the world. To be a professional Web developer today implies proficiency in Java. Therefore, if Internet-based programming is in your future, you have chosen the right language to learn—and this book will help you learn it.

The purpose of this book is to teach you the fundamentals of Java programming. It uses a step-by-step approach complete with numerous examples, self-tests, and projects. It assumes no previous programming experience. The book starts with the basics, such as how to compile and run a Java program. It then discusses the keywords, features, and constructs that form the core of the Java language. You'll also find coverage of some of Java's most advanced features, including multithreaded programming and generics. An introduction to Swing concludes the book. By the time you finish, you will have a firm grasp of the essentials of Java programming.

It is important to state at the outset that this book is just a starting point. Java is more than just the elements that define the language. Java also includes extensive libraries and tools that aid in the development of programs. To be a top-notch Java programmer implies mastery of these areas, too. After completing this book, you will have the knowledge to pursue any and all other aspects of Java.

The Evolution of Java

Only a few languages have fundamentally reshaped the very essence of programming. In this elite group, one stands out because its impact was both rapid and widespread. This language is, of course, Java. It is not an overstatement to say that the original release of Java 1.0 in 1995 by

Sun Microsystems, Inc. caused a revolution in programming. This revolution radically transformed the Web into a highly interactive environment. In the process, Java set a new standard in computer language design.

Over the years, Java continued to grow, evolve, and otherwise redefine itself. Unlike many other languages, which are slow to incorporate new features, Java has continually been at the forefront of computer language design. One reason for this is the culture of innovation and change that came to surround Java. As a result, Java has gone through several upgrades—some relatively small, others more significant.

The first major update to Java was version 1.1. The features added by Java 1.1 were more substantial than the increase in the minor revision number would have you think. For example, Java 1.1 added many new library elements, redefined the way events are handled, and reconfigured many features of the original 1.0 library.

The next major release of Java was Java 2, where the 2 indicates second generation. The creation of Java 2 was a watershed event, marking the beginning of Java's "modern age." The first release of Java 2 carried the version number 1.2. It may seem odd that the first release of Java 2 used the 1.2 version number. The reason is that it originally referred to the internal version number of the Java libraries, but then was generalized to refer to the entire release itself. With Java 2, Sun repackaged the Java product as J2SE (Java 2 Platform Standard Edition), and the version numbers began to be applied to that product.

The next upgrade of Java was J2SE 1.3. This version of Java was the first major upgrade to the original Java 2 release. For the most part it added to existing functionality and tightened up the development environment. The release of J2SE 1.4 further enhanced Java. This release contained several important new features, including chained exceptions, channel-based I/O, and the **assert** keyword.

The next release of Java was J2SE 5, and it created the second Java revolution. Unlike most of the previous Java upgrades, which offered important, but incremental improvements, J2SE 5 fundamentally expanded the scope, power, and range of the language. To give you an idea of the magnitude of the changes caused by J2SE 5, here is a list of its major new features that are discussed in this book:

- Generics
- Autoboxing/unboxing
- Enumerations
- The enhanced, "for-each" style **for** loop
- Variable-length arguments (varargs)
- Static import
- Annotations

This is not a list of minor tweaks or incremental upgrades. Each item in the list represents a significant addition to the Java language. Some, such as generics, the enhanced **for**, and varargs, introduce new syntax elements. Others, such as autoboxing and auto-unboxing, alter the semantics of the language. Annotations add an entirely new dimension to programming.

The importance of these new features is reflected in the use of the version number "5." The next version number for Java would normally have been 1.5. However, the new features were so significant that a shift from 1.4 to 1.5 just didn't seem to express the magnitude of the change. Instead, Sun elected to increase the version number to 5 as a way of emphasizing that a major event was taking place. Thus, it was named J2SE 5, and the developer's kit was called JDK 5. However, in order to maintain consistency, Sun decided to use 1.5 as its *internal version* number, which is also referred to as the *developer version* number. The "5" in J2SE 5 is called the *product version* number

The newest release of Java is called Java SE 6, and that is the version of Java described in this book. With the release of Java SE 6, Sun once again decided to change the name of the Java platform. First, notice that the "2" has been dropped. Thus, the platform now has the name *Java SE* and the official product name is *Java Platform, Standard Edition 6*. As with J2SE 5, the 6 in Java SE 6 is the product version number. The internal, developer version number is 1.6.

Java SE 6 builds on the base of J2SE 5, adding incremental improvements. Java SE 6 adds no major features to the Java language proper, but does enhance the API libraries, adds several new packages, and offers improvements to the runtime. In general, the release of Java SE 6 serves to further solidify the advances made by J2SE 5.

How This Book Is Organized

This book presents an evenly paced tutorial in which each section builds upon the previous one. It contains 15 modules, each discussing an aspect of Java. This book is unique because it includes several special elements that reinforce what you are learning.

Critical Skills

Each module begins with a set of critical skills that you will be learning. The location of each skill within the module is indicated.

Mastery Check

Each module concludes with a Mastery Check, a self-test that lets you test your knowledge. The answers are in Appendix A.

Progress Checks

At the end of each major section, Progress Checks are presented that test your understanding of the key points of the preceding section. The answers to these questions are at the bottom of the page.

Ask the Expert

Sprinkled throughout the book are special "Ask the Expert" boxes. These contain additional information or interesting commentary about a topic. They use a Question/Answer format.

Projects

Each Module contains one or more projects that show you how to apply what you are learning. These are real-world examples that you can use as starting points for your own programs.

No Previous Programming Experience Required

This book assumes no previous programming experience. Thus, if you have never programmed before, you can use this book. If you do have some previous programming experience, you will be able to advance a bit quicker. Keep in mind, however, that Java differs in several key ways from other popular computer languages. It is important not to jump to conclusions. Thus, even for the experienced programmer, a careful reading is advised.

Required Software

To compile and run all of the programs in this book you will need the latest Java Developers Kit (JDK) from Sun, which at the time of this writing is JDK 6. This is the JDK for Java SE 6. Instructions for obtaining the Java JDK are given in Module 1.

If you are using an earlier version of Java, such as Java 1.4, you will still be able to use this book, but you won't be able to compile and run the programs that use Java's newer features.

Don't Forget: Code on the Web

Remember, the source code for all of the examples and projects in this book is available free of charge on the Web at **www.osborne.com**.

For Further Study

Java: A Beginner's Guide is your gateway to the Herb Schildt series of programming books. Here are some others that you will find of interest.

To learn more about Java programming, we recommend the following:

Java: The Complete Reference

The Art of Java

Swing: A Beginner's Guide

To learn about C++, you will find these books especially helpful.

C++: The Complete Reference

C++ From the Ground Up

STL Programming From the Ground Up

The Art of C++

To learn about C# we suggest the following Schildt books:

C#: A Beginner's Guide

C#: The Complete Reference

If you want to learn about the C language, then the following title will be of interest.

C: The Complete Reference

When you need solid answers, fast, turn to Herbert Schildt, the recognized authority on programming.

Module 1

Java Fundamentals

The rise of the Internet and the World Wide Web fundamentally reshaped computing. Prior to the Web, the cyber landscape was dominated by stand-alone PCs. Today, nearly all PCs are connected to the Internet. The Internet, itself, was transformed—originally offering a convenient way to share files and information, today it is a vast, distributed computing universe. With these changes came a new way to program: Java.

Java is the preeminent language of the Internet, but it is more than that. Java revolutionized programming, changing the way that we think about both the form and the function of a program. To be a professional programmer today implies the ability to program in Java—it is that important. In the course of this book, you will learn the skills needed to master it.

The purpose of this module is to introduce you to Java, including its history, its design philosophy, and several of its most important features. By far, the hardest thing about learning a programming language is the fact that no element exists in isolation. Instead, the components of the language work in conjunction with each other. This interrelatedness is especially pronounced in Java. In fact, it is difficult to discuss one aspect of Java without involving others. To help overcome this problem, this module provides a brief overview of several Java features, including the general form of a Java program, some basic control structures, and operators. It does not go into too many details but, rather, concentrates on the general concepts common to any Java program.

CRITICAL SKILL
1.1 The Origins of Java

Computer language innovation is driven forward by two factors: improvements in the art of programming and changes in the computing environment. Java is no exception. Building upon the rich legacy inherited from C and C++, Java adds refinements and features that reflect the current state of the art in programming. Responding to the rise of the online environment, Java offers features that streamline programming for a highly distributed architecture.

Java was conceived by James Gosling, Patrick Naughton, Chris Warth, Ed Frank, and Mike Sheridan at Sun Microsystems in 1991. This language was initially called "Oak" but was renamed "Java" in 1995. Somewhat surprisingly, the original impetus for Java was not the Internet! Instead, the primary motivation was the need for a platform-independent language that could be used to create software to be embedded in various consumer electronic devices, such as toasters, microwave ovens, and remote controls. As you can probably guess, many different types of CPUs are used as controllers. The trouble was that (at that time) most computer languages were designed to be compiled for a specific target. For example, consider C++.

Although it was possible to compile a C++ program for just about any type of CPU, to do so required a full C++ compiler targeted for that CPU. The problem, however, is that compilers are expensive and time-consuming to create. In an attempt to find a better solution, Gosling and others worked on a portable, cross-platform language that could produce code that would run on a variety of CPUs under differing environments. This effort ultimately led to the creation of Java.

About the time that the details of Java were being worked out, a second, and ultimately more important, factor emerged that would play a crucial role in the future of Java. This second force was, of course, the World Wide Web. Had the Web not taken shape at about the same time that Java was being implemented, Java might have remained a useful but obscure language for programming consumer electronics. However, with the emergence of the Web, Java was propelled to the forefront of computer language design, because the Web, too, demanded portable programs.

Most programmers learn early in their careers that portable programs are as elusive as they are desirable. While the quest for a way to create efficient, portable (platform-independent) programs is nearly as old as the discipline of programming itself, it had taken a back seat to other, more pressing problems. However, with the advent of the Internet and the Web, the old problem of portability returned with a vengeance. After all, the Internet consists of a diverse, distributed universe populated with many types of computers, operating systems, and CPUs. What was once an irritating but a low-priority problem had become a high-profile necessity.

By 1993 it became obvious to members of the Java design team that the problems of portability frequently encountered when creating code for embedded controllers are also found when attempting to create code for the Internet. This realization caused the focus of Java to switch from consumer electronics to Internet programming. So, while it was the desire for an architecture-neutral programming language that provided the initial spark, it was the Internet that ultimately led to Java's large-scale success.

How Java Relates to C and C++

Java is directly related to both C and C++. Java inherits its syntax from C. Its object model is adapted from C++. Java's relationship with C and C++ is important for several reasons. First, many programmers are familiar with the C/C++ syntax. This makes it easy for a C/C++ programmer to learn Java and, conversely, for a Java programmer to learn C/C++.

Second, Java's designers did not "reinvent the wheel." Instead, they further refined an already highly successful programming paradigm. The modern age of programming began with C. It moved to C++, and now to Java. By inheriting and building upon that rich heritage, Java provides a powerful, logically consistent programming environment that takes the best of the past and adds new features required by the online environment. Perhaps most important, because of their similarities, C, C++, and Java define a common, conceptual framework for the professional programmer. Programmers do not face major rifts when switching from one language to another.

One of the central design philosophies of both C and C++ is that the programmer is in charge! Java also inherits this philosophy. Except for those constraints imposed by the Internet environment, Java gives you, the programmer, full control. If you program well, your programs reflect it. If you program poorly, your programs reflect that, too. Put differently, Java is not a language with training wheels. It is a language for professional programmers.

Java has one other attribute in common with C and C++: it was designed, tested, and refined by real, working programmers. It is a language grounded in the needs and experiences of the people who devised it. There is no better way to produce a top-flight professional programming language.

Because of the similarities between Java and C++, especially their support for object-oriented programming, it is tempting to think of Java as simply the "Internet version of C++." However, to do so would be a mistake. Java has significant practical and philosophical differences. Although Java was influenced by C++, it is not an enhanced version of C++. For example, it is neither upwardly nor downwardly compatible with C++. Of course, the similarities with C++ are significant, and if you are a C++ programmer, you will feel right at home with Java. Another point: Java was not designed to replace C++. Java was designed to solve a certain set of problems. C++ was designed to solve a different set of problems. Both will coexist for many years to come.

How Java Relates to C#

Recently a new language called C# has come on the scene. Created by Microsoft to support its .NET Framework, C# is closely reated to Java. In fact, many of C#'s features were directly adapted from Java. Both Java and C# share the same general C++-style syntax, support distributed programming, and utilize the same object model. There are, of course, differences between Java and C#, but the overall "look and feel" of these languages is very similar. This means that if you already know C#, then learning Java will be especially easy. Conversely, if C# is in your future, then your knowledge of Java will come in handy.

Given the similarity between Java and C#, one might naturally ask, "Will C# replace Java?" The answer is No. Java and C# are optimized for two different types of computing environments. Just as C++ and Java will co-exist for a long time to come, so will C# and Java.

Progress Check

1. Java is useful for the Internet because it can produce _____ programs.

2. Java is the direct descendent of what languages?

---

1. portable
2. C and C++.

CRITICAL SKILL
 1.2 Java's Contribution to the Internet

The Internet helped catapult Java to the forefront of programming, and Java, in turn, had a profound effect on the Internet. In addition to simplifying web programming in general, Java innovated a new type of networked program called the *applet* that changed the way the online world thought about content. Java also addressed some of the thorniest issues associated with the Internet: portability and security. Let's look more closely at each of these.

Java Applets

An applet is a special kind of Java program that is designed to be transmitted over the Internet and automatically executed by a Java-compatible web browser. Furthermore, an applet is downloaded on demand, without further interaction with the user. If the user clicks on a link that contains an applet, the applet will be automatically downloaded and run in the browser. Applets are intended to be small programs. They are typically used to display data provided by the server, handle user input, or provide simple functions, such as a loan calculator, that execute locally, rather than on the server. In essence, the applet allows some functionality to be moved from the server to the client.

The creation of the applet changed Internet programming because it expanded the universe of objects that can move about freely in cyberspace. In general, there are two very broad categories of objects that are transmitted between the server and the client: passive information and dynamic, active programs. For example, when you read your e-mail, you are viewing passive data. Even when you download a program, the program's code is still only passive data until you execute it. By contrast, the applet is a dynamic, self-executing program. Such a program is an active agent on the client computer, yet it is initiated by the server.

As desirable as dynamic, networked programs are, they also present serious problems in the areas of security and portability. Obviously, a program that downloads and executes automatically on the client computer must be prevented from doing harm. It must also be able to run in a variety of different environments and under different operating systems. As you will see, Java solved these problems in an effective and elegant way. Let's look a bit more closely at each.

Security

As you are likely aware, every time that you download a "normal" program, you are taking a risk because the code you are downloading might contain a virus, Trojan horse, or other harmful code. At the core of the problem is the fact that malicious code can cause its damage because it has gained unauthorized access to system resources. For example, a virus program might gather private information, such as credit card numbers, bank account balances, and passwords, by searching the contents of your computer's local file system. In order for Java to enable applets to be safely downloaded and executed on the client computer, it was necessary to prevent an applet from launching such an attack.

Java achieved this protection by confining an applet to the Java execution environment and not allowing it access to other parts of the computer. (You will see how this is accomplished shortly.) The ability to download applets with confidence that no harm will be done and that no security will be breached is considered by many to be the single most innovative aspect of Java.

Portability

Portability is a major aspect of the Internet because there are many different types of computers and operating systems connected to it. If a Java program was to be run on virtually any computer connected to the Internet, there needed to be some way to enable that program to execute on different systems. For example, in the case of an applet, the same applet must be able to be downloaded and executed by the wide variety of different CPUs, operating systems, and browsers connected to the Internet. It is not practical to have different versions of the applet for different computers. The *same* code must work in *all* computers. Therefore, some means of generating portable executable code was needed. As you will soon see, the same mechanism that helps ensure security also helps create portability.

CRITICAL SKILL
1.3 Java's Magic: The Bytecode

The key that allows Java to solve both the security and the portability problems just described is that the output of a Java compiler is not executable code. Rather, it is bytecode. *Bytecode* is a highly optimized set of instructions designed to be executed by the Java run-time system, which is called the *Java Virtual Machine (JVM)*. In essence, the original JVM was designed as an *interpreter for bytecode.* This may come as a bit of a surprise because many modern languages are designed to be compiled into executable code due to performance concerns. However, the fact that a Java program is executed by the JVM helps solve the major problems associated with web-based programs. Here is why.

Translating a Java program into bytecode makes it much easier to run a program in a wide variety of environments because only the JVM needs to be implemented for each platform. Once the run-time package exists for a given system, any Java program can run on it. Remember, although the details of the JVM will differ from platform to platform, all understand the same Java bytecode. If a Java program were compiled to native code, then different versions of the same program would have to exist for each type of CPU connected to the Internet. This is, of course, not a feasible solution. Thus, the execution of bytecode by the JVM is the easiest way to create truly portable programs.

The fact that a Java program is executed by the JVM also helps to make it secure. Because the JVM is in control, it can contain the program and prevent it from generating side effects outside of the system. Safety is also enhanced by certain restrictions that exist in the Java language.

When a program is interpreted, it generally runs slower than the same program would run if compiled to executable code. However, with Java, the differential between the two is not so

Ask the Expert

Q: I have heard about a special type of Java program called a servlet. What is it?

A: A *servlet* is a small program that executes on the server. Just as applets dynamically extend the functionality of a web browser, servlets dynamically extend the functionality of a web server. It is helpful to understand that as useful as applets can be, they are just one half of the client/server equation. Not long after the initial release of Java it became obvious that Java would also be useful on the server side. The result was the servlet. Thus, with the advent of the servlet, Java spanned both sides of the client/server connection. Although the creation of servlets is beyond the scope of this beginner's guide, they are something that you will want to study further as you advance in Java programming. (Coverage of servlets can be found in my book *Java: The Complete Reference*, published by McGraw-Hill/Osborne.)

great. Because bytecode has been highly optimized, the use of bytecode enables the JVM to execute programs much faster than you might expect.

Although Java was designed as an interpreted language, there is nothing about Java that prevents on-the-fly compilation of bytecode into native code in order to boost performance. For this reason, Sun began supplying its HotSpot technology not long after Java's initial release. HotSpot provides a just-in-time (JIT) compiler for bytecode. When a JIT compiler is part of the JVM, selected portions of bytecode are compiled into executable code in real time on a piece-by-piece, demand basis. It is important to understand that it is not practical to compile an entire Java program into executable code all at once because Java performs various run-time checks that can be done only at run time. Instead, a JIT compiler compiles code as it is needed, during execution. Furthermore, not all sequences of bytecode are compiled—only those that will benefit from compilation. The remaining code is simply interpreted. However, the just-in-time approach still yields a significant performance boost. Even when dynamic compilation is applied to bytecode, the portability and safety features still apply because the JVM is still in charge of the execution environment.

CRITICAL SKILL
1.4 The Java Buzzwords

No overview of Java is complete without a look at the Java buzzwords. Although the fundamental forces that necessitated the invention of Java are portability and security, other factors played an important role in molding the final form of the language. The key considerations were summed up by the Java design team in the following list of buzzwords.

Simple	Java has a concise, cohesive set of features that makes it easy to learn and use.
Secure	Java provides a secure means of creating Internet applications.
Portable	Java programs can execute in any environment for which there is a Java run-time system.
Object-oriented	Java embodies the modern, object-oriented programming philosophy.
Robust	Java encourages error-free programming by being strictly typed and performing run-time checks.
Multithreaded	Java provides integrated support for multithreaded programming.
Architecture-neutral	Java is not tied to a specific machine or operating system architecture.
Interpreted	Java supports cross-platform code through the use of Java bytecode.
High performance	The Java bytecode is highly optimized for speed of execution.
Distributed	Java was designed with the distributed environment of the Internet in mind.
Dynamic	Java programs carry with them substantial amounts of run-time type information that is used to verify and resolve accesses to objects at run time.

Progress Check

1. What is an applet?

2. What is Java bytecode?

3. The use of bytecode helps solve what two Internet programming problems?

Ask the Expert

Q: To address the issues of portability and security, why was it necessary to create a new computer language such as Java; couldn't a language like C++ be adapted? In other words, couldn't a C++ compiler that outputs bytecode be created?

A: While it would be possible for a C++ compiler to generate bytecode rather than executable code, C++ has features that discourage its use for the creation of Internet programs—the most important feature being C++'s support for pointers. A *pointer* is the address of some object stored in memory. Using a pointer, it would be possible to access resources outside the program itself, resulting in a security breach. Java does not support pointers, thus eliminating this problem.

1. An applet is a small program that is dynamically downloaded over the Web.

2. A highly optimized set of instructions that can be interpreted by the Java Interpreter.

3. Portability and security.

CRITICAL SKILL
1.5 Object-Oriented Programming

At the center of Java is object-oriented programming (OOP). The object-oriented methodology is inseparable from Java, and all Java programs are, to at least some extent, object-oriented. Because of OOP's importance to Java, it is useful to understand OOP's basic principles before you write even a simple Java program.

OOP is a powerful way to approach the job of programming. Programming methodologies have changed dramatically since the invention of the computer, primarily to accommodate the increasing complexity of programs. For example, when computers were first invented, programming was done by toggling in the binary machine instructions using the computer's front panel. As long as programs were just a few hundred instructions long, this approach worked. As programs grew, assembly language was invented so that a programmer could deal with larger, increasingly complex programs, using symbolic representations of the machine instructions. As programs continued to grow, high-level languages were introduced that gave the programmer more tools with which to handle complexity. The first widespread language was, of course, FORTRAN. Although FORTRAN was a very impressive first step, it is hardly a language that encourages clear, easy-to-understand programs.

The 1960s gave birth to structured programming. This is the method encouraged by languages such as C and Pascal. The use of structured languages made it possible to write moderately complex programs fairly easily. Structured languages are characterized by their support for stand-alone subroutines, local variables, rich control constructs, and their lack of reliance upon the GOTO. Although structured languages are a powerful tool, even they reach their limit when a project becomes too large.

Consider this: At each milestone in the development of programming, techniques and tools were created to allow the programmer to deal with increasingly greater complexity. Each step of the way, the new approach took the best elements of the previous methods and moved forward. Prior to the invention of OOP, many projects were nearing (or exceeding) the point where the structured approach no longer works. Object-oriented methods were created to help programmers break through these barriers.

Object-oriented programming took the best ideas of structured programming and combined them with several new concepts. The result was a different way of organizing a program. In the most general sense, a program can be organized in one of two ways: around its code (what is happening) or around its data (what is being affected). Using only structured programming techniques, programs are typically organized around code. This approach can be thought of as "code acting on data."

Object-oriented programs work the other way around. They are organized around data, with the key principle being "data controlling access to code." In an object-oriented language, you define the data and the routines that are permitted to act on that data. Thus, a data type defines precisely what sort of operations can be applied to that data.

To support the principles of object-oriented programming, all OOP languages, including Java, have three traits in common: encapsulation, polymorphism, and inheritance. Let's examine each.

Encapsulation

Encapsulation is a programming mechanism that binds together code and the data it manipulates, and that keeps both safe from outside interference and misuse. In an object-oriented language, code and data can be bound together in such a way that a self-contained *black box* is created. Within the box are all necessary data and code. When code and data are linked together in this fashion, an object is created. In other words, an object is the device that supports encapsulation.

Within an object, code, data, or both may be *private* to that object or *public*. Private code or data is known to and accessible by only another part of the object. That is, private code or data cannot be accessed by a piece of the program that exists outside the object. When code or data is public, other parts of your program can access it even though it is defined within an object. Typically, the public parts of an object are used to provide a controlled interface to the private elements of the object.

Java's basic unit of encapsulation is the *class*. Although the class will be examined in great detail later in this book, the following brief discussion will be helpful now. A class defines the form of an object. It specifies both the data and the code that will operate on that data. Java uses a class specification to construct *objects*. Objects are instances of a class. Thus, a class is essentially a set of plans that specify how to build an object.

The code and data that constitute a class are called *members* of the class. Specifically, the data defined by the class are referred to as *member variables* or *instance variables*. The code that operates on that data is referred to as *member methods* or just *methods*. *Method* is Java's term for a subroutine. If you are familiar with C/C++, it may help to know that what a Java programmer calls a *method,* a C/C++ programmer calls a *function.*

Polymorphism

Polymorphism (from Greek, meaning "many forms") is the quality that allows one interface to access a general class of actions. The specific action is determined by the exact nature of the situation. A simple example of polymorphism is found in the steering wheel of an automobile. The steering wheel (i.e., the interface) is the same no matter what type of actual steering mechanism is used. That is, the steering wheel works the same whether your car has manual steering, power steering, or rack-and-pinion steering. Therefore, once you know how to operate the steering wheel, you can drive any type of car.

The same principle can also apply to programming. For example, consider a stack (which is a first-in, last-out list). You might have a program that requires three different types of stacks. One stack is used for integer values, one for floating-point values, and one for characters. In this case, the algorithm that implements each stack is the same, even though the data being stored differs. In a non-object-oriented language, you would be required to create three different sets of stack routines, with each set using different names. However, because of polymorphism, in Java you can create one general set of stack routines that works for all three specific situations. This way, once you know how to use one stack, you can use them all.

More generally, the concept of polymorphism is often expressed by the phrase "one interface, multiple methods." This means that it is possible to design a generic interface to a group of related activities. Polymorphism helps reduce complexity by allowing the same interface to be used to specify a *general class of action*. It is the compiler's job to select the *specific action* (i.e., method) as it applies to each situation. You, the programmer, don't need to do this selection manually. You need only remember and utilize the general interface.

Inheritance

Inheritance is the process by which one object can acquire the properties of another object. This is important because it supports the concept of hierarchical classification. If you think about it, most knowledge is made manageable by hierarchical (i.e., top-down) classifications. For example, a Red Delicious apple is part of the classification *apple,* which in turn is part of the *fruit* class, which is under the larger class *food.* That is, the *food* class possesses certain qualities (edible, nutritious, etc.) which also, logically, apply to its subclass, *fruit.* In addition to these qualities, the *fruit* class has specific characteristics (juicy, sweet, etc.) that distinguish it from other food. The *apple* class defines those qualities specific to an apple (grows on trees, not tropical, etc.). A Red Delicious apple would, in turn, inherit all the qualities of all preceding classes, and would define only those qualities that make it unique.

Without the use of hierarchies, each object would have to explicitly define all of its characteristics. Using inheritance, an object need only define those qualities that make it unique within its class. It can inherit its general attributes from its parent. Thus, it is the inheritance mechanism that makes it possible for one object to be a specific instance of a more general case.

Progress Check

1. Name the principles of OOP.

2. What is the basic unit of encapsulation in Java?

---

1. Encapsulation, polymorphism, and inheritance.
2. The class.

Ask the Expert

Q: You state that object-oriented programming is an effective way to manage large programs. However, it seems that it might add substantial overhead to relatively small ones. Since you say that all Java programs are, to some extent, object-oriented, does this impose a penalty for smaller programs?

A: No. As you will see, for small programs, Java's object-oriented features are nearly transparent. Although it is true that Java follows a strict object model, you have wide latitude as to the degree to which you employ it. For smaller programs, their "object-orientedness" is barely perceptible. As your programs grow, you will integrate more object-oriented features effortlessly.

Obtaining the Java Development Kit

Now that the theoretical underpinning of Java has been explained, it is time to start writing Java programs. Before you can compile and run those programs, however, you must have a Java development system installed on your computer. The one used by this book is the standard JDK (Java Development Kit), which is available from Sun Microsystems. Several other Java development packages are available from other companies, but we will be using the JDK because it is available to all readers. It also constitutes the final authority on what is and isn't proper Java. At the time of this writing, the current release of the JDK is JDK 6. This is the development kit for Java SE 6, which stands for Java Platform, Standard Edition 6, and it is the version of Java described in this book. Because JDK 6 contains features that may not be supported by some earlier versions of Java, you should use JDK 6 (or later) to compile and run the programs in this book.

The JDK can be downloaded free of charge from **www.java.sun.com**. Just go to the download page and follow the instructions for the type of computer that you have. After you have installed the JDK, you will be ready to compile and run programs. The JDK supplies two primary programs. The first is **javac.exe**, which is the Java compiler. The second is **java.exe**, which is the standard Java interpreter, and is also referred to as the *application launcher*.

One other point: the JDK runs in the command prompt environment. It is not a windowed application.

CRITICAL SKILL
1.6 A First Simple Program

Let's start by compiling and running the short sample program shown here.

```
/*
   This is a simple Java program.

   Call this file Example.java.
*/
class Example {
  // A Java program begins with a call to main().
  public static void main(String args[]) {
    System.out.println("Java drives the Web.");
  }
}
```

You will follow these three steps:

1. Enter the program.

2. Compile the program.

3. Run the program.

Entering the Program

The programs shown in this book are available from Osborne's Web site: **www.osborne.com**.
However, if you want to enter the programs by hand, you are free to do so. In this case, you
must enter the program into your computer using a text editor, not a word processor. Word
processors typically store format information along with text. This format information will
confuse the Java compiler. If you are using a Windows platform, you can use WordPad or any
other programming editor that you like.

For most computer languages, the name of the file that holds the source code to a program
is arbitrary. However, this is not the case with Java. The first thing that you must learn about
Java is that *the name you give to a source file is very important*. For this example, the name of
the source file should be **Example.java**. Let's see why.

In Java, a source file is officially called a *compilation unit*. It is a text file that contains
one or more class definitions. The Java compiler requires that a source file use the **.java**
filename extension. As you can see by looking at the program, the name of the class defined
by the program is also **Example**. This is not a coincidence. In Java, all code must reside
inside a class. By convention, the name of that class should match the name of the file
that holds the program. You should also make sure that the capitalization of the filename
matches the class name. The reason for this is that Java is case sensitive. At this point, the
convention that filenames correspond to class names may seem arbitrary. However, this
convention makes it easier to maintain and organize your programs.

Compiling the Program

To compile the **Example** program, execute the compiler, **javac**, specifying the name of the source file on the command line, as shown here:

```
C:\>javac Example.java
```

The **javac** compiler creates a file called **Example.class** that contains the bytecode version of the program. Remember, bytecode is not executable code. Bytecode must be executed by a Java Virtual Machine. Thus, the output of **javac** is not code that can be directly executed.

To actually run the program, you must use the Java interpreter, **java**. To do so, pass the class name **Example** as a command-line argument, as shown here:

```
C:\>java Example
```

When the program is run, the following output is displayed:

```
Java drives the Web.
```

When Java source code is compiled, each individual class is put into its own output file named after the class and using the **.class** extension. This is why it is a good idea to give your Java source files the same name as the class they contain—the name of the source file will match the name of the **.class** file. When you execute the Java interpreter as just shown, you are actually specifying the name of the class that you want the interpreter to execute. It will automatically search for a file by that name that has the **.class** extension. If it finds the file, it will execute the code contained in the specified class.

The First Sample Program Line by Line

Although **Example.java** is quite short, it includes several key features that are common to all Java programs. Let's closely examine each part of the program.

The program begins with the following lines:

```
/*
   This is a simple Java program.

   Call this file Example.java.
*/
```

This is a *comment*. Like most other programming languages, Java lets you enter a remark into a program's source file. The contents of a comment are ignored by the compiler. Instead, a comment describes or explains the operation of the program to anyone who is reading its source code. In this case, the comment describes the program and reminds you that the source file should be called **Example.java**. Of course, in real applications, comments generally explain how some part of the program works or what a specific feature does.

Java supports three styles of comments. The one shown at the top of the program is called a *multiline comment.* This type of comment must begin with /* and end with */. Anything between these two comment symbols is ignored by the compiler. As the name suggests, a multiline comment may be several lines long.

The next line of code in the program is shown here:

```
class Example {
```

This line uses the keyword **class** to declare that a new class is being defined. As mentioned, the class is Java's basic unit of encapsulation. **Example** is the name of the class. The class definition begins with the opening curly brace ({) and ends with the closing curly brace (}). The elements between the two braces are members of the class. For the moment, don't worry too much about the details of a class except to note that in Java, all program activity occurs within one. This is one reason why all Java programs are (at least a little bit) object-oriented.

The next line in the program is the *single-line comment,* shown here:

```
// A Java program begins with a call to main().
```

This is the second type of comment supported by Java. A single-line comment begins with a // and ends at the end of the line. As a general rule, programmers use multiline comments for longer remarks and single-line comments for brief, line-by-line descriptions.

The next line of code is shown here:

```
public static void main (String args[]) {
```

This line begins the **main( )** method. As mentioned earlier, in Java, a subroutine is called a *method.* As the comment preceding it suggests, this is the line at which the program will begin executing. All Java applications begin execution by calling **main( )**. The exact meaning of each part of this line cannot be given now, since it involves a detailed understanding of several other of Java's features. However, since many of the examples in this book will use this line of code, let's take a brief look at each part now.

The **public** keyword is an *access specifier.* An access specifier determines how other parts of the program can access the members of the class. When a class member is preceded by **public**, then that member can be accessed by code outside the class in which it is declared. (The opposite of **public** is **private**, which prevents a member from being used by code defined outside of its class.) In this case, **main( )** must be declared as **public**, since it must be called by code outside of its class when the program is started. The keyword **static** allows **main( )** to be called before an object of the class has been created. This is necessary since **main( )** is called by the JVM before any objects are made. The keyword **void** simply tells the compiler that **main( )** does not return a value. As you will see, methods may also return values. If all this seems a bit confusing, don't worry. All of these concepts will be discussed in detail in subsequent modules.

As stated, **main( )** is the method called when a Java application begins. Any information that you need to pass to a method is received by variables specified within the set of parentheses that follow the name of the method. These variables are called *parameters*. If no parameters are required for a given method, you still need to include the empty parentheses. In **main( )** there is only one parameter, **String args[ ]**, which declares a parameter named **args**. This is an array of objects of type **String**. (*Arrays* are collections of similar objects.) Objects of type **String** store sequences of characters. In this case, **args** receives any command-line arguments present when the program is executed. This program does not make use of this information, but other programs shown later in this book will.

The last character on the line is the {. This signals the start of **main( )**'s body. All of the code included in a method will occur between the method's opening curly brace and its closing curly brace.

The next line of code is shown here. Notice that it occurs inside **main( )**.

```
System.out.println("Java drives the Web.");
```

This line outputs the string "Java drives the Web." followed by a new line on the screen. Output is actually accomplished by the built-in **println( )** method. In this case, **println( )** displays the string which is passed to it. As you will see, **println( )** can be used to display other types of information, too. The line begins with **System.out**. While too complicated to explain in detail at this time, briefly, **System** is a predefined class that provides access to the system, and **out** is the output stream that is connected to the console. Thus, **System.out** is an object that encapsulates console output. The fact that Java uses an object to define console output is further evidence of its object-oriented nature.

As you have probably guessed, console output (and input) is not used frequently in real-world Java programs and applets. Since most modern computing environments are windowed and graphical in nature, console I/O is used mostly for simple utility programs and for demonstration programs. Later in this book, you will learn other ways to generate output using Java, but for now, we will continue to use the console I/O methods.

Notice that the **println( )** statement ends with a semicolon. All statements in Java end with a semicolon. The reason that the other lines in the program do not end in a semicolon is that they are not, technically, statements.

The first } in the program ends **main( )**, and the last } ends the **Example** class definition.

One last point: Java is case sensitive. Forgetting this can cause you serious problems. For example, if you accidentally type **Main** instead of **main**, or **PrintLn** instead of **println**, the preceding program will be incorrect. Furthermore, although the Java compiler *will* compile classes that do not contain a **main( )** method, it has no way to execute them. So, if you had mistyped **main**, the compiler would still compile your program. However, the Java interpreter would report an error because it would be unable to find the **main( )** method.

Progress Check

   1. Where does a Java program begin execution?

   2. What does **System.out.println( )** do?

   3. What is the name of the Java compiler? Of the Java interpreter?

Handling Syntax Errors

If you have not yet done so, enter, compile, and run the preceding program. As you may
know from your previous programming experience, it is quite easy to accidentally type
something incorrectly when entering code into your computer. Fortunately, if you enter
something incorrectly into your program, the compiler will report a *syntax error* message
when it tries to compile it. The Java compiler attempts to make sense out of your source code
no matter what you have written. For this reason, the error that is reported may not always
reflect the actual cause of the problem. In the preceding program, for example, an accidental
omission of the opening curly brace after the **main( )** method causes the compiler to report the
following two errors.

```
Example.java:8: ';' expected
  public static void main(String args[])
                                        ^

Example.java:11: class, interface, or enum expected
}
^
```

Clearly, the first error message is completely wrong because what is missing is not a
semicolon, but a curly brace.

    The point of this discussion is that when your program contains a syntax error, you
shouldn't necessarily take the compiler's messages at face value. The messages may be
misleading. You may need to "second-guess" an error message in order to find the real
problem. Also, look at the last few lines of code in your program that precede the line being

---

1. **main( )**

2. Outputs information to the console.

3. The standard Java compiler is **javac.exe**; the interpreter is **java.exe**.

flagged. Sometimes an error will not be reported until several lines after the point at which the error actually occurred.

A Second Simple Program

Perhaps no other construct is as important to a programming language as the assignment of a value to a variable. A *variable* is a named memory location that can be assigned a value. Further, the value of a variable can be changed during the execution of a program. That is, the content of a variable is changeable, not fixed.

The following program creates two variables called **var1** and **var2**.

```
/*
   This demonstrates a variable.

   Call this file Example2.java.
*/
class Example2 {
  public static void main(String args[]) {
    int var1; // this declares a variable          ◄———— Declare variables.
    int var2; // this declares another variable

    var1 = 1024; // this assigns 1024 to var1 ◄————— Assign a variable a value.

    System.out.println("var1 contains " + var1);

    var2 = var1 / 2;

    System.out.print("var2 contains var1 / 2: ");
    System.out.println(var2);
  }
}
```

When you run this program, you will see the following output:

```
var1 contains 1024
var2 contains var1 / 2: 512
```

This program introduces several new concepts. First, the statement

```
int var1; // this declares a variable
```

declares a variable called **var1** of type integer. In Java, all variables must be declared before they are used. Further, the type of values that the variable can hold must also be specified. This is called the *type* of the variable. In this case, **var1** can hold integer values. These are whole number values. In Java, to declare a variable to be of type integer, precede its name with the keyword **int**. Thus, the preceding statement declares a variable called **var1** of type **int**.

The next line declares a second variable called **var2**.

```
int var2; // this declares another variable
```

Notice that this line uses the same format as the first line except that the name of the variable is different.

In general, to declare a variable you will use a statement like this:

type var-name;

Here, *type* specifies the type of variable being declared, and *var-name* is the name of the variable. In addition to **int**, Java supports several other data types.

The following line of code assigns **var1** the value 1024:

```
var1 = 1024; // this assigns 1024 to var1
```

In Java, the assignment operator is the single equal sign. It copies the value on its right side into the variable on its left.

The next line of code outputs the value of **var1** preceded by the string "var1 contains ":

```
System.out.println("var1 contains " + var1);
```

In this statement, the plus sign causes the value of **var1** to be displayed after the string that precedes it. This approach can be generalized. Using the + operator, you can chain together as many items as you want within a single **println( )** statement.

The next line of code assigns **var2** the value of **var1** divided by 2:

```
var2 = var1 / 2;
```

This line divides the value in **var1** by 2 and then stores that result in **var2**. Thus, after the line executes, **var2** will contain the value 512. The value of **var1** will be unchanged. Like most other computer languages, Java supports a full range of arithmetic operators, including those shown here:

+	Addition
−	Subtraction
*	Multiplication
/	Division

Here are the next two lines in the program:

```
System.out.print("var2 contains var1 / 2: ");
System.out.println(var2);
```

Two new things are occurring here. First, the built-in method **print( )** is used to display the string "var2 contains var1 / 2: ". This string is *not* followed by a new line. This means that when the next output is generated, it will start on the same line. The **print( )** method is just like **println( )**, except that it does not output a new line after each call. Second, in the call to **println( )**, notice that **var2** is used by itself. Both **print( )** and **println( )** can be used to output values of any of Java's built-in types.

One more point about declaring variables before we move on: It is possible to declare two or more variables using the same declaration statement. Just separate their names by commas. For example, **var1** and **var2** could have been declared like this:

```
int var1, var2; // both declared using one statement
```

Another Data Type

In the preceding program, a variable of type **int** was used. However, a variable of type **int** can hold only whole numbers. Thus, it cannot be used when a fractional component is required. For example, an **int** variable can hold the value 18, but not the value 18.3. Fortunately, **int** is only one of several data types defined by Java. To allow numbers with fractional components, Java defines two floating-point types: **float** and **double**, which represent single- and double-precision values, respectively. Of the two, **double** is the most commonly used.

To declare a variable of type **double**, use a statement similar to that shown here:

```
double x;
```

Here, **x** is the name of the variable, which is of type **double**. Because **x** has a floating-point type, it can hold values such as 122.23, 0.034, or −19.0.

To better understand the difference between **int** and **double**, try the following program:

```
/*
   This program illustrates the differences
   between int and double.

   Call this file Example3.java.
*/
class Example3 {
  public static void main(String args[]) {
    int var;  // this declares an int variable
    double x; // this declares a floating-point variable

    var = 10; // assign var the value 10

    x = 10.0; // assign x the value 10.0
```

```
System.out.println("Original value of var: " + var);
System.out.println("Original value of x: " + x);

System.out.println(); // print a blank line   ←————— Output a blank line.

// now, divide both by 4
var = var / 4;
x = x / 4;

System.out.println("var after division: " + var);
System.out.println("x after division: " + x);
  }
}
```

The output from this program is shown here:

```
Original value of var: 10
Original value of x: 10.0

var after division: 2   ←———Fractional component lost
x after division: 2.5   ←——————— Fractional component preserved
```

As you can see, when **var** is divided by 4, a whole-number division is performed, and the outcome is 2—the fractional component is lost. However, when **x** is divided by 4, the fractional component is preserved, and the proper answer is displayed.

There is one other new thing to notice in the program. To print a blank line, simply call **println( )** without any arguments.

Ask the Expert

Q: Why does Java have different data types for integers and floating-point values? That is, why aren't all numeric values just the same type?

A: Java supplies different data types so that you can write efficient programs. For example, integer arithmetic is faster than floating-point calculations. Thus, if you don't need fractional values, then you don't need to incur the overhead associated with types **float** or **double**. Second, the amount of memory required for one type of data might be less than that required for another. By supplying different types, Java enables you to make best use of system resources. Finally, some algorithms require (or at least benefit from) the use of a specific type of data. In general, Java supplies a number of built-in types to give you the greatest flexibility.

Project 1-1 Converting Gallons to Liters

GalToLit.java

Although the preceding sample programs illustrate several important features of the Java language, they are not very useful. Even though you do not know much about Java at this point, you can still put what you have learned to work to create a practical program. In this project, we will create a program that converts gallons to liters.

The program will work by declaring two **double** variables. One will hold the number of the gallons, and the second will hold the number of liters after the conversion. There are 3.7854 liters in a gallon. Thus, to convert gallons to liters, the gallon value is multiplied by 3.7854. The program displays both the number of gallons and the equivalent number of liters.

Step by Step

1. Create a new file called **GalToLit.java**.

2. Enter the following program into the file:

```
/*
    Project 1-1

    This program converts gallons to liters.

    Call this program GalToLit.java.
*/
class GalToLit {
  public static void main(String args[]) {
    double gallons; // holds the number of gallons
    double liters;  // holds conversion to liters

    gallons = 10; // start with 10 gallons

    liters = gallons * 3.7854; // convert to liters

      System.out.println(gallons + " gallons is " + liters + " liters.");
  }
}
```

3. Compile the program using the following command line:

```
C>javac GalToLit.java
```

4. Run the program using this command:

```
C>java GalToLit
```

You will see this output:

```
10.0 gallons is 37.854 liters.
```

5. As it stands, this program converts 10 gallons to liters. However, by changing the value assigned to **gallons**, you can have the program convert a different number of gallons into its equivalent number of liters.

Progress Check

1. What is Java's keyword for the integer data type?

2. What is **double**?

Two Control Statements

Inside a method, execution proceeds from one statement to the next, top to bottom. However, it is possible to alter this flow through the use of the various program control statements supported by Java. Although we will look closely at control statements later, two are briefly introduced here because we will be using them to write sample programs.

The if Statement

You can selectively execute part of a program through the use of Java's conditional statement: the **if**. The Java **if** statement works much like the IF statement in any other language. Its simplest form is shown here:

if*(condition) statement*;

Here, *condition* is a Boolean expression. If *condition* is true, then the statement is executed. If *condition* is false, then the statement is bypassed. Here is an example:

```
if(10 < 11) System.out.println("10 is less than 11");
```

In this case, since 10 is less than 11, the conditional expression is true, and **println( )** will execute. However, consider the following:

```
if(10 < 9) System.out.println("this won't be displayed");
```

In this case, 10 is not less than 9. Thus, the call to **println( )** will not take place.

---

1. **int**
2. The keyword for the **double** floating-point data type.

Java defines a full complement of relational operators that may be used in a conditional expression. They are shown here:

Operator	Meaning
<	Less than
<=	Less than or equal
>	Greater than
>=	Greater than or equal
==	Equal to
!=	Not equal

Notice that the test for equality is the double equal sign.

Here is a program that illustrates the **if** statement:

```java
/*
   Demonstrate the if.

   Call this file IfDemo.java.
*/
class IfDemo {
   public static void main(String args[]) {
      int a, b, c;

      a = 2;
      b = 3;

      if(a < b) System.out.println("a is less than b");

      // this won't display anything
      if(a == b) System.out.println("you won't see this");

      System.out.println();

      c = a - b; // c contains -1

      System.out.println("c contains -1");
      if(c >= 0) System.out.println("c is non-negative");
      if(c < 0) System.out.println("c is negative");

      System.out.println();

      c = b - a; // c now contains 1
```

```
        System.out.println("c contains 1");
        if(c >= 0) System.out.println("c is non-negative");
        if(c < 0) System.out.println("c is negative");

    }
}
```

The output generated by this program is shown here:

```
a is less than b

c contains -1
c is negative

c contains 1
c is non-negative
```

Notice one other thing in this program. The line

```
int a, b, c;
```

declares three variables, **a**, **b**, and **c**, by use of a comma-separated list. As mentioned earlier, when you need two or more variables of the same type, they can be declared in one statement. Just separate the variable names by commas.

The for Loop

You can repeatedly execute a sequence of code by creating a *loop*. Java supplies a powerful assortment of loop constructs. The one we will look at here is the **for** loop. The simplest form of the **for** loop is shown here:

for*(initialization; condition; iteration) statement*;

In its most common form, the *initialization* portion of the loop sets a loop control variable to an initial value. The *condition* is a Boolean expression that tests the loop control variable. If the outcome of that test is true, the **for** loop continues to iterate. If it is false, the loop terminates. The *iteration* expression determines how the loop control variable is changed each time the loop iterates. Here is a short program that illustrates the **for** loop:

```
/*
   Demonstrate the for loop.

   Call this file ForDemo.java.
```

```
*/
class ForDemo {
  public static void main(String args[]) {
    int count;

    for(count = 0; count < 5; count = count+1)  ⟵——— This loop iterates five times.
      System.out.println("This is count: " + count);

    System.out.println("Done!");
  }
}
```

The output generated by the program is shown here:

```
This is count: 0
This is count: 1
This is count: 2
This is count: 3
This is count: 4
Done!
```

In this example, **count** is the loop control variable. It is set to zero in the initialization portion of the **for**. At the start of each iteration (including the first one), the conditional test **count < 5** is performed. If the outcome of this test is true, the **println( )** statement is executed, and then the iteration portion of the loop is executed. This process continues until the conditional test is false, at which point execution picks up at the bottom of the loop.

As a point of interest, in professionally written Java programs, you will almost never see the iteration portion of the loop written as shown in the preceding program. That is, you will seldom see statements like this:

```
count = count + 1;
```

The reason is that Java includes a special increment operator that performs this operation more efficiently. The increment operator is **++** (that is, two plus signs back to back). The increment operator increases its operand by one. By use of the increment operator, the preceding statement can be written like this:

```
count++;
```

Thus, the **for** in the preceding program will usually be written like this:

```
for(count = 0; count < 5; count++)
```

You might want to try this. As you will see, the loop still runs exactly the same as it did before.

Java also provides a decrement operator, which is specified as – –. This operator decreases its operand by one.

Progress Check

1. What does the **if** statement do?

2. What does the **for** statement do?

3. What are Java's relational operators?

CRITICAL SKILL
1.9 Create Blocks of Code

Another key element of Java is the *code block*. A code block is a grouping of two or more statements. This is done by enclosing the statements between opening and closing curly braces. Once a block of code has been created, it becomes a logical unit that can be used any place that a single statement can. For example, a block can be a target for Java's **if** and **for** statements. Consider this **if** statement:

```
if(w < h) {  ◄──────── Start of block
  v = w * h;
  w = 0;
}  ◄──────── End of block
```

Here, if **w** is less than **h**, both statements inside the block will be executed. Thus, the two statements inside the block form a logical unit, and one statement cannot execute without the other also executing. The key point here is that whenever you need to logically link two or more statements, you do so by creating a block. Code blocks allow many algorithms to be implemented with greater clarity and efficiency.

---

1. The **if** is Java's conditional statement.
2. The **for** is one of Java's loop statements.
3. The relational operators are = =, !=, <, >, <=, and >=.

Here is a program that uses a block of code to prevent a division by zero:

```
/*
  Demonstrate a block of code.

  Call this file BlockDemo.java.
*/
class BlockDemo {
  public static void main(String args[]) {
    double i, j, d;

    i = 5;
    j = 10;

    // the target of this if is a block
    if(i != 0) {
      System.out.println("i does not equal zero");
      d = j / i;
      System.out.print("j / i is " + d);
    }
  }
}
```

The target of the **if** is this entire block.

The output generated by this program is shown here:

```
i does not equal zero
j / i is 2.0
```

In this case, the target of the **if** statement is a block of code and not just a single statement. If the condition controlling the **if** is true (as it is in this case), the three statements inside the block will be executed. Try setting **i** to zero and observe the result. You will see that the entire block is skipped.

As you will see later in this book, blocks of code have additional properties and uses. However, the main reason for their existence is to create logically inseparable units of code.

Ask the Expert

Q: Does the use of a code block introduce any run-time inefficiencies? In other words, does Java actually execute the { and }?

A: No. Code blocks do not add any overhead whatsoever. In fact, because of their ability to simplify the coding of certain algorithms, their use generally increases speed and efficiency. Also, the { and } exist only in your program's source code. Java does not, per se, execute the { or }.

CRITICAL SKILL
1.10 Semicolons and Positioning

In Java, the semicolon is a *separator* that is used to terminate a statement. That is, each individual statement must be ended with a semicolon. It indicates the end of one logical entity.

As you know, a block is a set of logically connected statements that are surrounded by opening and closing braces. A block is *not* terminated with a semicolon. Since a block is a group of statements, with a semicolon after each statement, it makes sense that a block is not terminated by a semicolon; instead, the end of the block is indicated by the closing brace.

Java does not recognize the end of the line as a terminator. For this reason, it does not matter where on a line you put a statement. For example,

```
x = y;
y = y + 1;
System.out.println(x + " " + y);
```

is the same as the following, to Java.

```
x = y;  y = y + 1;  System.out.println(x + " " + y);
```

Furthermore, the individual elements of a statement can also be put on separate lines. For example, the following is perfectly acceptable:

```
System.out.println("This is a long line of output" +
                x + y + z +
                "more output");
```

Breaking long lines in this fashion is often used to make programs more readable. It can also help prevent excessively long lines from wrapping.

Indentation Practices

You may have noticed in the previous examples that certain statements were indented. Java is a free-form language, meaning that it does not matter where you place statements relative to each other on a line. However, over the years, a common and accepted indentation style has developed that allows for very readable programs. This book follows that style, and it is recommended that you do so as well. Using this style, you indent one level after each opening brace, and move back out one level after each closing brace. Certain statements encourage some additional indenting; these will be covered later.

Progress Check

1. How is a block of code created? What does it do?

2. In Java, statements are terminated by a _____.

3. All Java statements must start and end on one line. True or False?

Project 1-2 Improving the Gallons-to-Liters Converter

GalToLitTable.java

You can use the **for** loop, the **if** statement, and code blocks to create an improved version of the gallons-to-liters converter that you developed in the first project. This new version will print a table of conversions, beginning with 1 gallon and ending at 100 gallons. After every 10 gallons, a blank line will be output. This is accomplished through the use of a variable called **counter** that counts the number of lines that have been output. Pay special attention to its use.

Step by Step

1. Create a new file called **GalToLitTable.java**.

2. Enter the following program into the file.

```
/*
    Project 1-2

    This program displays a conversion
    table of gallons to liters.

    Call this program "GalToLitTable.java".
*/
class GalToLitTable {
  public static void main(String args[]) {
    double gallons, liters;
    int counter;                       Line counter is initally set to zero.

    counter = 0;  ◄─────────────────────────┘
    for(gallons = 1; gallons <= 100; gallons++) {
      liters = gallons * 3.7854; // convert to liters
```

---

1. A block is started by a {. It is ended by a }. A block creates a logical unit of code.

2. Semicolon.

3. False.

```
System.out.println(gallons + " gallons is " +
                   liters + " liters.");

counter++;  ◄─────────────────────────────    Increment the line counter
// every 10th line, print a blank line           with each loop iteration.
if(counter == 10) {  ◄──────────────────       If counter is 10,
  System.out.println();                         output a blank line.
  counter = 0; // reset the line counter
  }
 }
 }
}
```

3. Compile the program using the following command line:

```
C>javac GalToLitTable.java
```

4. Run the program using this command:

```
C>java GalToLitTable
```

Here is a portion of the output that you will see:

```
1.0 gallons is 3.7854 liters.
2.0 gallons is 7.5708 liters.
3.0 gallons is 11.356200000000001 liters.
4.0 gallons is 15.1416 liters.
5.0 gallons is 18.927 liters.
6.0 gallons is 22.712400000000002 liters.
7.0 gallons is 26.4978 liters.
8.0 gallons is 30.2832 liters.
9.0 gallons is 34.0686 liters.
10.0 gallons is 37.854 liters.

11.0 gallons is 41.6394 liters.
12.0 gallons is 45.42480000000005 liters.
13.0 gallons is 49.2102 liters.
14.0 gallons is 52.9956 liters.
15.0 gallons is 56.781 liters.
16.0 gallons is 60.5664 liters.
17.0 gallons is 64.3518 liters.
18.0 gallons is 68.1372 liters.
19.0 gallons is 71.9226 liters.
20.0 gallons is 75.708 liters.

21.0 gallons is 79.4934000000001 liters.
22.0 gallons is 83.2788 liters.
23.0 gallons is 87.0642 liters.
24.0 gallons is 90.84960000000001 liters.
```

(continued)

```
25.0 gallons is 94.635 liters.
26.0 gallons is 98.4204 liters.
27.0 gallons is 102.2058 liters.
28.0 gallons is 105.9912 liters.
29.0 gallons is 109.7766 liters.
30.0 gallons is 113.562 liters.
```

CRITICAL SKILL

1.11 The Java Keywords

Fifty keywords are currently defined in the Java language (see Table 1-1). These keywords, combined with the syntax of the operators and separators, form the definition of the Java language. These keywords cannot be used as names for a variable, class, or method.

The keywords **const** and **goto** are reserved but not used. In the early days of Java, several other keywords were reserved for possible future use. However, the current specification for Java defines only the keywords shown in Table 1-1.

In addition to the keywords, Java reserves the following: **true**, **false**, and **null**. These are values defined by Java. You may not use these words for the names of variables, classes, and so on.

CRITICAL SKILL

1.12 Identifiers in Java

In Java an identifier is a name given to a method, a variable, or any other user-defined item. Identifiers can be from one to several characters long. Variable names may start with any letter of the alphabet, an underscore, or a dollar sign. Next may be either a letter, a digit, a dollar sign, or an underscore. The underscore can be used to enhance the readability of a variable

abstract	assert	boolean	break	byte	case
catch	char	class	const	continue	default
do	double	else	enum	extends	final
finally	float	for	goto	if	implements
import	instanceof	int	interface	long	native
new	package	private	protected	public	return
short	static	strictfp	super	switch	synchronized
this	throw	throws	transient	try	void
volatile	while				

Table 1-1 The Java Keywords

name, as in **line_count**. Uppercase and lowercase are different; that is, to Java, **myvar** and **MyVar** are separate names. Here are some examples of acceptable identifiers:

Test	x	y2	MaxLoad
$up	_top	my_var	sample23

Remember, you can't start an identifier with a digit. Thus, **12x** is invalid, for example.

You cannot use any of the Java keywords as identifier names. Also, you should not assign the name of any standard method, such as **println**, to an identifier. Beyond these two restrictions, good programming practice dictates that you use identifier names that reflect the meaning or usage of the items being named.

Progress Check

1. Which is the keyword: **for**, **For**, or **FOR**?

2. A Java identifier can contain what type of characters?

3. Are **index21** and **Index21** the same identifier?

The Java Class Libraries

The sample programs shown in this module make use of two of Java's built-in methods: **println( )** and **print( )**. These methods are members of the **System** class, which is a class predefined by Java that is automatically included in your programs. In the larger view, the Java environment relies on several built-in class libraries that contain many built-in methods that provide support for such things as I/O, string handling, networking, and graphics. The standard classes also provide support for windowed output. Thus, Java as a totality is a combination of the Java language itself, plus its standard classes. As you will see, the class libraries provide much of the functionality that comes with Java. Indeed, part of becoming a Java programmer is learning to use the standard Java classes. Throughout this book, various elements of the standard library classes and methods are described. However, the Java library is something that you will also want to explore more on your own.

---

1. The keyword is **for**. In Java, all keywords are in lowercase.
2. Letters, digits, the underscore, and the $.
3. No; Java is case sensitive.

Module 1 Mastery Check

1. What is bytecode and why is it important to Java's use for Internet programming?

2. What are the three main principles of object-oriented programming?

3. Where do Java programs begin execution?

4. What is a variable?

5. Which of the following variable names is invalid?

    A. count

    B. $count

    C. count27

    D. 67count

6. How do you create a single-line comment? How do you create a multiline comment?

7. Show the general form of the **if** statement. Show the general form of the **for** loop.

8. How do you create a block of code?

9. The moon's gravity is about 17 percent that of earth's. Write a program that computes your effective weight on the moon.

10. Adapt Project 1-2 so that it prints a conversion table of inches to meters. Display 12 feet of conversions, inch by inch. Output a blank line every 12 inches. (One meter equals approximately 39.37 inches.)

11. If you make a typing mistake when entering your program, what sort of error will result?

12. Does it matter where on a line you put a statement?

Module 2

Introducing Data Types
and Operators

A t the foundation of any programming language are its data types and operators, and Java is no exception. These elements define the limits of a language and determine the kind of tasks to which it can be applied. Fortunately, Java supports a rich assortment of both data types and operators, making it suitable for any type of programming.

Data types and operators are a large subject. We will begin here with an examination of Java's foundational data types and its most commonly used operators. We will also take a closer look at variables and examine the expression.

Why Data Types Are Important

Data types are especially important in Java because it is a strongly typed language. This means that all operations are type checked by the compiler for type compatibility. Illegal operations will not be compiled. Thus, strong type checking helps prevent errors and enhances reliability. To enable strong type checking, all variables, expressions, and values have a type. There is no concept of a "type-less" variable, for example. Furthermore, the type of a value determines what operations are allowed on it. An operation allowed on one type might not be allowed on another.

Java's Primitive Types

Java contains two general categories of built-in data types: object-oriented and non-object-oriented. Java's object-oriented types are defined by classes, and a discussion of classes is deferred until later. However, at the core of Java are eight primitive (also called elemental or simple) types of data, which are shown in Table 2-1. The term *primitive* is used here to indicate that these types are not objects in an object-oriented sense, but rather, normal binary values. These primitive types are not objects because of efficiency concerns. All of Java's other data types are constructed from these primitive types.

Java strictly specifies a range and behavior for each primitive type, which all implementations of the Java Virtual Machine must support. Because of Java's portability requirement, Java is uncompromising on this account. For example, an **int** is the same in all execution environments. This allows programs to be fully portable. There is no need to rewrite code to fit a specific platform. Although strictly specifying the size of the primitive types may cause a small loss of performance in some environments, it is necessary in order to achieve portability.

Type	Meaning
boolean	Represents true/false values
byte	8-bit integer
char	Character
double	Double-precision floating point
float	Single-precision floating point
int	Integer
long	Long integer
short	Short integer

Table 2-1   Java's Built-in Primitive Data Types

Integers

Java defines four integer types: **byte**, **short**, **int**, and **long**, which are shown here:

Type	Width in Bits	Range
byte	8	−128 to 127
short	16	−32,768 to 32,767
int	32	−2,147,483,648 to 2,147,483,647
long	64	−9,223,372,036,854,775,808 to 9,223,372,036,854,775,807

As the table shows, all of the integer types are signed positive and negative values. Java does not support unsigned (positive-only) integers. Many other computer languages support both signed and unsigned integers. However, Java's designers felt that unsigned integers were unnecessary.

NOTE

Technically, the Java run-time system can use any size it wants to store a primitive type. However, in all cases, types must act as specified.

The most commonly used integer type is **int**. Variables of type **int** are often employed to control loops, to index arrays, and to perform general-purpose integer math.

When you need an integer that has a range greater than **int**, use **long**. For example, here is a program that computes the number of cubic inches contained in a cube that is one mile by one mile, by one mile:

```
/*
    Compute the number of cubic inches
    in 1 cubic mile.
*/
class Inches {
  public static void main(String args[]) {
    long ci;
    long im;

    im = 5280 * 12;

    ci = im * im * im;

    System.out.println("There are " + ci +
                        " cubic inches in cubic mile.");

  }
}
```

Here is the output from the program:

```
There are 254358061056000 cubic inches in cubic mile.
```

Clearly, the result could not have been held in an **int** variable.

The smallest integer type is **byte**. Variables of type **byte** are especially useful when working with raw binary data that may not be directly compatible with Java's other built-in types. The **short** type creates a short integer. Variables of type **short** are appropriate when you don't need the larger range offered by **int**.

Ask the Expert

Q: You say that there are four integer types: int, short, long, **and** byte. **However, I have heard that** char **can also be categorized as an integer type in Java. Can you explain?**

A: The formal specification for Java defines a type category called *integral types,* which includes **byte**, **short**, **int**, **long**, and **char**. They are called integral types because they all hold whole-number, binary values. However, the purpose of the first four is to represent numeric integer quantities. The purpose of **char** is to represent characters. Therefore, the principal uses of **char** and the principal uses of the other integral types are fundamentally different. Because of the differences, the **char** type is treated separately in this book.

Floating-Point Types

As explained in Module 1, the floating-point types can represent numbers that have fractional components. There are two kinds of floating-point types, **float** and **double**, which represent single- and double-precision numbers, respectively. Type **float** is 32 bits wide and type **double** is 64 bits wide.

Of the two, **double** is the most commonly used because all of the math functions in Java's class library use **double** values. For example, the **sqrt( )** method (which is defined by the standard **Math** class) returns a **double** value that is the square root of its **double** argument. Here, **sqrt( )** is used to compute the length of the hypotenuse, given the lengths of the two opposing sides:

```
/*
   Use the Pythagorean theorem to
   find the length of the hypotenuse
   given the lengths of the two opposing
   sides.
*/
class Hypot {
  public static void main(String args[]) {
    double x, y, z;

    x = 3;
    y = 4;

    z = Math.sqrt(x*x + y*y);

    System.out.println("Hypotenuse is " +z);
  }
}
```

Notice how **sqrt( )** is called. It is preceded by the name of the class of which it is a member.

The output from the program is shown here:

```
Hypotenuse is 5.0
```

One other point about the preceding example: As mentioned, **sqrt( )** is a member of the standard **Math** class. Notice how **sqrt( )** is called; it is preceded by the name **Math**. This is similar to the way **System.out** precedes **println( )**. Although not all standard methods are called by specifying their class name first, several are.

Characters

In Java, characters are not 8-bit quantities like they are in many other computer languages. Instead, Java uses Unicode. *Unicode* defines a character set that can represent all of the characters found in all human languages. Thus, in Java, **char** is an unsigned 16-bit type having a range of 0 to 65,536. The standard 8-bit ASCII character set is a subset of Unicode and ranges from 0 to 127. Thus, the ASCII characters are still valid Java characters.

A character variable can be assigned a value by enclosing the character in single quotes. For example, this assigns the variable **ch** the letter X:

```
char ch;
ch = 'X';
```

You can output a **char** value using a **println( )** statement. For example, this line outputs the value in **ch**:

```
System.out.println("This is ch: " + ch);
```

Since **char** is an unsigned 16-bit type, it is possible to perform various arithmetic manipulations on a **char** variable. For example, consider the following program:

```
// Character variables can be handled like integers.
class CharArithDemo {
  public static void main(String args[]) {
    char ch;

    ch = 'X';
    System.out.println("ch contains " + ch);

    ch++; // increment ch  ←——————— A char can be incremented.
    System.out.println("ch is now " + ch);

    ch = 90; // give ch the value Z  ←——————— A char can be assigned an integer value.
    System.out.println("ch is now " + ch);
  }
}
```

The output generated by this program is shown here:

```
ch contains X
ch is now Y
ch is now Z
```

In the program, **ch** is first given the value X. Next, **ch** is incremented. This results in **ch** containing Y, the next character in the ASCII (and Unicode) sequence. Next, **ch** is assigned

Ask the Expert

Q: Why does Java use Unicode?

A: Java was designed for worldwide use. Thus, it needs to use a character set that can represent all the world's languages. Unicode is the standard character set designed expressly for this purpose. Of course, the use of Unicode is inefficient for languages such as English, German, Spanish, or French, whose characters can be contained within 8 bits. But such is the price that must be paid for global portability.

the value 90, which is the ASCII (and Unicode) value that corresponds to the letter Z. Since the ASCII character set occupies the first 127 values in the Unicode character set, all the "old tricks" that you may have used with characters in other languages will work in Java, too.

The Boolean Type

The **boolean** type represents true/false values. Java defines the values true and false using the reserved words **true** and **false**. Thus, a variable or expression of type **boolean** will be one of these two values.

Here is a program that demonstrates the **boolean** type:

```java
// Demonstrate boolean values.
class BoolDemo {
  public static void main(String args[]) {
    boolean b;

    b = false;
    System.out.println("b is " + b);
    b = true;
    System.out.println("b is " + b);

    // a boolean value can control the if statement
    if(b) System.out.println("This is executed.");

    b = false;
    if(b) System.out.println("This is not executed.");
```

```
    // outcome of a relational operator is a boolean value
    System.out.println("10 > 9 is " + (10 > 9));
  }
}
```

The output generated by this program is shown here:

```
b is false
b is true
This is executed.
10 > 9 is true
```

There are three interesting things to notice about this program. First, as you can see, when a **boolean** value is output by **println( )**, "true" or "false" is displayed. Second, the value of a **boolean** variable is sufficient, by itself, to control the **if** statement. There is no need to write an **if** statement like this:

```
if(b == true) ...
```

Third, the outcome of a relational operator, such as <, is a **boolean** value. This is why the expression **10 > 9** displays the value "true." Further, the extra set of parentheses around **10 > 9** is necessary because the + operator has a higher precedence than the >.

Progress Check

1. What are Java's integer types?

2. What is Unicode?

3. What values can a **boolean** variable have?

---

1. Java's integer types are **byte**, **short**, **int**, and **long**.
2. Unicode is an international character set.
3. Variables of type **boolean** can be either **true** or **false**.

Project 2-1 How Far Away Is the Lightning?

Sound.java   In this project you will create a program that computes how far away, in feet, a
listener is from a lightning strike. Sound travels approximately 1,100 feet per second
through air. Thus, knowing the interval between the time you see a lightning bolt and the time
the sound reaches you enables you to compute the distance to the lightning. For this project,
assume that the time interval is 7.2 seconds.

Step by Step

1. Create a new file called **Sound.java**.

2. To compute the distance, you will need to use floating-point values. Why? Because the time
   interval, 7.2, has a fractional component. Although it would be permissible to use a value of
   type **float**, we will use **double** in the example.

3. To compute the distance, you will multiply 7.2 by 1,100. You will then assign this value to
   a variable.

4. Finally, you will display the result.

   Here is the entire **Sound.java** program listing:

```
/*
   Project 2-1
   Compute the distance to a lightning
   strike whose sound takes 7.2 seconds
   to reach you.
*/
class Sound {
  public static void main(String args[]) {
    double dist;

    dist = 7.2 * 1100;

    System.out.println("The lightning is " + dist +
                       " feet away.");

  }
}
```

5. Compile and run the program. The following result is displayed:

```
The lightning is 7920.0 feet away.
```

(continued)

6. Extra challenge: You can compute the distance to a large object, such as a rock wall, by timing the echo. For example, if you clap your hands and time how long it takes for you to hear the echo, then you know the total round-trip time. Dividing this value by two yields the time it takes the sound to go one way. You can then use this value to compute the distance to the object. Modify the preceding program so that it computes the distance, assuming that the time interval is that of an echo.

Literals

In Java, *literals* refer to fixed values that are represented in their human-readable form. For example, the number 100 is a literal. Literals are also commonly called *constants*. For the most part, literals, and their usage, are so intuitive that they have been used in one form or another by all the preceding sample programs. Now the time has come to explain them formally.

Java literals can be of any of the primitive data types. The way each literal is represented depends upon its type. As explained earlier, character constants are enclosed in single quotes. For example, 'a' and ' %' are both character constants.

Integer constants are specified as numbers without fractional components. For example, 10 and –100 are integer constants. Floating-point constants require the use of the decimal point followed by the number's fractional component. For example, 11.123 is a floating-point constant. Java also allows you to use scientific notation for floating-point numbers.

By default, integer literals are of type **int**. If you want to specify a **long** literal, append an l or an L. For example, 12 is an **int**, but 12L is a **long**.

By default, floating-point literals are of type **double**. To specify a **float** literal, append an F or f to the constant. For example, 10.19F is of type **float**.

Although integer literals create an **int** value by default, they can still be assigned to variables of type **char**, **byte**, or **short** as long as the value being assigned can be represented by the target type. An integer literal can always be assigned to a **long** variable.

Hexadecimal and Octal Constants

As you probably know, in programming it is sometimes easier to use a number system based on 8 or 16 instead of 10. The number system based on 8 is called *octal,* and it uses the digits 0 through 7. In octal the number 10 is the same as 8 in decimal. The base 16 number system is called *hexadecimal* and uses the digits 0 through 9 plus the letters A through F, which stand for 10, 11, 12, 13, 14, and 15. For example, the hexadecimal number 10 is 16 in decimal. Because of the frequency with which these two number systems are used, Java allows you to specify integer constants in hexadecimal or octal instead of decimal. A hexadecimal constant must begin with 0x (a zero followed by an x). An octal constant begins with a zero. Here are some examples:

```
hex = 0xFF; // 255 in decimal
oct = 011;  // 9 in decimal
```

Character Escape Sequences

Enclosing character constants in single quotes works for most printing characters, but a few characters, such as the carriage return, pose a special problem when a text editor is used. In addition, certain other characters, such as the single and double quotes, have special meaning in Java, so you cannot use them directly. For these reasons, Java provides special *escape sequences*, sometimes referred to as backslash character constants, shown in Table 2-2. These sequences are used in place of the characters that they represent.

For example, this assigns **ch** the tab character:

```
ch = '\t';
```

The next example assigns a single quote to **ch**:

```
ch = '\'';
```

String Literals

Java supports one other type of literal: the string. A *string* is a set of characters enclosed by double quotes. For example,

```
"this is a test"
```

Escape Sequence	Description
\'	Single quote
\"	Double quote
\\	Backslash
\r	Carriage return
\n	New line
\f	Form feed
\t	Horizontal tab
\b	Backspace
\ddd	Octal constant (where *ddd* is an octal constant)
\uxxxx	Hexadecimal constant (where *xxxx* is a hexadecimal constant)

Table 2-2 Character Escape Sequences

is a string. You have seen examples of strings in many of the **println( )** statements in the preceding sample programs.

   In addition to normal characters, a string literal can also contain one or more of the escape sequences just described. For example, consider the following program. It uses the **\n** and **\t** escape sequences.

```
// Demonstrate escape sequences in strings.
class StrDemo {
  public static void main(String args[]) {
    System.out.println("First line\nSecond line");
    System.out.println("A\tB\tC");
    System.out.println("D\tE\tF")  ;
  }
}
```

Use \n to generate a new line.

Use tabs to align output.

   The output is shown here:

```
First line
Second line
A       B       C
D       E       F
```

   Notice how the **\n** escape sequence is used to generate a new line. You don't need to use multiple **println( )** statements to get multiline output. Just embed **\n** within a longer string at the points where you want the new lines to occur.

Progress Check

1. What is the type of the literal 10? What is the type of the literal 10.0?

2. How do you specify a **long** literal?

3. Is "x" a string or a character literal?

---

1. The literal 10 is an **int,** and 10.0 is a **double**.
2. A **long** literal is specified by adding the L or l suffix. For example, 100L.
3. The literal "x" is a string.

Ask the Expert

Q: Is a string consisting of a single character the same as a character literal? For example, is "k" the same as 'k'?

A: No. You must not confuse strings with characters. A character literal represents a single letter of type **char**. A string containing only one letter is still a string. Although strings consist of characters, they are not the same type.

CRITICAL SKILL
2.3 A Closer Look at Variables

Variables were introduced in Module 1. Here, we will take a closer look at them. As you learned earlier, variables are declared using this form of statement,

type var-name;

where *type* is the data type of the variable, and *var-name* is its name. You can declare a variable of any valid type, including the simple types just described. When you create a variable, you are creating an instance of its type. Thus, the capabilities of a variable are determined by its type. For example, a variable of type **boolean** cannot be used to store floating-point values. Furthermore, the type of a variable cannot change during its lifetime. An **int** variable cannot turn into a **char** variable, for example.

All variables in Java must be declared prior to their use. This is necessary because the compiler must know what type of data a variable contains before it can properly compile any statement that uses the variable. It also enables Java to perform strict type checking.

Initializing a Variable

In general, you must give a variable a value prior to using it. One way to give a variable a value is through an assignment statement, as you have already seen. Another way is by giving it an initial value when it is declared. To do this, follow the variable's name with an equal sign and the value being assigned. The general form of initialization is shown here:

type var = value;

Here, *value* is the value that is given to *var* when *var* is created. The value must be compatible with the specified type. Here are some examples:

```
int count = 10; // give count an initial value of 10
char ch = 'X'; // initialize ch with the letter X
float f = 1.2F; // f is initialized with 1.2
```

When declaring two or more variables of the same type using a comma-separated list, you can give one or more of those variables an initial value. For example:

```
int a, b = 8, c = 19, d; // b and c have initializations
```

In this case, only **b** and **c** are initialized.

Dynamic Initialization

Although the preceding examples have used only constants as initializers, Java allows variables to be initialized dynamically, using any expression valid at the time the variable is declared. For example, here is a short program that computes the volume of a cylinder given the radius of its base and its height:

```
// Demonstrate dynamic initialization.
class DynInit {
    public static void main(String args[]) {
        double radius = 4, height = 5;

        // dynamically initialize volume
        double volume = 3.1416 * radius * radius * height;

        System.out.println("Volume is " + volume);
    }
}
```

volume is dynamically initialized at run time.

Here, three local variables—**radius**, **height**, and **volume**—are declared. The first two, **radius** and **height**, are initialized by constants. However, **volume** is initialized dynamically to the volume of the cylinder. The key point here is that the initialization expression can use any element valid at the time of the initialization, including calls to methods, other variables, or literals.

CRITICAL SKILL
2.4 The Scope and Lifetime of Variables

So far, all of the variables that we have been using were declared at the start of the **main( )**
method. However, Java allows variables to be declared within any block. As explained in
Module 1, a block is begun with an opening curly brace and ended by a closing curly brace.
A block defines a *scope*. Thus, each time you start a new block, you are creating a new
scope. A scope determines what objects are visible to other parts of your program. It also
determines the lifetime of those objects.

Many other computer languages define two general categories of scopes: global and local.
Although supported by Java, these are not the best ways to categorize Java's scopes. The most
important scopes in Java are those defined by a class and those defined by a method. A discussion
of class scope (and variables declared within it) is deferred until later in this book, when classes
are described. For now, we will examine only the scopes defined by or within a method.

The scope defined by a method begins with its opening curly brace. However, if that
method has parameters, they too are included within the method's scope.

As a general rule, variables declared inside a scope are not visible (that is, accessible) to
code that is defined outside that scope. Thus, when you declare a variable within a scope, you
are localizing that variable and protecting it from unauthorized access and/or modification.
Indeed, the scope rules provide the foundation for encapsulation.

Scopes can be nested. For example, each time you create a block of code, you are creating
a new, nested scope. When this occurs, the outer scope encloses the inner scope. This means
that objects declared in the outer scope will be visible to code within the inner scope. However,
the reverse is not true. Objects declared within the inner scope will not be visible outside it.

To understand the effect of nested scopes, consider the following program:

```
// Demonstrate block scope.
class ScopeDemo {
  public static void main(String args[]) {
    int x; // known to all code within main

    x = 10;
    if(x == 10) { // start new scope

      int y = 20; // known only to this block

      // x and y both known here.
```

```
      System.out.println("x and y: " + x + " " + y);
      x = y * 2;
   }
   // y = 100; // Error! y not known here  ◄——— Here, y is outside of its scope.

   // x is still known here.
   System.out.println("x is " + x);
  }
}
```

As the comments indicate, the variable **x** is declared at the start of **main( )**'s scope and is accessible to all subsequent code within **main( )**. Within the **if** block, **y** is declared. Since a block defines a scope, **y** is visible only to other code within its block. This is why outside of its block, the line **y = 100;** is commented out. If you remove the leading comment symbol, a compile-time error will occur, because **y** is not visible outside of its block. Within the **if** block, **x** can be used because code within a block (that is, a nested scope) has access to variables declared by an enclosing scope.

Within a block, variables can be declared at any point, but are valid only after they are declared. Thus, if you define a variable at the start of a method, it is available to all of the code within that method. Conversely, if you declare a variable at the end of a block, it is effectively useless, because no code will have access to it.

Here is another important point to remember: variables are created when their scope is entered, and destroyed when their scope is left. This means that a variable will not hold its value once it has gone out of scope. Therefore, variables declared within a method will not hold their values between calls to that method. Also, a variable declared within a block will lose its value when the block is left. Thus, the lifetime of a variable is confined to its scope.

If a variable declaration includes an initializer, that variable will be reinitialized each time the block in which it is declared is entered. For example, consider this program:

```
// Demonstrate lifetime of a variable.
class VarInitDemo {
  public static void main(String args[]) {
    int x;

    for(x = 0; x < 3; x++) {
      int y = -1; // y is initialized each time block is entered
      System.out.println("y is: " + y); // this always prints -1
      y = 100;
      System.out.println("y is now: " + y);
    }
  }
}
```

The output generated by this program is shown here:

```
y is: -1
y is now: 100
y is: -1
y is now: 100
y is: -1
y is now: 100
```

As you can see, **y** is always reinitialized to –1 each time the inner **for** loop is entered. Even though it is subsequently assigned the value 100, this value is lost.

There is one quirk to Java's scope rules that may surprise you: although blocks can be nested, no variable declared within an inner scope can have the same name as a variable declared by an enclosing scope. For example, the following program, which tries to declare two separate variables with the same name, will not compile.

```
/*
   This program attempts to declare a variable
   in an inner scope with the same name as one
   defined in an outer scope.

   *** This program will not compile. ***
*/
class NestVar {
  public static void main(String args[]) {
    int count; ◄─────────────────────────────────┐
                                                  │
    for(count = 0; count < 10; count = count+1) { │
      System.out.println("This is count: " + count);
                                          Can't declare count again because
      int count; // illegal!!! ◄───────── it's already declared.
      for(count = 0; count < 2; count++)
        System.out.println("This program is in error!");
    }
  }
}
```

If you come from a C/C++ background, you know that there is no restriction on the names that you give variables declared in an inner scope. Thus, in C/C++ the declaration of **count** within the block of the outer **for** loop is completely valid, and such a declaration hides the outer variable. The designers of Java felt that this *name hiding* could easily lead to programming errors and disallowed it.

Progress Check

1. What is a scope? How can one be created?

2. Where in a block can variables be declared?

3. In a block, when is a variable created? When is it destroyed?

Operators

Java provides a rich operator environment. An *operator* is a symbol that tells the compiler to perform a specific mathematical or logical manipulation. Java has four general classes of operators: arithmetic, bitwise, relational, and logical. Java also defines some additional operators that handle certain special situations. This module will examine the arithmetic, relational, and logical operators. We will also examine the assignment operator. The bitwise and other special operators are examined later.

CRITICAL SKILL
2.5 Arithmetic Operators

Java defines the following arithmetic operators:

Operator	Meaning
+	Addition
–	Subtraction (also unary minus)
*	Multiplication
/	Division
%	Modulus
++	Increment
– –	Decrement

---

1. A scope defines the visibility and lifetime of an object. A block defines a scope.

2. A variable can be defined at any point within a block.

3. Inside a block, a variable is created when its declaration is encountered. It is destroyed when the block exits.

The operators +, –, *, and / all work the same way in Java as they do in any other computer language (or algebra, for that matter). These can be applied to any built-in numeric data type. They can also be used on objects of type **char**.

Although the actions of arithmetic operators are well known to all readers, a few special situations warrant some explanation. First, remember that when / is applied to an integer, any remainder will be truncated; for example, 10/3 will equal 3 in integer division. You can obtain the remainder of this division by using the modulus operator **%**. It works in Java the way it does in other languages: it yields the remainder of an integer division. For example, 10 % 3 is 1. In Java, the **%** can be applied to both integer and floating-point types. Thus, 10.0 % 3.0 is also 1. The following program demonstrates the modulus operator.

```
// Demonstrate the % operator.
class ModDemo {
  public static void main(String args[]) {
    int iresult, irem;
    double dresult, drem;

    iresult = 10 / 3;
    irem = 10 % 3;

    dresult = 10.0 / 3.0;
    drem = 10.0 % 3.0;

    System.out.println("Result and remainder of 10 / 3: " +
                       iresult + " " + irem);
    System.out.println("Result and remainder of 10.0 / 3.0: " +
                       dresult + " " + drem);

  }
}
```

The output from the program is shown here:

```
Result and remainder of 10 / 3: 3 1
Result and remainder of 10.0 / 3.0: 3.3333333333333335 1.0
```

As you can see, the **%** yields a remainder of 1 for both integer and floating-point operations.

Increment and Decrement

Introduced in Module 1, the ++ and the – – are Java's increment and decrement operators. As you will see, they have some special properties that make them quite interesting. Let's begin by reviewing precisely what the increment and decrement operators do.

The increment operator adds 1 to its operand, and the decrement operator subtracts 1. Therefore,

```
x = x + 1;
```

is the same as

```
x++;
```

and

```
x = x - 1;
```

is the same as

```
--x;
```

Both the increment and decrement operators can either precede (prefix) or follow (postfix) the operand. For example,

```
x = x + 1;
```

can be written as

```
++x; // prefix form
```

or as

```
x++; // postfix form
```

In the foregoing example, there is no difference whether the increment is applied as a prefix or a postfix. However, when an increment or decrement is used as part of a larger expression, there is an important difference. When an increment or decrement operator precedes its operand, Java will perform the corresponding operation prior to obtaining the operand's value for use by the rest of the expression. If the operator follows its operand, Java will obtain the operand's value before incrementing or decrementing it. Consider the following:

```
x = 10;
y = ++x;
```

In this case, **y** will be set to 11. However, if the code is written as

```
x = 10;
y = x++;
```

then **y** will be set to 10. In both cases, **x** is still set to 11; the difference is when it happens. There are significant advantages in being able to control when the increment or decrement operation takes place.

CRITICAL SKILL

2.6 Relational and Logical Operators

In the terms *relational operator* and *logical operator, relational* refers to the relationships that values can have with one another, and *logical* refers to the ways in which true and false values can be connected together. Since the relational operators produce true or false results, they often work with the logical operators. For this reason they will be discussed together here.

The relational operators are shown here:

Operator	Meaning
==	Equal to
!=	Not equal to
>	Greater than
<	Less than
>=	Greater than or equal to
<=	Less than or equal to

The logical operators are shown next:

Operator	Meaning
&	AND
|	OR
^	XOR (exclusive OR)
||	Short-circuit OR
&&	Short-circuit AND
!	NOT

The outcome of the relational and logical operators is a **boolean** value.

In Java, all objects can be compared for equality or inequality using == and !=. However, the comparison operators, <, >, <=, or >=, can be applied only to those types that support an ordering relationship. Therefore, all of the relational operators can be applied to all numeric types and to type **char**. However, values of type **boolean** can only be compared for equality or inequality, since the **true** and **false** values are not ordered. For example, **true** > **false** has no meaning in Java.

For the logical operators, the operands must be of type **boolean**, and the result of a logical operation is of type **boolean**. The logical operators, **&**, **|**, **^**, and **!**, support the basic logical operations AND, OR, XOR, and NOT, according to the following truth table.

p	q	p & q	p | q	p ^ q	!p
False	False	False	False	False	True
True	False	False	True	True	False
False	True	False	True	True	True
True	True	True	True	False	False

As the table shows, the outcome of an exclusive OR operation is true when exactly one and only one operand is true.

Here is a program that demonstrates several of the relational and logical operators:

```java
// Demonstrate the relational and logical operators.
class RelLogOps {
  public static void main(String args[]) {
    int i, j;
    boolean b1, b2;

    i = 10;
    j = 11;
    if(i < j) System.out.println("i < j");
    if(i <= j) System.out.println("i <= j");
    if(i != j) System.out.println("i != j");
    if(i == j) System.out.println("this won't execute");
    if(i >= j) System.out.println("this won't execute");
    if(i > j) System.out.println("this won't execute");

    b1 = true;
    b2 = false;
    if(b1 & b2) System.out.println("this won't execute");
    if(!(b1 & b2)) System.out.println("!(b1 & b2) is true");
    if(b1 | b2) System.out.println("b1 | b2 is true");
    if(b1 ^ b2) System.out.println("b1 ^ b2 is true");
  }
}
```

The output from the program is shown here:

```
i < j
i <= j
i != j
!(b1 & b2) is true
b1 | b2 is true
b1 ^ b2 is true
```

Short-Circuit Logical Operators

Java supplies special *short-circuit* versions of its AND and OR logical operators that can be used to produce more efficient code. To understand why, consider the following. In an AND operation, if the first operand is false, the outcome is false no matter what value the second operand has. In an OR operation, if the first operand is true, the outcome of the operation is true no matter what the value of the second operand. Thus, in these two cases there is no need to evaluate the second operand. By not evaluating the second operand, time is saved and more efficient code is produced.

The short-circuit AND operator is **&&**, and the short-circuit OR operator is **||**. Their normal counterparts are **&** and **|**. The only difference between the normal and short- circuit versions is that the normal operands will always evaluate each operand, but short-circuit versions will evaluate the second operand only when necessary.

Here is a program that demonstrates the short-circuit AND operator. The program determines whether the value in **d** is a factor of **n**. It does this by performing a modulus operation. If the remainder of **n / d** is zero, then **d** is a factor. However, since the modulus operation involves a division, the short-circuit form of the AND is used to prevent a divide-by-zero error.

```
// Demonstrate the short-circuit operators.
class SCops {
  public static void main(String args[]) {
    int n, d, q;

    n = 10;
    d = 2;
    if(d != 0 && (n % d) == 0)
      System.out.println(d + " is a factor of " + n);

    d = 0; // now, set d to zero

    // Since d is zero, the second operand is not evaluated.
    if(d != 0 && (n % d) == 0)          ← The short-circuit
      System.out.println(d + " is a factor of " + n);    operator prevents
                                                          a division by zero.

    /* Now, try same thing without short-circuit operator.
```

```
     This will cause a divide-by-zero error.
 */
 if(d != 0 & (n % d) == 0)
     System.out.println(d + " is a factor of " + n);
 }
}
```

Now both expressions are evaluated, allowing a division by zero to occur.

To prevent a divide-by-zero, the **if** statement first checks to see if **d** is equal to zero. If it is, the short-circuit AND stops at that point and does not perform the modulus division. Thus, in the first test, **d** is 2 and the modulus operation is performed. The second test fails because **d** is set to zero, and the modulus operation is skipped, avoiding a divide-by-zero error. Finally, the normal AND operator is tried. This causes both operands to be evaluated, which leads to a run-time error when the division by zero occurs.

Progress Check

1. What does the **%** operator do? To what types can it be applied?

2. What type of values can be used as operands of the logical operators?

3. Does a short-circuit operator always evaluate both of its operands?

CRITICAL SKILL
2.7 The Assignment Operator

You have been using the assignment operator since Module 1. Now it is time to take a formal look at it. The *assignment operator* is the single equal sign, =. This operator works in Java much as it does in any other computer language. It has this general form:

var = expression;

Here, the type of *var* must be compatible with the type of *expression*.

---

1. The **%** is the modulus operator, which returns the remainder of an integer division. It can be applied to all of the numeric types.

2. The logical operators must have operands of type **boolean**.

3. No, a short-circuit operator evaluates its second operand only if the outcome of the operation cannot be determined solely by its first operand.

Ask the Expert

Q: Since the short-circuit operators are, in some cases, more efficient than their normal counterparts, why does Java still offer the normal AND and OR operators?

A: In some cases you will want both operands of an AND or OR operation to be evaluated because of the side effects produced. Consider the following:

```
// Side effects can be important.
class SideEffects {
  public static void main(String args[]) {
    int i;

    i = 0;

    /* Here, i is still incremented even though
       the if statement fails. */
    if(false & (++i < 100))
       System.out.println("this won't be displayed");
    System.out.println("if statements executed: " + i); // displays 1

    /* In this case, i is not incremented because
       the short-circuit operator skips the increment. */
    if(false && (++i < 100))
      System.out.println("this won't be displayed");
    System.out.println("if statements executed: " + i); // still 1 !!
  }
}
```

As the comments indicate, in the first **if** statement, **i** is incremented whether the **if** succeeds or not. However, when the short-circuit operator is used, the variable **i** is not incremented when the first operand is false. The lesson here is that if your code expects the right-hand operand of an AND or OR operation to be evaluated, you must use Java's non-short-circuit forms of these operations.

The assignment operator does have one interesting attribute that you may not be familiar with: it allows you to create a chain of assignments. For example, consider this fragment:

```
int x, y, z;

x = y = z = 100; // set x, y, and z to 100
```

This fragment sets the variables **x**, **y**, and **z** to 100 using a single statement. This works because the = is an operator that yields the value of the right-hand expression. Thus, the value of **z = 100** is 100, which is then assigned to **y**, which in turn is assigned to **x**. Using a "chain of assignment" is an easy way to set a group of variables to a common value.

Shorthand Assignments

Java provides special *shorthand* assignment operators that simplify the coding of certain assignment statements. Let's begin with an example. The assignment statement shown here

```
x = x + 10;
```

can be written, using Java shorthand, as

```
x += 10;
```

The operator pair += tells the compiler to assign to **x** the value of **x** plus 10.
    Here is another example. The statement

```
x = x - 100;
```

is the same as

```
x -= 100;
```

Both statements assign to **x** the value of **x** minus 100.
    This shorthand will work for all the binary operators in Java (that is, those that require two operands). The general form of the shorthand is

var op = expression;

Thus, the arithmetic and logical assignment operators are the following:

+=	–=	*=	/=
%=	&=	|=	^=

Because these operators combine an operation with an assignment, they are formally referred to as *compound assignment operators*.
    The compound assignment operators provide two benefits. First, they are more compact than their "longhand" equivalents. Second, they are implemented more efficiently by the Java run-time system. For these reasons, you will often see the compound assignment operators used in professionally written Java programs.

CRITICAL SKILL
2.9 Type Conversion in Assignments

In programming, it is common to assign one type of variable to another. For example, you might want to assign an **int** value to a **float** variable, as shown here:

```
int i;
float f;

i = 10;
f = i; // assign an int to a float
```

When compatible types are mixed in an assignment, the value of the right side is automatically converted to the type of the left side. Thus, in the preceding fragment, the value in **i** is converted into a **float** and then assigned to **f**. However, because of Java's strict type checking, not all types are compatible, and thus, not all type conversions are implicitly allowed. For example, **boolean** and **int** are not compatible.

When one type of data is assigned to another type of variable, an *automatic type conversion* will take place if

●   The two types are compatible.

●   The destination type is larger than the source type.

When these two conditions are met, a *widening conversion* takes place. For example, the **int** type is always large enough to hold all valid **byte** values, and both **int** and **byte** are integer types, so an automatic conversion from **byte** to **int** can be applied.

For widening conversions, the numeric types, including integer and floating-point types, are compatible with each other. For example, the following program is perfectly valid since **long** to **double** is a widening conversion that is automatically performed.

```
// Demonstrate automatic conversion from long to double.
class LtoD {
  public static void main(String args[]) {
    long L;
    double D;

    L = 100123285L;
    D = L; ◀─────────────────── Automatic conversion from long to double

    System.out.println("L and D: " + L + " " + D);

  }
}
```

Although there is an automatic conversion from **long** to **double**, there is no automatic conversion from **double** to **long** since this is not a widening conversion. Thus, the following version of the preceding program is invalid.

```
// *** This program will not compile. ***
class LtoD {
  public static void main(String args[]) {
    long L;
    double D;

    D = 100123285.0;
    L = D; // Illegal!!!          No automatic conversion from double to long

    System.out.println("L and D: " + L + " " + D);

  }
}
```

There are no automatic conversions from the numeric types to **char** or **boolean**. Also, **char** and **boolean** are not compatible with each other. However, an integer literal can be assigned to **char**.

CRITICAL SKILL
2.10 Casting Incompatible Types

Although the automatic type conversions are helpful, they will not fulfill all programming needs because they apply only to widening conversions between compatible types. For all other cases you must employ a cast. A *cast* is an instruction to the compiler to convert one type into another. Thus, it requests an explicit type conversion. A cast has this general form:

(*target-type*) *expression*

Here, *target-type* specifies the desired type to convert the specified expression to. For example, if you want to convert the type of the expression **x/y** to **int**, you can write

```
double x, y;
// ...
(int) (x / y)
```

Here, even though **x** and **y** are of type **double**, the cast converts the outcome of the expression to **int**. The parentheses surrounding **x / y** are necessary. Otherwise, the cast to **int** would apply only to the **x** and not to the outcome of the division. The cast is necessary here because there is no automatic conversion from **double** to **int**.

When a cast involves a *narrowing conversion,* information might be lost. For example, when casting a **long** into a **short**, information will be lost if the **long**'s value is greater than the range of a **short** because its high-order bits are removed. When a floating-point value is cast to an integer type, the fractional component will also be lost due to truncation. For example, if the value 1.23 is assigned to an integer, the resulting value will simply be 1. The 0.23 is lost.

The following program demonstrates some type conversions that require casts:

```
// Demonstrate casting.
class CastDemo {
  public static void main(String args[]) {
    double x, y;
    byte b;
    int i;
    char ch;

    x = 10.0;
    y = 3.0;                                        Truncation will occur in this conversion.

    i = (int) (x / y); // cast double to int
    System.out.println("Integer outcome of x / y: " + i);

    i = 100;
    b = (byte) i;          No loss of info here. A byte can hold the value 100.
    System.out.println("Value of b: " + b);

    i = 257;
    b = (byte) i;          Information loss this time. A byte cannot hold the value 257.
    System.out.println("Value of b: " + b);

    b = 88; // ASCII code for X
    ch = (char) b;          Cast between incompatible types
    System.out.println("ch: " + ch);
  }
}
```

The output from the program is shown here:

```
Integer outcome of x / y: 3
Value of b: 100
Value of b: 1
ch: X
```

In the program, the cast of **(x / y)** to **int** results in the truncation of the fractional component, and information is lost. Next, no loss of information occurs when **b** is assigned the value 100 because a **byte** can hold the value 100. However, when the attempt is made to assign **b** the value 257, information loss occurs because 257 exceeds a **byte**'s maximum value. Finally, no information is lost, but a cast is needed when assigning a **byte** value to a **char**.

Progress Check

1. What is a cast?

2. Can a **short** be assigned to an **int** without a cast? Can a **byte** be assigned to a **char** without a cast?

3. How can the following statement be rewritten?

   ```
   x = x + 23;
   ```

Operator Precedence

The following table shows the order of precedence for all Java operators, from highest to lowest. This table includes several operators that will be discussed later in this book.

highest			
( )	[ ]	.	
++	--	~	!
*	/	%	
+	-		
>>	>>>	<<	
>	>=	<	<=
==	!=		
&			
^			
|			
&&			
||			
? :			
=	op=		
lowest			

---

1. A cast is an explicit conversion.

2. Yes. No.

3. x += 23;

Project 2-2 Display a Truth Table for the Logical Operators

LogicalOpTable.java   In this project you will create a program that displays the truth table for Java's logical operators. You must make the columns in the table line up. This project makes use of several features covered in this module, including one of Java's escape sequences and the logical operators. It also illustrates the differences in the precedence between the arithmetic + operator and the logical operators.

Step by Step

1. Create a new file called **LogicalOpTable.java**.

2. To ensure that the columns line up, you will use the **\t** escape sequence to embed tabs into each output string. For example, this **println( )** statement displays the header for the table:

```
System.out.println("P\tQ\tAND\tOR\tXOR\tNOT");
```

3. Each subsequent line in the table will use tabs to position the outcome of each operation under its proper heading.

4. Here is the entire **LogicalOpTable.java** program listing. Enter it at this time.

```
// Project 2-2: a truth table for the logical operators.
class LogicalOpTable {
  public static void main(String args[]) {

    boolean p, q;

    System.out.println("P\tQ\tAND\tOR\tXOR\tNOT");

    p = true; q = true;
    System.out.print(p + "\t" + q +"\t");
    System.out.print((p&q) + "\t" + (p|q) + "\t");
    System.out.println((p^q) + "\t" + (!p));

    p = true; q = false;
    System.out.print(p + "\t" + q +"\t");
    System.out.print((p&q) + "\t" + (p|q) + "\t");
    System.out.println((p^q) + "\t" + (!p));

    p = false; q = true;
    System.out.print(p + "\t" + q +"\t");
    System.out.print((p&q) + "\t" + (p|q) + "\t");
    System.out.println((p^q) + "\t" + (!p));
```

(continued)

```
        p = false; q = false;
        System.out.print(p + "\t" + q +"\t");
        System.out.print((p&q) + "\t" + (p|q) + "\t");
        System.out.println((p^q) + "\t" + (!p));
    }
}
```

Notice the parentheses surrounding the logical operations inside the **println( )** statements. They are necessary because of the precedence of Java's operators. The + operator is higher than the logical operators.

5. Compile and run the program. The following table is displayed.

P	Q	AND	OR	XOR	NOT
true	true	true	true	false	false
true	false	false	true	true	false
false	true	false	true	true	true
false	false	false	false	false	true

6. On your own, try modifying the program so that it uses and displays 1's and 0's, rather than true and false. This may involve a bit more effort than you might at first think!

Expressions

Operators, variables, and literals are the constituents of *expressions*. An expression in Java is any valid combination of those pieces. You probably already know the general form of an expression from your other programming experience, or from algebra. However, a few aspects of expressions will be discussed now.

Type Conversion in Expressions

Within an expression, it is possible to mix two or more different types of data as long as they are compatible with each other. For example, you can mix **short** and **long** within an expression because they are both numeric types. When different types of data are mixed within an expression, they are all converted to the same type. This is accomplished through the use of Java's *type promotion rules*.

First, all **char**, **byte**, and **short** values are promoted to **int**. Then, if one operand is a **long**, the whole expression is promoted to **long**. If one operand is a **float** operand, the entire expression is promoted to **float**. If any of the operands is **double**, the result is **double**.

It is important to understand that type promotions apply only to the values operated upon when an expression is evaluated. For example, if the value of a **byte** variable is promoted to **int** inside an expression, outside the expression, the variable is still a **byte**. Type promotion only affects the evaluation of an expression.

Type promotion can, however, lead to somewhat unexpected results. For example, when an arithmetic operation involves two **byte** values, the following sequence occurs: First, the **byte** operands are promoted to **int**. Then the operation takes place, yielding an **int** result. Thus, the outcome of an operation involving two **byte** values will be an **int**. This is not what you might intuitively expect. Consider the following program:

```
// A promotion surprise!
class PromDemo {
  public static void main(String args[]) {
    byte b;
    int i;

    b = 10;
    i = b * b; // OK, no cast needed

    b = 10;
    b = (byte) (b * b); // cast needed!!

    System.out.println("i and b: " + i + " " + b);
  }
}
```

No cast needed because result is already elevated to **int**.

Cast is needed here to assign an **int** to a **byte**!

Somewhat counterintuitively, no cast is needed when assigning **b * b** to **i**, because **b** is promoted to **int** when the expression is evaluated. However, when you try to assign **b * b** to **b**, you do need a cast—back to **byte**! Keep this in mind if you get unexpected type-incompatibility error messages on expressions that would otherwise seem perfectly OK.

This same sort of situation also occurs when performing operations on **char**s. For example, in the following fragment, the cast back to **char** is needed because of the promotion of **ch1** and **ch2** to **int** within the expression.

```
char ch1 = 'a', ch2 = 'b';

ch1 = (char) (ch1 + ch2);
```

Without the cast, the result of adding **ch1** to **ch2** would be **int**, which can't be assigned to a **char**.

Casts are not only useful when converting between types in an assignment. For example, consider the following program. It uses a cast to **double** to obtain a fractional component from an otherwise integer division.

```
// Using a cast.
class UseCast {
  public static void main(String args[]) {
    int i;
```

```
for(i = 0; i < 5; i++) {
  System.out.println(i + " / 3: " + i / 3);
  System.out.println(i + " / 3 with fractions: "
                        + (double) i / 3);
  System.out.println();
  }
 }
}
```

The output from the program is shown here:

```
0 / 3: 0
0 / 3 with fractions: 0.0

1 / 3: 0
1 / 3 with fractions: 0.3333333333333333

2 / 3: 0
2 / 3 with fractions: 0.6666666666666666

3 / 3: 1
3 / 3 with fractions: 1.0

4 / 3: 1
4 / 3 with fractions: 1.3333333333333333
```

Spacing and Parentheses

An expression in Java may have tabs and spaces in it to make it more readable. For example, the following two expressions are the same, but the second is easier to read:

```
x=10/y*(127/x);
```

```
x = 10 / y * (127/x);
```

Parentheses increase the precedence of the operations contained within them, just like in algebra. Use of redundant or additional parentheses will not cause errors or slow down the execution of the expression. You are encouraged to use parentheses to make clear the exact order of evaluation, both for yourself and for others who may have to figure out your program later. For example, which of the following two expressions is easier to read?

```
x = y/3-34*temp+127;
```

```
x = (y/3) - (34*temp) + 127;
```

Module 2 Mastery Check

1. Why does Java strictly specify the range and behavior of its primitive types?

2. What is Java's character type, and how does it differ from the character type used by many other programming languages?

3. A **boolean** value can have any value you like because any non-zero value is true. True or False?

4. Given this output,

   ```
   One
   Two
   Three
   ```

   using a single string, show the **println( )** statement that produced it.

5. What is wrong with this fragment?

   ```
   for(i = 0; i < 10; i++) {
     int sum;

     sum = sum + i;
   }
   System.out.println("Sum is: " + sum);
   ```

6. Explain the difference between the prefix and postfix forms of the increment operator.

7. Show how a short-circuit AND can be used to prevent a divide-by-zero error.

8. In an expression, what type are **byte** and **short** promoted to?

9. In general, when is a cast needed?

10. Write a program that finds all of the prime numbers between 2 and 100.

11. Does the use of redundant parentheses affect program performance?

12. Does a block define a scope?

Module 3

Program Control Statements

n this module you will learn about the statements that control a program's flow of execution. There are three categories of program control statements: *selection* statements, which include the **if** and the **switch**; *iteration* statements, which include the **for**, **while**, and **do-while** loops; and *jump* statements, which include **break**, **continue**, and **return**. Except for **return**, which is discussed later in this book, the remaining control statements, including the **if** and **for** statements to which you have already had a brief introduction, are examined in detail here. The module begins by explaining how to perform some simple keyboard input.

CRITICAL SKILL
3.1

Input Characters from the Keyboard

Before examining Java's control statements, we will make a short digression that will allow you to begin writing interactive programs. Up to this point, the sample programs in this book have displayed information *to* the user, but they have not received information *from* the user. Thus, you have been using console output, but not console (keyboard) input. The main reason for this is that Java's input system relies upon a rather complex system of classes, the use of which requires an understanding of various features, such as exception handling and classes, that are not discussed until later in this book. There is no direct parallel to the very convenient **println( )** method, for example, that allows you to read various types of data entered by the user. Frankly, Java's approach to console input is not as easy to use as one might like. Also, most real-world Java programs and applets will be graphical and window based, not console based. For these reasons, not much use of console input is found in this book. However, there is one type of console input that *is* easy to use: reading a character from the keyboard. Since several of the examples in this module will make use of this feature, it is discussed here.

The easiest way to read a character from the keyboard is to call **System.in.read( )**. **System.in** is the complement to **System.out**. It is the input object attached to the keyboard. The **read( )** method waits until the user presses a key and then returns the result. The character is returned as an integer, so it must be cast into a **char** to assign it to a **char** variable. By default, console input is line buffered, so you must press ENTER before any character that you type will be sent to your program. Here is a program that reads a character from the keyboard:

```
// Read a character from the keyboard.
class KbIn {
  public static void main(String args[])
    throws java.io.IOException {
```

```
    char ch;

    System.out.print("Press a key followed by ENTER: ");

    ch = (char) System.in.read(); // get a char ◄——— Read a character
                                                      from the keyboard.
    System.out.println("Your key is: " + ch);
  }
}
```

Here is a sample run:

```
Press a key followed by ENTER: t
Your key is: t
```

In the program, notice that **main( )** begins like this:

```
public static void main(String args[])
  throws java.io.IOException {
```

Because **System.in.read( )** is being used, the program must specify the **throws java.io.IOException** clause. This line is necessary to handle input errors. It is part of Java's exception handling mechanism, which is discussed in Module 9. For now, don't worry about its precise meaning.

The fact that **System.in** is line buffered is a source of annoyance at times. When you press ENTER, a carriage return, line feed sequence is entered into the input stream. Furthermore, these characters are left pending in the input buffer until you read them. Thus, for some applications, you may need to remove them (by reading them) before the next input operation. You will see an example of this later in this module.

Progress Check

1. What is **System.in**?

2. How can you read a character typed at the keyboard?

---

1. **System.in** is the input object linked to standard input, which is usually the keyboard.
2. To read a character, call **System.in.read( )**.

CRITICAL SKILL

3.2 The if Statement

Module 1 introduced the **if** statement. It is examined in detail here. The complete form of the **if** statement is

if(*condition*) *statement*;
else *statement*;

where the targets of the **if** and **else** are single statements. The **else** clause is optional. The targets of both the **if** and **else** can be blocks of statements. The general form of the **if**, using blocks of statements, is

if(*condition*)
{
   statement sequence
}
else
{
   statement sequence
}

If the conditional expression is true, the target of the **if** will be executed; otherwise, if it exists, the target of the **else** will be executed. At no time will both of them be executed. The conditional expression controlling the **if** must produce a **boolean** result.

To demonstrate the **if** (and several other control statements), we will create and develop a simple computerized guessing game that would be suitable for young children. In the first version of the game, the program asks the player for a letter between A and Z. If the player presses the correct letter on the keyboard, the program responds by printing the message **** Right ****. The program is shown here:

```
// Guess the letter game.
class Guess {
  public static void main(String args[])
    throws java.io.IOException {

    char ch, answer = 'K';

    System.out.println("I'm thinking of a letter between A and Z.");
    System.out.print("Can you guess it: ");

    ch = (char) System.in.read(); // read a char from the keyboard

    if(ch == answer) System.out.println("** Right **");
  }
}
```

This program prompts the player and then reads a character from the keyboard. Using an **if** statement, it then checks that character against the answer, which is K in this case. If K was entered, the message is displayed. When you try this program, remember that the K must be entered in uppercase.

Taking the guessing game further, the next version uses the **else** to print a message when the wrong letter is picked.

```java
// Guess the letter game, 2nd version.
class Guess2 {
  public static void main(String args[])
    throws java.io.IOException {

    char ch, answer = 'K';

    System.out.println("I'm thinking of a letter between A and Z.");
    System.out.print("Can you guess it: ");

    ch = (char) System.in.read(); // get a char

    if(ch == answer) System.out.println("** Right **");
    else System.out.println("...Sorry, you're wrong.");
  }
}
```

Nested ifs

A *nested if* is an **if** statement that is the target of another **if** or **else**. Nested **if**s are very common in programming. The main thing to remember about nested **if**s in Java is that an **else** statement always refers to the nearest **if** statement that is within the same block as the **else** and not already associated with an **else**. Here is an example:

```java
if(i == 10) {
  if(j < 20) a = b;
  if(k > 100) c = d;
  else a = c; // this else refers to if(k > 100)
}
else a = d; // this else refers to if(i == 10)
```

As the comments indicate, the final **else** is not associated with **if(j < 20)**, because it is not in the same block (even though it is the nearest **if** without an **else**). Rather, the final **else** is associated with **if(i == 10)**. The inner **else** refers to **if(k > 100)**, because it is the closest **if** within the same block.

You can use a nested **if** to add a further improvement to the guessing game. This addition provides the player with feedback about a wrong guess.

```
// Guess the letter game, 3rd version.
class Guess3 {
  public static void main(String args[])
    throws java.io.IOException {

    char ch, answer = 'K';

    System.out.println("I'm thinking of a letter between A and Z.");
    System.out.print("Can you guess it: ");

    ch = (char) System.in.read(); // get a char

    if(ch == answer) System.out.println("** Right **");
    else {
      System.out.print("...Sorry, you're ");

      // a nested if
      if(ch < answer) System.out.println("too low");
      else System.out.println("too high");
    }
  }
}
```

A sample run is shown here:

```
I'm thinking of a letter between A and Z.
Can you guess it: Z
...Sorry, you're too high
```

The if-else-if Ladder

A common programming construct that is based upon the nested **if** is the **if-else-if** *ladder*. It looks like this:

if(*condition*)
  statement;
else if(*condition*)
  statement;
else if(*condition*)
  statement;

```
.
.
.
else
    statement;
```

The conditional expressions are evaluated from the top downward. As soon as a true condition is found, the statement associated with it is executed, and the rest of the ladder is bypassed. If none of the conditions is true, the final **else** statement will be executed. The final **else** often acts as a default condition; that is, if all other conditional tests fail, the last **else** statement is performed. If there is no final **else** and all other conditions are false, no action will take place.

The following program demonstrates the **if-else-if** ladder:

```
// Demonstrate an if-else-if ladder.
class Ladder {
  public static void main(String args[]) {
    int x;

    for(x=0; x<6; x++) {
      if(x==1)
        System.out.println("x is one");
      else if(x==2)
        System.out.println("x is two");
      else if(x==3)
        System.out.println("x is three");
      else if(x==4)
        System.out.println("x is four");
      else
        System.out.println("x is not between 1 and 4");   ◄─── This is the
    }                                                            default statement.
  }
}
```

The program produces the following output:

```
x is not between 1 and 4
x is one
x is two
x is three
x is four
x is not between 1 and 4
```

As you can see, the default **else** is executed only if none of the preceding **if** statements succeeds.

Progress Check

1. The condition controlling the **if** must be of what type?

2. To what **if** does an **else** always associate?

3. What is an **if-else-if** ladder?

CRITICAL SKILL
3.3
The switch Statement

The second of Java's selection statements is the **switch**. The **switch** provides for a multiway branch. Thus, it enables a program to select among several alternatives. Although a series of nested **if** statements can perform multiway tests, for many situations the **switch** is a more efficient approach. It works like this: the value of an expression is successively tested against a list of constants. When a match is found, the statement sequence associated with that match is executed. The general form of the **switch** statement is

```
switch(expression) {
  case constant1:
      statement sequence
      break;
  case constant2:
      statement sequence
      break;
  case constant3:
      statement sequence
      break;
    .
    .
    .
  default:
      statement sequence
}
```

---

1. The condition controlling an **if** must be of type **boolean**.

2. An **else** always associates with the nearest **if** in the same block that is not already associated with an **else**.

3. An **if-else-if** ladder is a sequence of nested **if-else** statements.

The **switch** expression can be of type **char**, **byte**, **short**, or **int**. (Floating-point expressions, for example, are not allowed.) Frequently, the expression controlling the **switch** is simply a variable. The **case** constants must be literals of a type compatible with the expression. No two **case** constants in the same **switch** can have identical values.

The **default** statement sequence is executed if no **case** constant matches the expression. The **default** is optional; if it is not present, no action takes place if all matches fail. When a match is found, the statements associated with that **case** are executed until the **break** is encountered or, in the case of **default** or the last **case**, until the end of the **switch** is reached.

The following program demonstrates the **switch**.

```java
// Demonstrate the switch.
class SwitchDemo {
  public static void main(String args[]) {
    int i;

    for(i=0; i<10; i++)
      switch(i) {
        case 0:
          System.out.println("i is zero");
          break;
        case 1:
          System.out.println("i is one");
          break;
        case 2:
          System.out.println("i is two");
          break;
        case 3:
          System.out.println("i is three");
          break;
        case 4:
          System.out.println("i is four");
          break;
        default:
          System.out.println("i is five or more");
      }

  }
}
```

The output produced by this program is shown here:

```
i is zero
i is one
i is two
i is three
i is four
i is five or more
i is five or more
i is five or more
i is five or more
i is five or more
```

As you can see, each time through the loop, the statements associated with the **case** constant that matches **i** are executed. All others are bypassed. When **i** is five or greater, no **case** statements match, so the **default** statement is executed.

Technically, the **break** statement is optional, although most applications of the **switch** will use it. When encountered within the statement sequence of a **case**, the **break** statement causes program flow to exit from the entire **switch** statement and resume at the next statement outside the **switch**. However, if a **break** statement does not end the statement sequence associated with a **case**, then all the statements *at and following* the matching **case** will be executed until a **break** (or the end of the **switch**) is encountered.

For example, study the following program carefully. Before looking at the output, can you figure out what it will display on the screen?

```java
// Demonstrate the switch without break statements.
class NoBreak {
  public static void main(String args[]) {
    int i;

    for(i=0; i<=5; i++) {
      switch(i) {
        case 0:
          System.out.println("i is less than one");
        case 1:
          System.out.println("i is less than two");
        case 2:
          System.out.println("i is less than three");
        case 3:
          System.out.println("i is less than four");
        case 4:
          System.out.println("i is less than five");
```

The **case** statements fall through here.

```
      }
    System.out.println();
  }
 }
}
```

This program displays the following output:

```
i is less than one
i is less than two
i is less than three
i is less than four
i is less than five

i is less than two
i is less than three
i is less than four
i is less than five

i is less than three
i is less than four
i is less than five

i is less than four
i is less than five

i is less than five
```

As this program illustrates, execution will continue into the next **case** if no **break** statement is present.

You can have empty **case**s, as shown in this example:

```
switch(i) {
  case 1:
  case 2:
  case 3: System.out.println("i is 1, 2 or 3");
    break;
  case 4: System.out.println("i is 4");
    break;
}
```

In this fragment, if **i** has the value 1, 2, or 3, the first **println( )** statement executes. If it is 4, the second **println( )** statement executes. The "stacking" of **case**s, as shown in this example, is common when several **case**s share common code.

Nested switch Statements

It is possible to have a **switch** as part of the statement sequence of an outer **switch**. This is called a nested **switch**. Even if the **case** constants of the inner and outer **switch** contain common values, no conflicts will arise. For example, the following code fragment is perfectly acceptable.

```
switch(ch1) {
  case 'A': System.out.println("This A is part of outer switch.");
    switch(ch2) {
      case 'A':
        System.out.println("This A is part of inner switch");
        break;
      case 'B': // ...
    } // end of inner switch
    break;
  case 'B': // ...
```

Progress Check

1. The expression controlling the **switch** can be of what type?

2. When the **switch** expression matches a **case** constant, what happens?

3. If a **case** sequence does not end in **break**, what happens?

---

1. The **switch** expression can be of type **char**, **short**, **int**, or **byte**.

2. When a matching **case** constant is found, the statement sequence associated with that **case** is executed.

3. If a **case** sequence does not end with **break**, execution continues into the next **case** sequence, if one exists.

Project 3-1   Start Building a Java Help System

`Help.java`   This project builds a simple help system that displays the syntax for the Java control statements. The program displays a menu containing the control statements and then waits for you to choose one. After one is chosen, the syntax of the statement is displayed. In this first version of the program, help is available for only the **if** and **switch** statements. The other control statements are added in subsequent projects.

Step by Step

1. Create a file called **Help.java**.

2. The program begins by displaying the following menu:

```
Help on:
  1. if
  2. switch
Choose one:
```

To accomplish this, you will use the statement sequence shown here:

```
System.out.println("Help on:");
System.out.println("  1. if");
System.out.println("  2. switch");
System.out.print("Choose one: ");
```

3. Next, the program obtains the user's selection by calling **System.in.read( )**, as shown here:

```
choice = (char) System.in.read();
```

4. Once the selection has been obtained, the program uses the **switch** statement shown here to display the syntax for the selected statement.

```
switch(choice) {
  case '1':
    System.out.println("The if:\n");
    System.out.println("if(condition) statement;");
    System.out.println("else statement;");
    break;
  case '2':
    System.out.println("The switch:\n");
    System.out.println("switch(expression) {");
    System.out.println("  case constant:");
    System.out.println("    statement sequence");
    System.out.println("    break;");
    System.out.println("  // ...");
    System.out.println("}");
```

(continued)

```
      break;
    default:
      System.out.print("Selection not found.");
}
```

Notice how the **default** clause catches invalid choices. For example, if the user enters 3, no **case** constants will match, causing the **default** sequence to execute.

5. Here is the entire **Help.java** program listing:

```
/*
   Project 3-1

   A simple help system.
*/
class Help {
  public static void main(String args[])
    throws java.io.IOException {
    char choice;

    System.out.println("Help on:");
    System.out.println("  1. if");
    System.out.println("  2. switch");
    System.out.print("Choose one: ");
    choice = (char) System.in.read();

    System.out.println("\n");

    switch(choice) {
      case '1':
        System.out.println("The if:\n");
        System.out.println("if(condition) statement;");
        System.out.println("else statement;");
        break;
      case '2':
        System.out.println("The switch:\n");
        System.out.println("switch(expression) {");
        System.out.println("  case constant:");
        System.out.println("    statement sequence");
        System.out.println("    break;");
        System.out.println("  // ...");
        System.out.println("}");
```

```
        break;
      default:
        System.out.print("Selection not found.");
    }
  }
}
```

6. Here is a sample run.

```
Help on:
  1. if
  2. switch
Choose one: 1

The if:

if(condition) statement;
else statement;
```

Ask the Expert

Q: Under what conditions should I use an if-else-if **ladder rather than a** switch **when coding a multiway branch?**

A: In general, use an **if-else-if** ladder when the conditions controlling the selection process do not rely upon a single value. For example, consider the following **if-else-if** sequence:

```
if(x < 10) // ...
else if(y != 0) // ...
else if(!done) // ...
```

This sequence cannot be recoded into a **switch** because all three conditions involve different variables—and differing types. What variable would control the **switch**? Also, you will need to use an **if-else-if** ladder when testing floating-point values or other objects that are not of types valid for use in a **switch** expression.

CRITICAL SKILL
3.4 The for Loop

You have been using a simple form of the **for** loop since Module 1. You might be surprised at just how powerful and flexible the **for** loop is. Let's begin by reviewing the basics, starting with the most traditional forms of the **for**.

The general form of the **for** loop for repeating a single statement is

for(*initialization*; *condition*; *iteration*) *statement*;

For repeating a block, the general form is

for(*initialization*; *condition*; *iteration*)
{
    statement sequence
}

The *initialization* is usually an assignment statement that sets the initial value of the *loop control variable,* which acts as the counter that controls the loop. The *condition* is a Boolean expression that determines whether or not the loop will repeat. The *iteration* expression defines the amount by which the loop control variable will change each time the loop is repeated. Notice that these three major sections of the loop must be separated by semicolons. The **for** loop will continue to execute as long as the condition tests true. Once the condition becomes false, the loop will exit, and program execution will resume on the statement following the **for**.

The following program uses a **for** loop to print the square roots of the numbers between 1 and 99. It also displays the rounding error present for each square root.

```
// Show square roots of 1 to 99 and the rounding error.
class SqrRoot {
  public static void main(String args[]) {
    double num, sroot, rerr;

    for(num = 1.0; num < 100.0; num++) {
      sroot = Math.sqrt(num);
      System.out.println("Square root of " + num +
                         " is " + sroot);

      // compute rounding error
      rerr = num - (sroot * sroot);
      System.out.println("Rounding error is " + rerr);
      System.out.println();
    }
  }
}
```

Notice that the rounding error is computed by squaring the square root of each number. This result is then subtracted from the original number, thus yielding the rounding error.

The **for** loop can proceed in a positive or negative fashion, and it can change the loop control variable by any amount. For example, the following program prints the numbers 100 to –95, in decrements of 5.

```java
// A negatively running for loop.
class DecrFor {
  public static void main(String args[]) {
    int x;

    for(x = 100; x > -100; x -= 5)        ←——— Loop control variable is
      System.out.println(x);                     decremented by 5 each time.
  }
}
```

An important point about **for** loops is that the conditional expression is always tested at the top of the loop. This means that the code inside the loop may not be executed at all if the condition is false to begin with. Here is an example:

```java
for(count=10; count < 5; count++)
  x += count; // this statement will not execute
```

This loop will never execute because its control variable, **count**, is greater than 5 when the loop is first entered. This makes the conditional expression, **count < 5**, false from the outset; thus, not even one iteration of the loop will occur.

Some Variations on the for Loop

The **for** is one of the most versatile statements in the Java language because it allows a wide range of variations. For example, multiple loop control variables can be used. Consider the following program:

```java
// Use commas in a for statement.
class Comma {
  public static void main(String args[]) {
    int i, j;

    for(i=0, j=10; i < j; i++, j--)          ←——— Notice the two loop
      System.out.println("i and j: " + i + " " + j);    control variables.



  }
}
```

The output from the program is shown here:

```
i and j: 0 10
i and j: 1 9
i and j: 2 8
i and j: 3 7
i and j: 4 6
```

Here, commas separate the two initialization statements and the two iteration expressions. When the loop begins, both **i** and **j** are initialized. Each time the loop repeats, **i** is incremented and **j** is decremented. Multiple loop control variables are often convenient and can simplify certain algorithms. You can have any number of initialization and iteration statements, but in practice, more than two or three make the **for** loop unwieldy.

The condition controlling the loop can be any valid Boolean expression. It does not need to involve the loop control variable. In the next example, the loop continues to execute until the user types the letter S at the keyboard.

```
// Loop until an S is typed.
class ForTest {
  public static void main(String args[])
    throws java.io.IOException {

    int i;

    System.out.println("Press S to stop.");

    for(i = 0; (char) System.in.read() != 'S'; i++)
      System.out.println("Pass #" + i);
  }
}
```

Missing Pieces

Some interesting **for** loop variations are created by leaving pieces of the loop definition empty. In Java, it is possible for any or all of the initialization, condition, or iteration portions of the **for** loop to be blank. For example, consider the following program.

```
// Parts of the for can be empty.
class Empty {
  public static void main(String args[]) {
    int i;

    for(i = 0; i < 10; ) {          ◄──────── The iteration expression is missing.
      System.out.println("Pass #" + i);
```

```
      i++; // increment loop control var
    }
  }
}
```

Here, the iteration expression of the **for** is empty. Instead, the loop control variable **i** is incremented inside the body of the loop. This means that each time the loop repeats, **i** is tested to see whether it equals 10, but no further action takes place. Of course, since **i** is still incremented within the body of the loop, the loop runs normally, displaying the following output:

```
Pass #0
Pass #1
Pass #2
Pass #3
Pass #4
Pass #5
Pass #6
Pass #7
Pass #8
Pass #9
```

In the next example, the initialization portion is also moved out of the **for**.

```
// Move more out of the for loop.
class Empty2 {
  public static void main(String args[]) {
    int i;

    i = 0; // move initialization out of loop          The initialization expression
    for(; i < 10; ) {                                   is moved out of the loop.
      System.out.println("Pass #" + i);
      i++; // increment loop control var
    }
  }
}
```

In this version, **i** is initialized before the loop begins, rather than as part of the **for**. Normally, you will want to initialize the loop control variable inside the **for**. Placing the initialization outside of the loop is generally done only when the initial value is derived through a complex process that does not lend itself to containment inside the **for** statement.

The Infinite Loop

You can create an *infinite loop* (a loop that never terminates) using the **for** by leaving the conditional expression empty. For example, the following fragment shows the way most Java programmers create an infinite loop.

```
for(;;) // intentionally infinite loop
{
  //...
}
```

This loop will run forever. Although there are some programming tasks, such as operating system command processors, that require an infinite loop, most "infinite loops" are really just loops with special termination requirements. Near the end of this module you will see how to halt a loop of this type. (Hint: it's done using the **break** statement.)

Loops with No Body

In Java, the body associated with a **for** loop (or any other loop) can be empty. This is because a *null statement* is syntactically valid. Body-less loops are often useful. For example, the following program uses one to sum the numbers 1 through 5.

```
// The body of a loop can be empty.
class Empty3 {
  public static void main(String args[]) {
    int i;
    int sum = 0;

    // sum the numbers through 5
    for(i = 1; i <= 5; sum += i++) ;    ◄──────── No body in this loop!

    System.out.println("Sum is " + sum);
  }
}
```

The output from the program is shown here:

```
Sum is 15
```

Notice that the summation process is handled entirely within the **for** statement, and no body is needed. Pay special attention to the iteration expression:

```
sum += i++
```

Don't be intimidated by statements like this. They are common in professionally written Java programs and are easy to understand if you break them down into their parts. In words, this statement says "add to **sum** the value of **sum** plus **i**, then increment **i**." Thus, it is the same as this sequence of statements:

```
sum = sum + i;
i++;
```

Declaring Loop Control Variables Inside the for Loop

Often the variable that controls a **for** loop is needed only for the purposes of the loop and is not used elsewhere. When this is the case, it is possible to declare the variable inside the initialization portion of the **for**. For example, the following program computes both the summation and the factorial of the numbers 1 through 5. It declares its loop control variable **i** inside the **for**.

```
// Declare loop control variable inside the for.
class ForVar {
  public static void main(String args[]) {
    int sum = 0;
    int fact = 1;

    // compute the factorial of the numbers through 5
    for(int i = 1; i <= 5; i++) {          The variable i is declared
      sum += i;  // i is known throughout the loop    inside the for statement.
      fact *= i;
    }

    // but, i is not known here.

    System.out.println("Sum is " + sum);
    System.out.println("Factorial is " + fact);
  }
}
```

When you declare a variable inside a **for** loop, there is one important point to remember: the scope of that variable ends when the **for** statement does. (That is, the scope of the variable is limited to the **for** loop.) Outside the **for** loop, the variable will cease to exist. Thus, in the preceding example, **i** is not accessible outside the **for** loop. If you need to use the loop control variable elsewhere in your program, you will not be able to declare it inside the **for** loop.

Before moving on, you might want to experiment with your own variations on the **for** loop. As you will find, it is a fascinating loop.

The Enhanced for Loop

Recently, a new form of the **for** loop, called the *enhanced for*, was added to Java. The enhanced **for** provides a streamlined way to cycle through the contents of a collection of objects, such as an array. The enhanced **for** loop is discussed in Chapter 5, after arrays have been introduced.

Progress Check

1. Can portions of a **for** statement be empty?

2. Show how to create an infinite loop using **for**.

3. What is the scope of a variable declared within a **for** statement?

CRITICAL SKILL
3.5 The while Loop

Another of Java's loops is the **while**. The general form of the **while** loop is

while(*condition*) *statement*;

where *statement* may be a single statement or a block of statements, and *condition* defines the condition that controls the loop, and it may be any valid Boolean expression. The loop repeats while the condition is true. When the condition becomes false, program control passes to the line immediately following the loop.

Here is a simple example in which a **while** is used to print the alphabet:

```
// Demonstrate the while loop.
class WhileDemo {
  public static void main(String args[]) {
    char ch;

    // print the alphabet using a while loop
    ch = 'a';
    while(ch <= 'z') {
```

1. Yes. All three parts of the **for**—initialization, condition, and iteration—can be empty.
2. for(;;)
3. The scope of a variable declared within a **for** is limited to the loop. Outside the loop, it is unknown.

```
      System.out.print(ch);
      ch++;
    }
  }
}
```

Here, **ch** is initialized to the letter a. Each time through the loop, **ch** is output and then incremented. This process continues until **ch** is greater than z.

As with the **for** loop, the **while** checks the conditional expression at the top of the loop, which means that the loop code may not execute at all. This eliminates the need for performing a separate test before the loop. The following program illustrates this characteristic of the **while** loop. It computes the integer powers of 2, from 0 to 9.

```
// Compute integer powers of 2.
class Power {
  public static void main(String args[]) {
    int e;
    int result;

    for(int i=0; i < 10; i++) {
      result = 1;
      e = i;
      while(e > 0) {
        result *= 2;
        e--;
      }

      System.out.println("2 to the " + i +
                          " power is " + result);
    }
  }
}
```

The output from the program is shown here:

```
2 to the 0 power is 1
2 to the 1 power is 2
2 to the 2 power is 4
2 to the 3 power is 8
2 to the 4 power is 16
2 to the 5 power is 32
2 to the 6 power is 64
2 to the 7 power is 128
2 to the 8 power is 256
2 to the 9 power is 512
```

Ask the Expert

Q: Given the flexibility inherent in all of Java's loops, what criteria should I use when selecting a loop? That is, how do I choose the right loop for a specific job?

A: Use a **for** loop when performing a known number of iterations. Use the **do-while** when you need a loop that will always perform at least one iteration. The **while** is best used when the loop will repeat an unknown number of times.

Notice that the **while** loop executes only when **e** is greater than 0. Thus, when **e** is zero, as it is in the first iteration of the **for** loop, the **while** loop is skipped.

CRITICAL SKILL
3.6 # The do-while Loop

The last of Java's loops is the **do-while**. Unlike the **for** and the **while** loops, in which the condition is tested at the top of the loop, the **do-while** loop checks its condition at the bottom of the loop. This means that a **do-while** loop will always execute at least once. The general form of the **do-while** loop is

do {
    statements;
} while(*condition*);

Although the braces are not necessary when only one statement is present, they are often used to improve readability of the **do-while** construct, thus preventing confusion with the **while**. The **do-while** loop executes as long as the conditional expression is true.

The following program loops until the user enters the letter q.

```
// Demonstrate the do-while loop.
class DWDemo {
  public static void main(String args[])
    throws java.io.IOException {

    char ch;

    do {
      System.out.print("Press a key followed by ENTER: ");
```

```
      ch = (char) System.in.read(); // get a char
    } while(ch != 'q');
  }
}
```

Using a **do-while** loop, we can further improve the guessing game program from earlier in this module. This time, the program loops until you guess the letter.

```
// Guess the letter game, 4th version.
class Guess4 {
  public static void main(String args[])
    throws java.io.IOException {

    char ch, answer = 'K';

    do {
      System.out.println("I'm thinking of a letter between A and Z.");
      System.out.print("Can you guess it: ");

      // read a letter, but skip cr/lf
      do {
        ch = (char) System.in.read(); // get a char
      } while(ch == '\n' | ch == '\r');

      if(ch == answer) System.out.println("** Right **");
      else {
        System.out.print("...Sorry, you're ");
        if(ch < answer) System.out.println("too low");
        else System.out.println("too high");
        System.out.println("Try again!\n");
      }
    } while(answer != ch);
  }
}
```

Here is a sample run:

```
I'm thinking of a letter between A and Z.
Can you guess it: A
...Sorry, you're too low
Try again!
```

```
I'm thinking of a letter between A and Z.
Can you guess it: Z
...Sorry, you're too high
Try again!

I'm thinking of a letter between A and Z.
Can you guess it: K
** Right **
```

Notice one other thing of interest in this program. The **do-while** loop shown here obtains the next character, skipping over any carriage return and line feed characters that might be in the input stream:

```
// read a letter, but skip cr/lf
do {
  ch = (char) System.in.read(); // get a char
} while(ch == '\n' | ch == '\r');
```

Here is why this loop is needed: As explained earlier, **System.in** is line buffered—you have to press ENTER before characters are sent. Pressing ENTER causes a carriage return and a line feed character to be generated. These characters are left pending in the input buffer. This loop discards those characters by continuing to read input until neither is present.

Progress Check

1. What is the main difference between the **while** and the **do-while** loops?

2. The condition controlling the **while** can be of any type. True or False?

---

1. The **while** checks its condition at the top of the loop. The **do-while** checks its condition at the bottom of the loop. Thus, a **do-while** will always execute at least once.
2. False. The condition must be of type **boolean**.

Project 3-2   Improve the Java Help System

Help2.java   This project expands on the Java help system that was created in Project 3-1. This
version adds the syntax for the **for**, **while**, and **do-while** loops. It also checks the
user's menu selection, looping until a valid response is entered.

Step by Step

1. Copy **Help.java** to a new file called **Help2.java**.

2. Change the portion of the program that displays the choices so that it uses the loop shown
here:

```
do {
  System.out.println("Help on:");
  System.out.println("  1. if");
  System.out.println("  2. switch");
  System.out.println("  3. for");
  System.out.println("  4. while");
  System.out.println("  5. do-while\n");
  System.out.print("Choose one: ");
  do {
    choice = (char) System.in.read();
  } while(choice == '\n' | choice == '\r');
} while( choice < '1' | choice > '5');
```

Notice that a nested **do-while** loop is used to discard any spurious carriage return or line
feed characters that may be present in the input stream. After making this change, the
program will loop, displaying the menu until the user enters a response that is between
1 and 5.

3. Expand the **switch** statement to include the **for**, **while**, and **do-while** loops, as shown here:

```
switch(choice) {
  case '1':
    System.out.println("The if:\n");
    System.out.println("if(condition) statement;");
    System.out.println("else statement;");
    break;
```

(continued)

```
    case '2':
      System.out.println("The switch:\n");
      System.out.println("switch(expression) {");
      System.out.println("  case constant:");
      System.out.println("    statement sequence");
      System.out.println("    break;");
      System.out.println("  // ...");
      System.out.println("}");
      break;
    case '3':
      System.out.println("The for:\n");
      System.out.print("for(init; condition; iteration)");
      System.out.println(" statement;");
      break;
    case '4':
      System.out.println("The while:\n");
      System.out.println("while(condition) statement;");
      break;
    case '5':
      System.out.println("The do-while:\n");
      System.out.println("do {");
      System.out.println("  statement;");
      System.out.println("} while (condition);");
      break;
  }
```

Notice that no **default** statement is present in this version of the **switch**. Since the menu loop ensures that a valid response will be entered, it is no longer necessary to include a **default** statement to handle an invalid choice.

4. Here is the entire **Help2.java** program listing:

```
/*
   Project 3-2

   An improved Help system that uses a
   do-while to process a menu selection.
*/
class Help2 {
  public static void main(String args[])
    throws java.io.IOException {
    char choice;

    do {
      System.out.println("Help on:");
```

```
    System.out.println("  1. if");
    System.out.println("  2. switch");
    System.out.println("  3. for");
    System.out.println("  4. while");
    System.out.println("  5. do-while\n");
    System.out.print("Choose one: ");
    do {
      choice = (char) System.in.read();
    } while(choice == '\n' | choice == '\r');
  } while( choice < '1' | choice > '5');

  System.out.println("\n");

  switch(choice) {
    case '1':
      System.out.println("The if:\n");
      System.out.println("if(condition) statement;");
      System.out.println("else statement;");
      break;
    case '2':
      System.out.println("The switch:\n");
      System.out.println("switch(expression) {");
      System.out.println("  case constant:");
      System.out.println("    statement sequence");
      System.out.println("    break;");
      System.out.println("  // ...");
      System.out.println("}");
      break;
    case '3':
      System.out.println("The for:\n");
      System.out.print("for(init; condition; iteration)");
      System.out.println(" statement;");
      break;
    case '4':
      System.out.println("The while:\n");
      System.out.println("while(condition) statement;");
      break;
    case '5':
      System.out.println("The do-while:\n");
      System.out.println("do {");
      System.out.println("  statement;");
      System.out.println("} while (condition);");
      break;
    }
  }
}
```

Use break to Exit a Loop

It is possible to force an immediate exit from a loop, bypassing any remaining code in the body of the loop and the loop's conditional test, by using the **break** statement. When a **break** statement is encountered inside a loop, the loop is terminated and program control resumes at the next statement following the loop. Here is a simple example:

```
// Using break to exit a loop.
class BreakDemo {
  public static void main(String args[]) {
    int num;

    num = 100;

    // loop while i-squared is less than num
    for(int i=0; i < num; i++) {
      if(i*i >= num) break; // terminate loop if i*i >= 100
      System.out.print(i + " ");
    }
    System.out.println("Loop complete.");
  }
}
```

This program generates the following output:

```
0 1 2 3 4 5 6 7 8 9 Loop complete.
```

As you can see, although the **for** loop is designed to run from 0 to **num** (which in this case is 100), the **break** statement causes it to terminate early, when **i** squared is greater than or equal to **num**.

The **break** statement can be used with any of Java's loops, including intentionally infinite loops. For example, the following program simply reads input until the user types the letter q.

```
// Read input until a q is received.
class Break2 {
  public static void main(String args[])
    throws java.io.IOException {

    char ch;

    for( ; ; ) {                              ──────────── This "infinite" loop is
      ch = (char) System.in.read(); // get a char    terminated by the break.
      if(ch == 'q') break;  ◄────────────────────────┘
```

```
    }
    System.out.println("You pressed q!");
  }
}
```

When used inside a set of nested loops, the **break** statement will break out of only the innermost loop. For example:

```
// Using break with nested loops.
class Break3 {
  public static void main(String args[]) {

    for(int i=0; i<3; i++) {
      System.out.println("Outer loop count: " + i);
      System.out.print("    Inner loop count: ");

      int t = 0;
      while(t < 100) {
        if(t == 10) break; // terminate loop if t is 10
        System.out.print(t + " ");
        t++;
      }
      System.out.println();
    }
    System.out.println("Loops complete.");
  }
}
```

This program generates the following output:

```
Outer loop count: 0
    Inner loop count: 0 1 2 3 4 5 6 7 8 9
Outer loop count: 1
    Inner loop count: 0 1 2 3 4 5 6 7 8 9
Outer loop count: 2
    Inner loop count: 0 1 2 3 4 5 6 7 8 9
Loops complete.
```

As you can see, the **break** statement in the inner loop causes the termination of only that loop. The outer loop is unaffected.

Here are two other points to remember about **break**. First, more than one **break** statement may appear in a loop. However, be careful. Too many **break** statements have the tendency to destructure your code. Second, the **break** that terminates a **switch** statement affects only that **switch** statement and not any enclosing loops.

Use break as a Form of goto

In addition to its uses with the **switch** statement and loops, the **break** statement can be employed by itself to provide a "civilized" form of the goto statement. Java does not have a goto statement, because it provides an unstructured way to alter the flow of program execution. Programs that make extensive use of the goto are usually hard to understand and hard to maintain. There are, however, a few places where the goto is a useful and legitimate device. For example, the goto can be helpful when exiting from a deeply nested set of loops. To handle such situations, Java defines an expanded form of the **break** statement. By using this form of **break**, you can, for example, break out of one or more blocks of code. These blocks need not be part of a loop or a **switch**. They can be any block. Further, you can specify precisely where execution will resume, because this form of **break** works with a label. As you will see, **break** gives you the benefits of a goto without its problems.

The general form of the labeled **break** statement is shown here:

break *label*;

Typically, *label* is the name of a label that identifies a block of code. When this form of **break** executes, control is transferred out of the named block of code. The labeled block of code must enclose the **break** statement, but it does not need to be the immediately enclosing block. This means that you can use a labeled **break** statement to exit from a set of nested blocks. But you cannot use **break** to transfer control to a block of code that does not enclose the **break** statement.

To name a block, put a label at the start of it. The block being labeled can be a stand-alone block, or a statement that has a block as its target. A *label* is any valid Java identifier followed by a colon. Once you have labeled a block, you can then use this label as the target of a **break** statement. Doing so causes execution to resume at the *end* of the labeled block. For example, the following program shows three nested blocks.

```java
// Using break with a label.
class Break4 {
  public static void main(String args[]) {
    int i;

    for(i=1; i<4; i++) {
one:   {
two:     {
three:     {
            System.out.println("\ni is " + i);
```

```
      if(i==1) break one;   ◄─────────── Break to a label.
      if(i==2) break two;
      if(i==3) break three;

      // this is never reached
      System.out.println("won't print");
    }
    System.out.println("After block three.");
  }
  System.out.println("After block two.");
}
System.out.println("After block one.");
}
System.out.println("After for.");

}
}
```

The output from the program is shown here:

```
i is 1
After block one.

i is 2
After block two.
After block one.

i is 3
After block three.
After block two.
After block one.
After for.
```

Let's look closely at the program to understand precisely why this output is produced. When **i** is 1, the first **if** statement succeeds, causing a **break** to the end of the block of code defined by label **one**. This causes **After block one.** to print. When **i** is 2, the second **if** succeeds, causing control to be transferred to the end of the block labeled by **two**. This causes the messages **After block two.** and **After block one.** to be printed, in that order. When **i** is 3, the third **if** succeeds, and control is transferred to the end of the block labeled by **three**. Now, all three messages are displayed.

Here is another example. This time, **break** is being used to jump outside of a series of nested **for** loops. When the **break** statement in the inner loop is executed, program control jumps to the end of the block defined by the outer **for** loop, which is labeled by **done**. This causes the remainder of all three loops to be bypassed.

```
// Another example of using break with a label.
class Break5 {
  public static void main(String args[]) {

done:
    for(int i=0; i<10; i++) {
      for(int j=0; j<10; j++) {
        for(int k=0; k<10; k++) {
          System.out.println(k + " ");
          if(k == 5) break done; // jump to done
        }
        System.out.println("After k loop"); // won't execute
      }
      System.out.println("After j loop"); // won't execute
    }
    System.out.println("After i loop");
  }
}
```

The output from the program is shown here:

```
0
1
2
3
4
5
After i loop
```

Precisely where you put a label is very important—especially when working with loops. For example, consider the following program:

```
// Where you put a label is important.
class Break6 {
  public static void main(String args[]) {
    int x=0, y=0;

// here, put label before for statement.
stop1: for(x=0; x < 5; x++) {
         for(y = 0; y < 5; y++) {
```

```
            if(y == 2) break stop1;
            System.out.println("x and y: " + x + " " + y);
        }
    }

    System.out.println();

// now, put label immediately before {
        for(x=0; x < 5; x++)
stop2: {
            for(y = 0; y < 5; y++) {
            if(y == 2) break stop2;
            System.out.println("x and y: " + x + " " + y);
        }
    }

    }
}
```

The output from this program is shown here:

```
x and y: 0 0
x and y: 0 1

x and y: 0 0
x and y: 0 1
x and y: 1 0
x and y: 1 1
x and y: 2 0
x and y: 2 1
x and y: 3 0
x and y: 3 1
x and y: 4 0
x and y: 4 1
```

In the program, both sets of nested loops are the same except for one point. In the first set, the label precedes the outer **for** loop. In this case, when the **break** executes, it transfers control to the end of the entire **for** block, skipping the rest of the outer loop's iterations. In the second set, the label precedes the outer **for**'s opening curly brace. Thus, when **break stop2** executes, control is transferred to the end of the outer **for**'s block, causing the next iteration to occur.

Keep in mind that you cannot **break** to any label that is not defined for an enclosing block. For example, the following program is invalid and will not compile.

```
// This program contains an error.
class BreakErr {
  public static void main(String args[]) {

    one: for(int i=0; i<3; i++) {
      System.out.print("Pass " + i + ": ");
    }

    for(int j=0; j<100; j++) {
      if(j == 10) break one; // WRONG
      System.out.print(j + " ");
    }
  }
}
```

Since the loop labeled **one** does not enclose the **break** statement, it is not possible to transfer control to that block.

Ask the Expert

Q: You say that the goto is unstructured and that the break with a label offers a better alternative. But really, doesn't breaking to a label, which might be many lines of code and levels of nesting removed from the break, also destructure code?

A: The short answer is yes! However, in those cases in which a jarring change in program flow is required, breaking to a label still retains some structure. A **goto** has none!

CRITICAL SKILL
3.9 Use continue

It is possible to force an early iteration of a loop, bypassing the loop's normal control structure. This is accomplished using **continue**. The **continue** statement forces the next iteration of the loop to take place, skipping any code between itself and the conditional expression that controls the loop. Thus, **continue** is essentially the complement of **break**. For example, the following program uses **continue** to help print the even numbers between 0 and 100.

```
// Use continue.
class ContDemo {
  public static void main(String args[]) {
    int i;

    // print even numbers between 0 and 100
    for(i = 0; i<=100; i++) {
      if((i%2) != 0) continue; // iterate
      System.out.println(i);
    }
  }
}
```

Only even numbers are printed, because an odd one will cause the loop to iterate early, bypassing the call to **println( )**.

In **while** and **do-while** loops, a **continue** statement will cause control to go directly to the conditional expression and then continue the looping process. In the case of the **for**, the iteration expression of the loop is evaluated, then the conditional expression is executed, and then the loop continues.

As with the **break** statement, **continue** may specify a label to describe which enclosing loop to continue. Here is an example program that uses **continue** with a label:

```
// Use continue with a label.
class ContToLabel {
  public static void main(String args[]) {

outerloop:
    for(int i=1; i < 10; i++) {
      System.out.print("\nOuter loop pass " + i +
                       ", Inner loop: ");
      for(int j = 1; j < 10; j++) {
        if(j == 5) continue outerloop; // continue outer loop
        System.out.print(j);
      }
    }
  }
}
```

The output from the program is shown here:

```
Outer loop pass 1, Inner loop: 1234
Outer loop pass 2, Inner loop: 1234
```

```
Outer loop pass 3, Inner loop: 1234
Outer loop pass 4, Inner loop: 1234
Outer loop pass 5, Inner loop: 1234
Outer loop pass 6, Inner loop: 1234
Outer loop pass 7, Inner loop: 1234
Outer loop pass 8, Inner loop: 1234
Outer loop pass 9, Inner loop: 1234
```

As the output shows, when the **continue** executes, control passes to the outer loop, skipping the remainder of the inner loop.

Good uses of **continue** are rare. One reason is that Java provides a rich set of loop statements that fit most applications. However, for those special circumstances in which early iteration is needed, the **continue** statement provides a structured way to accomplish it.

Progress Check

1. Within a loop, what happens when a **break** (with no label) is executed?

2. What happens when a **break** with a label is executed?

3. What does **continue** do?

---

1. Within a loop, a **break** without a label causes immediate termination of the loop. Execution resumes at the first line of code after the loop.

2. When a labeled **break** is executed, execution resumes at the end of the labeled block.

3. The **continue** statement causes a loop to iterate immediately, bypassing any remaining code. If the **continue** includes a label, the labeled loop is continued.

Project 3-3 Finish the Java Help System

Help3.java   This project puts the finishing touches on the Java help system that was created in the previous projects. This version adds the syntax for **break** and **continue**. It also allows the user to request the syntax for more than one statement. It does this by adding an outer loop that runs until the user enters **q** as a menu selection.

Step by Step

1. Copy **Help2.java** to a new file called **Help3.java**.

2. Surround all of the program code with an infinite **for** loop. Break out of this loop, using **break**, when a letter **q** is entered. Since this loop surrounds all of the program code, breaking out of this loop causes the program to terminate.

3. Change the menu loop as shown here:

```
do {
  System.out.println("Help on:");
  System.out.println("  1. if");
  System.out.println("  2. switch");
  System.out.println("  3. for");
  System.out.println("  4. while");
  System.out.println("  5. do-while");
  System.out.println("  6. break");
  System.out.println("  7. continue\n");
  System.out.print("Choose one (q to quit): ");
  do {
    choice = (char) System.in.read();
  } while(choice == '\n' | choice == '\r');
} while( choice < '1' | choice > '7' & choice != 'q');
```

Notice that this loop now includes the **break** and **continue** statements. It also accepts the letter **q** as a valid choice.

4. Expand the **switch** statement to include the **break** and **continue** statements, as shown here:

```
case '6':
  System.out.println("The break:\n");
  System.out.println("break; or break label;");
  break;
case '7':
  System.out.println("The continue:\n");
  System.out.println("continue; or continue label;");
  break;
```

(continued)

5. Here is the entire **Help3.java** program listing:

```
/*
   Project 3-3

   The finished Java statement Help system
   that processes multiple requests.
*/
class Help3 {
  public static void main(String args[])
    throws java.io.IOException {
    char choice;

    for(;;) {
      do {
        System.out.println("Help on:");
        System.out.println("  1. if");
        System.out.println("  2. switch");
        System.out.println("  3. for");
        System.out.println("  4. while");
        System.out.println("  5. do-while");
        System.out.println("  6. break");
        System.out.println("  7. continue\n");
        System.out.print("Choose one (q to quit): ");
        do {
          choice = (char) System.in.read();
        } while(choice == '\n' | choice == '\r');
      } while( choice < '1' | choice > '7' & choice != 'q');

      if(choice == 'q') break;

      System.out.println("\n");

      switch(choice) {
        case '1':
          System.out.println("The if:\n");
          System.out.println("if(condition) statement;");
          System.out.println("else statement;");
          break;
        case '2':
          System.out.println("The switch:\n");
          System.out.println("switch(expression) {");
          System.out.println("  case constant:");
          System.out.println("    statement sequence");
          System.out.println("    break;");
          System.out.println("  // ...");
          System.out.println("}");
          break;
```

```
      case '3':
        System.out.println("The for:\n");
        System.out.print("for(init; condition; iteration)");
        System.out.println(" statement;");
        break;
      case '4':
        System.out.println("The while:\n");
        System.out.println("while(condition) statement;");
        break;
      case '5':
        System.out.println("The do-while:\n");
        System.out.println("do {");
        System.out.println("  statement;");
        System.out.println("} while (condition);");
        break;
      case '6':
        System.out.println("The break:\n");
        System.out.println("break; or break label;");
        break;
      case '7':
        System.out.println("The continue:\n");
        System.out.println("continue; or continue label;");
        break;
    }
    System.out.println();
  }
 }
}
```

6. Here is a sample run:

```
Help on:
  1. if
  2. switch
  3. for
  4. while
  5. do-while
  6. break
  7. continue

Choose one (q to quit): 1

The if:

if(condition) statement;
else statement;

Help on:
```

(continued)

```
   1. if
   2. switch
   3. for
   4. while
   5. do-while
   6. break
   7. continue

Choose one (q to quit): 6

The break:

break; or break label;

Help on:
   1. if
   2. switch
   3. for
   4. while
   5. do-while
   6. break
   7. continue

Choose one (q to quit): q
```

CRITICAL SKILL
3.10 Nested Loops

As you have seen in some of the preceding examples, one loop can be nested inside of another. Nested loops are used to solve a wide variety of programming problems and are an essential part of programming. So, before leaving the topic of Java's loop statements, let's look at one more nested loop example. The following program uses a nested **for** loop to find the factors of the numbers from 2 to 100.

```
/*
   Use nested loops to find factors of numbers
   between 2 and 100.
*/
class FindFac {
  public static void main(String args[]) {

    for(int i=2; i <= 100; i++) {
      System.out.print("Factors of " + i + ": ");
      for(int j = 2; j < i; j++)
        if((i%j) == 0) System.out.print(j + " ");
      System.out.println();
    }
```

```
   }
}
```

Here is a portion of the output produced by the program:

```
Factors of 2:
Factors of 3:
Factors of 4: 2
Factors of 5:
Factors of 6: 2 3
Factors of 7:
Factors of 8: 2 4
Factors of 9: 3
Factors of 10: 2 5
Factors of 11:
Factors of 12: 2 3 4 6
Factors of 13:
Factors of 14: 2 7
Factors of 15: 3 5
Factors of 16: 2 4 8
Factors of 17:
Factors of 18: 2 3 6 9
Factors of 19:
Factors of 20: 2 4 5 10
```

In the program, the outer loop runs **i** from 2 through 100. The inner loop successively tests all numbers from 2 up to **i**, printing those that evenly divide **i**. Extra challenge: The preceding program can be made more efficient. Can you see how? (Hint: the number of iterations in the inner loop can be reduced.)

✓ Module 3 Mastery Check

1. Write a program that reads characters from the keyboard until a period is received. Have the program count the number of spaces. Report the total at the end of the program.

2. Show the general form of the **if-else-if** ladder.

3. Given

```
if(x < 10)
  if(y > 100) {
    if(!done) x = z;
    else y = z;
  }
else System.out.println("error"); // what if?
```

to what **if** does the last **else** associate?

4. Show the **for** statement for a loop that counts from 1000 to 0 by –2.

5. Is the following fragment valid?

```
for(int i = 0; i < num; i++)
  sum += i;

count = i;
```

6. Explain what **break** does. Be sure to explain both of its forms.

7. In the following fragment, after the **break** statement executes, what is displayed?

```
for(i = 0; i < 10; i++) {
  while(running) {
    if(x<y) break;
    // ...
  }
  System.out.println("after while");
}
System.out.println("After for");
```

8. What does the following fragment print?

```
for(int i = 0; i<10; i++) {
  System.out.print(i + " ");
  if((i%2) == 0) continue;
  System.out.println();
}
```

9. The iteration expression in a **for** loop need not always alter the loop control variable by a fixed amount. Instead, the loop control variable can change in any arbitrary way. Using this concept, write a program that uses a **for** loop to generate and display the progression 1, 2, 4, 8, 16, 32, and so on.

10. The ASCII lowercase letters are separated from the uppercase letters by 32. Thus, to convert a lowercase letter to uppercase, subtract 32 from it. Use this information to write a program that reads characters from the keyboard. Have it convert all lowercase letters to uppercase, and all uppercase letters to lowercase, displaying the result. Make no changes to any other character. Have the program stop when the user presses period. At the end, have the program display the number of case changes that have taken place.

11. What is an infinite loop?

12. When using **break** with a label, must the label be on a block that contains the **break**?

Module 4

Introducing Classes, Objects, and Methods

B efore you can go much further in your study of Java, you need to learn about the class. The class is the essence of Java. It is the foundation upon which the entire Java language is built because the class defines the nature of an object. As such, the class forms the basis for object-oriented programming in Java. Within a class are defined data and code that acts upon that data. The code is contained in methods. Because classes, objects, and methods are fundamental to Java, they are introduced in this module. Having a basic understanding of these features will allow you to write more sophisticated programs and better understand certain key Java elements described in the following module.

CRITICAL SKILL
4.1 Class Fundamentals

Since all Java program activity occurs within a class, we have been using classes since the start of this book. Of course, only extremely simple classes have been used, and we have not taken advantage of the majority of their features. As you will see, classes are substantially more powerful than the limited ones presented so far.

Let's begin by reviewing the basics. A class is a template that defines the form of an object. It specifies both the data and the code that will operate on that data. Java uses a class specification to construct *objects*. Objects are *instances* of a class. Thus, a class is essentially a set of plans that specify how to build an object. It is important to be clear on one issue: a class is a logical abstraction. It is not until an object of that class has been created that a physical representation of that class exists in memory.

One other point: recall that the methods and variables that constitute a class are called *members* of the class. The data members are also referred to as *instance variables*.

The General Form of a Class

When you define a class, you declare its exact form and nature. You do this by specifying the instance variables that it contains and the methods that operate on them. Although very simple classes might contain only methods or only instance variables, most real-world classes contain both.

A class is created by using the keyword **class**. The general form of a **class** definition is shown here:

```
class classname {
    // declare instance variables
    type var1;
    type var2;
    // ...
    type varN;

    // declare methods
    type method1(parameters) {
```

```
    // body of method
  }
  type method2(parameters) {
    // body of method
  }
    // ...
  type methodN(parameters) {
    // body of method
  }
}
```

Although there is no syntactic rule that enforces it, a well-designed class should define one and only one logical entity. For example, a class that stores names and telephone numbers will not normally also store information about the stock market, average rainfall, sunspot cycles, or other unrelated information. The point here is that a well-designed class groups logically connected information. Putting unrelated information into the same class will quickly destructure your code!

Up to this point, the classes that we have been using have only had one method: **main( )**. Soon you will see how to create others. However, notice that the general form of a class does not specify a **main( )** method. A **main( )** method is required only if that class is the starting point for your program. Also, applets don't require a **main( )**.

Defining a Class

To illustrate classes we will develop a class that encapsulates information about vehicles, such as cars, vans, and trucks. This class is called **Vehicle**, and it will store three items of information about a vehicle: the number of passengers that it can carry, its fuel capacity, and its average fuel consumption (in miles per gallon).

The first version of **Vehicle** is shown next. It defines three instance variables: **passengers**, **fuelcap**, and **mpg**. Notice that **Vehicle** does not contain any methods. Thus, it is currently a data-only class. (Subsequent sections will add methods to it.)

```
class Vehicle {
  int passengers; // number of passengers
  int fuelcap;    // fuel capacity in gallons
  int mpg;        // fuel consumption in miles per gallon
}
```

A **class** definition creates a new data type. In this case, the new data type is called **Vehicle**. You will use this name to declare objects of type **Vehicle**. Remember that a **class** declaration is only a type description; it does not create an actual object. Thus, the preceding code does not cause any objects of type **Vehicle** to come into existence.

To actually create a **Vehicle** object, you will use a statement like the following:

```
Vehicle minivan = new Vehicle(); // create a Vehicle object called minivan
```

After this statement executes, **minivan** will be an instance of **Vehicle**. Thus, it will have "physical" reality. For the moment, don't worry about the details of this statement.

Each time you create an instance of a class, you are creating an object that contains its own copy of each instance variable defined by the class. Thus, every **Vehicle** object will contain its own copies of the instance variables **passengers**, **fuelcap**, and **mpg**. To access these variables, you will use the dot (.) operator. The *dot operator* links the name of an object with the name of a member. The general form of the dot operator is shown here:

object.member

Thus, the object is specified on the left, and the member is put on the right. For example, to assign the **fuelcap** variable of **minivan** the value 16, use the following statement:

```
minivan.fuelcap = 16;
```

In general, you can use the dot operator to access both instance variables and methods.

Here is a complete program that uses the **Vehicle** class:

```
/* A program that uses the Vehicle class.

   Call this file VehicleDemo.java
*/
class Vehicle {
  int passengers; // number of passengers
  int fuelcap;    // fuel capacity in gallons
  int mpg;        // fuel consumption in miles per gallon
}

// This class declares an object of type Vehicle.
class VehicleDemo {
  public static void main(String args[]) {
    Vehicle minivan = new Vehicle();
    int range;

    // assign values to fields in minivan
    minivan.passengers = 7;
    minivan.fuelcap = 16;        ←——————— Notice the use of the dot
    minivan.mpg = 21;                      operator to access a member.

    // compute the range assuming a full tank of gas
    range = minivan.fuelcap * minivan.mpg;
```

```
    System.out.println("Minivan can carry " + minivan.passengers +
                       " with a range of " + range);
  }
}
```

You should call the file that contains this program **VehicleDemo.java** because the **main( )** method is in the class called **VehicleDemo**, not the class called **Vehicle**. When you compile this program, you will find that two **.class** files have been created, one for **Vehicle** and one for **VehicleDemo**. The Java compiler automatically puts each class into its own **.class** file. It is not necessary for both the **Vehicle** and the **VehicleDemo** class to be in the same source file. You could put each class in its own file, called **Vehicle.java** and **VehicleDemo.java**, respectively.

To run this program, you must execute **VehicleDemo.class**. The following output is displayed:

```
Minivan can carry 7 with a range of 336
```

Before moving on, let's review a fundamental principle: each object has its own copies of the instance variables defined by its class. Thus, the contents of the variables in one object can differ from the contents of the variables in another. There is no connection between the two objects except for the fact that they are both objects of the same type. For example, if you have two **Vehicle** objects, each has its own copy of **passengers**, **fuelcap**, and **mpg**, and the contents of these can differ between the two objects. The following program demonstrates this fact. (Notice that the class with **main( )** is now called **TwoVehicles**.)

```
// This program creates two Vehicle objects.

class Vehicle {
  int passengers; // number of passengers
  int fuelcap;    // fuel capacity in gallons
  int mpg;        // fuel consumption in miles per gallon
}

// This class declares an object of type Vehicle.
class TwoVehicles {
  public static void main(String args[]) {
    Vehicle minivan = new Vehicle();          ─────── Remember,
    Vehicle sportscar = new Vehicle();                **minivan** and
                                                      **sportscar** refer
    int range1, range2;                               to separate
                                                      objects.

    // assign values to fields in minivan
    minivan.passengers = 7;
    minivan.fuelcap = 16;
    minivan.mpg = 21;
```

```
// assign values to fields in sportscar
sportscar.passengers = 2;
sportscar.fuelcap = 14;
sportscar.mpg = 12;

// compute the ranges assuming a full tank of gas
range1 = minivan.fuelcap * minivan.mpg;
range2 = sportscar.fuelcap * sportscar.mpg;

System.out.println("Minivan can carry " + minivan.passengers +
                   " with a range of " + range1);

System.out.println("Sportscar can carry " + sportscar.passengers +
                   " with a range of " + range2);
  }
}
```

The output produced by this program is shown here:

```
Minivan can carry 7 with a range of 336
Sportscar can carry 2 with a range of 168
```

As you can see, **minivan**'s data is completely separate from the data contained in **sportscar**. The following illustration depicts this situation.

	passengers	7
minivan →	fuelcap	16
	mpg	21

	passengers	2
sportscar →	fuelcap	14
	mpg	12

Progress Check

1. A class contains what two things?

2. What operator is used to access the members of a class through an object?

3. Each object has its own copies of the class' _____.

---

1. Code and data. In Java, this means methods and instance variables.
2. The dot operator.
3. instance variables

CRITICAL SKILL
4.2 # How Objects Are Created

In the preceding programs, the following line was used to declare an object of type **Vehicle**:

```
Vehicle minivan = new Vehicle();
```

This declaration performs two functions. First, it declares a variable called **minivan** of the class type **Vehicle**. This variable does not define an object. Instead, it is simply a variable that can *refer to* an object. Second, the declaration creates a physical copy of the object and assigns to **minivan** a reference to that object. This is done by using the **new** operator.

The **new** operator dynamically allocates (that is, allocates at run time) memory for an object and returns a reference to it. This reference is, more or less, the address in memory of the object allocated by **new**. This reference is then stored in a variable. Thus, in Java, all class objects must be dynamically allocated.

The two steps combined in the preceding statement can be rewritten like this to show each step individually:

```
Vehicle minivan; // declare reference to object
minivan = new Vehicle(); // allocate a Vehicle object
```

The first line declares **minivan** as a reference to an object of type **Vehicle**. Thus, **minivan** is a variable that can refer to an object, but it is not an object, itself. At this point, **minivan** contains the value **null**, which means that it does not refer to an object. The next line creates a new **Vehicle** object and assigns a reference to it to **minivan**. Now, **minivan** is linked with an object.

CRITICAL SKILL
4.3 # Reference Variables and Assignment

In an assignment operation, object reference variables act differently than do variables of a primitive type, such as **int**. When you assign one primitive-type variable to another, the situation is straightforward. The variable on the left receives a *copy* of the *value* of the variable on the right. When you assign an object reference variable to another, the situation is a bit more complicated because you are changing the object that the reference variable refers to. The effect of this difference can cause some counterintuitive results. For example, consider the following fragment:

```
Vehicle car1 = new Vehicle();
Vehicle car2 = car1;
```

At first glance, it is easy to think that **car1** and **car2** refer to different objects, but this is not the case. Instead, **car1** and **car2** will both refer to the *same* object. The assignment of **car1** to

car2 simply makes **car2** refer to the same object as does **car1**. Thus, the object can be acted upon by either **car1** or **car2**. For example, after the assignment

```
car1.mpg = 26;
```

executes, both of these **println( )** statements

```
System.out.println(car1.mpg);
System.out.println(car2.mpg);
```

display the same value: 26.

Although **car1** and **car2** both refer to the same object, they are not linked in any other way. For example, a subsequent assignment to **car2** simply changes the object to which **car2** refers. For example:

```
Vehicle car1 = new Vehicle();
Vehicle car2 = car1;
Vehicle car3 = new Vehicle();

car2 = car3; // now car2 and car3 refer to the same object.
```

After this sequence executes, **car2** refers to the same object as **car3**. The object referred to by **car1** is unchanged.

Progress Check

1. Explain what occurs when one object reference variable is assigned to another.

2. Assuming a class called **MyClass**, show how an object called **ob** is created.

CRITICAL SKILL
4.4 Methods

As explained, instance variables and methods are the constituents of classes. So far, the **Vehicle** class contains data, but no methods. Although data-only classes are perfectly valid, most classes will have methods. Methods are subroutines that manipulate the data defined by the class and, in many cases, provide access to that data. In most cases, other parts of your program will interact with a class through its methods.

---

1. When one object reference variable is assigned to another object reference variable, both variables will refer to the same object. A copy of the object *is not* made.

2. Myclass ob = new MyClass( );

A method contains one or more statements. In well-written Java code, each method performs only one task. Each method has a name, and it is this name that is used to call the method. In general, you can give a method whatever name you please. However, remember that **main( )** is reserved for the method that begins execution of your program. Also, don't use Java's keywords for method names.

When denoting methods in text, this book has used and will continue to use a convention that has become common when writing about Java. A method will have parentheses after its name. For example, if a method's name is **getval**, it will be written **getval( )** when its name is used in a sentence. This notation will help you distinguish variable names from method names in this book.

The general form of a method is shown here:

ret-type name(*parameter-list*) {
  // body of method
}

Here, *ret-type* specifies the type of data returned by the method. This can be any valid type, including class types that you create. If the method does not return a value, its return type must be **void**. The name of the method is specified by *name*. This can be any legal identifier other than those already used by other items within the current scope. The *parameter-list* is a sequence of type and identifier pairs separated by commas. Parameters are essentially variables that receive the value of the *arguments* passed to the method when it is called. If the method has no parameters, the parameter list will be empty.

Adding a Method to the Vehicle Class

As just explained, the methods of a class typically manipulate and provide access to the data of the class. With this in mind, recall that **main( )** in the preceding examples computed the range of a vehicle by multiplying its fuel consumption rate by its fuel capacity. While technically correct, this is not the best way to handle this computation. The calculation of a vehicle's range is something that is best handled by the **Vehicle** class itself. The reason for this conclusion is easy to understand: the range of a vehicle is dependent upon the capacity of the fuel tank and the rate of fuel consumption, and both of these quantities are encapsulated by **Vehicle**. By adding a method to **Vehicle** that computes the range, you are enhancing its object-oriented structure.

To add a method to **Vehicle**, specify it within **Vehicle**'s declaration. For example, the following version of **Vehicle** contains a method called **range( )** that displays the range of the vehicle.

```
// Add range to Vehicle.

class Vehicle {
  int passengers; // number of passengers
  int fuelcap;    // fuel capacity in gallons
```

```
    int mpg;          // fuel consumption in miles per gallon

  // Display the range.
  void range() {           The range( ) method is contained within the Vehicle class.
    System.out.println("Range is " + fuelcap * mpg);
  }
}
```

Notice that **fuelcap** and **mpg** are used directly, without the dot operator.

```
class AddMeth {
  public static void main(String args[]) {
    Vehicle minivan = new Vehicle();
    Vehicle sportscar = new Vehicle();

    int range1, range2;

    // assign values to fields in minivan
    minivan.passengers = 7;
    minivan.fuelcap = 16;
    minivan.mpg = 21;

    // assign values to fields in sportscar
    sportscar.passengers = 2;
    sportscar.fuelcap = 14;
    sportscar.mpg = 12;

    System.out.print("Minivan can carry " + minivan.passengers +
                     ". ");

    minivan.range(); // display range of minivan

    System.out.print("Sportscar can carry " + sportscar.passengers +
                     ". ");

    sportscar.range(); // display range of sportscar.
  }
}
```

This program generates the following output:

```
Minivan can carry 7. Range is 336
Sportscar can carry 2. Range is 168
```

Let's look at the key elements of this program, beginning with the **range( )** method itself. The first line of **range( )** is

```
void range() {
```

This line declares a method called **range** that has no parameters. Its return type is **void**. Thus, **range( )** does not return a value to the caller. The line ends with the opening curly brace of the method body.

The body of **range( )** consists solely of this line:

```
System.out.println("Range is " + fuelcap * mpg);
```

This statement displays the range of the vehicle by multiplying **fuelcap** by **mpg**. Since each object of type **Vehicle** has its own copy of **fuelcap** and **mpg**, when **range( )** is called, the range computation uses the calling object's copies of those variables.

The **range( )** method ends when its closing curly brace is encountered. This causes program control to transfer back to the caller.

Next, look closely at this line of code from inside **main( )**:

```
minivan.range();
```

This statement invokes the **range( )** method on **minivan**. That is, it calls **range( )** relative to the **minivan** object, using the object's name followed by the dot operator. When a method is called, program control is transferred to the method. When the method terminates, control is transferred back to the caller, and execution resumes with the line of code following the call.

In this case, the call to **minivan.range( )** displays the range of the vehicle defined by **minivan**. In similar fashion, the call to **sportscar.range( )** displays the range of the vehicle defined by **sportscar**. Each time **range( )** is invoked, it displays the range for the specified object.

There is something very important to notice inside the **range( )** method: the instance variables **fuelcap** and **mpg** are referred to directly, without preceding them with an object name or the dot operator. When a method uses an instance variable that is defined by its class, it does so directly, without explicit reference to an object and without use of the dot operator. This is easy to understand if you think about it. A method is always invoked relative to some object of its class. Once this invocation has occurred, the object is known. Thus, within a method, there is no need to specify the object a second time. This means that **fuelcap** and **mpg** inside **range( )** implicitly refer to the copies of those variables found in the object that invokes **range( )**.

CRITICAL SKILL

4.5 Returning from a Method

In general, there are two conditions that cause a method to return—first, as the **range( )** method in the preceding example shows, when the method's closing curly brace is encountered. The second is when a **return** statement is executed. There are two forms of **return**—one for use in **void** methods (those that do not return a value) and one for returning values. The first form is examined here. The next section explains how to return values.

In a **void** method, you can cause the immediate termination of a method by using this form of **return**:

return ;

When this statement executes, program control returns to the caller, skipping any remaining code in the method. For example, consider this method:

```
void myMeth() {
  int i;

  for(i=0; i<10; i++) {
    if(i == 5) return; // stop at 5
    System.out.println();
  }
}
```

Here, the **for** loop will only run from 0 to 5, because once **i** equals 5, the method returns.

It is permissible to have multiple return statements in a method, especially when there are two or more routes out of it. For example:

```
void myMeth() {
  // ...
  if(done) return;
  // ...
  if(error) return;
  // ...
}
```

Here, the method returns if it is done or if an error occurs. Be careful, however, because having too many exit points in a method can destructure your code; so avoid using them casually. A well-designed method has well-defined exit points.

To review: a **void** method can return in one of two ways—its closing curly brace is reached, or a **return** statement is executed.

CRITICAL SKILL
4.6 Returning a Value

Although methods with a return type of **void** are not rare, most methods will return a value. In fact, the ability to return a value is one of the most useful features of a method. You have already seen one example of a return value: when we used the **sqrt( )** function to obtain a square root.

Return values are used for a variety of purposes in programming. In some cases, such as with **sqrt( )**, the return value contains the outcome of some calculation. In other cases, the return value may simply indicate success or failure. In still others, it may contain a status code. Whatever the purpose, using method return values is an integral part of Java programming.

Methods return a value to the calling routine using this form of **return**:

return *value*;

Here, *value* is the value returned. This form of **return** can be used only with methods that have a non-**void** return type. Furthermore, a non-**void** method *must* return a value by using this form of **return**.

You can use a return value to improve the implementation of **range( )**. Instead of displaying the range, a better approach is to have **range( )** compute the range and return this value. Among the advantages to this approach is that you can use the value for other calculations. The following example modifies **range( )** to return the range rather than displaying it.

```java
// Use a return value.

class Vehicle {
  int passengers; // number of passengers
  int fuelcap;    // fuel capacity in gallons
  int mpg;        // fuel consumption in miles per gallon

  // Return the range.
  int range() {
    return mpg * fuelcap;   // ←——————— Return the range for a given vehicle.
  }
}

class RetMeth {
  public static void main(String args[]) {
    Vehicle minivan = new Vehicle();
    Vehicle sportscar = new Vehicle();

    int range1, range2;

    // assign values to fields in minivan
    minivan.passengers = 7;
    minivan.fuelcap = 16;
    minivan.mpg = 21;

    // assign values to fields in sportscar
    sportscar.passengers = 2;
    sportscar.fuelcap = 14;
    sportscar.mpg = 12;
```

```
         // get the ranges
         range1 = minivan.range();
         range2 = sportscar.range();
```
— Assign the value returned to a variable.

```
      System.out.println("Minivan can carry " + minivan.passengers +
                      " with range of " + range1 + " Miles");


      System.out.println("Sportscar can carry " + sportscar.passengers +
                      " with range of " + range2 + " miles");

   }
}
```

The output is shown here:

```
Minivan can carry 7 with range of 336 Miles
Sportscar can carry 2 with range of 168 miles
```

In the program, notice that when **range( )** is called, it is put on the right side of an assignment statement. On the left is a variable that will receive the value returned by **range( )**. Thus, after

```
range1 = minivan.range();
```

executes, the range of the **minivan** object is stored in **range1**.

Notice that **range( )** now has a return type of **int**. This means that it will return an integer value to the caller. The return type of a method is important because the type of data returned by a method must be compatible with the return type specified by the method. Thus, if you want a method to return data of type **double**, its return type must be type **double**.

Although the preceding program is correct, it is not written as efficiently as it could be. Specifically, there is no need for the **range1** or **range2** variables. A call to **range( )** can be used in the **println( )** statement directly, as shown here:

```
System.out.println("Minivan can carry " + minivan.passengers +
                   " with range of " + minivan.range() + " Miles");
```

In this case, when **println( )** is executed, **minivan.range( )** is called automatically and its value will be passed to **println( )**. Furthermore, you can use a call to **range( )** whenever the range of a **Vehicle** object is needed. For example, this statement compares the ranges of two vehicles:

```
if(v1.range() > v2.range()) System.out.println("v1 has greater range");
```

CRITICAL SKILL
4.7 Using Parameters

It is possible to pass one or more values to a method when the method is called. As explained, a value passed to a method is called an *argument*. Inside the method, the variable that receives the argument is called a *parameter*. Parameters are declared inside the parentheses that follow the method's name. The parameter declaration syntax is the same as that used for variables. A parameter is within the scope of its method, and aside from its special task of receiving an argument, it acts like any other local variable.

Here is a simple example that uses a parameter. Inside the **ChkNum** class, the method **isEven( )** returns **true** if the value that it is passed is even. It returns **false** otherwise. Therefore, **isEven( )** has a return type of **boolean**.

```
// A simple example that uses a parameter.

class ChkNum {
  // return true if x is even
  boolean isEven(int x) {              Here, x is an integer parameter of isEven( ).
    if((x%2) == 0) return true;
    else return false;
  }
}

class ParmDemo {
  public static void main(String args[]) {
    ChkNum e = new ChkNum();

    if(e.isEven(10)) System.out.println("10 is even.");     Pass arguments
                                                            to isEven( ).
    if(e.isEven(9)) System.out.println("9 is even.");

    if(e.isEven(8)) System.out.println("8 is even.");

  }
}
```

Here is the output produced by the program:

```
10 is even.
8 is even.
```

In the program, **isEven( )** is called three times, and each time a different value is passed. Let's look at this process closely. First, notice how **isEven( )** is called. The argument is specified between the parentheses. When **isEven( )** is called the first time, it is passed the value 10. Thus, when **isEven( )** begins executing, the parameter **x** receives the value 10. In the second call, 9 is the argument, and **x**, then, has the value 9. In the third call, the argument is 8, which is the value that **x** receives. The point is that the value passed as an argument when **isEven( )** is called is the value received by its parameter, **x**.

A method can have more than one parameter. Simply declare each parameter, separating one from the next with a comma. For example, the **Factor** class defines a method called **isFactor( )** that determines whether the first parameter is a factor of the second.

```
class Factor {
  boolean isFactor(int a, int b) {  ◄——————— This method has two parameters.
    if( (b % a) == 0) return true;
    else return false;
  }
}
class IsFact {
  public static void main(String args[]) {
    Factor x = new Factor();
                                                          Pass two arguments
                                                          to isFactor( ).
    if(x.isFactor(2, 20)) System.out.println("2 is factor");
    if(x.isFactor(3, 20)) System.out.println("this won't be displayed");

  }
}
```

Notice that when **isFactor( )** is called, the arguments are also separated by commas.

When using multiple parameters, each parameter specifies its own type, which can differ from the others. For example, this is perfectly valid:

```
int myMeth(int a, double b, float c) {
  // ...
```

Adding a Parameterized Method to Vehicle

You can use a parameterized method to add a new feature to the **Vehicle** class: the ability to compute the amount of fuel needed for a given distance. This new method is called **fuelneeded( )**. This method takes the number of miles that you want to drive and returns the number of gallons of gas required. The **fuelneeded( )** method is defined like this:

```
double fuelneeded(int miles) {
  return (double) miles / mpg;
}
```

Notice that this method returns a value of type **double**. This is useful since the amount of fuel needed for a given distance might not be an even number.

The entire **Vehicle** class that includes **fuelneeded( )** is shown here:

```java
/*
   Add a parameterized method that computes the
   fuel required for a given distance.
*/

class Vehicle {
  int passengers; // number of passengers
  int fuelcap;    // fuel capacity in gallons
  int mpg;        // fuel consumption in miles per gallon

  // Return the range.
  int range() {
    return mpg * fuelcap;
  }

  // Compute fuel needed for a given distance.
  double fuelneeded(int miles) {
    return (double) miles / mpg;
  }
}

class CompFuel {
  public static void main(String args[]) {
    Vehicle minivan = new Vehicle();
    Vehicle sportscar = new Vehicle();
    double gallons;
    int dist = 252;

    // assign values to fields in minivan
    minivan.passengers = 7;
    minivan.fuelcap = 16;
    minivan.mpg = 21;

    // assign values to fields in sportscar
    sportscar.passengers = 2;
    sportscar.fuelcap = 14;
    sportscar.mpg = 12;
```

```
gallons = minivan.fuelneeded(dist);

System.out.println("To go " + dist + " miles minivan needs " +
                   gallons + " gallons of fuel.");

gallons = sportscar.fuelneeded(dist);

System.out.println("To go " + dist + " miles sportscar needs " +
                   gallons + " gallons of fuel.");

  }
}
```

The output from the program is shown here:

```
To go 252 miles minivan needs 12.0 gallons of fuel.
To go 252 miles sportscar needs 21.0 gallons of fuel.
```

Progress Check

1. When must an instance variable or method be accessed through an object reference using the dot operator? When can a variable or method be used directly?

2. Explain the difference between an argument and a parameter.

3. Explain the two ways that a method can return to its caller.

---

1. When an instance variable is accessed by code that is not part of the class in which that instance variable is defined, it must be done through an object, by use of the dot operator. However, when an instance variable is accessed by code that is part of the same class as the instance variable, that variable can be referred to directly. The same thing applies to methods.

2. An *argument* is a value that is passed to a method when it is invoked. A *parameter* is a variable defined by a method that receives the value of the argument.

3. A method can be made to return through the use of the **return** statement. If the method has a **void** return type, it will also return when its closing curly brace is reached. Non-**void** methods must return a value, so returning by reaching the closing curly brace is not an option.

Project 4-1 Creating a Help Class

`HelpClassDemo.java`

If one were to try to summarize the essence of the class in one sentence, it might be this: a class encapsulates functionality. Of course, sometimes the trick is knowing where one "functionality" ends and another begins. As a general rule, you will want your classes to be the building blocks of your larger application. In order to do this, each class must represent a single functional unit that performs clearly delineated actions. Thus, you will want your classes to be as small as possible—but no smaller! That is, classes that contain extraneous functionality confuse and destructure code, but classes that contain too little functionality are fragmented. What is the balance? It is at this point that the *science* of programming becomes the *art* of programming. Fortunately, most programmers find that this balancing act becomes easier with experience.

To begin to gain that experience you will convert the help system from Project 3-3 in the preceding module into a Help class. Let's examine why this is a good idea. First, the help system defines one logical unit. It simply displays the syntax for Java's control statements. Thus, its functionality is compact and well defined. Second, putting help in a class is an esthetically pleasing approach. Whenever you want to offer the help system to a user, simply instantiate a help-system object. Finally, because help is encapsulated, it can be upgraded or changed without causing unwanted side effects in the programs that use it.

Step by Step

1. Create a new file called **HelpClassDemo.java.** To save you some typing, you might want to copy the file from Project 3-3, **Help3.java**, into **HelpClassDemo.java**.

2. To convert the help system into a class, you must first determine precisely what constitutes the help system. For example, in **Help3.java**, there is code to display a menu, input the user's choice, check for a valid response, and display information about the item selected. The program also loops until the letter q is pressed. If you think about it, it is clear that the menu, the check for a valid response, and the display of the information are integral to the help system. How user input is obtained, and whether repeated requests should be processed, are not. Thus, you will create a class that displays the help information, the help menu, and checks for a valid selection. Its methods will be called **helpon( )**, **showmenu( )**, and **isvalid( )**, respectively.

(continued)

3. Create the **helpon( )** method as shown here:

```
void helpon(int what) {
  switch(what) {
    case '1':
      System.out.println("The if:\n");
      System.out.println("if(condition) statement;");
      System.out.println("else statement;");
      break;
    case '2':
      System.out.println("The switch:\n");
      System.out.println("switch(expression) {");
      System.out.println("  case constant:");
      System.out.println("    statement sequence");
      System.out.println("    break;");
      System.out.println("  // ...");
      System.out.println("}");
      break;
    case '3':
      System.out.println("The for:\n");
      System.out.print("for(init; condition; iteration)");
      System.out.println(" statement;");
      break;
    case '4':
      System.out.println("The while:\n");
      System.out.println("while(condition) statement;");
      break;
    case '5':
      System.out.println("The do-while:\n");
      System.out.println("do {");
      System.out.println("  statement;");
      System.out.println("} while (condition);");
      break;
    case '6':
      System.out.println("The break:\n");
      System.out.println("break; or break label;");
      break;
    case '7':
      System.out.println("The continue:\n");
      System.out.println("continue; or continue label;");
      break;
  }
  System.out.println();
}
```

4. Next, create the **showmenu( )** method:

```
void showmenu() {
  System.out.println("Help on:");
```

```
    System.out.println("  1. if");
    System.out.println("  2. switch");
    System.out.println("  3. for");
    System.out.println("  4. while");
    System.out.println("  5. do-while");
    System.out.println("  6. break");
    System.out.println("  7. continue\n");
    System.out.print("Choose one (q to quit): ");
}
```

5. Create the **isvalid( )** method, shown here:

```
boolean isvalid(int ch) {
  if(ch < '1' | ch > '7' & ch != 'q') return false;
  else return true;
}
```

6. Assemble the foregoing methods into the **Help** class, shown here:

```
class Help {
  void helpon(int what) {
    switch(what) {
      case '1':
        System.out.println("The if:\n");
        System.out.println("if(condition) statement;");
        System.out.println("else statement;");
        break;
      case '2':
        System.out.println("The switch:\n");
        System.out.println("switch(expression) {");
        System.out.println("  case constant:");
        System.out.println("    statement sequence");
        System.out.println("    break;");
        System.out.println("  // ...");
        System.out.println("}");
        break;
      case '3':
        System.out.println("The for:\n");
        System.out.print("for(init; condition; iteration)");
        System.out.println(" statement;");
        break;
      case '4':
        System.out.println("The while:\n");
        System.out.println("while(condition) statement;");
        break;
      case '5':
        System.out.println("The do-while:\n");
```

(continued)

```
        System.out.println("do {");
        System.out.println("  statement;");
        System.out.println("} while (condition);");
        break;
    case '6':
        System.out.println("The break:\n");
        System.out.println("break; or break label;");
        break;
    case '7':
        System.out.println("The continue:\n");
        System.out.println("continue; or continue label;");
        break;
    }
    System.out.println();
  }

  void showmenu() {
    System.out.println("Help on:");
    System.out.println("  1. if");
    System.out.println("  2. switch");
    System.out.println("  3. for");
    System.out.println("  4. while");
    System.out.println("  5. do-while");
    System.out.println("  6. break");
    System.out.println("  7. continue\n");
    System.out.print("Choose one (q to quit): ");
  }

  boolean isvalid(int ch) {
    if(ch < '1' | ch > '7' & ch != 'q') return false;
    else return true;
  }

}
```

7. Finally, rewrite the **main( )** method from Project 3-3 so that it uses the new **Help** class. Call this class **HelpClassDemo.java**. The entire listing for **HelpClassDemo.java** is shown here:

```
/*
   Project 4-1

   Convert the help system from Project 3-3 into
   a Help class.
*/

class Help {
  void helpon(int what) {
```

```
    switch(what) {
      case '1':
        System.out.println("The if:\n");
        System.out.println("if(condition) statement;");
        System.out.println("else statement;");
        break;
      case '2':
        System.out.println("The switch:\n");
        System.out.println("switch(expression) {");
        System.out.println("  case constant:");
        System.out.println("    statement sequence");
        System.out.println("    break;");
        System.out.println("  // ...");
        System.out.println("}");
        break;
      case '3':
        System.out.println("The for:\n");
        System.out.print("for(init; condition; iteration)");
        System.out.println(" statement;");
        break;
      case '4':
        System.out.println("The while:\n");
        System.out.println("while(condition) statement;");
        break;
      case '5':
        System.out.println("The do-while:\n");
        System.out.println("do {");
        System.out.println("  statement;");
        System.out.println("} while (condition);");
        break;
      case '6':
        System.out.println("The break:\n");
        System.out.println("break; or break label;");
        break;
      case '7':
        System.out.println("The continue:\n");
        System.out.println("continue; or continue label;");
        break;
    }
    System.out.println();
  }

  void showmenu() {
    System.out.println("Help on:");
    System.out.println("  1. if");
```

(continued)

```
        System.out.println("  2. switch");
        System.out.println("  3. for");
        System.out.println("  4. while");
        System.out.println("  5. do-while");
        System.out.println("  6. break");
        System.out.println("  7. continue\n");
        System.out.print("Choose one (q to quit): ");
    }

  boolean isvalid(int ch) {
    if(ch < '1' | ch > '7' & ch != 'q') return false;
    else return true;
  }

}

class HelpClassDemo {
  public static void main(String args[])
    throws java.io.IOException {
    char choice;
    Help hlpobj = new Help();

    for(;;) {
      do {
        hlpobj.showmenu();
        do {
          choice = (char) System.in.read();
        } while(choice == '\n' | choice == '\r');

      } while( !hlpobj.isvalid(choice) );

      if(choice == 'q') break;

      System.out.println("\n");

      hlpobj.helpon(choice);
    }
  }
}
```

When you try the program, you will find that it is functionally the same as before. The advantage to this approach is that you now have a help system component that can be reused whenever it is needed.

CRITICAL SKILL
4.8 Constructors

In the preceding examples, the instance variables of each **Vehicle** object had to be set manually using a sequence of statements, such as:

```
minivan.passengers = 7;
minivan.fuelcap = 16;
minivan.mpg = 21;
```

An approach like this would never be used in professionally written Java code. Aside from being error prone (you might forget to set one of the fields), there is simply a better way to accomplish this task: the constructor.

A *constructor* initializes an object when it is created. It has the same name as its class and is syntactically similar to a method. However, constructors have no explicit return type. Typically, you will use a constructor to give initial values to the instance variables defined by the class, or to perform any other startup procedures required to create a fully formed object.

All classes have constructors, whether you define one or not, because Java automatically provides a default constructor that initializes all member variables to zero. However, once you define your own constructor, the default constructor is no longer used.

Here is a simple example that uses a constructor:

```
// A simple constructor.

class MyClass {
  int x;

  MyClass() {           ◄——————— This is the constructor for MyClass.
    x = 10;
  }
}

class ConsDemo {
  public static void main(String args[]) {
    MyClass t1 = new MyClass();
    MyClass t2 = new MyClass();

    System.out.println(t1.x + " " + t2.x);
  }
}
```

In this example, the constructor for **MyClass** is

```
MyClass() {
  x = 10;
}
```

This constructor assigns the instance variable **x** of **MyClass** the value 10. This constructor is called by **new** when an object is created. For example, in the line

```
MyClass t1 = new MyClass();
```

the constructor **MyClass( )** is called on the **t1** object, giving **t1.x** the value 10. The same is true for **t2**. After construction, **t2.x** has the value 10. Thus, the output from the program is

```
10 10
```

CRITICAL SKILL
4.9 Parameterized Constructors

In the preceding example, a parameter-less constructor was used. Although this is fine for some situations, most often you will need a constructor that accepts one or more parameters. Parameters are added to a constructor in the same way that they are added to a method: just declare them inside the parentheses after the constructor's name. For example, here, **MyClass** is given a parameterized constructor:

```
// A parameterized constructor.

class MyClass {
  int x;

  MyClass(int i) {  ◄─────────── This constructor has a parameter.
    x = i;
  }
}

class ParmConsDemo {
  public static void main(String args[]) {
    MyClass t1 = new MyClass(10);
    MyClass t2 = new MyClass(88);

    System.out.println(t1.x + " " + t2.x);
  }
}
```

The output from this program is shown here:

```
10 88
```

In this version of the program, the **MyClass( )** constructor defines one parameter called **i**, which is used to initialize the instance variable, **x**. Thus, when the line

```
MyClass t1 = new MyClass(10);
```

executes, the value 10 is passed to **i**, which is then assigned to **x**.

Adding a Constructor to the Vehicle Class

We can improve the **Vehicle** class by adding a constructor that automatically initializes the **passengers**, **fuelcap**, and **mpg** fields when an object is constructed. Pay special attention to how **Vehicle** objects are created.

```java
// Add a constructor.

class Vehicle {
  int passengers; // number of passengers
  int fuelcap;    // fuel capacity in gallons
  int mpg;        // fuel consumption in miles per gallon

  // This is a constructor for Vehicle.
  Vehicle(int p, int f, int m) {          Constructor for Vehicle.
    passengers = p;
    fuelcap = f;
    mpg = m;
  }

  // Return the range.
  int range() {
    return mpg * fuelcap;
  }

  // Compute fuel needed for a given distance.
  double fuelneeded(int miles) {
    return (double) miles / mpg;
  }
}

class VehConsDemo {
  public static void main(String args[]) {

    // construct complete vehicles
    Vehicle minivan = new Vehicle(7, 16, 21);
    Vehicle sportscar = new Vehicle(2, 14, 12);
    double gallons;
    int dist = 252;

    gallons = minivan.fuelneeded(dist);

    System.out.println("To go " + dist + " miles minivan needs " +
                       gallons + " gallons of fuel.");
```

```
      gallons = sportscar.fuelneeded(dist);

      System.out.println("To go " + dist + " miles sportscar needs " +
                         gallons + " gallons of fuel.");

    }
  }
```

Both **minivan** and **sportscar** are initialized by the **Vehicle( )** constructor when they are created. Each object is initialized as specified in the parameters to its constructor. For example, in the following line,

```
Vehicle minivan = new Vehicle(7, 16, 21);
```

the values 7, 16, and 21 are passed to the **Vehicle( )** constructor when **new** creates the object. Thus, **minivan**'s copy of **passengers**, **fuelcap**, and **mpg** will contain the values 7, 16, and 21, respectively. The output from this program is the same as the previous version.

Progress Check

1. What is a constructor, and when is it executed?

2. Does a constructor have a return type?

CRITICAL SKILL
4.10 The new Operator Revisited

Now that you know more about classes and their constructors, let's take a closer look at the **new** operator. The **new** operator has this general form:

class-var = new *class-name*(*arg-list*);

Here, *class-var* is a variable of the class type being created. The *class-name* is the name of the class that is being instantiated. The class name followed by a parenthesized argument list (which can be empty) specifies the constructor for the class. If a class does not define its own constructor, **new** will use the default constructor supplied by Java. Thus, **new** can be used to create an object of any class type.

---

1. A constructor is a method that is executed when an object of its class is instantiated. A constructor is used to initialize the object being created.

2. No.

Ask the Expert

Q: **Why don't I need to use** new **for variables of the primitive types, such as** int **or** float?

A: Java's primitive types are not implemented as objects. Rather, because of efficiency concerns, they are implemented as "normal" variables. A variable of a primitive type actually contains the value that you have given it. As explained, object variables are references to the object. This layer of indirection (and other object features) adds overhead to an object that is avoided by a primitive type.

Since memory is finite, it is possible that **new** will not be able to allocate memory for an object because insufficient memory exists. If this happens, a run-time exception will occur. (You will learn how to handle this and other exceptions in Module 9.) For the sample programs in this book, you won't need to worry about running out of memory, but you will need to consider this possibility in real-world programs that you write.

CRITICAL SKILL
4.11 Garbage Collection and Finalizers

As you have seen, objects are dynamically allocated from a pool of free memory by using the **new** operator. As explained, memory is not infinite, and the free memory can be exhausted. Thus, it is possible for **new** to fail because there is insufficient free memory to create the desired object. For this reason, a key component of any dynamic allocation scheme is the recovery of free memory from unused objects, making that memory available for subsequent reallocation. In many programming languages, the release of previously allocated memory is handled manually. For example, in C++, you use the **delete** operator to free memory that was allocated. However, Java uses a different, more trouble-free approach: *garbage collection.*

Java's garbage collection system reclaims objects automatically—occurring transparently, behind the scenes, without any programmer intervention. It works like this: when no references to an object exist, that object is assumed to be no longer needed, and the memory occupied by the object is released. This recycled memory can then be used for a subsequent allocation.

Garbage collection occurs only sporadically during the execution of your program. It will not occur simply because one or more objects exist that are no longer used. For efficiency, the garbage collector will usually run only when two conditions are met: there are objects to recycle, and there is a need to recycle them. Remember, garbage collection takes time, so the Java run-time system does it only when necessary. Thus, you can't know precisely when garbage collection will take place.

The finalize( ) Method

It is possible to define a method that will be called just before an object's final destruction by the garbage collector. This method is called **finalize( )**, and it can be used to ensure that an object terminates cleanly. For example, you might use **finalize( )** to make sure that an open file owned by that object is closed.

To add a finalizer to a class, you simply define the **finalize( )** method. The Java runtime calls that method whenever it is about to recycle an object of that class. Inside the **finalize( )** method you will specify those actions that must be performed before an object is destroyed.

The **finalize( )** method has this general form:

```
protected void finalize( )
{
  // finalization code here
}
```

Here, the keyword **protected** is a specifier that prevents access to **finalize( )** by code defined outside its class. This and the other access specifiers are explained in Module 6.

It is important to understand that **finalize( )** is called just before garbage collection. It is not called when an object goes out of scope, for example. This means that you cannot know when—or even if—**finalize( )** will be executed. For example, if your program ends before garbage collection occurs, **finalize( )** will not execute. Therefore, it should be used as a "backup" procedure to ensure the proper handling of some resource, or for special-use applications, not as the means that your program uses in its normal operation.

Ask the Expert

Q: I know that C++ defines things called *destructors*, which are automatically executed when an object is destroyed. Is finalize( ) **similar to a destructor?**

A: Java does not have destructors. Although it is true that the **finalize( )** method approximates the function of a destructor, it is not the same. For example, a C++ destructor is always called just before an object goes out of scope, but you can't know when **finalize( )** will be called for any specific object. Frankly, because of Java's use of garbage collection, there is little need for a destructor.

Project 4-2 Demonstrate Finalization

`Finalize.java`

Because garbage collection runs sporadically, in the background, it is not trivial to demonstrate the **finalize( )** method. Recall that **finalize( )** is called when an object is about to be recycled. As explained, objects are not necessarily recycled as soon as they are no longer needed. Instead, the garbage collector waits until it can perform its collection efficiently, usually when there are many unused objects. Thus, to demonstrate the **finalize( )** method, you often need to create and destroy a large number of objects—and this is precisely what you will do in this project.

Step by Step

1. Create a new file called **Finalize.java.**

2. Create the **FDemo** class shown here:

```java
class FDemo {
  int x;

  FDemo(int i) {
    x = i;
  }

  // called when object is recycled
  protected void finalize() {
    System.out.println("Finalizing " + x);
  }

  // generates an object that is immediately destroyed
  void generator(int i) {
    FDemo o = new FDemo(i);
  }

}
```

The constructor sets the instance variable **x** to a known value. In this example, **x** is used as an object ID. The **finalize( )** method displays the value of **x** when an object is recycled. Of special interest is **generator( )**. This method creates and then promptly discards an **FDemo** object. You will see how this is used in the next step.

(continued)

3. Create the **Finalize** class, shown here:

```
class Finalize {
  public static void main(String args[]) {
    int count;

    FDemo ob = new FDemo(0);

    /* Now, generate a large number of objects. At
       some point, garbage collection will occur.
       Note: you might need to increase the number
       of objects generated in order to force
       garbage collection. */

    for(count=1; count < 100000; count++)
      ob.generator(count);
  }
}
```

This class creates an initial **FDemo** object called **ob**. Then, using **ob**, it creates 100,000 objects by calling **generator( )** on **ob**. This has the net effect of creating and discarding 100,000 objects. At various points in the middle of this process, garbage collection will take place. Precisely how often or when depends upon several factors, such as the initial amount of free memory and the operating system. However, at some point, you will start to see the messages generated by **finalize( )**. If you don't see the messages, try increasing the number of objects being generated by raising the count in the **for** loop.

4. Here is the entire **Finalize.java** program:

```
/*
   Project 4-2

   Demonstrate the finalize() method.
*/

class FDemo {
  int x;

  FDemo(int i) {
    x = i;
  }

  // called when object is recycled
  protected void finalize() {
    System.out.println("Finalizing " + x);
  }
```

```
    // generates an object that is immediately destroyed
    void generator(int i) {
      FDemo o = new FDemo(i);
    }

}

class Finalize {
  public static void main(String args[]) {
    int count;

    FDemo ob = new FDemo(0);

    /* Now, generate a large number of objects. At
       some point, garbage collection will occur.
       Note: you might need to increase the number
       of objects generated in order to force
       garbage collection. */

    for(count=1; count < 100000; count++)
      ob.generator(count);
  }
}
```

CRITICAL SKILL
4.12 The this Keyword

Before concluding this module it is necessary to introduce **this**. When a method is called, it is automatically passed an implicit argument that is a reference to the invoking object (that is, the object on which the method is called). This reference is called **this**. To understand **this**, first consider a program that creates a class called **Pwr** that computes the result of a number raised to some integer power:

```
class Pwr {
  double b;
  int e;
  double val;

  Pwr(double base, int exp) {
    b = base;
    e = exp;

    val = 1;
    if(exp==0) return;
    for( ; exp>0; exp--) val = val * base;
```

```
    }

    double get_pwr() {
      return val;
    }
  }

class DemoPwr {
  public static void main(String args[]) {
    Pwr x = new Pwr(4.0, 2);
    Pwr y = new Pwr(2.5, 1);
    Pwr z = new Pwr(5.7, 0);

    System.out.println(x.b + " raised to the " + x.e +
                       " power is " + x.get_pwr());
    System.out.println(y.b + " raised to the " + y.e +
                       " power is " + y.get_pwr());
    System.out.println(z.b + " raised to the " + z.e +
                       " power is " + z.get_pwr());
  }
}
```

As you know, within a method, the other members of a class can be accessed directly, without any object or class qualification. Thus, inside **get_pwr( )**, the statement

```
return val;
```

means that the copy of **val** associated with the invoking object will be returned. However, the same statement can also be written like this:

```
return this.val;
```

Here, **this** refers to the object on which **get_pwr( )** was called. Thus, **this.val** refers to that object's copy of **val**. For example, if **get_pwr( )** had been invoked on **x**, then **this** in the preceding statement would have been referring to **x**. Writing the statement without using **this** is really just shorthand.

Here is the entire **Pwr** class written using the **this** reference:

```
class Pwr {
  double b;
  int e;
  double val;

  Pwr(double base, int exp) {
    this.b = base;
```

```
    this.e = exp;

    this.val = 1;
    if(exp==0) return;
    for( ; exp>0; exp--) this.val = this.val * base;
  }

  double get_pwr() {
    return this.val;
  }
}
```

Actually, no Java programmer would write **Pwr** as just shown because nothing is gained, and the standard form is easier. However, **this** has some important uses. For example, the Java syntax permits the name of a parameter or a local variable to be the same as the name of an instance variable. When this happens, the local name *hides* the instance variable. You can gain access to the hidden instance variable by referring to it through **this**. For example, although not recommended style, the following is a syntactically valid way to write the **Pwr( )** constructor.

```
Pwr(double b, int e) {
  this.b = b;                    ── This refers to the b instance
  this.e = e;                        variable, not the parameter.

  val = 1;
  if(e==0) return;
  for( ; e>0; e--) val = val * b;
}
```

In this version, the names of the parameters are the same as the names of the instance variables, thus hiding them. However, **this** is used to "uncover" the instance variables.

✓

Module 4 Mastery Check

1. What is the difference between a class and an object?

2. How is a class defined?

3. What does each object have its own copy of?

4. Using two separate statements, show how to declare an object called **counter** of a class called **MyCounter**.

5. Show how a method called **myMeth( )** is declared if it has a return type of **double** and has two **int** parameters called **a** and **b**.

6. How must a method return if it returns a value?

7. What name does a constructor have?

8. What does **new** do?

9. What is garbage collection, and how does it work? What is **finalize( )**?

10. What is **this**?

11. Can a constructor have one or more parameters?

12. If a method returns no value, what must its return type be?

Module 5

More Data Types and Operators

This module returns to the subject of Java's data types and operators. It discusses arrays, the **String** type, the bitwise operators, and the **?** ternary operator. It also covers Java's new for-each style **for** loop. Along the way, command-line arguments are described.

Arrays

An array is a collection of variables of the same type, referred to by a common name. In Java, arrays can have one or more dimensions, although the one-dimensional array is the most common. Arrays are used for a variety of purposes because they offer a convenient means of grouping together related variables. For example, you might use an array to hold a record of the daily high temperature for a month, a list of stock price averages, or a list of your collection of programming books.

The principal advantage of an array is that it organizes data in such a way that it can be easily manipulated. For example, if you have an array containing the incomes for a selected group of households, it is easy to compute the average income by cycling through the array. Also, arrays organize data in such a way that it can be easily sorted.

Although arrays in Java can be used just like arrays in other programming languages, they have one special attribute: they are implemented as objects. This fact is one reason that a discussion of arrays was deferred until objects had been introduced. By implementing arrays as objects, several important advantages are gained, not the least of which is that unused arrays can be garbage collected.

One-Dimensional Arrays

A one-dimensional array is a list of related variables. Such lists are common in programming. For example, you might use a one-dimensional array to store the account numbers of the active users on a network. Another array might be used to store the current batting averages for a baseball team.

To declare a one-dimensional array, you will use this general form:

type array-name[ ] = new *type*[*size*];

Here, *type* declares the base type of the array. The base type determines the data type of each element contained in the array. The number of elements that the array will hold is determined by *size*. Since arrays are implemented as objects, the creation of an array is a two-step process. First, you declare an array reference variable. Second, you allocate memory for the array, assigning a reference to that memory to the array variable. Thus, arrays in Java are dynamically allocated using the **new** operator.

Here is an example. The following creates an **int** array of 10 elements and links it to an array reference variable named **sample**.

```
int sample[] = new int[10];
```

This declaration works just like an object declaration. The **sample** variable holds a reference to the memory allocated by **new**. This memory is large enough to hold 10 elements of type **int**.

As with objects, it is possible to break the preceding declaration in two. For example:

```
int sample[];
sample = new int[10];
```

In this case, when **sample** is first created, it is **null**, because it refers to no physical object. It is only after the second statement executes that **sample** is linked with an array.

An individual element within an array is accessed by use of an index. An *index* describes the position of an element within an array. In Java, all arrays have zero as the index of their first element. Because **sample** has 10 elements, it has index values of 0 through 9. To index an array, specify the number of the element you want, surrounded by square brackets. Thus, the first element in **sample** is **sample[0]**, and the last element is **sample[9]**. For example, the following program loads **sample** with the numbers 0 through 9.

```
// Demonstrate a one-dimensional array.
class ArrayDemo {
  public static void main(String args[]) {
    int sample[] = new int[10];
    int i;

    for(i = 0; i < 10; i = i+1)       ◄───────────────┐
      sample[i] = i;                      Arrays are indexed from zero.

    for(i = 0; i < 10; i = i+1)       ◄───────────────┘
      System.out.println("This is sample[" + i + "]: " +
                        sample[i]);
  }
}
```

The output from the program is shown here:

```
This is sample[0]: 0
This is sample[1]: 1
This is sample[2]: 2
This is sample[3]: 3
```

```
This is sample[4]: 4
This is sample[5]: 5
This is sample[6]: 6
This is sample[7]: 7
This is sample[8]: 8
This is sample[9]: 9
```

Conceptually, the **sample** array looks like this:

0	1	2	3	4	5	6	7	8	9
Sample [0]	Sample [1]	Sample [2]	Sample [3]	Sample [4]	Sample [5]	Sample [6]	Sample [7]	Sample [8]	Sample [9]

Arrays are common in programming because they let you deal easily with large numbers of related variables. For example, the following program finds the minimum and maximum values stored in the **nums** array by cycling through the array using a **for** loop.

```
// Find the minimum and maximum values in an array.
class MinMax {
  public static void main(String args[]) {
    int nums[] = new int[10];
    int min, max;

    nums[0] = 99;
    nums[1] = -10;
    nums[2] = 100123;
    nums[3] = 18;
    nums[4] = -978;
    nums[5] = 5623;
    nums[6] = 463;
    nums[7] = -9;
    nums[8] = 287;
    nums[9] = 49;

    min = max = nums[0];
    for(int i=1; i < 10; i++) {
      if(nums[i] < min) min = nums[i];
      if(nums[i] > max) max = nums[i];
    }
    System.out.println("min and max: " + min + " " + max);
  }
}
```

The output from the program is shown here:

```
min and max: -978 100123
```

In the preceding program, the **nums** array was given values by hand, using 10 separate assignment statements. Although perfectly correct, there is an easier way to accomplish this. Arrays can be initialized when they are created. The general form for initializing a one-dimensional array is shown here:

type array-name[ ] = { *val1, val2, val3, ... , valN* };

Here, the initial values are specified by *val1* through *valN*. They are assigned in sequence, left to right, in index order. Java automatically allocates an array large enough to hold the initializers that you specify. There is no need to explicitly use the **new** operator. For example, here is a better way to write the **MinMax** program:

```java
// Use array initializers.
class MinMax2 {
  public static void main(String args[]) {
    int nums[] = { 99, -10, 100123, 18, -978,
                   5623, 463, -9, 287, 49 };          ←———— Array initializers
    int min, max;

    min = max = nums[0];
    for(int i=1; i < 10; i++) {
      if(nums[i] < min) min = nums[i];
      if(nums[i] > max) max = nums[i];
    }
    System.out.println("Min and max: " + min + " " + max);
  }
}
```

Array boundaries are strictly enforced in Java; it is a run-time error to overrun or underrun the end of an array. If you want to confirm this for yourself, try the following program that purposely overruns an array.

```java
// Demonstrate an array overrun.
class ArrayErr {
  public static void main(String args[]) {
    int sample[] = new int[10];
    int i;

    // generate an array overrun
    for(i = 0; i < 100; i = i+1)
      sample[i] = i;
  }
}
```

As soon as **i** reaches 10, an **ArrayIndexOutOfBoundsException** is generated and the program is terminated.

Progress Check

1. Arrays are accessed via an _____.

2. How is a 10-element **char** array declared?

3. Java does not check for array overruns at run time. True or False?

Project 5-1 Sorting an Array

`Bubble.java`

Because a one-dimensional array organizes data into an indexable linear list, it is the perfect data structure for sorting. In this project you will learn a simple way to sort an array. As you may know, there are a number of different sorting algorithms. There are the quick sort, the shaker sort, and the shell sort, to name just three. However, the best known, simplest, and easiest to understand is called the Bubble sort. Although the Bubble sort is not very efficient—in fact, its performance is unacceptable for sorting large arrays—it may be used effectively for sorting small arrays.

Step by Step

1. Create a file called **Bubble.java**.

2. The Bubble sort gets its name from the way it performs the sorting operation. It uses the repeated comparison and, if necessary, exchange of adjacent elements in the array. In this process, small values move toward one end and large ones toward the other end. The process is conceptually similar to bubbles finding their own level in a tank of water. The Bubble sort operates by making several passes through the array, exchanging out-of-place elements

---

1. index
2. char a[] = new char[10];
3. False. Java does not allow array overruns at run time.

when necessary. The number of passes required to ensure that the array is sorted is equal to one less than the number of elements in the array.

Here is the code that forms the core of the Bubble sort. The array being sorted is called **nums**.

```java
// This is the Bubble sort.
for(a=1; a < size; a++)
  for(b=size-1; b >= a; b--) {
    if(nums[b-1] > nums[b]) { // if out of order
      // exchange elements
      t = nums[b-1];
      nums[b-1] = nums[b];
      nums[b] = t;
    }
  }
```

Notice that sort relies on two **for** loops. The inner loop checks adjacent elements in the array, looking for out-of-order elements. When an out-of-order element pair is found, the two elements are exchanged. With each pass, the smallest of the remaining elements moves into its proper location. The outer loop causes this process to repeat until the entire array has been sorted.

3. Here is the entire **Bubble** program:

```java
/*
   Project 5-1

   Demonstrate the Bubble sort.
*/

class Bubble {
  public static void main(String args[]) {
    int nums[] = { 99, -10, 100123, 18, -978,
                   5623, 463, -9, 287, 49 };
    int a, b, t;
    int size;

    size = 10; // number of elements to sort

    // display original array
    System.out.print("Original array is:");
    for(int i=0; i < size; i++)
```

(continued)

```
      System.out.print(" " + nums[i]);
    System.out.println();

    // This is the Bubble sort.
    for(a=1; a < size; a++)
      for(b=size-1; b >= a; b--) {
        if(nums[b-1] > nums[b]) { // if out of order
          // exchange elements
          t = nums[b-1];
          nums[b-1] = nums[b];
          nums[b] = t;
        }
      }

    // display sorted array
    System.out.print("Sorted array is:");
    for(int i=0; i < size; i++)
      System.out.print(" " + nums[i]);
    System.out.println();
  }
}
```

The output from the program is shown here:

```
Original array is: 99 -10 100123 18 -978 5623 463 -9 287 49
Sorted array is: -978 -10 -9 18 49 99 287 463 5623 100123
```

4. Although the Bubble sort is good for small arrays, it is not efficient when used on larger ones. The best general-purpose sorting algorithm is the Quicksort. The Quicksort, however, relies on features of Java that you have not yet learned about.

CRITICAL SKILL
5.2 Multidimensional Arrays

Although the one-dimensional array is the most commonly used array in programming, multidimensional arrays (arrays of two or more dimensions) are certainly not rare. In Java, a multidimensional array is an array of arrays.

Two-Dimensional Arrays

The simplest form of the multidimensional array is the two-dimensional array. A two-dimensional array is, in essence, a list of one-dimensional arrays. To declare a two-dimensional integer array **table** of size 10, 20 you would write

```
int table[][] = new int[10][20];
```

Pay careful attention to the declaration. Unlike some other computer languages, which use commas to separate the array dimensions, Java places each dimension in its own set of brackets. Similarly, to access point 3, 5 of array **table**, you would use **table[3][5]**.

In the next example, a two-dimensional array is loaded with the numbers 1 through 12.

```
// Demonstrate a two-dimensional array.
class TwoD {
  public static void main(String args[]) {
    int t, i;
    int table[][] = new int[3][4];

    for(t=0; t < 3; ++t) {
      for(i=0; i < 4; ++i) {
        table[t][i] = (t*4)+i+1;
        System.out.print(table[t][i] + " ");
      }
      System.out.println();
    }
  }
}
```

In this example, **table[0][0]** will have the value 1, **table[0][1]** the value 2, **table[0][2]** the value 3, and so on. The value of **table[2][3]** will be 12. Conceptually, the array will look like that shown in Figure 5-1.

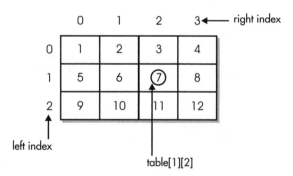

Figure 5-1 Conceptual view of the table array created by the TwoD program

Irregular Arrays

When you allocate memory for a multidimensional array, you need to specify only the memory for the first (leftmost) dimension. You can allocate the remaining dimensions separately. For example, the following code allocates memory for the first dimension of **table** when it is declared. It allocates the second dimension manually.

```
int table[][] = new int[3][];
table[0] = new int[4];
table[1] = new int[4];
table[2] = new int[4];
```

Although there is no advantage to individually allocating the second dimension arrays in this situation, there may be in others. For example, when you allocate dimensions separately, you do not need to allocate the same number of elements for each index. Since multidimensional arrays are implemented as arrays of arrays, the length of each array is under your control. For example, assume you are writing a program that stores the number of passengers that ride an airport shuttle. If the shuttle runs 10 times a day during the week and twice a day on Saturday and Sunday, you could use the **riders** array shown in the following program to store the information. Notice that the length of the second dimension for the first five indices is 10 and the length of the second dimension for the last two indices is 2.

```
// Manually allocate differing size second dimensions.
class Ragged {
  public static void main(String args[]) {
    int riders[][] = new int[7][];
    riders[0] = new int[10];
    riders[1] = new int[10];
    riders[2] = new int[10];          Here, the second dimensions
    riders[3] = new int[10];          are 10 elements long.
    riders[4] = new int[10];
    riders[5] = new int[2];           But here, they are
    riders[6] = new int[2];           2 elements long.

    int i, j;

    // fabricate some fake data
    for(i=0; i < 5; i++)
      for(j=0; j < 10; j++)
        riders[i][j] = i + j + 10;
    for(i=5; i < 7; i++)
      for(j=0; j < 2; j++)
        riders[i][j] = i + j + 10;
```

```
      System.out.println("Riders per trip during the week:");
      for(i=0; i < 5; i++) {
        for(j=0; j < 10; j++)
          System.out.print(riders[i][j] + " ");
        System.out.println();
      }
      System.out.println();

      System.out.println("Riders per trip on the weekend:");
      for(i=5; i < 7; i++) {
        for(j=0; j < 2; j++)
          System.out.print(riders[i][j] + " ");
        System.out.println();
      }
    }
  }
```

The use of irregular (or ragged) multidimensional arrays is not recommended for most applications, because it runs contrary to what people expect to find when a multidimensional array is encountered. However, irregular arrays can be used effectively in some situations. For example, if you need a very large two-dimensional array that is sparsely populated (that is, one in which not all of the elements will be used), an irregular array might be a perfect solution.

Arrays of Three or More Dimensions

Java allows arrays with more than two dimensions. Here is the general form of a multidimensional array declaration:

type name[ ][ ]...[ ] = new *type*[*size1*][*size2*]...[*sizeN*];

For example, the following declaration creates a 4 x 10 x 3 three-dimensional integer array.

```
int multidim[][][] = new int[4][10][3];
```

Initializing Multidimensional Arrays

A multidimensional array can be initialized by enclosing each dimension's initializer list within its own set of curly braces. For example, the general form of array initialization for a two-dimensional array is shown here:

type-specifier array_name[ ][ ] = {
   { *val, val, val, ..., val* },
   { *val, val, val, ..., val* },
.
.
.

```
    { val, val, val, ..., val }
};
```

Here, *val* indicates an initialization value. Each inner block designates a row. Within each row, the first value will be stored in the first position of the subarray, the second value in the second position, and so on. Notice that commas separate the initializer blocks and that a semicolon follows the closing **}**.

For example, the following program initializes an array called **sqrs** with the numbers 1 through 10 and their squares.

```
// Initialize a two-dimensional array.
class Squares {
  public static void main(String args[]) {
    int sqrs[][] = {
      { 1, 1 },
      { 2, 4 },
      { 3, 9 },
      { 4, 16 },
      { 5, 25 },          Notice how each row has
      { 6, 36 },          its own set of initializers.
      { 7, 49 },
      { 8, 64 },
      { 9, 81 },
      { 10, 100 }
    };
    int i, j;

    for(i=0; i < 10; i++) {
      for(j=0; j < 2; j++)
        System.out.print(sqrs[i][j] + " ");
      System.out.println();
    }
  }
}
```

Here is the output from the program:

```
1 1
2 4
3 9
4 16
5 25
6 36
7 49
8 64
9 81
10 100
```

Progress Check

1. For multidimensional arrays, each dimension is specified how?

2. In a two-dimensional array, which is an array of arrays, can the length of each array differ?

3. How are multidimensional arrays initialized?

CRITICAL SKILL
5.4 Alternative Array Declaration Syntax

There is a second form that can be used to declare an array:

type[ ] *var-name;*

Here, the square brackets follow the type specifier, not the name of the array variable. For example, the following two declarations are equivalent:

```
int counter[] = new int[3];
int[] counter = new int[3];
```

The following declarations are also equivalent:

```
char table[][] = new char[3][4];
char[][] table = new char[3][4];
```

This alternative declaration form offers convenience when declaring several arrays at the same time. For example,

```
int[] nums, nums2, nums3; // create three arrays
```

This creates three array variables of type **int**. It is the same as writing

```
int nums[], nums2[], nums3[]; // also, create three arrays
```

The alternative declaration form is also useful when specifying an array as a return type for a method. For example,

```
int[] someMeth( ) { ...
```

This declares that **someMeth( )** returns an array of type **int**.

---

1. Each dimension is specified within its own set of square brackets.
2. Yes.
3. Multidimensional arrays are initialized by putting each subarray's initializers inside their own set of curly braces.

Assigning Array References

Like other objects, when you assign one array reference variable to another, you are simply changing what object that variable refers to. You are not causing a copy of the array to be made, nor are you causing the contents of one array to be copied to the other. For example, consider this program:

```
// Assigning array reference variables.
class AssignARef {
  public static void main(String args[]) {
    int i;

    int nums1[] = new int[10];
    int nums2[] = new int[10];

    for(i=0; i < 10; i++)
      nums1[i] = i;

    for(i=0; i < 10; i++)
      nums2[i] = -i;

    System.out.print("Here is nums1: ");
    for(i=0; i < 10; i++)
      System.out.print(nums1[i] + " ");
    System.out.println();

    System.out.print("Here is nums2: ");
    for(i=0; i < 10; i++)
      System.out.print(nums2[i] + " ");
    System.out.println();

    nums2 = nums1; // now nums2 refers to nums1  ◄──────── Assign an array
                                                            reference
    System.out.print("Here is nums2 after assignment: ");
    for(i=0; i < 10; i++)
      System.out.print(nums2[i] + " ");
    System.out.println();

    // now operate on nums1 array through nums2
    nums2[3] = 99;

    System.out.print("Here is nums1 after change through nums2: ");
```

```
      for(i=0; i < 10; i++)
        System.out.print(nums1[i] + " ");
      System.out.println();
    }
}
```

The output from the program is shown here:

```
Here is nums1: 0 1 2 3 4 5 6 7 8 9
Here is nums2: 0 -1 -2 -3 -4 -5 -6 -7 -8 -9
Here is nums2 after assignment: 0 1 2 3 4 5 6 7 8 9
Here is nums1 after change through nums2: 0 1 2 99 4 5 6 7 8 9
```

As the output shows, after the assignment of **nums1** to **nums2**, both array reference variables refer to the same object.

CRITICAL SKILL
5.6 Using the length Member

Because arrays are implemented as objects, each array has associated with it a **length** instance variable that contains the number of elements that the array can hold. (In other words, **length** contains the size of the array.) Here is a program that demonstrates this property:

```
// Use the length array member.
class LengthDemo {
  public static void main(String args[]) {
    int list[] = new int[10];
    int nums[] = { 1, 2, 3 };
    int table[][] = { // a variable-length table
      {1, 2, 3},
      {4, 5},
      {6, 7, 8, 9}
    };

    System.out.println("length of list is " + list.length);
    System.out.println("length of nums is " + nums.length);
    System.out.println("length of table is " + table.length);
    System.out.println("length of table[0] is " + table[0].length);
    System.out.println("length of table[1] is " + table[1].length);
    System.out.println("length of table[2] is " + table[2].length);
    System.out.println();
```

```
    // use length to initialize list
    for(int i=0; i < list.length; i++)
      list[i] = i * i;

    System.out.print("Here is list: ");
    // now use length to display list
    for(int i=0; i < list.length; i++)
      System.out.print(list[i] + " ");
    System.out.println();
  }
}
```

Use **length** to control a **for** loop.

This program displays the following output:

```
length of list is 10
length of nums is 3
length of table is 3
length of table[0] is 3
length of table[1] is 2
length of table[2] is 4

Here is list: 0 1 4 9 16 25 36 49 64 81
```

Pay special attention to the way **length** is used with the two-dimensional array **table**. As explained, a two-dimensional array is an array of arrays. Thus, when the expression

```
table.length
```

is used, it obtains the number of *arrays* stored in **table**, which is 3 in this case. To obtain the length of any individual array in **table**, you will use an expression such as this,

```
table[0].length
```

which, in this case, obtains the length of the first array.

One other thing to notice in **LengthDemo** is the way that **list.length** is used by the **for** loops to govern the number of iterations that take place. Since each array carries with it its own length, you can use this information rather than manually keeping track of an array's size. Keep in mind that the value of **length** has nothing to do with the number of elements that are actually in use. It contains the number of elements that the array is capable of holding.

The inclusion of the **length** member simplifies many algorithms by making certain types of array operations easier—and safer—to perform. For example, the following program uses **length** to copy one array to another while preventing an array overrun and its attendant run-time exception.

```
// Use length variable to help copy an array.
class ACopy {
  public static void main(String args[]) {
    int i;
    int nums1[] = new int[10];
    int nums2[] = new int[10];

    for(i=0; i < nums1.length; i++)
      nums1[i] = i;

    // copy nums1 to nums2
    if(nums2.length >= nums1.length)
      for(i = 0; i < nums2.length; i++)
        nums2[i] = nums1[i];

    for(i=0; i < nums2.length; i++)
      System.out.print(nums2[i] + " ");
  }
}
```

Use **length** to compare array sizes.

Here, **length** helps perform two important functions. First, it is used to confirm that the target array is large enough to hold the contents of the source array. Second, it provides the termination condition of the **for** loop that performs the copy. Of course, in this simple example, the sizes of the arrays are easily known, but this same approach can be applied to a wide range of more challenging situations.

Progress Check

1. How can the following be rewritten?

```
int x[]  = new int[10];
```

2. When one array reference is assigned to another, the elements of the first array are copied to the second. True or False?

3. As it pertains to arrays, what is **length**?

---

1. `int[] x = new int[10];`
2. False. Only the reference is changed.
3. **length** is an instance variable that all arrays have. It contains the number of elements that the array can hold.

Project 5-2 A Queue Class

QDemo.java   As you may know, a data structure is a means of organizing data. The simplest
data structure is the array, which is a linear list that supports random access to its
elements. Arrays are often used as the underpinning for more sophisticated data structures,
such as stacks and queues. A *stack* is a list in which elements can be accessed in first-in,
last-out (FILO) order only. A *queue* is a list in which elements can be accessed in first-in,
first-out (FIFO) order only. Thus, a stack is like a stack of plates on a table—the first down
is the last to be used. A queue is like a line at a bank—the first in line is the first served.

What makes data structures such as stacks and queues interesting is that they combine
storage for information with the methods that access that information. Thus, stacks and queues
are *data engines* in which storage and retrieval are provided by the data structure itself, not
manually by your program. Such a combination is, obviously, an excellent choice for a class,
and in this project you will create a simple queue class.

In general, queues support two basic operations: put and get. Each put operation places a
new element on the end of the queue. Each get operation retrieves the next element from the
front of the queue. Queue operations are *consumptive*: once an element has been retrieved, it
cannot be retrieved again. The queue can also become full, if there is no space available to
store an item, and it can become empty, if all of the elements have been removed.

One last point: there are two basic types of queues—circular and noncircular. A *circular
queue* reuses locations in the underlying array when elements are removed. A *noncircular queue*
does not reuse locations and eventually becomes exhausted. For the sake of simplicity, this
example creates a noncircular queue, but with a little thought and effort, you can easily
transform it into a circular queue.

Step by Step

1. Create a file called **QDemo.java**.

2. Although there are other ways to support a queue, the method we will use is based upon
   an array. That is, an array will provide the storage for the items put into the queue. This
   array will be accessed through two indices. The *put* index determines where the next
   element of data will be stored. The *get* index indicates at what location the next element
   of data will be obtained. Keep in mind that the get operation is consumptive, and it is not
   possible to retrieve the same element twice. Although the queue that we will be creating
   stores characters, the same logic can be used to store any type of object. Begin creating the
   Queue class with these lines:

```
class Queue {
   char q[]; // this array holds the queue
   int putloc, getloc; // the put and get indices
```

3. The constructor for the **Queue** class creates a queue of a given size. Here is the **Queue** constructor:

```
Queue(int size) {
  q = new char[size+1]; // allocate memory for queue
  putloc = getloc = 0;
}
```

Notice that the queue is created one larger than the size specified in **size**. Because of the way the queue algorithm will be implemented, one array location will be unused, so the array must be created one larger than the requested queue size. The put and get indices are initially set to zero.

4. The **put( )** method, which stores elements, is shown next:

```
// put a character into the queue
void put(char ch) {
  if(putloc==q.length-1) {
    System.out.println(" - Queue is full.");
    return;
  }

  putloc++;
  q[putloc] = ch;
}
```

The method begins by checking for a queue-full condition. If **putloc** is equal to the last location in the **q** array, there is no more room in which to store elements. Otherwise, **putloc** is incremented and the new element is stored at that location. Thus, **putloc** is always the index of the last element stored.

5. To retrieve elements, use the **get( )** method, shown next:

```
// get a character from the queue
char get() {
  if(getloc == putloc) {
    System.out.println(" - Queue is empty.");
    return (char) 0;
  }

  getloc++;
  return q[getloc];
}
```

Notice first the check for queue-empty. If **getloc** and **putloc** both index the same element, the queue is assumed to be empty. This is why **getloc** and **putloc** were both initialized to zero by the **Queue** constructor. Next, **getloc** is incremented and the next element is returned. Thus, **getloc** always indicates the location of the last element retrieved.

(continued)

6. Here is the entire **QDemo.java** program:

```
/*
   Project 5-2

   A queue class for characters.
*/

class Queue {
  char q[]; // this array holds the queue
  int putloc, getloc; // the put and get indices

  Queue(int size) {
    q = new char[size+1]; // allocate memory for queue
    putloc = getloc = 0;
  }

  // put a character into the queue
  void put(char ch) {
    if(putloc==q.length-1) {
      System.out.println(" - Queue is full.");
      return;
    }

    putloc++;
    q[putloc] = ch;
  }

  // get a character from the queue
  char get() {
    if(getloc == putloc) {
      System.out.println(" - Queue is empty.");
      return (char) 0;
    }

    getloc++;
    return q[getloc];
  }
}

// Demonstrate the Queue class.
class QDemo {
  public static void main(String args[]) {
    Queue bigQ = new Queue(100);
    Queue smallQ = new Queue(4);
```

```
     char ch;
     int i;

     System.out.println("Using bigQ to store the alphabet.");
     // put some numbers into bigQ
     for(i=0; i < 26; i++)
       bigQ.put((char) ('A' + i));

     // retrieve and display elements from bigQ
     System.out.print("Contents of bigQ: ");
     for(i=0; i < 26; i++) {
       ch = bigQ.get();
       if(ch != (char) 0) System.out.print(ch);
     }

     System.out.println("\n");


     System.out.println("Using smallQ to generate errors.");
     // Now, use smallQ to generate some errors
     for(i=0; i < 5; i++) {
       System.out.print("Attempting to store " +
                         (char) ('Z' - i));

       smallQ.put((char) ('Z' - i));

       System.out.println();
     }
     System.out.println();

     // more errors on smallQ
     System.out.print("Contents of smallQ: ");
     for(i=0; i < 5; i++) {
       ch = smallQ.get();

       if(ch != (char) 0) System.out.print(ch);
     }
   }
 }
```

7. The output produced by the program is shown here:

```
Using bigQ to store the alphabet.
Contents of bigQ: ABCDEFGHIJKLMNOPQRSTUVWXYZ

Using smallQ to generate errors.
```

(continued)

```
Attempting to store Z
Attempting to store Y
Attempting to store X
Attempting to store W
Attempting to store V - Queue is full.


Contents of smallQ: ZYXW - Queue is empty.
```

8. On your own, try modifying **Queue** so that it stores other types of objects. For example, have it store **int**s or **double**s.

The For-Each Style for Loop

When working with arrays, it is common to encounter situations in which each element in an array must be examined, from start to finish. For example, to compute the sum of the values held in an array, each element in the array must be examined. The same situation occurs when computing an average, searching for a value, copying an array, and so on. Because such "start to finish" operations are so common, Java defines a second form of the **for** loop that streamlines this operation.

The second form of the **for** implements a "for-each" style loop. A for-each loop cycles through a collection of objects, such as an array, in strictly sequential fashion, from start to finish. In recent years, for-each style loops have gained popularity among both computer language designers and programmers. Originally, Java did not offer a for-each style loop. However, with the release of JDK 5, the **for** loop was enhanced to provide this option. The for-each style of **for** is also referred to as the *enhanced for loop*. Both terms are used in this book.

The general form of the for-each style **for** is shown here.

for(*type itr-var* : *collection*) *statement-block*

Here, *type* specifies the type, and *itr-var* specifies the name of an *iteration variable* that will receive the elements from a collection, one at a time, from beginning to end. The collection being cycled through is specified by *collection*. There are various types of collections that can be used with the **for**, but the only type used in this book is the array. With each iteration of the loop, the next element in the collection is retrieved and stored in *itr-var*. The loop repeats until all elements in the collection have been obtained. Thus, when iterating over an array of size *N*, the enhanced **for** obtains the elements in the array in index order, from 0 to *N*-1.

Because the iteration variable receives values from the collection, *type* must be the same as (or compatible with) the elements stored in the collection. Thus, when iterating over arrays, *type* must be compatible with the base type of the array.

Ask the Expert

Q: Aside from arrays, what other types of collections can the for-each style for **loop cycle through?**

A: One of the most important uses of the for-each style **for** is to cycle through the contents of a collection defined by the Collections Framework. The Collections Framework is a set of classes that implement various data structures, such as lists, vectors, sets, and maps. A discussion of the Collections Framework is beyond the scope of this book, but complete coverage of the Collections Framework can be found in my book *Java: The Complete Reference, 7th Edition* (McGraw-Hill, 2007).

To understand the motivation behind a for-each style loop, consider the type of **for** loop that it is designed to replace. The following fragment uses a traditional **for** loop to compute the sum of the values in an array:

```
int nums[] = { 1, 2, 3, 4, 5, 6, 7, 8, 9, 10 };
int sum = 0;

for(int i=0; i < 10; i++) sum += nums[i];
```

To compute the sum, each element in **nums** is read, in order, from start to finish. Thus, the entire array is read in strictly sequential order. This is accomplished by manually indexing the **nums** array by **i**, the loop control variable. Furthermore, the starting and ending value for the loop control variable, and its increment, must be explicitly specified.

The for-each style **for** automates the preceding loop. Specifically, it eliminates the need to establish a loop counter, specify a starting and ending value, and manually index the array. Instead, it automatically cycles through the entire array, obtaining one element at a time, in sequence, from beginning to end. For example, here is the preceding fragment rewritten using a for-each version of the **for:**

```
int nums[] = { 1, 2, 3, 4, 5, 6, 7, 8, 9, 10 };
int sum = 0;

for(int x: nums) sum += x;
```

With each pass through the loop, **x** is automatically given a value equal to the next element in **nums**. Thus, on the first iteration, **x** contains 1, on the second iteration, **x** contains 2, and so on. Not only is the syntax streamlined, it also prevents boundary errors.

Here is an entire program that demonstrates the for-each version of the **for** just described:

```
// Use a for-each style for loop.
class ForEach {
  public static void main(String args[]) {
    int nums[] = { 1, 2, 3, 4, 5, 6, 7, 8, 9, 10 };
    int sum = 0;

    // Use for-each style for to display and sum the values.
    for(int x : nums) {
      System.out.println("Value is: " + x);
      sum += x;                          A for-each style for loop
    }

    System.out.println("Summation: " + sum);
  }
}
```

The output from the program is shown here:

```
Value is: 1
Value is: 2
Value is: 3
Value is: 4
Value is: 5
Value is: 6
Value is: 7
Value is: 8
Value is: 9
Value is: 10
Summation: 55
```

As this output shows, the for-each style **for** automatically cycles through an array in sequence from the lowest index to the highest.

Although the for-each **for** loop iterates until all elements in an array have been examined, it is possible to terminate the loop early by using a **break** statement. For example, this loop sums only the first five elements of **nums**.

```
// Sum only the first 5 elements.
for(int x : nums) {
  System.out.println("Value is: " + x);
  sum += x;
  if(x == 5) break; // stop the loop when 5 is obtained
}
```

There is one important point to understand about the for-each style **for** loop. Its iteration variable is "read-only" as it relates to the underlying array. An assignment to the iteration variable has no effect on the underlying array. In other words, you can't change the contents of the array by assigning the iteration variable a new value. For example, consider this program:

```java
// The for-each loop is essentially read-only.
class NoChange {
  public static void main(String args[]) {
    int nums[] = { 1, 2, 3, 4, 5, 6, 7, 8, 9, 10 };

    for(int x : nums) {
      System.out.print(x + " ");
      x = x * 10; // no effect on nums  ◄─────── This does not change nums.
    }

    System.out.println();

    for(int x : nums)
      System.out.print(x + " ");

    System.out.println();
  }
}
```

The first **for** loop increases the value of the iteration variable by a factor of 10. However, this assignment has no effect on the underlying array **nums**, as the second **for** loop illustrates. The output, shown here, proves this point.

```
1 2 3 4 5 6 7 8 9 10
1 2 3 4 5 6 7 8 9 10
```

Iterating Over Multidimensional Arrays

The enhanced **for** also works on multidimensional arrays. Remember, however, that in Java, multidimensional arrays consist of *arrays of arrays*. (For example, a two-dimensional array is an array of one-dimensional arrays.) This is important when iterating over a multidimensional array because each iteration obtains the *next array*, not an individual element. Furthermore, the iteration variable in the **for** loop must be compatible with the type of array being obtained. For example, in the case of a two-dimensional array, the iteration variable must be a reference to a one-dimensional array. In general, when using the for-each **for** to iterate over an array of *N* dimensions, the objects obtained will be arrays of *N*-1 dimensions. To understand the implications of this, consider the following program. It uses nested **for** loops to obtain the elements of a two-dimensional array in row-order, from first to last.

Notice how **x** is declared.

```java
// Use for-each style for on a two-dimensional array.
class ForEach2 {
  public static void main(String args[]) {
    int sum = 0;
    int nums[][] = new int[3][5];

    // give nums some values
    for(int i = 0; i < 3; i++)
      for(int j=0; j < 5; j++)
        nums[i][j] = (i+1)*(j+1);

    // Use for-each for loop to display and sum the values.
    for(int x[] : nums) {
      for(int y : x) {
        System.out.println("Value is: " + y);
        sum += y;
      }
    }
    System.out.println("Summation: " + sum);
  }
}
```

Notice how **x** is declared.

The output from this program is shown here:

```
Value is: 1
Value is: 2
Value is: 3
Value is: 4
Value is: 5
Value is: 2
Value is: 4
Value is: 6
Value is: 8
Value is: 10
Value is: 3
Value is: 6
Value is: 9
Value is: 12
Value is: 15
Summation: 90
```

In the program, pay special attention to this line:

```java
for(int x[] : nums) {
```

Notice how **x** is declared. It is a reference to a one-dimensional array of integers. This is necessary because each iteration of the **for** obtains the next *array* in **nums**, beginning with the array specified by **nums[0]**. The inner **for** loop then cycles through each of these arrays, displaying the values of each element.

Applying the Enhanced for

Since the for-each style **for** can only cycle through an array sequentially, from start to finish, you might think that its use is limited. However, this is not true. A large number of algorithms require exactly this mechanism. One of the most common is searching. For example, the following program uses a **for** loop to search an unsorted array for a value. It stops if the value is found.

```java
// Search an array using for-each style for.
class Search {
  public static void main(String args[]) {
    int nums[] = { 6, 8, 3, 7, 5, 6, 1, 4 };
    int val = 5;
    boolean found = false;

    // Use for-each style for to search nums for val.
    for(int x : nums) {
      if(x == val) {
        found = true;
        break;
      }
    }

    if(found)
      System.out.println("Value found!");
  }
}
```

The for-each style **for** is an excellent choice in this application because searching an unsorted array involves examining each element in sequence. (Of course, if the array were sorted, a binary search could be used, which would require a different style loop.) Other types of applications that benefit from for-each style loops include computing an average, finding the minimum or maximum of a set, looking for duplicates, and so on.

Now that the for-each style **for** has been introduced, it will be used where appropriate throughout the remainder of this book.

Progress Check

1. What does the for-each style **for** loop do?

2. Given an array of **double** called **nums**, show a for-each style **for** that cycles through it.

3. Can the for-each style **for** cycle through the contents of a multidimensional array?

Strings

From a day-to-day programming standpoint, one of the most important of Java's data types is **String**. **String** defines and supports character strings. In many other programming languages a string is an array of characters. This is not the case with Java. In Java, strings are objects.

Actually, you have been using the **String** class since Module 1, but you did not know it. When you create a string literal, you are actually creating a **String** object. For example, in the statement

```
System.out.println("In Java, strings are objects.");
```

the string "In Java, strings are objects." is automatically made into a **String** object by Java. Thus, the use of the **String** class has been "below the surface" in the preceding programs. In the following sections you will learn to handle it explicitly. Be aware, however, that the **String** class is quite large, and we will only scratch its surface here. It is a class that you will want to explore on its own.

Constructing Strings

You can construct a **String** just like you construct any other type of object: by using **new** and calling the **String** constructor. For example:

```
String str = new String("Hello");
```

This creates a **String** object called **str** that contains the character string "Hello". You can also construct a **String** from another **String**. For example:

```
String str = new String("Hello");
String str2 = new String(str);
```

After this sequence executes, **str2** will also contain the character string "Hello".

---

1. A for-each style **for** cycles through the contents of a collection, such as an array, from start to finish.
2. `for(double d : nums) ...`
3. Yes; however, each iteration obtains the next sub-array.

Another easy way to create a **String** is shown here:

```
String str = "Java strings are powerful.";
```

In this case, **str** is initialized to the character sequence "Java strings are powerful."

Once you have created a **String** object, you can use it anywhere that a quoted string is allowed. For example, you can use a **String** object as an argument to **println( )**, as shown in this example:

```
// Introduce String.
class StringDemo {
  public static void main(String args[]) {
    // declare strings in various ways
    String str1 = new String("Java strings are objects.");
    String str2 = "They are constructed various ways.";
    String str3 = new String(str2);

    System.out.println(str1);
    System.out.println(str2);
    System.out.println(str3);
  }
}
```

The output from the program is shown here:

```
Java strings are objects.
They are constructed various ways.
They are constructed various ways.
```

Operating on Strings

The **String** class contains several methods that operate on strings. Here are a few:

boolean equals(String *str*)	Returns true if the invoking string contains the same character sequence as *str*.
int length( )	Obtains the length of a string.
char charAt(int *index*)	Obtains the character at the index specified by *index*.
int compareTo(String *str*)	Returns less than zero if the invoking string is less than *str*, greater than zero if the invoking string is greater than *str*, and zero if the strings are equal.
int indexOf(String *str*)	Searches the invoking string for the substring specified by *str*. Returns the index of the first match or −1 on failure.
int lastIndexOf(String *str*)	Searches the invoking string for the substring specified by *str*. Returns the index of the last match or −1 on failure.

Here is a program that demonstrates these methods:

```java
// Some String operations.
class StrOps {
  public static void main(String args[]) {
    String str1 =
      "When it comes to Web programming, Java is #1.";
    String str2 = new String(str1);
    String str3 = "Java strings are powerful.";
    int result, idx;
    char ch;

    System.out.println("Length of str1: " +
                        str1.length());

    // display str1, one char at a time.
    for(int i=0; i < str1.length(); i++)
      System.out.print(str1.charAt(i));
    System.out.println();

    if(str1.equals(str2))
      System.out.println("str1 equals str2");
    else
      System.out.println("str1 does not equal str2");

    if(str1.equals(str3))
      System.out.println("str1 equals str3");
    else
      System.out.println("str1 does not equal str3");

    result = str1.compareTo(str3);
    if(result == 0)
      System.out.println("str1 and str3 are equal");
    else if(result < 0)
      System.out.println("str1 is less than str3");
    else
      System.out.println("str1 is greater than str3");


    // assign a new string to str2
    str2 = "One Two Three One";

    idx = str2.indexOf("One");
    System.out.println("Index of first occurrence of One: " + idx);
    idx = str2.lastIndexOf("One");
    System.out.println("Index of last occurrence of One: " + idx);

  }
}
```

Ask the Expert

Q: Why does String **define the** equals( ) **method? Can't I just use** ==?

A: The **equals( )** method compares the character sequences of two **String** objects for equality. Applying the == to two **String** references simply determines whether the two references refer to the same object.

This program generates the following output:

```
Length of str1: 45
When it comes to Web programming, Java is #1.
str1 equals str2
str1 does not equal str3
str1 is greater than str3
Index of first occurrence of One: 0
Index of last occurrence of One: 14
```

You can *concatenate* (join together) two strings using the + operator. For example, this statement

```
String str1 = "One";
String str2 = "Two";
String str3 = "Three";
String str4 = str1 + str2 + str3;
```

initializes **str4** with the string "OneTwoThree".

Arrays of Strings

Like any other data type, strings can be assembled into arrays. For example:

```
// Demonstrate String arrays.
class StringArrays {
  public static void main(String args[]) {
    String strs[] = { "This", "is", "a", "test." };

    System.out.println("Original array: ");
    for(String s : strs)
      System.out.print(s + " ");
    System.out.println("\n");
```

An array of strings

```
    // change a string
    strs[1] = "was";
    strs[3] = "test, too!";

    System.out.println("Modified array: ");
    for(String s : strs)
      System.out.print(s + " ");
  }
}
```

Here is the output from this program:

```
Original array:
This is a test.

Modified array:
This was a test, too!
```

Strings Are Immutable

The contents of a **String** object are immutable. That is, once created, the character sequence that makes up the string cannot be altered. This restriction allows Java to implement strings more efficiently. Even though this probably sounds like a serious drawback, it isn't. When you need a string that is a variation on one that already exists, simply create a new string that contains the desired changes. Since unused **String** objects are automatically garbage collected, you don't even need to worry about what happens to the discarded strings.

It must be made clear, however, that **String** reference variables may, of course, change the object to which they refer. It is just that the contents of a specific **String** object cannot be changed after it is created.

Ask the Expert

Q: You say that once created, String **objects are immutable. I understand that, from a practical point of view, this is not a serious restriction, but what if I want to create a string that *can* be changed?**

A: You're in luck. Java offers a class called **StringBuffer**, which creates string objects that can be changed. For example, in addition to the **charAt( )** method, which obtains the character at a specific location, **StringBuffer** defines **setCharAt( )**, which sets a character within the string. However, for most purposes you will want to use **String**, not **StringBuffer**.

To fully understand why immutable strings are not a hindrance, we will use another of **String**'s methods: **substring( )**. The **substring( )** method returns a new string that contains a specified portion of the invoking string. Because a new **String** object is manufactured that contains the substring, the original string is unaltered, and the rule of immutability remains intact. The form of **substring( )** that we will be using is shown here:

String substring(int *startIndex*, int *endIndex*)

Here, *startIndex* specifies the beginning index, and *endIndex* specifies the stopping point.

Here is a program that demonstrates **substring( )** and the principle of immutable strings:

```
// Use substring().
class SubStr {
  public static void main(String args[]) {
    String orgstr = "Java makes the Web move.";

    // construct a substring
    String substr = orgstr.substring(5, 18);

    System.out.println("orgstr: " + orgstr);
    System.out.println("substr: " + substr);

  }
}
```

This creates a new string that contains the desired substring.

Here is the output from the program:

```
orgstr: Java makes the Web move.
substr: makes the Web
```

As you can see, the original string **orgstr** is unchanged, and **substr** contains the substring.

CRITICAL SKILL
5.9 Using Command-Line Arguments

Now that you know about the **String** class, you can understand the **args** parameter to **main( )** that has been in every program shown so far. Many programs accept what are called *command-line arguments*. A command-line argument is the information that directly follows the program's name on the command line when it is executed. To access the command-line arguments inside a Java program is quite easy—they are stored as strings in the **String** array passed to **main( )**. For example, the following program displays all of the command-line arguments that it is called with:

```
// Display all command-line information.
class CLDemo {
  public static void main(String args[]) {
    System.out.println("There are " + args.length +
                       " command-line arguments.");

    System.out.println("They are: ");
    for(int i=0; i<args.length; i++)
      System.out.println("arg[" + i + "]: " + args[i]);
  }
}
```

If **CLDemo** is executed like this,

```
java CLDemo one two three
```

you will see the following output:

```
There are 3 command-line arguments.
They are:
arg[0]: one
arg[1]: two
arg[2]: three
```

Notice that the first argument is stored at index 0, the second argument is stored at index 1, and so on.

To get a taste of the way command-line arguments can be used, consider the next program. It takes one command-line argument that specifies a person's name. It then searches through a two-dimensional array of strings for that name. If it finds a match, it displays that person's telephone number.

```
// A simple automated telephone directory.
class Phone {
  public static void main(String args[]) {
    String numbers[][] = {
      { "Tom", "555-3322" },
      { "Mary", "555-8976" },
      { "Jon", "555-1037" },
      { "Rachel", "555-1400" }
    };
    int i;
```

```
    if(args.length != 1)                                    To use the program, one
      System.out.println("Usage: java Phone <name>");        command-line argument
    else {                                                   must be present.
      for(i=0; i<numbers.length; i++) {
        if(numbers[i][0].equals(args[0])) {
          System.out.println(numbers[i][0] + ": " +
                             numbers[i][1]);
          break;
        }
      }
      if(i == numbers.length)
        System.out.println("Name not found.");
    }
  }
}
```

Here is a sample run:

```
C>java Phone Mary
Mary: 555-8976
```

Progress Check

1. In Java, all strings are objects. True or False?

2. How can you obtain the length of a string?

3. What are command-line arguments?

CRITICAL SKILL
5.10 The Bitwise Operators

In Module 2 you learned about Java's arithmetic, relational, and logical operators. Although these are the most commonly used, Java provides additional operators that expand the set of problems to which Java can be applied: the bitwise operators. The bitwise operators can be used on values of type **long**, **int**, **short**, **char**, or **byte**. Bitwise operations cannot be used on **boolean**, **float**, or

1. True.

2. The length of a string can be obtained by calling the **length( )** method.

3. Command-line arguments are specified on the command line when a program is executed. They are passed as strings to the **args** parameter of **main( )**.

double, or class types. They are called the *bitwise* operators because they are used to test, set, or shift the individual bits that make up a value. Bitwise operations are important to a wide variety of systems-level programming tasks in which status information from a device must be interrogated or constructed. Table 5-1 lists the bitwise operators.

The Bitwise AND, OR, XOR, and NOT Operators

The bitwise operators AND, OR, XOR, and NOT are **&**, **|**, **^**, and **~**. They perform the same operations as their Boolean logical equivalents described in Module 2. The difference is that the bitwise operators work on a bit-by-bit basis. The following table shows the outcome of each operation using 1's and 0's.

p	q	p & q	p | q	p ^ q	~p
0	0	0	0	0	1
1	0	0	1	1	0
0	1	0	1	1	1
1	1	1	1	0	0

In terms of its most common usage, you can think of the bitwise AND as a way to turn bits off. That is, any bit that is 0 in either operand will cause the corresponding bit in the outcome to be set to 0. For example:

```
    1 1 0 1  0 0 1 1
&   1 0 1 0  1 0 1 0
    1 0 0 0  0 0 1 0
```

The following program demonstrates the **&** by turning any lowercase letter into uppercase by resetting the 6th bit to 0. As the Unicode/ASCII character set is defined, the lowercase

Operator	Result
&	Bitwise AND
|	Bitwise OR
^	Bitwise exclusive OR
>>	Shift right
>>>	Unsigned shift right
<<	Shift left
~	One's complement (unary NOT)

Table 5-1 The Bitwise Operators

letters are the same as the uppercase ones except that the lowercase ones are greater in value by exactly 32. Therefore, to transform a lowercase letter to uppercase, just turn off the 6th bit, as this program illustrates.

```
// Uppercase letters.
class UpCase {
  public static void main(String args[]) {
    char ch;

    for(int i=0; i < 10; i++) {
      ch = (char) ('a' + i);
      System.out.print(ch);

      // This statement turns off the 6th bit.
      ch = (char) ((int) ch & 65503); // ch is now uppercase

      System.out.print(ch + " ");
    }
  }
}
```

The output from this program is shown here:

```
aA bB cC dD eE fF gG hH iI jJ
```

The value 65,503 used in the AND statement is the decimal representation of 1111 1111 1101 1111. Thus, the AND operation leaves all bits in **ch** unchanged except for the 6th one, which is set to 0.

The AND operator is also useful when you want to determine whether a bit is on or off. For example, this statement determines whether bit 4 in **status** is set:

```
if(status & 8) System.out.println("bit 4 is on");
```

The number 8 is used because it translates into a binary value that has only the 4th bit set. Therefore, the **if** statement can succeed only when bit 4 of **status** is also on. An interesting use of this concept is to show the bits of a **byte** value in binary format.

```
// Display the bits within a byte.
class ShowBits {
  public static void main(String args[]) {
    int t;
    byte val;

    val = 123;
```

```
    for(t=128; t > 0; t = t/2) {
      if((val & t) != 0) System.out.print("1 ");
      else System.out.print("0 ");
    }
  }
}
```

The output is shown here:

```
0 1 1 1 1 0 1 1
```

The **for** loop successively tests each bit in **val**, using the bitwise AND, to determine whether it is on or off. If the bit is on, the digit **1** is displayed; otherwise **0** is displayed. In Project 5-3, you will see how this basic concept can be expanded to create a class that will display the bits in any type of integer.

The bitwise OR, as the reverse of AND, can be used to turn bits on. Any bit that is set to 1 in either operand will cause the corresponding bit in the result to be set to 1. For example:

```
    1 1 0 1 0 0 1 1
  | 1 0 1 0 1 0 1 0
    1 1 1 1 1 0 1 1
```

We can make use of the OR to change the uppercasing program into a lowercasing program, as shown here:

```
// Lowercase letters.
class LowCase {
  public static void main(String args[]) {
    char ch;

    for(int i=0; i < 10; i++) {
      ch = (char) ('A' + i);
      System.out.print(ch);

      // This statement turns on the 6th bit.
      ch = (char) ((int) ch | 32); // ch is now lowercase

      System.out.print(ch + " ");
    }
  }
}
```

The output from this program is shown here:

```
Aa Bb Cc Dd Ee Ff Gg Hh Ii Jj
```

The program works by ORing each character with the value 32, which is 0000 0000 0010 0000 in binary. Thus, 32 is the value that produces a value in binary in which only the 6th bit is set. When this value is ORed with any other value, it produces a result in which the 6th bit is set and all other bits remain unchanged. As explained, for characters this means that each uppercase letter is transformed into its lowercase equivalent.

An exclusive OR, usually abbreviated XOR, will set a bit on if, and only if, the bits being compared are different, as illustrated here:

```
  0 1 1 1 1 1 1 1
^ 1 0 1 1 1 0 0 1
  1 1 0 0 0 1 1 0
```

The XOR operator has an interesting property that makes it a simple way to encode a message. When some value X is XORed with another value Y, and then that result is XORed with Y again, X is produced. That is, given the sequence

R1 = X ^ Y;
R2 = R1 ^ Y;

then R2 is the same value as X. Thus, the outcome of a sequence of two XORs using the same value produces the original value.

You can use this principle to create a simple cipher program in which some integer is the key that is used to both encode and decode a message by XORing the characters in that message. To encode, the XOR operation is applied the first time, yielding the cipher text. To decode, the XOR is applied a second time, yielding the plain text. Here is a simple example that uses this approach to encode and decode a short message:

```
// Use XOR to encode and decode a message.
class Encode {
  public static void main(String args[]) {
    String msg = "This is a test";
    String encmsg = "";
    String decmsg = "";
    int key = 88;

    System.out.print("Original message: ");
    System.out.println(msg);

    // encode the message
    for(int i=0; i < msg.length(); i++)          This constructs the encoded string.
      encmsg = encmsg + (char) (msg.charAt(i) ^ key);

    System.out.print("Encoded message: ");
    System.out.println(encmsg);

    // decode the message
```

```
    for(int i=0; i < msg.length(); i++)
      decmsg = decmsg + (char) (encmsg.charAt(i) ^ key);

    System.out.print("Decoded message: ");
    System.out.println(decmsg);
  }
}
```

This constructs the decoded string.

Here is the output:

```
Original message: This is a test
Encoded message: 01+x1+x9x,=+,
Decoded message: This is a test
```

As you can see, the result of two XORs using the same key produces the decoded message.

The unary one's complement (NOT) operator reverses the state of all the bits of the operand. For example, if some integer called **A** has the bit pattern 1001 0110, then ~**A** produces a result with the bit pattern 0110 1001.

The following program demonstrates the NOT operator by displaying a number and its complement in binary.

```
// Demonstrate the bitwise NOT.
class NotDemo {
  public static void main(String args[]) {
    byte b = -34;

    for(int t=128; t > 0; t = t/2) {
      if((b & t) != 0) System.out.print("1 ");
      else System.out.print("0 ");
    }
    System.out.println();

    // reverse all bits
    b = (byte) ~b;

    for(int t=128; t > 0; t = t/2) {
      if((b & t) != 0) System.out.print("1 ");
      else System.out.print("0 ");
    }
  }
}
```

Here is the output:

```
1 1 0 1 1 1 1 0
0 0 1 0 0 0 0 1
```

The Shift Operators

In Java it is possible to shift the bits that make up a value to the left or to the right by a specified amount. Java defines the three bit-shift operators shown here:

<<	Left shift
>>	Right shift
>>>	Unsigned right shift

The general forms for these operators are shown here:

value << *num-bits*

value >> *num-bits*

value >>> *num-bits*

Here, *value* is the value being shifted by the number of bit positions specified by *num-bits*.

Each left shift causes all bits within the specified value to be shifted left one position and a 0 bit to be brought in on the right. Each right shift shifts all bits to the right one position and preserves the sign bit. As you may know, negative numbers are usually represented by setting the high-order bit of an integer value to 1, and this is the approach used by Java. Thus, if the value being shifted is negative, each right shift brings in a 1 on the left. If the value is positive, each right shift brings in a 0 on the left.

In addition to the sign bit, there is something else to be aware of when right shifting. Java uses *two's complement* to represent negative values. In this approach negative values are stored by first reversing the bits in the value and then adding 1. Thus, the byte value for –1 in binary is 1111 1111. Right shifting this value will always produce –1!

If you don't want to preserve the sign bit when shifting right, you can use an unsigned right shift (>>>), which always brings in a 0 on the left. For this reason, the >>> is also called the *zero-fill* right shift. You will use the unsigned right shift when shifting bit patterns, such as status codes, that do not represent integers.

For all of the shifts, the bits shifted out are lost. Thus, a shift is not a rotate, and there is no way to retrieve a bit that has been shifted out.

Shown next is a program that graphically illustrates the effect of a left and right shift. Here, an integer is given an initial value of 1, which means that its low-order bit is set. Then, a series of eight shifts are performed on the integer. After each shift, the lower 8 bits of the value are shown. The process is then repeated, except that a 1 is put in the 8th bit position, and right shifts are performed.

```
// Demonstrate the shift << and >> operators.
class ShiftDemo {
  public static void main(String args[]) {
```

```
int val = 1;

for(int i = 0; i < 8; i++) {
  for(int t=128; t > 0; t = t/2) {
    if((val & t) != 0) System.out.print("1 ");
    else System.out.print("0 ");
  }
  System.out.println();
  val = val << 1; // left shift
}
System.out.println();

val = 128;
for(int i = 0; i < 8; i++) {
  for(int t=128; t > 0; t = t/2) {
    if((val & t) != 0) System.out.print("1 ");
    else System.out.print("0 ");
  }
  System.out.println();
  val = val >> 1; // right shift
  }
 }
}
```

The output from the program is shown here:

```
0 0 0 0 0 0 0 1
0 0 0 0 0 0 1 0
0 0 0 0 0 1 0 0
0 0 0 0 1 0 0 0
0 0 0 1 0 0 0 0
0 0 1 0 0 0 0 0
0 1 0 0 0 0 0 0
1 0 0 0 0 0 0 0

1 0 0 0 0 0 0 0
0 1 0 0 0 0 0 0
0 0 1 0 0 0 0 0
0 0 0 1 0 0 0 0
0 0 0 0 1 0 0 0
0 0 0 0 0 1 0 0
0 0 0 0 0 0 1 0
0 0 0 0 0 0 0 1
```

You need to be careful when shifting **byte** and **short** values because Java will automatically promote these types to **int** when evaluating an expression. For example, if you right shift a **byte** value, it will first be promoted to **int** and then shifted. The result of the shift will also be

Ask the Expert

Q: **Since binary is based on powers of two, can the shift operators be used as a shortcut for multiplying or dividing an integer by two?**

A: Yes. The bitwise shift operators can be used to perform very fast multiplication or division by two. A shift left doubles a value. A shift right halves it. Of course, this only works as long as you are not shifting bits off one end or the other.

of type **int**. Often this conversion is of no consequence. However, if you shift a negative **byte** or **short** value, it will be sign-extended when it is promoted to **int**. Thus, the high-order bits of the resulting integer value will be filled with ones. This is fine when performing a normal right shift. But when you perform a zero-fill right shift, there are 24 ones to be shifted before the byte value begins to see zeros.

Bitwise Shorthand Assignments

All of the binary bitwise operators have a shorthand form that combines an assignment with the bitwise operation. For example, the following two statements both assign to **x** the outcome of an XOR of **x** with the value 127.

```
x = x ^ 127;
x ^= 127;
```

Project 5-3   A ShowBits Class

ShowBitsDemo.java

This project creates a class called **ShowBits** that enables you to display in binary the bit pattern for any integer value. Such a class can be quite useful in programming. For example, if you are debugging device-driver code, then being able to monitor the data stream in binary is often a benefit.

Step by Step

1. Create a file called **ShowBitsDemo.java**.

2. Begin the **ShowBits** class as shown here:

```
class ShowBits {
  int numbits;
```

(continued)

```
ShowBits(int n) {
  numbits = n;
}
```

ShowBits creates objects that display a specified number of bits. For example, to create an object that will display the low-order 8 bits of some value, use

```
ShowBits byteval = new ShowBits(8)
```

The number of bits to display is stored in **numbits**.

3. To actually display the bit pattern, **ShowBits** provides the method **show( )**, which is shown here:

```
void show(long val) {
  long mask = 1;

  // left-shift a 1 into the proper position
  mask <<= numbits-1;

  int spacer = 0;
  for(; mask != 0; mask >>>= 1) {
    if((val & mask) != 0) System.out.print("1");
    else System.out.print("0");
    spacer++;
    if((spacer % 8) == 0) {
      System.out.print(" ");
      spacer = 0;
    }
  }
  System.out.println();
}
```

Notice that **show( )** specifies one **long** parameter. This does not mean that you always have to pass **show( )** a **long** value, however. Because of Java's automatic type promotions, any integer type can be passed to **show( )**. The number of bits displayed is determined by the value stored in **numbits**. After each group of 8 bits, **show( )** outputs a space. This makes it easier to read the binary values of long bit patterns.

4. The **ShowBitsDemo** program is shown here:

```
/*
   Project 5-3

   A class that displays the binary representation of a value.
*/

class ShowBits {
```

5

More Data Types and Operators

```
      int numbits;

   ShowBits(int n) {
     numbits = n;
   }

   void show(long val) {
     long mask = 1;

     // left-shift a 1 into the proper position
     mask <<= numbits-1;

     int spacer = 0;
     for(; mask != 0; mask >>>= 1) {
       if((val & mask) != 0) System.out.print("1");
       else System.out.print("0");
       spacer++;
       if((spacer % 8) == 0) {
         System.out.print(" ");
         spacer = 0;
       }
     }
     System.out.println();
   }
}

// Demonstrate ShowBits.
class ShowBitsDemo {
  public static void main(String args[]) {
    ShowBits b = new ShowBits(8);
    ShowBits i = new ShowBits(32);
    ShowBits li = new ShowBits(64);

    System.out.println("123 in binary: ");
    b.show(123);

    System.out.println("\n87987 in binary: ");
    i.show(87987);

    System.out.println("\n237658768 in binary: ");
    li.show(237658768);


    // you can also show low-order bits of any integer
    System.out.println("\nLow order 8 bits of 87987 in binary: ");
    b.show(87987);
```

(continued)

Project
5-3

A ShowBits Class

```
      }
   }
```

5. The output from **ShowBitsDemo** is shown here:

```
123 in binary:
01111011

87987 in binary:
00000000 00000001 01010111 10110011

237658768 in binary:
00000000 00000000 00000000 00000000 00001110 00101010 01100010 10010000

Low order 8 bits of 87987 in binary:
10110011
```

Progress Check

1. To what types can the bitwise operators be applied?

2. What is >>>?

5.11 The ? Operator

One of Java's most fascinating operators is the **?**. The **?** operator is often used to replace **if-else** statements of this general form:

if (*condition*)
    var = *expression1*;
else
    var = *expression2*;

Here, the value assigned to *var* depends upon the outcome of the condition controlling the **if**.
    The **?** is called a *ternary operator* because it requires three operands. It takes the general form

Exp1 ? *Exp2* : *Exp3*;

---

1. **byte**, **short**, **int**, **long**, and **char**.

2. >>> performs an unsigned right shift. This causes a zero to be shifted into the leftmost bit position. It differs from >>, which preserves the sign bit.

where *Exp1* is a **boolean** expression, and *Exp2* and *Exp3* are expressions of any type other than **void**. The type of *Exp2* and *Exp3* must be the same, though. Notice the use and placement of the colon.

The value of a **?** expression is determined like this: *Exp1* is evaluated. If it is true, then *Exp2* is evaluated and becomes the value of the entire **?** expression. If *Exp1* is false, then *Exp3* is evaluated and its value becomes the value of the expression. Consider this example, which assigns **absval** the absolute value of **val**:

```
absval = val < 0 ? -val : val; // get absolute value of val
```

Here, **absval** will be assigned the value of **val** if **val** is zero or greater. If **val** is negative, then **absval** will be assigned the negative of that value (which yields a positive value). The same code written using the **if-else** structure would look like this:

```
if(val < 0) absval  = -val;
else absval = val;
```

Here is another example of the **?** operator. This program divides two numbers, but will not allow a division by zero.

```
// Prevent a division by zero using the ?.
class NoZeroDiv {
  public static void main(String args[]) {
    int result;

    for(int i = -5; i < 6; i++) {
      result = i != 0 ? 100 / i : 0;  ←——————— This prevents a divide-by-zero.
      if(i != 0)
        System.out.println("100 / " + i + " is " + result);
    }
  }
}
```

The output from the program is shown here:

```
100 / -5 is -20
100 / -4 is -25
100 / -3 is -33
100 / -2 is -50
100 / -1 is -100
100 / 1 is 100
100 / 2 is 50
100 / 3 is 33
100 / 4 is 25
100 / 5 is 20
```

Pay special attention to this line from the program:

```
result = i != 0 ? 100 / i : 0;
```

Here, **result** is assigned the outcome of the division of 100 by **i**. However, this division takes place only if **i** is not zero. When **i** is zero, a placeholder value of zero is assigned to **result**.

You don't actually have to assign the value produced by the **?** to some variable. For example, you could use the value as an argument in a call to a method. Or, if the expressions are all of type **boolean**, the **?** can be used as the conditional expression in a loop or **if** statement. For example, here is the preceding program rewritten a bit more efficiently. It produces the same output as before.

```
// Prevent a division by zero using the ?.
class NoZeroDiv2 {
  public static void main(String args[]) {

    for(int i = -5; i < 6; i++)
      if(i != 0 ? true : false)
        System.out.println("100 / " + i +
                              " is " + 100 / i);
  }
}
```

Notice the **if** statement. If **i** is zero, then the outcome of the **if** is false, the division by zero is prevented, and no result is displayed. Otherwise the division takes place.

Module 5 Mastery Check

1. Show two ways to declare a one-dimensional array of 12 **double**s.

2. Show how to initialize a one-dimensional array of integers to the values 1 through 5.

3. Write a program that uses an array to find the average of 10 **double** values. Use any 10 values you like.

4. Change the sort in Project 5-1 so that it sorts an array of strings. Demonstrate that it works.

5. What is the difference between the **String** methods **indexOf( )** and **lastIndexOf( )**?

6. Since all strings are objects of type **String**, show how you can call the **length( )** and **charAt( )** methods on this string literal: "I like Java".

7. Expanding on the **Encode** cipher class, modify it so that it uses an eight-character string as the key.

8. Can the bitwise operators be applied to the **double** type?

9. Show how this sequence can be rewritten using the **?** operator.

```
if(x < 0) y = 10;
else y = 20;
```

10. In the following fragment, is the **&** a bitwise or logical operator? Why?

```
boolean a, b;
// ...
if(a & b) ...
```

11. Is it an error to overrun the end of an array? Is it an error to index an array with a negative value?

12. What is the unsigned right-shift operator?

13. Rewrite the **MinMax** class shown earlier in this chapter so that it uses a for-each style **for** loop.

14. Can the **for** loops that perform sorting in the **Bubble** class shown in Project 5-1 be converted into for-each style loops? If not, why not?

Module 6

A Closer Look at Methods and Classes

This module resumes our examination of classes and methods. It begins by explaining how to control access to the members of a class. It then discusses the passing and returning of objects, method overloading, recursion, and the use of the keyword **static**. Also described are nested classes and variable-length arguments, one of Java's newest features.

Controlling Access to Class Members

In its support for encapsulation, the class provides two major benefits. First, it links data with the code that manipulates it. You have been taking advantage of this aspect of the class since Module 4. Second, it provides the means by which access to members can be controlled. It is this feature that is examined here.

Although Java's approach is a bit more sophisticated, in essence, there are two basic types of class members: public and private. A public member can be freely accessed by code defined outside of its class. This is the type of class member that we have been using up to this point. A private member can be accessed only by other methods defined by its class. It is through the use of private members that access is controlled.

Restricting access to a class' members is a fundamental part of object-oriented programming because it helps prevent the misuse of an object. By allowing access to private data only through a well-defined set of methods, you can prevent improper values from being assigned to that data—by performing a range check, for example. It is not possible for code outside the class to set the value of a private member directly. You can also control precisely how and when the data within an object is used. Thus, when correctly implemented, a class creates a "black box" that can be used, but the inner workings of which are not open to tampering.

Up to this point, you haven't had to worry about access control because Java provides a default access setting in which the members of a class are freely available to the other code in your program. (Thus, the default access setting is essentially public.) Although convenient for simple classes (and example programs in books such as this one), this default setting is inadequate for many real-world situations. Here you will see how to use Java's other access control features.

Java's Access Specifiers

Member access control is achieved through the use of three *access specifiers*: **public**, **private**, and **protected**. As explained, if no access specifier is used, the default access setting is assumed. In this module we will be concerned with **public** and **private**. The **protected** specifier applies only when inheritance is involved and is described in Module 8.

When a member of a class is modified by the **public** specifier, that member can be accessed by any other code in your program. This includes methods defined inside other classes.

When a member of a class is specified as **private**, that member can be accessed only by other members of its class. Thus, methods in other classes cannot access a **private** member of another class.

The default access setting (in which no access specifier is used) is the same as **public** unless your program is broken down into packages. A *package* is, essentially, a grouping of classes. Packages are both an organizational and an access control feature, but a discussion of packages must wait until Module 8. For the types of programs shown in this and the preceding modules, **public** access is the same as default access.

An access specifier precedes the rest of a member's type specification. That is, it must begin a member's declaration statement. Here are some examples:

```
public String errMsg;
private accountBalance bal;

private boolean isError(byte status) { // ...
```

To understand the effects of **public** and **private**, consider the following program:

```
// Public vs private access.
class MyClass {
  private int alpha; // private access
  public int beta; // public access
  int gamma; // default access (essentially public)

  /* Methods to access alpha. It is OK for a
     member of a class to access a private member
     of the same class.
  */
  void setAlpha(int a) {
    alpha = a;
  }

  int getAlpha() {
    return alpha;
  }
}

class AccessDemo {
  public static void main(String args[]) {
    MyClass ob = new MyClass();
```

```
      /* Access to alpha is allowed only through
         its accessor methods. */
      ob.setAlpha(-99);
      System.out.println("ob.alpha is " + ob.getAlpha());

      // You cannot access alpha like this:
//    ob.alpha = 10; // Wrong! alpha is private!  ◄────── Wrong—alpha is private!

      // These are OK because beta and gamma are public.
      ob.beta = 88;  ◄────────── OK because these are public.
      ob.gamma = 99;
    }
}
```

As you can see, inside the **MyClass** class, **alpha** is specified as **private**, **beta** is explicitly specified as **public**, and **gamma** uses the default access, which for this example is the same as specifying **public**. Because **alpha** is private, it cannot be accessed by code outside of its class. Therefore, inside the **AccessDemo** class, **alpha** cannot be used directly. It must be accessed through its public accessor methods: **setAlpha( )** and **getAlpha( )**. If you were to remove the comment symbol from the beginning of the following line,

```
//   ob.alpha = 10; // Wrong! alpha is private!
```

you would not be able to compile this program because of the access violation. Although access to **alpha** by code outside of **MyClass** is not allowed, methods defined within **MyClass** can freely access it, as the **setAlpha( )** and **getAlpha( )** methods show.

The key point is this: a private member can be used freely by other members of its class, but it cannot be accessed by code outside its class.

To see how access control can be applied to a more practical example, consider the following program that implements a "fail-soft" **int** array, in which boundary errors are prevented, thus avoiding a run-time exception from being generated. This is accomplished by encapsulating the array as a private member of a class, allowing access to the array only through member methods. With this approach, any attempt to access the array beyond its boundaries can be prevented, with such an attempt failing gracefully (resulting in a "soft" landing rather than a "crash"). The fail-soft array is implemented by the **FailSoftArray** class, shown here:

```
/* This class implements a "fail-soft" array which prevents
   runtime errors.
 */
class FailSoftArray {
  private int a[]; // reference to array
  private int errval; // value to return if get() fails
```

```java
  public int length; // length is public

  /* Construct array given its size and the value to
     return if get() fails. */
  public FailSoftArray(int size, int errv) {
    a = new int[size];
    errval = errv;
    length = size;
  }

  // Return value at given index.
  public int get(int index) {
    if(ok(index)) return a[index];          Trap an out-of-bounds index.
    return errval;
  }

  // Put a value at an index. Return false on failure.
  public boolean put(int index, int val) {
    if(ok(index)) {
      a[index] = val;
      return true;
    }
    return false;
  }

  // Return true if index is within bounds.
  private boolean ok(int index) {
   if(index >= 0 & index < length) return true;
   return false;
  }
}

// Demonstrate the fail-soft array.
class FSDemo {
  public static void main(String args[]) {
    FailSoftArray fs = new FailSoftArray(5, -1);
    int x;

    // show quiet failures
    System.out.println("Fail quietly.");
    for(int i=0; i < (fs.length * 2); i++)
      fs.put(i, i*10);          Access to array must be through its accessor methods.

    for(int i=0; i < (fs.length * 2); i++) {
      x = fs.get(i);
```

```
      if(x != -1) System.out.print(x + " ");
    }
    System.out.println("");

    // now, handle failures
    System.out.println("\nFail with error reports.");
    for(int i=0; i < (fs.length * 2); i++)
      if(!fs.put(i, i*10))
        System.out.println("Index " + i + " out-of-bounds");

    for(int i=0; i < (fs.length * 2); i++) {
      x = fs.get(i);
      if(x != -1) System.out.print(x + " ");
      else
        System.out.println("Index " + i + " out-of-bounds");
    }
  }
}
```

The output from the program is shown here:

```
Fail quietly.
0 10 20 30 40

Fail with error reports.
Index 5 out-of-bounds
Index 6 out-of-bounds
Index 7 out-of-bounds
Index 8 out-of-bounds
Index 9 out-of-bounds
0 10 20 30 40 Index 5 out-of-bounds
Index 6 out-of-bounds
Index 7 out-of-bounds
Index 8 out-of-bounds
Index 9 out-of-bounds
```

Let's look closely at this example. Inside **FailSoftArray** are defined three **private** members. The first is **a**, which stores a reference to the array that will actually hold information. The second is **errval**, which is the value that will be returned when a call to **get( )** fails. The third is the **private** method **ok( )**, which determines whether an index is within bounds. Thus, these three members can be used only by other members of the **FailSoftArray** class. Specifically, **a** and **errval** can be used only by other methods in the class, and **ok( )** can be called only by other members of **FailSoftArray**. The rest of the class members are **public** and can be called by any other code in a program that uses **FailSoftArray**.

When a **FailSoftArray** object is constructed, you must specify the size of the array and the value that you want to return if a call to **get( )** fails. The error value must be a value that would otherwise not be stored in the array. Once constructed, the actual array referred to by **a** and the error value stored in **errval** cannot be accessed by users of the **FailSoftArray** object. Thus, they are not open to misuse. For example, the user cannot try to index **a** directly, possibly exceeding its bounds. Access is available only through the **get( )** and **put( )** methods.

The **ok( )** method is **private** mostly for the sake of illustration. It would be harmless to make it **public** because it does not modify the object. However, since it is used internally by the **FailSoftArray** class, it can be **private**.

Notice that the **length** instance variable is **public**. This is in keeping with the way Java implements arrays. To obtain the length of a **FailSoftArray**, simply use its **length** member.

To use a **FailSoftArray** array, call **put( )** to store a value at the specified index. Call **get( )** to retrieve a value from a specified index. If the index is out-of-bounds, **put( )** returns **false** and **get( )** returns **errval**.

For the sake of convenience, the majority of the examples in this book will continue to use default access for most members. Remember, however, that in the real world, restricting access to members—especially instance variables—is an important part of successful object-oriented programming. As you will see in Module 7, access control is even more vital when inheritance is involved.

Progress Check

1. Name Java's access specifiers.

2. Explain what **private** does.

---

1. **private**, **public**, and **protected**. A default access is also available.
2. When a member is specified as **private**, it can be accessed only by other members of its class.

Project 6-1 Improving the Queue Class

Queue.java

You can use the **private** specifier to make a rather important improvement to the **Queue** class developed in Module 5, Project 5-2. In that version, all members of the **Queue** class use the default access, which is essentially public. This means that it would be possible for a program that uses a **Queue** to directly access the underlying array, possibly accessing its elements out of turn. Since the entire point of a queue is to provide a first-in, first-out list, allowing out-of-order access is not desirable. It would also be possible for a malicious programmer to alter the values stored in the **putloc** and **getloc** indices, thus corrupting the queue. Fortunately, these types of problems are easy to prevent by applying the **private** specifier.

Step by Step

1. Copy the original **Queue** class in Project 5-2 to a new file called **Queue.java**.

2. In the **Queue** class, add the **private** specifier to the **q** array, and the indices **putloc** and **getloc**, as shown here:

```
// An improved queue class for characters.
class Queue {
  // these members are now private
  private char q[]; // this array holds the queue
  private int putloc, getloc; // the put and get indices

  Queue(int size) {
    q = new char[size+1]; // allocate memory for queue
    putloc = getloc = 0;
  }

  // Put a character into the queue.
  void put(char ch) {
    if(putloc==q.length-1) {
      System.out.println(" - Queue is full.");
      return;
    }

    putloc++;
    q[putloc] = ch;
  }

  // Get a character from the queue.
```

```
    char get() {
      if(getloc == putloc) {
        System.out.println(" - Queue is empty.");
        return (char) 0;
      }

      getloc++;
      return q[getloc];
    }
  }
```

3. Changing **q**, **putloc**, and **getloc** from default access to private access has no effect on a program that properly uses **Queue**. For example, it still works fine with the **QDemo** class from Project 5-2. However, it prevents the improper use of a **Queue**. For example, the following types of statements are illegal:

```
Queue test = new Queue(10);

test.q[0] = 99; // wrong!
test.putloc = -100; // won't work!
```

4. Now that **q**, **putloc**, and **getloc** are private, the **Queue** class strictly enforces the first-in, first-out attribute of a queue.

Pass Objects to Methods

Up to this point, the examples in this book have been using simple types as parameters to methods. However, it is both correct and common to pass objects to methods. For example, the following program defines a class called **Block** that stores the dimensions of a three-dimensional block:

```
// Objects can be passed to methods.
class Block {
  int a, b, c;
  int volume;

  Block(int i, int j, int k) {
    a = i;
    b = j;
    c = k;
    volume = a * b * c;
  }
```

```
    // Return true if ob defines same block.
    boolean sameBlock(Block ob) {          ◄——————— Use object type for parameter.
      if((ob.a == a) & (ob.b == b) & (ob.c == c)) return true;
      else return false;
    }

    // Return true if ob has same volume.
    boolean sameVolume(Block ob) {  ◄
      if(ob.volume == volume) return true;
      else return false;
    }
}

class PassOb {
  public static void main(String args[]) {
    Block ob1 = new Block(10, 2, 5);
    Block ob2 = new Block(10, 2, 5);
    Block ob3 = new Block(4, 5, 5);

    System.out.println("ob1 same dimensions as ob2: " +
                   ob1.sameBlock(ob2));  ◄——————— Pass an object.
    System.out.println("ob1 same dimensions as ob3: " +
                   ob1.sameBlock(ob3));  ◄
    System.out.println("ob1 same volume as ob3: " +
                   ob1.sameVolume(ob3));  ◄
  }
}
```

This program generates the following output:

```
ob1 same dimensions as ob2: true
ob1 same dimensions as ob3: false
ob1 same volume as ob3: true
```

The **sameBlock( )** and **sameVolume( )** methods compare the **Block** object passed as a parameter to the invoking object. For **sameBlock( )**, the dimensions of the objects are compared and **true** is returned only if the two blocks are the same. For **sameVolume( )**, the two blocks are compared only to determine whether they have the same volume. In both cases, notice that the parameter **ob** specifies **Block** as its type. Although **Block** is a class type created by the program, it is used in the same way as Java's built-in types.

How Arguments Are Passed

As the preceding example demonstrated, passing an object to a method is a straightforward task. However, there are some nuances of passing an object that are not shown in the example. In certain cases, the effects of passing an object will be different from those experienced when passing non-object arguments. To see why, you need to understand the two ways in which an argument can be passed to a subroutine.

The first way is *call-by-value*. This approach copies the *value* of an argument into the formal parameter of the subroutine. Therefore, changes made to the parameter of the subroutine have no effect on the argument in the call. The second way an argument can be passed is *call-by-reference*. In this approach, a reference to an argument (not the value of the argument) is passed to the parameter. Inside the subroutine, this reference is used to access the actual argument specified in the call. This means that changes made to the parameter *will* affect the argument used to call the subroutine. As you will see, Java uses both approaches, depending upon what is passed.

In Java, when you pass a primitive type, such as **int** or **double**, to a method, it is passed by value. Thus, what occurs to the parameter that receives the argument has no effect outside the method. For example, consider the following program:

```java
// Primitive types are passed by value.
class Test {
  /* This method causes no change to the arguments
     used in the call. */
  void noChange(int i, int j) {
    i = i + j;
    j = -j;
  }
}

class CallByValue {
  public static void main(String args[]) {
    Test ob = new Test();

    int a = 15, b = 20;

    System.out.println("a and b before call: " +
                       a + " " + b);

    ob.noChange(a, b);
```

```
    System.out.println("a and b after call: " +
                        a + " " + b);
  }
}
```

The output from this program is shown here:

```
a and b before call: 15 20
a and b after call: 15 20
```

As you can see, the operations that occur inside **noChange( )** have no effect on the values of **a** and **b** used in the call.

When you pass an object to a method, the situation changes dramatically, because objects are implicitly passed by reference. Keep in mind that when you create a variable of a class type, you are only creating a reference to an object. Thus, when you pass this reference to a method, the parameter that receives it will refer to the same object as that referred to by the argument. This effectively means that objects are passed to methods by use of call-by-reference. Changes to the object inside the method *do* affect the object used as an argument. For example, consider the following program:

```
// Objects are passed by reference.
class Test {
  int a, b;

  Test(int i, int j) {
    a = i;
    b = j;
  }
  /* Pass an object. Now, ob.a and ob.b in object
     used in the call will be changed. */
  void change(Test ob) {
    ob.a = ob.a + ob.b;
    ob.b = -ob.b;
  }
}

class CallByRef {
  public static void main(String args[]) {
    Test ob = new Test(15, 20);

    System.out.println("ob.a and ob.b before call: " +
                       ob.a + " " + ob.b);

    ob.change(ob);
```

```
System.out.println("ob.a and ob.b after call: " +
                   ob.a + " " + ob.b);
  }
}
```

This program generates the following output:

```
ob.a and ob.b before call: 15 20
ob.a and ob.b after call: 35 -20
```

As you can see, in this case, the actions inside **change( )** have affected the object used as an argument.

As a point of interest, when an object reference is passed to a method, the reference itself is passed by use of call-by-value. However, since the value being passed refers to an object, the copy of that value will still refer to the same object referred to by its corresponding argument.

Ask the Expert

Q: Is there any way that I can pass a primitive type by reference?

A: Not directly. However, Java defines a set of classes that *wrap* the primitive types in objects. These are **Double**, **Float**, **Byte**, **Short**, **Integer**, **Long**, and **Character**. In addition to allowing a primitive type to be passed by reference, these wrapper classes define several methods that enable you to manipulate their values. For example, the numeric type wrappers include methods that convert a numeric value from its binary form into its human-readable **String** form, and vice versa.

Progress Check

1. What is the difference between call-by-value and call-by-reference?

2. How does Java pass primitive types? How does it pass objects?

---

1. In call-by-value, a copy of the argument is passed to a subroutine. In call-by-reference, a reference to the argument is passed.

2. Java passes primitive types by value and object types by reference.

Returning Objects

A method can return any type of data, including class types. For example, the class **ErrorMsg** shown here could be used to report errors. Its method, **getErrorMsg( )**, returns a **String** object that contains a description of an error based upon the error code that it is passed.

```
// Return a String object.
class ErrorMsg {
  String msgs[] = {
    "Output Error",
    "Input Error",
    "Disk Full",
    "Index Out-Of-Bounds"
  };

  // Return the error message.
  String getErrorMsg(int i) {  ←——————— Return an object of type String.
    if(i >=0 & i < msgs.length)
      return msgs[i];
    else
      return "Invalid Error Code";
  }
}

class ErrMsg {
  public static void main(String args[]) {
    ErrorMsg err = new ErrorMsg();

    System.out.println(err.getErrorMsg(2));
    System.out.println(err.getErrorMsg(19));
  }
}
```

Its output is shown here:

```
Disk Full
Invalid Error Code
```

You can, of course, also return objects of classes that you create. For example, here is a reworked version of the preceding program that creates two error classes. One is called **Err**, and it encapsulates an error message along with a severity code. The second is called **ErrorInfo**. It defines a method called **getErrorInfo( )**, which returns an **Err** object.

```java
// Return a programmer-defined object.
class Err {
  String msg; // error message
  int severity; // code indicating severity of error

  Err(String m, int s) {
    msg = m;
    severity = s;
  }
}

class ErrorInfo {
  String msgs[] = {
    "Output Error",
    "Input Error",
    "Disk Full",
    "Index Out-Of-Bounds"
  };
  int howbad[] = { 3, 3, 2, 4 };

  Err getErrorInfo(int i) {                    ◄──────── Return an object of type Err.
    if(i >=0 & i < msgs.length)
      return new Err(msgs[i], howbad[i]);
    else
      return new Err("Invalid Error Code", 0);
  }
}

class ErrInfo {
  public static void main(String args[]) {
    ErrorInfo err = new ErrorInfo();
    Err e;

    e = err.getErrorInfo(2);
    System.out.println(e.msg + " severity: " + e.severity);

    e = err.getErrorInfo(19);
    System.out.println(e.msg + " severity: " + e.severity);
  }
}
```

Here is the output:

```
Disk Full severity: 2
Invalid Error Code severity: 0
```

Each time **getErrorInfo( )** is invoked, a new **Err** object is created, and a reference to it is returned to the calling routine. This object is then used within **main( )** to display the error message and severity code.

When an object is returned by a method, it remains in existence until there are no more references to it. At that point it is subject to garbage collection. Thus, an object won't be destroyed just because the method that created it terminates.

Method Overloading

In this section, you will learn about one of Java's most exciting features: method overloading. In Java, two or more methods within the same class can share the same name, as long as their parameter declarations are different. When this is the case, the methods are said to be *overloaded,* and the process is referred to as *method overloading.* Method overloading is one of the ways that Java implements polymorphism.

In general, to overload a method, simply declare different versions of it. The compiler takes care of the rest. You must observe one important restriction: the type and/or number of the parameters of each overloaded method must differ. It is not sufficient for two methods to differ only in their return types. (Return types do not provide sufficient information in all cases for Java to decide which method to use.) Of course, overloaded methods *may* differ in their return types, too. When an overloaded method is called, the version of the method whose parameters match the arguments is executed.

Here is a simple example that illustrates method overloading:

```java
// Demonstrate method overloading.
class Overload {
  void ovlDemo() {                                    First version
    System.out.println("No parameters");
  }

  // Overload ovlDemo for one integer parameter.
  void ovlDemo(int a) {                               Second version
    System.out.println("One parameter: " + a);
  }

  // Overload ovlDemo for two integer parameters.
  int ovlDemo(int a, int b) {                         Third version
    System.out.println("Two parameters: " + a + " " + b);
    return a + b;
  }

  // Overload ovlDemo for two double parameters.
  double ovlDemo(double a, double b) {                Fourth version
```

```
      System.out.println("Two double parameters: " +
                          a + " "+ b);
      return a + b;
    }
}

class OverloadDemo {
  public static void main(String args[]) {
    Overload ob = new Overload();
    int resI;
    double resD;

    // call all versions of ovlDemo()
    ob.ovlDemo();
    System.out.println();

    ob.ovlDemo(2);
    System.out.println();

    resI = ob.ovlDemo(4, 6);
    System.out.println("Result of ob.ovlDemo(4, 6): " +
                        resI);
    System.out.println();


    resD = ob.ovlDemo(1.1, 2.32);
    System.out.println("Result of ob.ovlDemo(1.1, 2.32): " +
                        resD);
  }
}
```

This program generates the following output:

```
No parameters

One parameter: 2

Two parameters: 4 6
Result of ob.ovlDemo(4, 6): 10

Two double parameters: 1.1 2.32
Result of ob.ovlDemo(1.1, 2.32): 3.42
```

As you can see, **ovlDemo( )** is overloaded four times. The first version takes no parameters, the second takes one integer parameter, the third takes two integer parameters, and the fourth takes two **double** parameters. Notice that the first two versions of **ovlDemo( )** return **void**, and the second two return a value. This is perfectly valid, but as explained, overloading is not affected one way or the other by the return type of a method. Thus, attempting to use these two versions of **ovlDemo( )** will cause an error.

```
// One ovlDemo(int) is OK.
void ovlDemo(int a) {                    ◄─────────────────────  Return types cannot be used to
  System.out.println("One parameter: " + a);                     differentiate overloaded methods.
}

/* Error! Two ovlDemo(int)s are not OK even though
    return types differ.
*/
int ovlDemo(int a) {      ◄─────────────────────────────────┘
  System.out.println("One parameter: " + a);
  return a * a;
}
```

As the comments suggest, the difference in their return types is insufficient for the purposes of overloading.

As you will recall from Module 2, Java provides certain automatic type conversions. These conversions also apply to parameters of overloaded methods. For example, consider the following:

```
/* Automatic type conversions can affect
    overloaded method resolution.
*/
class Overload2 {
  void f(int x) {
    System.out.println("Inside f(int): " + x);
  }

  void f(double x) {
    System.out.println("Inside f(double): " + x);
  }
}

class TypeConv {
  public static void main(String args[]) {
    Overload2 ob = new Overload2();

    int i = 10;
    double d = 10.1;
```

```
    byte b = 99;
    short s = 10;
    float f = 11.5F;


    ob.f(i); // calls ob.f(int)
    ob.f(d); // calls ob.f(double)

    ob.f(b); // calls ob.f(int) - type conversion
    ob.f(s); // calls ob.f(int) - type conversion
    ob.f(f); // calls ob.f(double) - type conversion
  }
}
```

The output from the program is shown here:

```
Inside f(int): 10
Inside f(double): 10.1
Inside f(int): 99
Inside f(int): 10
Inside f(double): 11.5
```

In this example, only two versions of **f( )** are defined: one that has an **int** parameter and one that has a **double** parameter. However, it is possible to pass **f( )** a **byte**, **short**, or **float** value. In the case of **byte** and **short**, Java automatically converts them to **int**. Thus, **f(int)** is invoked. In the case of **float**, the value is converted to **double** and **f(double)** is called.

It is important to understand, however, that the automatic conversions apply only if there is no direct match between a parameter and an argument. For example, here is the preceding program with the addition of a version of **f( )** that specifies a **byte** parameter:

```
// Add f(byte).
class Overload2 {
  void f(byte x) {
    System.out.println("Inside f(byte): " + x);
  }

  void f(int x) {
    System.out.println("Inside f(int): " + x);
  }

  void f(double x) {
    System.out.println("Inside f(double): " + x);
```

```
    }
}

class TypeConv {
  public static void main(String args[]) {
    Overload2 ob = new Overload2();

    int i = 10;
    double d = 10.1;

    byte b = 99;
    short s = 10;
    float f = 11.5F;


    ob.f(i); // calls ob.f(int)
    ob.f(d); // calls ob.f(double)

    ob.f(b); // calls ob.f(byte) - now, no type conversion

    ob.f(s); // calls ob.f(int) - type conversion
    ob.f(f); // calls ob.f(double) - type conversion
  }
}
```

Now when the program is run, the following output is produced:

```
Inside f(int): 10
Inside f(double): 10.1
Inside f(byte): 99
Inside f(int): 10
Inside f(double): 11.5
```

In this version, since there is a version of **f( )** that takes a **byte** argument, when **f( )** is called with a **byte** argument, **f(byte)** is invoked and the automatic conversion to **int** does not occur.

Method overloading supports polymorphism because it is one way that Java implements the "one interface, multiple methods" paradigm. To understand how, consider the following: In languages that do not support method overloading, each method must be given a unique name. However, frequently you will want to implement essentially the same method for different types of data. Consider the absolute value function. In languages that do not support overloading, there are usually three or more versions of this function, each with a slightly different name. For instance, in C, the function **abs( )** returns the absolute value of an integer, **labs( )** returns the absolute value of a long integer, and **fabs( )** returns the absolute value of a floating-point value. Since C does not support overloading, each function has to have its own name, even though all three functions do essentially the same thing. This makes the situation more complex, conceptually, than it actually is. Although the underlying concept of each function is the same, you still have three names to remember. This situation does not occur in Java, because each absolute value method can use the same name. Indeed, Java's standard class library includes an absolute value method, called **abs( )**. This method is overloaded by Java's **Math** class to handle all of the numeric types. Java determines which version of **abs( )** to call based upon the type of argument.

The value of overloading is that it allows related methods to be accessed by use of a common name. Thus, the name **abs** represents the *general action* that is being performed. It is left to the compiler to choose the correct *specific* version for a particular circumstance. You, the programmer, need only remember the general operation being performed. Through the application of polymorphism, several names have been reduced to one. Although this example is fairly simple, if you expand the concept, you can see how overloading can help manage greater complexity.

When you overload a method, each version of that method can perform any activity you desire. There is no rule stating that overloaded methods must relate to one another. However, from a stylistic point of view, method overloading implies a relationship. Thus, while you can use the same name to overload unrelated methods, you should not. For example, you could use the name **sqr** to create methods that return the *square* of an integer and the *square root* of a floating-point value. But these two operations are fundamentally different. Applying method overloading in this manner defeats its original purpose. In practice, you should only overload closely related operations.

Ask the Expert

Q: I've heard the term *signature* used by Java programmers. What is it?

A: As it applies to Java, a signature is the name of a method plus its parameter list. Thus, for the purposes of overloading, no two methods within the same class can have the same signature. Notice that a signature does not include the return type since it is not used by Java for overload resolution.

Progress Check

1. In order for a method to be overloaded, what condition must be met?

2. Does the return type play a role in method overloading?

3. How does Java's automatic type conversion affect overloading?

Overloading Constructors

Like methods, constructors can also be overloaded. Doing so allows you to construct objects in a variety of ways. For example, consider the following program:

```
// Demonstrate an overloaded constructor.
class MyClass {
  int x;

  MyClass() {                                          Construct objects in a variety of ways.
    System.out.println("Inside MyClass().");
    x = 0;
  }

  MyClass(int i) {
    System.out.println("Inside MyClass(int).");
    x = i;
  }

  MyClass(double d) {
    System.out.println("Inside MyClass(double).");
    x = (int) d;
  }

  MyClass(int i, int j) {
    System.out.println("Inside MyClass(int, int).");
```

1. For one method to overload another, the type and/or number of parameters must differ.

2. No. The return type can differ between overloaded methods, but it does not affect method overloading one way or another.

3. When there is no direct match between a set of arguments and a set of parameters, the method with the closest matching set of parameters is used if the arguments can be automatically converted to the type of the parameters.

```
      x = i * j;
  }
}

class OverloadConsDemo {
  public static void main(String args[]) {
    MyClass t1 = new MyClass();
    MyClass t2 = new MyClass(88);
    MyClass t3 = new MyClass(17.23);
    MyClass t4 = new MyClass(2, 4);

    System.out.println("t1.x: " + t1.x);
    System.out.println("t2.x: " + t2.x);
    System.out.println("t3.x: " + t3.x);
    System.out.println("t4.x: " + t4.x);
  }
}
```

The output from the program is shown here:

```
Inside MyClass().
Inside MyClass(int).
Inside MyClass(double).
Inside MyClass(int, int).
t1.x: 0
t2.x: 88
t3.x: 17
t4.x: 8
```

MyClass( ) is overloaded four ways, each constructing an object differently. The proper constructor is called based upon the parameters specified when **new** is executed. By overloading a class' constructor, you give the user of your class flexibility in the way objects are constructed.

One of the most common reasons that constructors are overloaded is to allow one object to initialize another. For example, consider this program that uses the **Summation** class to compute the summation of an integer value.

```
// Initialize one object with another.
class Summation {
  int sum;
```

```
    // Construct from an int.
    Summation(int num) {
      sum = 0;
      for(int i=1; i <= num; i++)
        sum += i;
    }

    // Construct from another object.
    Summation(Summation ob) {                Construct one object from another.
      sum = ob.sum;
    }
}

class SumDemo {
  public static void main(String args[]) {
    Summation s1 = new Summation(5);
    Summation s2 = new Summation(s1);

    System.out.println("s1.sum: " + s1.sum);
    System.out.println("s2.sum: " + s2.sum);
  }
}
```

The output is shown here:

```
s1.sum: 15
s2.sum: 15
```

Often, as this example shows, an advantage of providing a constructor that uses one object to initialize another is efficiency. In this case, when **s2** is constructed, it is not necessary to recompute the summation. Of course, even in cases when efficiency is not an issue, it is often useful to provide a constructor that makes a copy of an object.

Progress Check

1. Can a constructor take an object of its own class as a parameter?

2. Why might you want to provide overloaded constructors?

1. Yes.
2. To provide convenience and flexibility to the user of your class.

Project 6-2 Overloading the Queue Constructor

`QDemo2.java` In this project you will enhance the **Queue** class by giving it two additional
constructors. The first will construct a new queue from another queue. The second
will construct a queue, giving it initial values. As you will see, adding these constructors
enhances the usability of **Queue** substantially.

Step by Step

1. Create a file called **QDemo2.java** and copy the updated **Queue** class from Project 6-1 into it.

2. First, add the following constructor, which constructs a queue from a queue.

```java
// Construct a Queue from a Queue.
Queue(Queue ob) {
  putloc = ob.putloc;
  getloc = ob.getloc;
  q = new char[ob.q.length];

  // copy elements
  for(int i=getloc+1; i <= putloc; i++)
    q[i] = ob.q[i];
}
```

Look closely at this constructor. It initializes **putloc** and **getloc** to the values contained
in the **ob** parameter. It then allocates a new array to hold the queue and copies the elements
from **ob** into that array. Once constructed, the new queue will be an identical copy of the
original, but both will be completely separate objects.

3. Now add the constructor that initializes the queue from a character array, as shown here:

```java
// Construct a Queue with initial values.
Queue(char a[]) {
  putloc = 0;
  getloc = 0;
  q = new char[a.length+1];

  for(int i = 0; i < a.length; i++) put(a[i]);
}
```

This constructor creates a queue large enough to hold the characters in **a** and then stores
those characters in the queue. Because of the way the queue algorithm works, the length of
the queue must be 1 greater than the array.

(continued)

4. Here is the complete updated **Queue** class along with the **QDemo2** class, which demonstrates it:

```
// A queue class for characters.
class Queue {
  private char q[]; // this array holds the queue
  private int putloc, getloc; // the put and get indices

  // Construct an empty Queue given its size.
  Queue(int size) {
    q = new char[size+1]; // allocate memory for queue
    putloc = getloc = 0;
  }

  // Construct a Queue from a Queue.
  Queue(Queue ob) {
    putloc = ob.putloc;
    getloc = ob.getloc;
    q = new char[ob.q.length];

    // copy elements
    for(int i=getloc+1; i <= putloc; i++)
      q[i] = ob.q[i];
  }

  // Construct a Queue with initial values.
  Queue(char a[]) {
    putloc = 0;
    getloc = 0;
    q = new char[a.length+1];

    for(int i = 0; i < a.length; i++) put(a[i]);
  }

  // Put a character into the queue.
  void put(char ch) {
    if(putloc==q.length-1) {
      System.out.println(" - Queue is full.");
      return;
    }

    putloc++;
    q[putloc] = ch;
  }

  // Get a character from the queue.
```

```
      char get() {
        if(getloc == putloc) {
          System.out.println(" - Queue is empty.");
          return (char) 0;
        }

        getloc++;
        return q[getloc];
      }
    }

    // Demonstrate the Queue class.
    class QDemo2 {
      public static void main(String args[]) {
        // construct 10-element empty queue
        Queue q1 = new Queue(10);

        char name[] = {'T', 'o', 'm'};
        // construct queue from array
        Queue q2 = new Queue(name);

        char ch;
        int i;

        // put some characters into q1
        for(i=0; i < 10; i++)
          q1.put((char) ('A' + i));

        // construct queue from another queue
        Queue q3 = new Queue(q1);

        // Show the queues.
        System.out.print("Contents of q1: ");
        for(i=0; i < 10; i++) {
          ch = q1.get();
          System.out.print(ch);
        }

        System.out.println("\n");

        System.out.print("Contents of q2: ");
        for(i=0; i < 3; i++) {
          ch = q2.get();
          System.out.print(ch);
        }
```

(continued)

6

A Closer Look at Methods and Classes

Project
6-2

Overloading the **Queue Constructor**

```
        System.out.println("\n");

        System.out.print("Contents of q3: ");
        for(i=0; i < 10; i++) {
          ch = q3.get();
          System.out.print(ch);
        }
      }
    }
  }
```

The output from the program is shown here:

```
Contents of q1: ABCDEFGHIJ

Contents of q2: Tom

Contents of q3: ABCDEFGHIJ
```

6.6 Recursion

In Java, a method can call itself. This process is called *recursion,* and a method that calls itself is said to be *recursive.* In general, recursion is the process of defining something in terms of itself and is somewhat similar to a circular definition. The key component of a recursive method is a statement that executes a call to itself. Recursion is a powerful control mechanism.

The classic example of recursion is the computation of the factorial of a number. The *factorial* of a number *N* is the product of all the whole numbers between 1 and *N*. For example, 3 factorial is 1 x 2 x 3, or 6. The following program shows a recursive way to compute the factorial of a number. For comparison purposes, a nonrecursive equivalent is also included.

```
// A simple example of recursion.
class Factorial {
  // This is a recursive function.
  int factR(int n) {
    int result;

    if(n==1) return 1;
    result = factR(n-1) * n;
    return result;           ──── Execute the recursive call to factR( ).
  }

  // This is an iterative equivalent.
  int factI(int n) {
    int t, result;
```

```
      result = 1;
      for(t=1; t <= n; t++) result *= t;
      return result;
  }
}

class Recursion {
  public static void main(String args[]) {
    Factorial f = new Factorial();

    System.out.println("Factorials using recursive method.");
    System.out.println("Factorial of 3 is " + f.factR(3));
    System.out.println("Factorial of 4 is " + f.factR(4));
    System.out.println("Factorial of 5 is " + f.factR(5));
    System.out.println();

    System.out.println("Factorials using iterative method.");
    System.out.println("Factorial of 3 is " + f.factI(3));
    System.out.println("Factorial of 4 is " + f.factI(4));
    System.out.println("Factorial of 5 is " + f.factI(5));
  }
}
```

The output from this program is shown here:

```
Factorials using recursive method.
Factorial of 3 is 6
Factorial of 4 is 24
Factorial of 5 is 120

Factorials using iterative method.
Factorial of 3 is 6
Factorial of 4 is 24
Factorial of 5 is 120
```

The operation of the nonrecursive method **factI( )** should be clear. It uses a loop starting at 1 and progressively multiplies each number by the moving product.

The operation of the recursive **factR( )** is a bit more complex. When **factR( )** is called with an argument of 1, the method returns 1; otherwise it returns the product of **factR(n–1)*n**. To evaluate this expression, **factR( )** is called with **n–1**. This process repeats until **n** equals 1 and the calls to the method begin returning. For example, when the factorial of 2 is calculated, the first call to **factR( )** will cause a second call to be made with an argument of 1. This call will return 1, which is then multiplied by 2 (the original value of **n**). The answer is then 2. You might find it interesting to insert **println( )** statements into **factR( )** that show at what level each call is, and what the intermediate results are.

When a method calls itself, new local variables and parameters are allocated storage on the stack, and the method code is executed with these new variables from the start. A recursive call does not make a new copy of the method. Only the arguments are new. As each recursive call returns, the old local variables and parameters are removed from the stack, and execution resumes at the point of the call inside the method. Recursive methods could be said to "telescope" out and back.

Recursive versions of many routines may execute a bit more slowly than the iterative equivalent because of the added overhead of the additional method calls. Too many recursive calls to a method could cause a stack overrun. Because storage for parameters and local variables is on the stack and each new call creates a new copy of these variables, it is possible that the stack could be exhausted. If this occurs, the Java run-time system will cause an exception. However, you probably will not have to worry about this unless a recursive routine runs wild.

The main advantage to recursion is that some types of algorithms can be implemented more clearly and simply recursively than they can be iteratively. For example, the Quicksort sorting algorithm is quite difficult to implement in an iterative way. Also, some problems, especially AI-related ones, seem to lend themselves to recursive solutions.

When writing recursive methods, you must have a conditional statement, such as an **if**, somewhere to force the method to return without the recursive call being executed. If you don't do this, once you call the method, it will never return. This type of error is very common when working with recursion. Use **println( )** statements liberally so that you can watch what is going on and abort execution if you see that you have made a mistake.

CRITICAL SKILL
6.7 Understanding static

There will be times when you will want to define a class member that will be used independently of any object of that class. Normally a class member must be accessed through an object of its class, but it is possible to create a member that can be used by itself, without reference to a specific instance. To create such a member, precede its declaration with the keyword **static**. When a member is declared **static**, it can be accessed before any objects of its class are created, and without reference to any object. You can declare both methods and variables to be **static**. The most common example of a **static** member is **main( )**. **main( )** is declared as **static** because it must be called by the operating system when your program begins.

Outside the class, to use a **static** member, you need only specify the name of its class followed by the dot operator. No object needs to be created. For example, if you want to assign the value 10 to a **static** variable called **count** that is part of the **Timer** class, use this line:

```
Timer.count = 10;
```

This format is similar to that used to access normal instance variables through an object, except that the class name is used. A **static** method can be called in the same way—by use of the dot operator on the name of the class.

Variables declared as **static** are, essentially, global variables. When an object is declared, no copy of a **static** variable is made. Instead, all instances of the class share the same **static** variable. Here is an example that shows the differences between a **static** variable and an instance variable:

```
// Use a static variable.
class StaticDemo {
  int x; // a normal instance variable
  static int y; // a static variable
}
```

There is one copy of **y** for all objects to share.

```
class SDemo {
  public static void main(String args[]) {
    StaticDemo ob1 = new StaticDemo();
    StaticDemo ob2 = new StaticDemo();

    /* Each object has its own copy of
       an instance variable. */
    ob1.x = 10;
    ob2.x = 20;
    System.out.println("Of course, ob1.x and ob2.x " +
                       "are independent.");
    System.out.println("ob1.x: " + ob1.x +
                       "\nob2.x: " + ob2.x);
    System.out.println();

    /* Each object shares one copy of
       a static variable. */
    System.out.println("The static variable y is shared.");
    ob1.y = 19;
    System.out.println("ob1.y: " + ob1.y +
                       "\nob2.y: " + ob2.y);
    System.out.println();

    System.out.println("The static variable y can be" +
                       " accessed through its class.");
    StaticDemo.y = 11; // Can refer to y through class name
    System.out.println("StaticDemo.y: " + StaticDemo.y +
                       "\nob1.y: " + ob1.y +
                       "\nob2.y: " + ob2.y);
  }
}
```

The output from the program is shown here:

```
Of course, ob1.x and ob2.x are independent.
ob1.x: 10
ob2.x: 20

The static variable y is shared.
ob1.y: 19
ob2.y: 19


The static variable y can be accessed through its class.
StaticDemo.y: 11
ob1.y: 11
ob2.y: 11
```

As you can see, the **static** variable **y** is shared by both **ob1** and **ob2**. Changing it through one instance implies that it is changed for all instances. Furthermore, **y** can be accessed either through an object name, as in **ob2.y**, or through its class name, as in **StaticDemo.y**.

The difference between a **static** method and a normal method is that the **static** method can be called through its class name, without any object of that class being created. You have seen an example of this already: the **sqrt( )** method, which is a **static** method within Java's standard **Math** class. Here is an example that creates a **static** method:

```
// Use a static method.
class StaticMeth {
  static int val = 1024; // a static variable

  // a static method
  static int valDiv2() {
    return val/2;
  }
}

class SDemo2 {
  public static void main(String args[]) {

    System.out.println("val is " + StaticMeth.val);
    System.out.println("StaticMeth.valDiv2(): " +
                       StaticMeth.valDiv2());

    StaticMeth.val = 4;
    System.out.println("val is " + StaticMeth.val);
    System.out.println("StaticMeth.valDiv2(): " +
                       StaticMeth.valDiv2());
```

```
  }
}
```

The output is shown here:

```
val is 1024
StaticMeth.valDiv2(): 512
val is 4
StaticMeth.valDiv2(): 2
```

Methods declared as **static** have several restrictions:

● They can call only other **static** methods.

● They must access only **static** data.

● They do not have a **this** reference.

For example, in the following class, the **static** method **valDivDenom( )** is illegal.

```
class StaticError {
  int denom = 3; // a normal instance variable
  static int val = 1024; // a static variable

  /* Error! Can't access a non-static variable
     from within a static method. */
  static int valDivDenom() {
    return val/denom; // won't compile!
  }
}
```

Here, **denom** is a normal instance variable that cannot be accessed within a **static** method.

Static Blocks

Sometimes a class will require some type of initialization before it is ready to create objects. For example, it might need to establish a connection to a remote site. It also might need to initialize certain **static** variables before any of the class' **static** methods are used. To handle these types of situations Java allows you to declare a **static** block. A **static** block is executed when the class is first loaded. Thus, it is executed before the class can be used for any other purpose. Here is an example of a **static** block:

```
// Use a static block
class StaticBlock {
  static double rootOf2;
  static double rootOf3;
```

```
  static {                                           This block is executed
    System.out.println("Inside static block.");      when the class is loaded.
    rootOf2 = Math.sqrt(2.0);
    rootOf3 = Math.sqrt(3.0);
  }

  StaticBlock(String msg) {
    System.out.println(msg);
  }
}

class SDemo3 {
  public static void main(String args[]) {
    StaticBlock ob = new StaticBlock("Inside Constructor");

    System.out.println("Square root of 2 is " +
                       StaticBlock.rootOf2);
    System.out.println("Square root of 3 is " +
                       StaticBlock.rootOf3);

  }
}
```

The output is shown here:

```
Inside static block.
Inside Constructor
Square root of 2 is 1.4142135623730951
Square root of 3 is 1.7320508075688772
```

As you can see, the **static** block is executed before any objects are constructed.

Progress Check

1. Define recursion.

2. Explain the difference between **static** variables and instance variables.

3. When is a **static** block executed?

---

1. Recursion is the process of a method calling itself.

2. Each object of a class has its own copy of the instance variables defined by the class. Each object of a class shares one copy of a **static** variable.

3. A **static** block is executed when its class is first loaded, before its first use.

Project 6-3   The Quicksort

QSDemo.java   In Module 5 you were shown a simple sorting method called the Bubble sort. It was mentioned at the time that substantially better sorts exist. Here you will develop a version of one of the best: the Quicksort. The Quicksort, invented and named by C.A.R. Hoare, is the best general-purpose sorting algorithm currently available. The reason it could not be shown in Module 5 is that the best implementations of the Quicksort rely on recursion. The version we will develop sorts a character array, but the logic can be adapted to sort any type of object you like.

The Quicksort is built on the idea of partitions. The general procedure is to select a value, called the *comparand*, and then to partition the array into two sections. All elements greater than or equal to the partition value are put on one side, and those less than the value are put on the other. This process is then repeated for each remaining section until the array is sorted. For example, given the array **fedacb** and using the value **d** as the comparand, the first pass of the Quicksort would rearrange the array as follows:

Initial	f e d a c b
Pass 1	b c a d e f

This process is then repeated for each section—that is, **bca** and **def**. As you can see, the process is essentially recursive in nature, and indeed, the cleanest implementation of Quicksort is recursive.

You can select the comparand value in two ways. You can either choose it at random, or you can select it by averaging a small set of values taken from the array. For optimal sorting, you should select a value that is precisely in the middle of the range of values. However, this is not easy to do for most sets of data. In the worst case, the value chosen is at one extremity. Even in this case, however, Quicksort still performs correctly. The version of Quicksort that we will develop selects the middle element of the array as the comparand.

Step by Step

1. Create a file called **QSDemo.java**.

2. First, create the **Quicksort** class shown here:

```java
// Project 6-3: A simple version of the Quicksort.
class Quicksort {

  // Set up a call to the actual Quicksort method.
  static void qsort(char items[]) {
    qs(items, 0, items.length-1);
  }
```

(continued)

```
// A recursive version of Quicksort for characters.
private static void qs(char items[], int left, int right)
{
  int i, j;
  char x, y;

  i = left; j = right;
  x = items[(left+right)/2];

  do {
    while((items[i] < x) && (i < right)) i++;
    while((x < items[j]) && (j > left)) j--;

    if(i <= j) {
      y = items[i];
      items[i] = items[j];
      items[j] = y;
      i++; j--;
    }
  } while(i <= j);

  if(left < j) qs(items, left, j);
  if(i < right) qs(items, i, right);
}
}
```

To keep the interface to the Quicksort simple, the **Quicksort** class provides the **qsort( )** method, which sets up a call to the actual Quicksort method, **qs( )**. This enables the Quicksort to be called with just the name of the array to be sorted, without having to provide an initial partition. Since **qs( )** is only used internally, it is specified as **private**.

3. To use the **Quicksort**, simply call **Quicksort.qsort( )**. Since **qsort( )** is specified as **static**, it can be called through its class rather than on an object. Thus, there is no need to create a **Quicksort** object. After the call returns, the array will be sorted. Remember, this version works only for character arrays, but you can adapt the logic to sort any type of arrays you want.

4. Here is a program that demonstrates **Quicksort**:

```
// Project 6-3: A simple version of the Quicksort.
class Quicksort {

  // Set up a call to the actual Quicksort method.
  static void qsort(char items[]) {
    qs(items, 0, items.length-1);
  }
```

```java
// A recursive version of Quicksort for characters.
private static void qs(char items[], int left, int right)
{
  int i, j;
  char x, y;

  i = left; j = right;
  x = items[(left+right)/2];

  do {
    while((items[i] < x) && (i < right)) i++;
    while((x < items[j]) && (j > left)) j--;

    if(i <= j) {
      y = items[i];
      items[i] = items[j];
      items[j] = y;
      i++; j--;
    }
  } while(i <= j);

  if(left < j) qs(items, left, j);
  if(i < right) qs(items, i, right);
  }
}

class QSDemo {
  public static void main(String args[]) {
    char a[] = { 'd', 'x', 'a', 'r', 'p', 'j', 'i' };
    int i;

    System.out.print("Original array: ");
    for(i=0; i < a.length; i++)
      System.out.print(a[i]);

    System.out.println();

    // now, sort the array
    Quicksort.qsort(a);

    System.out.print("Sorted array: ");
    for(i=0; i < a.length; i++)
      System.out.print(a[i]);
  }
}
```

Introducing Nested and Inner Classes

In Java you can define a *nested class*. This is a class that is declared within another class. Frankly, the nested class is a somewhat advanced topic. In fact, nested classes were not even allowed in the first version of Java. It was not until Java 1.1 that they were added. However, it is important that you know what they are and the mechanics of how they are used because they play an important role in many real-world programs.

A nested class does not exist independently of its enclosing class. Thus, the scope of a nested class is bounded by its outer class. A nested class has access to the members, including private members, of the class in which it is nested. However, the enclosing class does not have access to the members of the nested class. A nested class that is declared directly within its enclosing class scope is a member of its enclosing class. It is also possible to declare a nested class that is local to a block.

There are two general types of nested classes: those that are preceded by the **static** modifier and those that are not. The only type that we are concerned about in this book is the non-static variety. This type of nested class is also called an *inner class*. It has access to all of the variables and methods of its outer class and may refer to them directly in the same way that other non-**static** members of the outer class do.

Sometimes an inner class is used to provide a set of services that is used only by its enclosing class. Here is an example that uses an inner class to compute various values for its enclosing class:

```java
// Use an inner class.
class Outer {
  int nums[];

  Outer(int n[]) {
    nums = n;
  }

  void Analyze() {
    Inner inOb = new Inner();

    System.out.println("Minimum: " + inOb.min());
    System.out.println("Maximum: " + inOb.max());
    System.out.println("Average: " + inOb.avg());
  }

  // This is an inner class.
  class Inner {          ◄──────── An inner class
    int min() {
      int m = nums[0];
```

```
      for(int i=1; i < nums.length; i++)
        if(nums[i] < m) m = nums[i];

      return m;
    }

    int max() {
      int m = nums[0];
      for(int i=1; i < nums.length; i++)
        if(nums[i] > m) m = nums[i];

      return m;
    }

    int avg() {
      int a = 0;
      for(int i=0; i < nums.length; i++)
        a += nums[i];

      return a / nums.length;
    }
  }
}

class NestedClassDemo {
  public static void main(String args[]) {
    int x[] = { 3, 2, 1, 5, 6, 9, 7, 8 };
    Outer outOb = new Outer(x);

    outOb.Analyze();
  }
}
```

The output from the program is shown here:

```
Minimum: 1
Maximum: 9
Average: 5
```

In this example, the inner class **Inner** computes various values from the array **nums**, which is a member of **Outer**. As explained, a nested class has access to the members of its enclosing class, so it is perfectly acceptable for **Inner** to access the **nums** array directly. Of course, the opposite is not true. For example, it would not be possible for **analyze( )** to invoke the **min( )** method directly, without creating an **Inner** object.

As mentioned, it is possible to nest a class within any block scope. Doing so simply creates a localized class that is not known outside its block. The following example adapts the **ShowBits** class developed in Project 5-3 for use as a local class.

```
// Use ShowBits as a local class.
class LocalClassDemo {
  public static void main(String args[]) {

    // An inner class version of ShowBits.
    class ShowBits {  ←————————————————— A local class nested within a method
      int numbits;

      ShowBits(int n) {
        numbits = n;
      }

      void show(long val) {
        long mask = 1;

        // left-shift a 1 into the proper position
        mask <<= numbits-1;

        int spacer = 0;
        for(; mask != 0; mask >>>= 1) {
          if((val & mask) != 0) System.out.print("1");
          else System.out.print("0");
          spacer++;
          if((spacer % 8) == 0) {
            System.out.print(" ");
            spacer = 0;
          }
        }
        System.out.println();
      }
    }


    for(byte b = 0; b < 10; b++) {
      ShowBits byteval = new ShowBits(8);

      System.out.print(b + " in binary: ");
      byteval.show(b);
    }
  }
}
```

The output from this version of the program is shown here:

```
0 in binary: 00000000
1 in binary: 00000001
2 in binary: 00000010
3 in binary: 00000011
4 in binary: 00000100
5 in binary: 00000101
6 in binary: 00000110
7 in binary: 00000111
8 in binary: 00001000
9 in binary: 00001001
```

In this example, the **ShowBits** class is not known outside of **main( )**, and any attempt to access it by any method other than **main( )** will result in an error.

One last point: you can create an inner class that does not have a name. This is called an *anonymous inner class*. An object of an anonymous inner class is instantiated when the class is declared, using **new**. Anonymous inner classes are discussed further in Module 15.

Ask the Expert

Q: What makes a static **nested class different from a non-**static **one?**

A: A **static** nested class is one that has the **static** modifier applied. Because it is **static**, it can access only other **static** members of the enclosing class directly. It must access other members of its outer class through an object reference.

Progress Check

1. A nested class has access to the other members of its enclosing class. True or False?

2. A nested class does not exist independently of its enclosing class. True or False?

1. True.
2. True.

Varargs: Variable-Length Arguments

Sometimes you will want to create a method that takes a variable number of arguments, based on its precise usage. For example, a method that opens an Internet connection might take a user name, password, file name, protocol, and so on, but supply defaults if some of this information is not provided. In this situation, it would be convenient to pass only the arguments to which the defaults did not apply. To create such a method implies that there must be some way to create a list of arguments that is variable in length, rather than fixed.

In the past, methods that required a variable-length argument list could be handled two ways, neither of which was particularly pleasing. First, if the maximum number of arguments was small and known, then you could create overloaded versions of the method, one for each way the method could be called. Although this works and is suitable for some situations, it applies to only a narrow class of situations. In cases where the maximum number of potential arguments is larger, or unknowable, a second approach was used in which the arguments were put into an array, and then the array was passed to the method. Frankly, both of these approaches often resulted in clumsy solutions, and it was widely acknowledged that a better approach was needed.

To address this need, a new feature was recently added to Java that simplified the creation of methods that require a variable number of arguments. This feature is called *varargs*, and it is short for variable-length arguments. A method that takes a variable number of arguments is called a *variable-arity method*, or simply a *varargs method*. The parameter list for a varargs method is not fixed, but rather variable in length. Thus, a varargs method can take a variable number of arguments.

Varargs Basics

A variable-length argument is specified by three periods (**...**). For example, here is how to write a method called **vaTest( )** that takes a variable number of arguments:

```
// vaTest() uses a vararg.          Declare a variable-length argument list.
static void vaTest(int ... v) {  ◄─────────────────────┘
  System.out.println("Number of args: " + v.length);
  System.out.println("Contents: ");

  for(int i=0; i < v.length; i++)
    System.out.println("  arg " + i + ": " + v[i]);

  System.out.println();
}
```

Notice that **v** is declared as shown here:

```
int ... v
```

This syntax tells the compiler that **vaTest( )** can be called with zero or more arguments. Furthermore, it causes **v** to be implicitly declared as an array of type **int[ ]**. Thus, inside **vaTest( )**, **v** is accessed using the normal array syntax.

Here is a complete program that demonstrates **vaTest( )**:

```
// Demonstrate variable-length arguments.
class VarArgs {

  // vaTest() uses a vararg.
  static void vaTest(int ... v) {
    System.out.println("Number of args: " + v.length);
    System.out.println("Contents: ");

    for(int i=0; i < v.length; i++)
      System.out.println("  arg " + i + ": " + v[i]);

    System.out.println();
  }

  public static void main(String args[])
  {

    // Notice how vaTest() can be called with a
    // variable number of arguments.
    vaTest(10);        // 1 arg
    vaTest(1, 2, 3);   // 3 args          Call with different numbers
    vaTest();          // no args         of arguments.
  }
}
```

The output from the program is shown here:

```
Number of args: 1
Contents:
  arg 0: 10

Number of args: 3
Contents:
  arg 0: 1
  arg 1: 2
  arg 2: 3

Number of args: 0
Contents:
```

There are two important things to notice about this program. First, as explained, inside **vaTest( )**, **v** is operated on as an array. This is because **v** *is an array*. The **...** syntax simply tells the compiler that a variable number of arguments will be used, and that these arguments will be stored in the array referred to by **v**. Second, in **main( )**, **vaTest( )** is called with different numbers of arguments, including no arguments at all. The arguments are automatically put in an array and passed to **v**. In the case of no arguments, the length of the array is zero.

A method can have "normal" parameters along with a variable-length parameter. However, the variable-length parameter must be the last parameter declared by the method. For example, this method declaration is perfectly acceptable:

```
int doIt(int a, int b, double c, int ... vals) {
```

In this case, the first three arguments used in a call to **doIt( )** are matched to the first three parameters. Then, any remaining arguments are assumed to belong to **vals**.

Here is a reworked version of the **vaTest( )** method that takes a regular argument and a variable-length argument:

```
// Use varargs with standard arguments.
class VarArgs2 {

  // Here, msg is a normal parameter and v is a
  // varargs parameter.
  static void vaTest(String msg, int ... v) {    ←————— A "normal" and vararg
    System.out.println(msg + v.length);                  parameter
    System.out.println("Contents: ");

    for(int i=0; i < v.length; i++)
      System.out.println("  arg " + i + ": " + v[i]);

    System.out.println();
  }

  public static void main(String args[])
  {
    vaTest("One vararg: ", 10);
    vaTest("Three varargs: ", 1, 2, 3);
    vaTest("No varargs: ");
  }
}
```

The output from this program is shown here:

```
One vararg: 1
Contents:
```

```
   arg 0: 10

Three varargs: 3
Contents:
   arg 0: 1
   arg 1: 2
   arg 2: 3

No varargs: 0
Contents:
```

Remember, the varargs parameter must be last. For example, the following declaration is incorrect:

```
int doIt(int a, int b, double c, int ... vals, boolean stopFlag) { // Error!
```

Here, there is an attempt to declare a regular parameter after the varargs parameter, which is illegal.

There is one more restriction to be aware of: there must be only one varargs parameter. For example, this declaration is also invalid:

```
int doIt(int a, int b, double c, int ... vals, double ... morevals) { // Error!
```

The attempt to declare the second varargs parameter is illegal.

Progress Check

1. Show how to declare a method called **sum( )** that takes a variable number of **int** arguments. (Use a return type of **int**.)

2. Given this declaration,
   ```
   void m(double ... x)
   ```
   the parameter **x** is implicitly declared as a/an _____.

---

1. `int sum(int ... n)`
2. array of **double**

Overloading Varargs Methods

You can overload a method that takes a variable-length argument. For example, the following program overloads **vaTest( )** three times:

```java
// Varargs and overloading.
class VarArgs3 {                          // First version of vaTest( )

  static void vaTest(int ... v) {  ←
    System.out.println("vaTest(int ...): " +
                       "Number of args: " + v.length);
    System.out.println("Contents: ");

    for(int i=0; i < v.length; i++)
      System.out.println("  arg " + i + ": " + v[i]);

    System.out.println();
  }                                       // Second version of vaTest( )

  static void vaTest(boolean ... v) {  ←
    System.out.println("vaTest(boolean ...): " +
                       "Number of args: " + v.length);
    System.out.println("Contents: ");

    for(int i=0; i < v.length; i++)
      System.out.println("  arg " + i + ": " + v[i]);

    System.out.println();
  }                                       // Third version of vaTest( )

  static void vaTest(String msg, int ... v) {  ←
    System.out.println("vaTest(String, int ...): " +
                       msg + v.length);
    System.out.println("Contents: ");

    for(int i=0; i < v.length; i++)
      System.out.println("  arg " + i + ": " + v[i]);

    System.out.println();
  }

  public static void main(String args[])
  {
    vaTest(1, 2, 3);
    vaTest("Testing: ", 10, 20);
    vaTest(true, false, false);
  }
}
```

The output produced by this program is shown here:

```
vaTest(int ...): Number of args: 3
Contents:
  arg 0: 1
  arg 1: 2
  arg 2: 3

vaTest(String, int ...): Testing: 2
Contents:
  arg 0: 10
  arg 1: 20

vaTest(boolean ...): Number of args: 3
Contents:
  arg 0: true
  arg 1: false
  arg 2: false
```

This program illustrates both ways that a varargs method can be overloaded. First, the types of its vararg parameter can differ. This is the case for **vaTest(int ...)** and **vaTest(boolean ...)**. Remember, the **...** causes the parameter to be treated as an array of the specified type. Therefore, just as you can overload methods by using different types of array parameters, you can overload varargs methods by using different types of varargs. In this case, Java uses the type difference to determine which overloaded method to call.

The second way to overload a varargs method is to add a normal parameter. This is what was done with **vaTest(String, int ...)**. In this case, Java uses both the number of arguments and the type of the arguments to determine which method to call.

Varargs and Ambiguity

Somewhat unexpected errors can result when overloading a method that takes a variable-length argument. These errors involve ambiguity because it is possible to create an ambiguous call to an overloaded varargs method. For example, consider the following program:

```
// Varargs, overloading, and ambiguity.
//
// This program contains an error and will
// not compile!
class VarArgs4 {

  // Use an int vararg parameter.
  static void vaTest(int ... v) {  ◄─────── An int vararg
    // ...
  }
```

```
// Use a boolean vararg parameter.
static void vaTest(boolean ... v) {  ◄────────── A boolean vararg
  // ...
}


public static void main(String args[])
{
  vaTest(1, 2, 3);  // OK
  vaTest(true, false, false); // OK

  vaTest(); // Error: Ambiguous!  ◄─────── Ambiguous!
}
}
```

In this program, the overloading of **vaTest( )** is perfectly correct. However, this program will not compile because of the following call:

```
vaTest(); // Error: Ambiguous!
```

Because the vararg parameter can be empty, this call could be translated into a call to **vaTest(int ...)** or to **vaTest(boolean ...)**. Both are equally valid. Thus, the call is inherently ambiguous.

Here is another example of ambiguity. The following overloaded versions of **vaTest( )** are inherently ambiguous even though one takes a normal parameter:

```
static void vaTest(int ... v) { // ...

static void vaTest(int n, int ... v) { // ...
```

Although the parameter lists of **vaTest( )** differ, there is no way for the compiler to resolve the following call:

```
vaTest(1)
```

Does this translate into a call to **vaTest(int ...)**, with one varargs argument, or into a call to **vaTest(int, int ...)** with no varargs arguments? There is no way for the compiler to answer this question. Thus, the situation is ambiguous.

Because of ambiguity errors like those just shown, sometimes you will need to forego overloading and simply use two different method names. Also, in some cases, ambiguity errors expose a conceptual flaw in your code, which you can remedy by more carefully crafting a solution.

✓

Module 6 Mastery Check

1. Given this fragment,

```
class X {
  private int count;
```

   is the following fragment correct?

```
class Y {
  public static void main(String args[]) {
    X ob = new X();

    ob.count = 10;
```

2. An access specifier must _____ a member's declaration.

3. The complement of a queue is a stack. It uses first-in, last-out accessing and is often likened to a stack of plates. The first plate put on the table is the last plate used. Create a stack class called **Stack** that can hold characters. Call the methods that access the stack **push( )** and **pop( )**. Allow the user to specify the size of the stack when it is created. Keep all other members of the **Stack** class private. (Hint: you can use the **Queue** class as a model; just change the way the data is accessed.)

4. Given this class,

```
class Test {
  int a;
  Test(int i) { a = i; }
}
```

   write a method called **swap( )** that exchanges the contents of the objects referred to by two **Test** object references.

5. Is the following fragment correct?

```
class X {
  int meth(int a, int b) { ... }
  String meth(int a, int b) { ... }
```

6. Write a recursive method that displays the contents of a string backwards.

7. If all objects of a class need to share the same variable, how must you declare that variable?

8. Why might you need to use a **static** block?

9. What is an inner class?

10. To make a member accessible by only other members of its class, what access specifier must be used?

11. The name of a method plus its parameter list constitutes the method's _____.

12. An **int** argument is passed to a method by using call-by-_____.

13. Create a varargs method called **sum( )** that sums the **int** values passed to it. Have it return the result. Demonstrate its use.

14. Can a varargs method be overloaded?

15. Show an example of an overloaded varargs method that is ambiguous.

Module 7

Inheritance

I nheritance is one of the three foundation principles of object-oriented programming because it allows the creation of hierarchical classifications. Using inheritance, you can create a general class that defines traits common to a set of related items. This class can then be inherited by other, more specific classes, each adding those things that are unique to it.

In the language of Java, a class that is inherited is called a *superclass*. The class that does the inheriting is called a *subclass*. Therefore, a subclass is a specialized version of a superclass. It inherits all of the variables and methods defined by the superclass and adds its own, unique elements.

CRITICAL SKILL
7.1 Inheritance Basics

Java supports inheritance by allowing one class to incorporate another class into its declaration. This is done by using the **extends** keyword. Thus, the subclass adds to (extends) the superclass.

Let's begin with a short example that illustrates several of the key features of inheritance. The following program creates a superclass called **TwoDShape**, which stores the width and height of a two-dimensional object, and a subclass called **Triangle**. Notice how the keyword **extends** is used to create a subclass.

```
// A simple class hierarchy.

// A class for two-dimensional objects.
class TwoDShape {
  double width;
  double height;

  void showDim() {
    System.out.println("Width and height are " +
                        width + " and " + height);
  }
}

// A subclass of TwoDShape for triangles.
class Triangle extends TwoDShape {
  String style;

  double area() {
    return width * height / 2;
  }

  void showStyle() {
    System.out.println("Triangle is " + style);
```

Triangle inherits **TwoDShape**.

Triangle can refer to the members of **TwoDShape** as if they were part of **Triangle**.

```
      }
}

class Shapes {
  public static void main(String args[]) {
    Triangle t1 = new Triangle();
    Triangle t2 = new Triangle();

    t1.width = 4.0;              ◄──── All members of Triangle are available to Triangle objects,
    t1.height = 4.0;                   even those inherited from TwoDShape.
    t1.style = "isosceles";

    t2.width = 8.0;
    t2.height = 12.0;
    t2.style = "right";

    System.out.println("Info for t1: ");
    t1.showStyle();
    t1.showDim();
    System.out.println("Area is " + t1.area());

    System.out.println();

    System.out.println("Info for t2: ");
    t2.showStyle();
    t2.showDim();
    System.out.println("Area is " + t2.area());
  }
}
```

The output from this program is shown here:

```
Info for t1:
Triangle is isosceles
Width and height are 4.0 and 4.0
Area is 8.0

Info for t2:
Triangle is right
Width and height are 8.0 and 12.0
Area is 48.0
```

Here, **TwoDShape** defines the attributes of a "generic" two-dimensional shape, such as a square, rectangle, triangle, and so on. The **Triangle** class creates a specific type of **TwoDShape**, in this case, a triangle. The **Triangle** class includes all of **TwoDObject** and adds the field **style**, the method **area( )**, and the method **showStyle( )**. A description of the type of triangle is stored in **style**, **area( )** computes and returns the area of the triangle, and **showStyle( )** displays the triangle style.

Because **Triangle** includes all of the members of its superclass, **TwoDShape**, it can access **width** and **height** inside **area( )**. Also, inside **main( )**, objects **t1** and **t2** can refer to **width** and **height** directly, as if they were part of **Triangle**. Figure 7-1 depicts conceptually how **TwoDShape** is incorporated into **Triangle**.

Even though **TwoDShape** is a superclass for **Triangle**, it is also a completely independent, stand-alone class. Being a superclass for a subclass does not mean that the superclass cannot be used by itself. For example, the following is perfectly valid.

```
TwoDShape shape = new TwoDShape();

shape.width = 10;
shape.height = 20;

shape.showDim();
```

Of course, an object of **TwoDShape** has no knowledge of or access to any subclasses of **TwoDShape**.

The general form of a **class** declaration that inherits a superclass is shown here:

class *subclass-name* extends *superclass-name* {
  // body of class
}

You can specify only one superclass for any subclass that you create. Java does not support the inheritance of multiple superclasses into a single subclass. (This differs from C++, in which you can inherit multiple base classes. Be aware of this when converting C++ code to Java.) You can, however, create a hierarchy of inheritance in which a subclass becomes a superclass of another subclass. Of course, no class can be a superclass of itself.

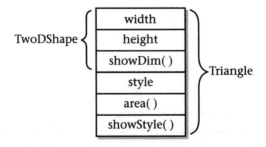

Figure 7-1 A conceptual depiction of the **Triangle** class

A major advantage of inheritance is that once you have created a superclass that defines the attributes common to a set of objects, it can be used to create any number of more specific subclasses. Each subclass can precisely tailor its own classification. For example, here is another subclass of **TwoDShape** that encapsulates rectangles.

```
// A subclass of TwoDShape for rectangles.
class Rectangle extends TwoDShape {
  boolean isSquare() {
    if(width == height) return true;
    return false;
  }

  double area() {
    return width * height;
  }
}
```

The **Rectangle** class includes **TwoDShape** and adds the methods **isSquare( )**, which determines if the rectangle is square, and **area( )**, which computes the area of a rectangle.

Member Access and Inheritance

As you learned in Module 6, often an instance variable of a class will be declared **private** to prevent its unauthorized use or tampering. Inheriting a class *does not* overrule the **private** access restriction. Thus, even though a subclass includes all of the members of its superclass, it cannot access those members of the superclass that have been declared **private**. For example, if, as shown here, **width** and **height** are made private in **TwoDShape**, then **Triangle** will not be able to access them.

```
// Private members are not inherited.

// This example will not compile.

// A class for two-dimensional objects.
class TwoDShape {
  private double width;  // these are
  private double height; // now private

  void showDim() {
    System.out.println("Width and height are " +
                       width + " and " + height);
  }
}
```

```java
// A subclass of TwoDShape for triangles.
class Triangle extends TwoDShape {
  String style;

  double area() {
    return width * height / 2; // Error! can't access
  }

  void showStyle() {
    System.out.println("Triangle is " + style);
  }
}
```

Can't access a **private** member of a superclass.

The **Triangle** class will not compile because the reference to **width** and **height** inside the **area( )** method causes an access violation. Since **width** and **height** are declared **private**, they are accessible only by other members of their own class. Subclasses have no access to them.

Remember that a class member that has been declared **private** will remain private to its class. It is not accessible by any code outside its class, including subclasses.

At first, you might think that the fact that subclasses do not have access to the private members of superclasses is a serious restriction that would prevent the use of private members in many situations. However this is not true. As explained in Module 6, Java programmers typically use accessor methods to provide access to the private methods of a class. Here is a rewrite of the **TwoDShape** and **Triangle** classes that uses methods to access the private instance variables **width** and **height**.

```java
// Use accessor methods to set and get private members.

// A class for two-dimensional objects.
class TwoDShape {
  private double width;  // these are
  private double height; // now private

  // Accessor methods for width and height.
  double getWidth() { return width; }
  double getHeight() { return height; }
  void setWidth(double w) { width = w; }
  void setHeight(double h) { height = h; }

  void showDim() {
    System.out.println("Width and height are " +
                       width + " and " + height);
  }
}
```

Accessor methods for **width** and **height**

```
// A subclass of TwoDShape for triangles.
class Triangle extends TwoDShape {
  String style;

  double area() {
    return getWidth() * getHeight() / 2;
  }

  void showStyle() {
    System.out.println("Triangle is " + style);
  }
}

class Shapes2 {
  public static void main(String args[]) {
    Triangle t1 = new Triangle();
    Triangle t2 = new Triangle();

    t1.setWidth(4.0);
    t1.setHeight(4.0);
    t1.style = "isosceles";

    t2.setWidth(8.0);
    t2.setHeight(12.0);
    t2.style = "right";

    System.out.println("Info for t1: ");
    t1.showStyle();
    t1.showDim();
    System.out.println("Area is " + t1.area());

    System.out.println();

    System.out.println("Info for t2: ");
    t2.showStyle();
    t2.showDim();
    System.out.println("Area is " + t2.area());
  }
}
```

Use accessor methods provided by superclass.

Ask the Expert

Q: When should I make an instance variable private?

A: There are no hard and fast rules, but here are two general principles. If an instance variable is to be used only by methods defined within its class, then it should be made private. If an instance variable must be within certain bounds, then it should be private and made available only through accessor methods. This way, you can prevent invalid values from being assigned.

Progress Check

1. When creating a subclass, what keyword is used to include a superclass?

2. Does a subclass include the members of its superclass?

3. Does a subclass have access to the private members of its superclass?

CRITICAL SKILL
7.2 Constructors and Inheritance

In a hierarchy, it is possible for both superclasses and subclasses to have their own constructors. This raises an important question: what constructor is responsible for building an object of the subclass—the one in the superclass, the one in the subclass, or both? The answer is this: the constructor for the superclass constructs the superclass portion of the object, and the constructor for the subclass constructs the subclass part. This makes sense because the superclass has no knowledge of or access to any element in a subclass. Thus, their construction must be separate. The preceding examples have relied upon the default constructors created automatically by Java, so this was not an issue. However, in practice, most classes will have explicit constructors. Here you will see how to handle this situation.

1. **extends**
2. Yes.
3. No.

When only the subclass defines a constructor, the process is straightforward: simply construct the subclass object. The superclass portion of the object is constructed automatically using its default constructor. For example, here is a reworked version of **Triangle** that defines a constructor. It also makes **style** private since it is now set by the constructor.

```java
// Add a constructor to Triangle.

// A class for two-dimensional objects.
class TwoDShape {
  private double width;  // these are
  private double height; // now private

  // Accessor methods for width and height.
  double getWidth() { return width; }
  double getHeight() { return height; }
  void setWidth(double w) { width = w; }
  void setHeight(double h) { height = h; }

  void showDim() {
    System.out.println("Width and height are " +
                       width + " and " + height);
  }
}

// A subclass of TwoDShape for triangles.
class Triangle extends TwoDShape {
  private String style;

  // Constructor
  Triangle(String s, double w, double h) {
    setWidth(w);  ◄─────────────────────── Initialize TwoDShape
    setHeight(h);                           portion of object.

    style = s;
  }

  double area() {
    return getWidth() * getHeight() / 2;
  }

  void showStyle() {
    System.out.println("Triangle is " + style);
  }
}
```

```
class Shapes3 {
  public static void main(String args[]) {
    Triangle t1 = new Triangle("isosceles", 4.0, 4.0);
    Triangle t2 = new Triangle("right", 8.0, 12.0);

    System.out.println("Info for t1: ");
    t1.showStyle();
    t1.showDim();
    System.out.println("Area is " + t1.area());

    System.out.println();

    System.out.println("Info for t2: ");
    t2.showStyle();
    t2.showDim();
    System.out.println("Area is " + t2.area());
  }
}
```

Here, **Triangle**'s constructor initializes the members of **TwoDClass** that it inherits along with its own **style** field.

When both the superclass and the subclass define constructors, the process is a bit more complicated because both the superclass and subclass constructors must be executed. In this case you must use another of Java's keywords, **super**, which has two general forms. The first calls a superclass constructor. The second is used to access a member of the superclass that has been hidden by a member of a subclass. Here, we will look at its first use.

Using super to Call Superclass Constructors

A subclass can call a constructor defined by its superclass by use of the following form of **super**:

super(*parameter-list*);

Here, *parameter-list* specifies any parameters needed by the constructor in the superclass. **super( )** must always be the first statement executed inside a subclass constructor.

To see how **super( )** is used, consider the version of **TwoDShape** in the following program. It defines a constructor that initializes **width** and **height**.

```
// Add constructors to TwoDShape.
class TwoDShape {
  private double width;
  private double height;

  // Parameterized constructor.
  TwoDShape(double w, double h) {          A constructor for TwoDShape.
    width = w;
    height = h;
  }

  // Accessor methods for width and height.
  double getWidth() { return width; }
  double getHeight() { return height; }
  void setWidth(double w) { width = w; }
  void setHeight(double h) { height = h; }

  void showDim() {
    System.out.println("Width and height are " +
                       width + " and " + height);
  }
}

// A subclass of TwoDShape for triangles.
class Triangle extends TwoDShape {
  private String style;

  Triangle(String s, double w, double h) {
    super(w, h); // call superclass constructor

    style = s;
  }                              Use super( ) to execute the
                                 TwoDShape constructor.

  double area() {
    return getWidth() * getHeight() / 2;
  }

  void showStyle() {
    System.out.println("Triangle is " + style);
  }
}
```

```
class Shapes4 {
  public static void main(String args[]) {
    Triangle t1 = new Triangle("isosceles", 4.0, 4.0);
    Triangle t2 = new Triangle("right", 8.0, 12.0);

    System.out.println("Info for t1: ");
    t1.showStyle();
    t1.showDim();
    System.out.println("Area is " + t1.area());

    System.out.println();

    System.out.println("Info for t2: ");
    t2.showStyle();
    t2.showDim();
    System.out.println("Area is " + t2.area());
  }
}
```

Here, **Triangle( )** calls **super( )** with the parameters **w** and **h**. This causes the **TwoDShape( )** constructor to be called, which initializes **width** and **height** using these values. **Triangle** no longer initializes these values itself. It need only initialize the value unique to it: **style**. This leaves **TwoDShape** free to construct its subobject in any manner that it so chooses. Furthermore, **TwoDShape** can add functionality about which existing subclasses have no knowledge, thus preventing existing code from breaking.

Any form of constructor defined by the superclass can be called by **super( )**. The constructor executed will be the one that matches the arguments. For example, here are expanded versions of both **TwoDShape** and **Triangle** that include default constructors and constructors that take one argument.

```
// Add more constructors to TwoDShape.
class TwoDShape {
  private double width;
  private double height;

  // A default constructor.
  TwoDShape() {
    width = height = 0.0;
  }
```

```
  // Parameterized constructor.
  TwoDShape(double w, double h) {
    width = w;
    height = h;
  }

  // Construct object with equal width and height.
  TwoDShape(double x) {
    width = height = x;
  }

  // Accessor methods for width and height.
  double getWidth() { return width; }
  double getHeight() { return height; }
  void setWidth(double w) { width = w; }
  void setHeight(double h) { height = h; }

  void showDim() {
    System.out.println("Width and height are " +
                        width + " and " + height);
  }
}

// A subclass of TwoDShape for triangles.
class Triangle extends TwoDShape {
  private String style;

  // A default constructor.
  Triangle() {
    super();
    style = "null";
  }

  // Constructor
  Triangle(String s, double w, double h) {
    super(w, h); // call superclass constructor

    style = s;
  }

  // Construct an isosceles triangle.
  Triangle(double x) {
    super(x); // call superclass constructor
```

Use **super( )** to call the various forms of the **TwoDShape** constructor.

```java
      style = "isosceles";
  }

  double area() {
    return getWidth() * getHeight() / 2;
  }

  void showStyle() {
    System.out.println("Triangle is " + style);
  }
}

class Shapes5 {
  public static void main(String args[]) {
    Triangle t1 = new Triangle();
    Triangle t2 = new Triangle("right", 8.0, 12.0);
    Triangle t3 = new Triangle(4.0);

    t1 = t2;

    System.out.println("Info for t1: ");
    t1.showStyle();
    t1.showDim();
    System.out.println("Area is " + t1.area());

    System.out.println();

    System.out.println("Info for t2: ");
    t2.showStyle();
    t2.showDim();
    System.out.println("Area is " + t2.area());

    System.out.println();

    System.out.println("Info for t3: ");
    t3.showStyle();
    t3.showDim();
    System.out.println("Area is " + t3.area());

    System.out.println();
  }
}
```

Here is the output from this version.

```
Info for t1:
Triangle is right
Width and height are 8.0 and 12.0
Area is 48.0

Info for t2:
Triangle is right
Width and height are 8.0 and 12.0
Area is 48.0

Info for t3:
Triangle is isosceles
Width and height are 4.0 and 4.0
Area is 8.0
```

Let's review the key concepts behind **super( )**. When a subclass calls **super( )**, it is calling the constructor of its immediate superclass. Thus, **super( )** always refers to the superclass immediately above the calling class. This is true even in a multilevel hierarchy. Also, **super( )** must always be the first statement executed inside a subclass constructor.

Progress Check

1. How does a subclass execute its superclass' constructor?

2. Can parameters be passed via **super( )**?

3. Can **super( )** go anywhere within a subclass' constructor?

1. It calls **super( )**.
2. Yes.
3. No, it must be the first statement executed.

7.3 Using super to Access Superclass Members

There is a second form of **super** that acts somewhat like **this**, except that it always refers to the superclass of the subclass in which it is used. This usage has the following general form:

super.*member*

Here, *member* can be either a method or an instance variable.

This form of **super** is most applicable to situations in which member names of a subclass hide members by the same name in the superclass. Consider this simple class hierarchy:

```
// Using super to overcome name hiding.
class A {
  int i;
}

// Create a subclass by extending class A.
class B extends A {
  int i; // this i hides the i in A

  B(int a, int b) {
    super.i = a; // i in A         Here, super.i refers
    i = b; // i in B                to the i in A.
  }

  void show() {
    System.out.println("i in superclass: " + super.i);
    System.out.println("i in subclass: " + i);
  }
}

class UseSuper {
  public static void main(String args[]) {
    B subOb = new B(1, 2);

    subOb.show();
  }
}
```

This program displays the following:

```
i in superclass: 1
i in subclass: 2
```

Although the instance variable **i** in **B** hides the **i** in **A**, **super** allows access to the **i** defined in the superclass. **super** can also be used to call methods that are hidden by a subclass.

Project 7-1   Extending the Vehicle Class

TruckDemo.java

To illustrate the power of inheritance, we will extend the **Vehicle** class first developed in Module 4. As you should recall, **Vehicle** encapsulates information about vehicles, including the number of passengers they can carry, their fuel capacity, and fuel consumption rate. We can use the **Vehicle** class as a starting point from which more specialized classes are developed. For example, one type of vehicle is a truck. An important attribute of a truck is its cargo capacity. Thus, to create a **Truck** class, you can extend **Vehicle**, adding an instance variable that stores the carrying capacity. Here is a version of **Vehicle** that does this. In the process, the instance variables in **Vehicle** will be made **private**, and accessor methods are provided to get and set their values.

Step by Step

1. Create a file called **TruckDemo.java** and copy the last implementation of **Vehicle** from Module 4 into the file.

2. Create the **Truck** class as shown here.

```java
// Extend Vehicle to create a Truck specialization.
class Truck extends Vehicle {
  private int cargocap; // cargo capacity in pounds

  // This is a constructor for Truck.
  Truck(int p, int f, int m, int c) {
    /* Initialize Vehicle members using
       Vehicle's constructor. */
    super(p, f, m);

    cargocap = c;
  }

  // Accessor methods for cargocap.
  int getCargo() { return cargocap; }
  void putCargo(int c) { cargocap = c; }
}
```

Here, **Truck** inherits **Vehicle**, adding **cargocap**, **getCargo( )**, and **putCargo( )**. Thus, **Truck** includes all of the general vehicle attributes defined by **Vehicle**. It need add only those items that are unique to its own class.

(continued)

3. Next, make the instance variables of **Vehicle** private, as shown here.

```
private int passengers; // number of passengers
private int fuelcap;    // fuel capacity in gallons
private int mpg;        // fuel consumption in miles per gallon
```

4. Here is an entire program that demonstrates the **Truck** class.

```
// Build a subclass of Vehicle for trucks.
class Vehicle {
  private int passengers; // number of passengers
  private int fuelcap;    // fuel capacity in gallons
  private int mpg;        // fuel consumption in miles per gallon

  // This is a constructor for Vehicle.
  Vehicle(int p, int f, int m) {
    passengers = p;
    fuelcap = f;
    mpg = m;
  }

  // Return the range.
  int range() {
    return mpg * fuelcap;
  }

  // Compute fuel needed for a given distance.
  double fuelneeded(int miles) {
    return (double) miles / mpg;
  }

  // Access methods for instance variables.
  int getPassengers() { return passengers; }
  void setPassengers(int p) { passengers = p; }
  int getFuelcap() { return fuelcap; }
  void setFuelcap(int f) { fuelcap = f; }
  int getMpg() { return mpg; }
  void setMpg(int m) { mpg = m; }

}

// Extend Vehicle to create a Truck specialization.
class Truck extends Vehicle {
  private int cargocap; // cargo capacity in pounds

  // This is a constructor for Truck.
  Truck(int p, int f, int m, int c) {
```

```
      /* Initialize Vehicle members using
         Vehicle's constructor. */
      super(p, f, m);

      cargocap = c;
    }

    // Accessor methods for cargocap.
    int getCargo() { return cargocap; }
    void putCargo(int c) { cargocap = c; }
}

class TruckDemo {
  public static void main(String args[]) {

    // construct some trucks
    Truck semi = new Truck(2, 200, 7, 44000);
    Truck pickup = new Truck(3, 28, 15, 2000);
    double gallons;
    int dist = 252;

    gallons = semi.fuelneeded(dist);

    System.out.println("Semi can carry " + semi.getCargo() +
                       " pounds.");
    System.out.println("To go " + dist + " miles semi needs " +
                       gallons + " gallons of fuel.\n");

    gallons = pickup.fuelneeded(dist);

    System.out.println("Pickup can carry " + pickup.getCargo() +
                       " pounds.");
    System.out.println("To go " + dist + " miles pickup needs " +
                       gallons + " gallons of fuel.");
  }
}
```

5. The output from this program is shown here:

```
Semi can carry 44000 pounds.
To go 252 miles semi needs 36.0 gallons of fuel.

Pickup can carry 2000 pounds.
To go 252 miles pickup needs 16.8 gallons of fuel.
```

(continued)

6. Many other types of classes can be derived from **Vehicle**. For example, the following skeleton creates an off-road class that stores the ground clearance of the vehicle.

```
// Create an off-road vehicle class
class OffRoad extends Vehicle {
  private int groundClearance; // ground clearance in inches

  // ...
}
```

The key point is that once you have created a superclass that defines the general aspects of an object, that superclass can be inherited to form specialized classes. Each subclass simply adds its own, unique attributes. This is the essence of inheritance.

CRITICAL SKILL
7.4 # Creating a Multilevel Hierarchy

Up to this point, we have been using simple class hierarchies that consist of only a superclass and a subclass. However, you can build hierarchies that contain as many layers of inheritance as you like. As mentioned, it is perfectly acceptable to use a subclass as a superclass of another. For example, given three classes called **A**, **B**, and **C**, **C** can be a subclass of **B**, which is a subclass of **A**. When this type of situation occurs, each subclass inherits all of the traits found in all of its superclasses. In this case, **C** inherits all aspects of **B** and **A**.

To see how a multilevel hierarchy can be useful, consider the following program. In it, the subclass **Triangle** is used as a superclass to create the subclass called **ColorTriangle**. **ColorTriangle** inherits all of the traits of **Triangle** and **TwoDShape** and adds a field called **color**, which holds the color of the triangle.

```
// A multilevel hierarchy.
class TwoDShape {
  private double width;
  private double height;

  // A default constructor.
  TwoDShape() {
    width = height = 0.0;
  }

  // Parameterized constructor.
  TwoDShape(double w, double h) {
    width = w;
    height = h;
  }
```

```java
  // Construct object with equal width and height.
  TwoDShape(double x) {
    width = height = x;
  }

  // Accessor methods for width and height.
  double getWidth() { return width; }
  double getHeight() { return height; }
  void setWidth(double w) { width = w; }
  void setHeight(double h) { height = h; }

  void showDim() {
    System.out.println("Width and height are " +
                       width + " and " + height);
  }
}

// Extend TwoDShape.
class Triangle extends TwoDShape {
  private String style;

  // A default constructor.
  Triangle() {
    super();
    style = "null";
  }

  Triangle(String s, double w, double h) {
    super(w, h); // call superclass constructor

    style = s;
  }

  // Construct an isosceles triangle.
  Triangle(double x) {
    super(x); // call superclass constructor

    style = "isosceles";
  }

  double area() {
    return getWidth() * getHeight() / 2;
  }
```

```
  void showStyle() {
    System.out.println("Triangle is " + style);
  }
}

// Extend Triangle.
class ColorTriangle extends Triangle {
  private String color;

  ColorTriangle(String c, String s,
                double w, double h) {
    super(s, w, h);

    color = c;
  }

  String getColor() { return color; }

  void showColor() {
    System.out.println("Color is " + color);
  }
}

class Shapes6 {
  public static void main(String args[]) {
    ColorTriangle t1 =
        new ColorTriangle("Blue", "right", 8.0, 12.0);
    ColorTriangle t2 =
        new ColorTriangle("Red", "isosceles", 2.0, 2.0);

    System.out.println("Info for t1: ");
    t1.showStyle();
    t1.showDim();
    t1.showColor();
    System.out.println("Area is " + t1.area());

    System.out.println();

    System.out.println("Info for t2: ");
    t2.showStyle();
    t2.showDim();
    t2.showColor();
    System.out.println("Area is " + t2.area());
  }
}
```

ColorTriangle inherits **Triangle**, which is descended from **TwoDShape**, so **ColorTriangle** includes all members of **Triangle** and **TwoDShape**.

A **ColorTriangle** object can call methods defined by itself and its superclasses.

The output of this program is shown here:

```
Info for t1:
Triangle is right
Width and height are 8.0 and 12.0
Color is Blue
Area is 48.0

Info for t2:
Triangle is isosceles
Width and height are 2.0 and 2.0
Color is Red
Area is 2.0
```

Because of inheritance, **ColorTriangle** can make use of the previously defined classes of **Triangle** and **TwoDShape**, adding only the extra information it needs for its own, specific application. This is part of the value of inheritance; it allows the reuse of code.

This example illustrates one other important point: **super( )** always refers to the constructor in the closest superclass. The **super( )** in **ColorTriangle** calls the constructor in **Triangle**. The **super( )** in **Triangle** calls the constructor in **TwoDShape**. In a class hierarchy, if a superclass constructor requires parameters, then all subclasses must pass those parameters "up the line." This is true whether or not a subclass needs parameters of its own.

CRITICAL SKILL
7.5 When Are Constructors Called?

In the foregoing discussion of inheritance and class hierarchies, an important question may have occurred to you: When a subclass object is created, whose constructor is executed first, the one in the subclass or the one defined by the superclass? For example, given a subclass called **B** and a superclass called **A**, is **A**'s constructor called before **B**'s, or vice versa? The answer is that in a class hierarchy, constructors are called in order of derivation, from superclass to subclass. Further, since **super( )** must be the first statement executed in a subclass' constructor, this order is the same whether or not **super( )** is used. If **super( )** is not used, then the default (parameterless) constructor of each superclass will be executed. The following program illustrates when constructors are executed:

```
// Demonstrate when constructors are called.

// Create a super class.
class A {
  A() {
    System.out.println("Constructing A.");
  }
}
```

```
// Create a subclass by extending class A.
class B extends A {
  B() {
    System.out.println("Constructing B.");
  }
}

// Create another subclass by extending B.
class C extends B {
  C() {
    System.out.println("Constructing C.");
  }
}

class OrderOfConstruction {
  public static void main(String args[]) {
    C c = new C();
  }
}
```

The output from this program is shown here:

```
Constructing A.
Constructing B.
Constructing C.
```

As you can see, the constructors are called in order of derivation.

If you think about it, it makes sense that constructors are executed in order of derivation. Because a superclass has no knowledge of any subclass, any initialization it needs to perform is separate from and possibly prerequisite to any initialization performed by the subclass. Therefore, it must be executed first.

CRITICAL SKILL
7.6

Superclass References and Subclass Objects

As you know, Java is a strongly typed language. Aside from the standard conversions and automatic promotions that apply to its primitive types, type compatibility is strictly enforced. Therefore, a reference variable for one class type cannot normally refer to an object of another class type. For example, consider the following program.

```
// This will not compile.
class X {
  int a;
```

```
  X(int i) { a = i; }
}

class Y {
  int a;

  Y(int i) { a = i; }
}

class IncompatibleRef {
  public static void main(String args[]) {
    X x = new X(10);
    X x2;
    Y y = new Y(5);

    x2 = x; // OK, both of same type

    x2 = y; // Error, not of same type
  }
}
```

Here, even though class **X** and class **Y** are physically the same, it is not possible to assign an **X** reference to a **Y** object because they have different types. In general, an object reference variable can refer only to objects of its type.

There is, however, an important exception to Java's strict type enforcement. A reference variable of a superclass can be assigned a reference to any subclass derived from that superclass. Here is an example:

```
// A superclass reference can refer to a subclass object.
class X {
  int a;

  X(int i) { a = i; }
}

class Y extends X {
  int b;

  Y(int i, int j) {
    super(j);
    b = i;
  }
}
```

```
class SupSubRef {
  public static void main(String args[]) {
    X x = new X(10);
    X x2;
    Y y = new Y(5, 6);

    x2 = x; // OK, both of same type
    System.out.println("x2.a: " + x2.a);

    x2 = y; // still Ok because Y is derived from X
    System.out.println("x2.a: " + x2.a);

    // X references know only about X members
    x2.a = 19; // OK
//    x2.b = 27; // Error, X doesn't have a b member
  }
}
```

OK because **Y** is a subclass of **X**; thus **x2** can refer to **y**.

Here, **Y** is now derived from **X**; thus it is permissible for **x2** to be assigned a reference to a **Y** object.

It is important to understand that it is the type of the reference variable— not the type of the object that it refers to—that determines what members can be accessed. That is, when a reference to a subclass object is assigned to a superclass reference variable, you will have access only to those parts of the object defined by the superclass. This is why **x2** can't access **b** even when it refers to a **Y** object. If you think about it, this makes sense, because the superclass has no knowledge of what a subclass adds to it. This is why the last line of code in the program is commented out.

Although the preceding discussion may seem a bit esoteric, it has some important practical applications. One is described here. The other is discussed later in this module, when method overriding is covered.

An important place where subclass references are assigned to superclass variables is when constructors are called in a class hierarchy. As you know, it is common for a class to define a constructor that takes an object of the class as a parameter. This allows the class to construct a copy of an object. Subclasses of such a class can take advantage of this feature. For example, consider the following versions of **TwoDShape** and **Triangle**. Both add constructors that take an object as a parameter.

```
class TwoDShape {
  private double width;
  private double height;
```

```
  // A default constructor.
  TwoDShape() {
    width = height = 0.0;
  }

  // Parameterized constructor.
  TwoDShape(double w, double h) {
    width = w;
    height = h;
  }

  // Construct an object with equal width and height.
  TwoDShape(double x) {
    width = height = x;
  }

  // Construct an object from an object.
  TwoDShape(TwoDShape ob) {               Construct object from an object.
    width = ob.width;
    height = ob.height;
  }

  // Accessor methods for width and height.
  double getWidth() { return width; }
  double getHeight() { return height; }
  void setWidth(double w) { width = w; }
  void setHeight(double h) { height = h; }

  void showDim() {
    System.out.println("Width and height are " +
                       width + " and " + height);
  }
}

// A subclass of TwoDShape for triangles.
class Triangle extends TwoDShape {
  private String style;

  // A default constructor.
  Triangle() {
    super();
    style = "null";
  }
```

```
// Constructor for Triangle.
Triangle(String s, double w, double h) {
  super(w, h); // call superclass constructor

  style = s;
}

// Construct an isosceles triangle.
Triangle(double x) {
  super(x); // call superclass constructor

  style = "isosceles";
}

// Construct an object from an object.
Triangle(Triangle ob) {
  super(ob); // pass object to TwoDShape constructor
  style = ob.style;
}

double area() {
  return getWidth() * getHeight() / 2;
}

void showStyle() {
  System.out.println("Triangle is " + style);
}
}

class Shapes7 {
  public static void main(String args[]) {
    Triangle t1 =
        new Triangle("right", 8.0, 12.0);

    // make a copy of t1
    Triangle t2 = new Triangle(t1);

    System.out.println("Info for t1: ");
    t1.showStyle();
    t1.showDim();
    System.out.println("Area is " + t1.area());

    System.out.println();
```

Pass a **Triangle** reference to **TwoDShape**'s constructor.

```
    System.out.println("Info for t2: ");
    t2.showStyle();
    t2.showDim();
    System.out.println("Area is " + t2.area());
  }
}
```

In this program, **t2** is constructed from **t1** and is, thus, identical. The output is shown here.

```
Info for t1:
Triangle is right
Width and height are 8.0 and 12.0
Area is 48.0

Info for t2:
Triangle is right
Width and height are 8.0 and 12.0
Area is 48.0
```

Pay special attention to this **Triangle** constructor:

```
// Construct an object from an object.
Triangle(Triangle ob) {
  super(ob); // pass object to TwoDShape constructor
  style = ob.style;
}
```

It receives an object of type **Triangle** and it passes that object (through **super**) to this **TwoDShape** constructor:

```
// Construct an object from an object.
TwoDShape(TwoDShape ob) {
  width = ob.width;
  height = ob.height;
}
```

The key point is that **TwoDshape( )** is expecting a **TwoDShape** object. However, **Triangle( )** passes it a **Triangle** object. The reason this works is because, as explained, a superclass reference can refer to a subclass object. Thus it is perfectly acceptable to pass **TwoDShape( )** a reference to an object of a class derived from **TwoDShape**. Because the **TwoDShape( )** constructor is initializing only those portions of the subclass object that are members of **TwoDShape**, it doesn't matter that the object might also contain other members added by derived classes.

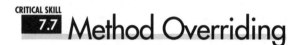

Progress Check

1. Can a subclass be used as a superclass for another subclass?

2. In a class hierarchy, in what order are the constructors called?

3. Given that **Jet** extends **Airplane**, can an **Airplane** reference refer to a **Jet** object?

CRITICAL SKILL
7.7 Method Overriding

In a class hierarchy, when a method in a subclass has the same return type and signature as a method in its superclass, then the method in the subclass is said to *override* the method in the superclass. When an overridden method is called from within a subclass, it will always refer to the version of that method defined by the subclass. The version of the method defined by the superclass will be hidden. Consider the following:

```
// Method overriding.
class A {
  int i, j;
  A(int a, int b) {
    i = a;
    j = b;
  }

  // display i and j
  void show() {
    System.out.println("i and j: " + i + " " + j);
  }
}

class B extends A {
  int k;

  B(int a, int b, int c) {
    super(a, b);
    k = c;
  }
```

1. Yes.

2. Constructors are called in order of derivation.

3. Yes. In all cases, a superclass reference can refer to a subclass object, but not vice versa.

```
// display k - this overrides show() in A
void show() {                                              This show( ) in B overrides
  System.out.println("k: " + k);                           the one defined by A.
}
}

class Override {
  public static void main(String args[]) {
    B subOb = new B(1, 2, 3);

    subOb.show(); // this calls show() in B
  }
}
```

The output produced by this program is shown here:

```
k: 3
```

When **show( )** is invoked on an object of type **B**, the version of **show( )** defined within **B** is used. That is, the version of **show( )** inside **B** overrides the version declared in **A**.

If you want to access the superclass version of an overridden method, you can do so by using **super**. For example, in this version of **B**, the superclass version of **show( )** is invoked within the subclass' version. This allows all instance variables to be displayed.

```
class B extends A {
  int k;

  B(int a, int b, int c) {
    super(a, b);
    k = c;                                    Use super to call the version of
  }                                           show( ) defined by superclass A.
  void show() {
    super.show(); // this calls A's show()
    System.out.println("k: " + k);
  }
}
```

If you substitute this version of **show( )** into the previous program, you will see the following output:

```
i and j: 1 2
k: 3
```

Here, **super.show( )** calls the superclass version of **show( )**.

Method overriding occurs *only* when the signatures of the two methods are identical. If they are not, then the two methods are simply overloaded. For example, consider this modified version of the preceding example:

```
/* Methods with differing signatures are
   overloaded and not overridden. */
class A {
  int i, j;

  A(int a, int b) {
    i = a;
    j = b;
  }

  // display i and j
  void show() {
    System.out.println("i and j: " + i + " " + j);
  }
}

// Create a subclass by extending class A.
class B extends A {
  int k;

  B(int a, int b, int c) {
    super(a, b);
    k = c;  }

  // overload show()
  void show(String msg) {
    System.out.println(msg + k);
  }
}

class Overload {
  public static void main(String args[]) {
    B subOb = new B(1, 2, 3);

    subOb.show("This is k: "); // this calls show() in B
    subOb.show(); // this calls show() in A
  }
}
```

Because signatures differ, this **show( )** simply overloads **show( )** in superclass **A**.

The output produced by this program is shown here:

```
This is k: 3
i and j: 1 2
```

The version of **show( )** in **B** takes a string parameter. This makes its signature different from the one in **A**, which takes no parameters. Therefore, no overriding (or name hiding) takes place.

CRITICAL SKILL
7.8

Overridden Methods Support Polymorphism

While the examples in the preceding section demonstrate the mechanics of method overriding, they do not show its power. Indeed, if there were nothing more to method overriding than a name space convention, then it would be, at best, an interesting curiosity but of little real value. However, this is not the case. Method overriding forms the basis for one of Java's most powerful concepts: *dynamic method dispatch.* Dynamic method dispatch is the mechanism by which a call to an overridden method is resolved at run time rather than compile time. Dynamic method dispatch is important because this is how Java implements run-time polymorphism.

Let's begin by restating an important principle: a superclass reference variable can refer to a subclass object. Java uses this fact to resolve calls to overridden methods at run time. Here's how. When an overridden method is called through a superclass reference, Java determines which version of that method to execute based upon the type of the object being referred to at the time the call occurs. Thus, this determination is made at run time. When different types of objects are referred to, different versions of an overridden method will be called. In other words, *it is the type of the object being referred to* (not the type of the reference variable) that determines which version of an overridden method will be executed. Therefore, if a superclass contains a method that is overridden by a subclass, then when different types of objects are referred to through a superclass reference variable, different versions of the method are executed.

Here is an example that illustrates dynamic method dispatch:

```
// Demonstrate dynamic method dispatch.

class Sup {
  void who() {
    System.out.println("who() in Sup");
  }
}
```

```
class Sub1 extends Sup {
  void who() {
    System.out.println("who() in Sub1");
  }
}

class Sub2 extends Sup {
  void who() {
    System.out.println("who() in Sub2");
  }
}

class DynDispDemo {
  public static void main(String args[]) {
    Sup superOb = new Sup();
    Sub1 subOb1 = new Sub1();
    Sub2 subOb2 = new Sub2();

    Sup supRef;

    supRef = superOb;
    supRef.who();          ◄─────────── In each case,
                                        the version of
    supRef = subOb1;                    who( ) to call
    supRef.who();          ◄─────────── is determined
                                        at run time by
                                        the type of
    supRef = subOb2;                    object being
    supRef.who();          ◄─────────── referred to.
  }
}
```

The output from the program is shown here:

```
who() in Sup
who() in Sub1
who() in Sub2
```

This program creates a superclass called **Sup** and two subclasses of it, called **Sub1** and **Sub2**. **Sup** declares a method called **who( )**, and the subclasses override it. Inside the **main( )** method, objects of type **Sup**, **Sub1**, and **Sub2** are declared. Also, a reference of type **Sup**, called **supRef**, is declared. The program then assigns a reference to each type of object to **supRef** and uses that reference to call **who( )**. As the output shows, the version of **who( )** executed is determined by the type of object being referred to at the time of the call, not by the class type of **supRef**.

Ask the Expert

Q: Overridden methods in Java look a lot like virtual functions in C++. Is there a similarity?

A: Yes. Readers familiar with C++ will recognize that overridden methods in Java are equivalent in purpose and similar in operation to virtual functions in C++.

Why Overridden Methods?

As stated earlier, overridden methods allow Java to support run-time polymorphism. Polymorphism is essential to object-oriented programming for one reason: it allows a general class to specify methods that will be common to all of its derivatives, while allowing subclasses to define the specific implementation of some or all of those methods. Overridden methods are another way that Java implements the "one interface, multiple methods" aspect of polymorphism.

Part of the key to successfully applying polymorphism is understanding that the superclasses and subclasses form a hierarchy that moves from lesser to greater specialization. Used correctly, the superclass provides all elements that a subclass can use directly. It also defines those methods that the derived class must implement on its own. This allows the subclass the flexibility to define its own methods, yet still enforces a consistent interface. Thus, by combining inheritance with overridden methods, a superclass can define the general form of the methods that will be used by all of its subclasses.

Applying Method Overriding to TwoDShape

To better understand the power of method overriding, we will apply it to the **TwoDShape** class. In the preceding examples, each class derived from **TwoDShape** defines a method called **area( )**. This suggests that it might be better to make **area( )** part of the **TwoDShape** class, allowing each subclass to override it, defining how the area is calculated for the type of shape that the class encapsulates. The following program does this. For convenience, it also adds a name field to **TwoDShape**. (This makes it easier to write demonstration programs.)

```
// Use dynamic method dispatch.
class TwoDShape {
  private double width;
  private double height;
  private String name;
```

```
// A default constructor.
TwoDShape() {
  width = height = 0.0;
  name = "null";
}

// Parameterized constructor.
TwoDShape(double w, double h, String n) {
  width = w;
  height = h;
  name = n;
}

// Construct object with equal width and height.
TwoDShape(double x, String n) {
  width = height = x;
  name = n;
}

// Construct an object from an object.
TwoDShape(TwoDShape ob) {
  width = ob.width;
  height = ob.height;
  name = ob.name;
}

// Accessor methods for width and height.
double getWidth() { return width; }
double getHeight() { return height; }
void setWidth(double w) { width = w; }
void setHeight(double h) { height = h; }

String getName() { return name; }

void showDim() {
  System.out.println("Width and height are " +
                     width + " and " + height);
}
```

The **area( )** method defined by **TwoDShape.**

```
double area() {
  System.out.println("area() must be overridden");
  return 0.0;
}
}
```

```
// A subclass of TwoDShape for triangles.
class Triangle extends TwoDShape {
  private String style;

  // A default constructor.
  Triangle() {
    super();
    style = "null";
  }

  // Constructor for Triangle.
  Triangle(String s, double w, double h) {
    super(w, h, "triangle");

    style = s;
  }

  // Construct an isosceles triangle.
  Triangle(double x) {
    super(x, "triangle"); // call superclass constructor

    style = "isosceles";
  }

  // Construct an object from an object.
  Triangle(Triangle ob) {
    super(ob); // pass object to TwoDShape constructor
    style = ob.style;
  }

  // Override area() for Triangle.
  double area() {                                        Override area( ) for Triangle.
    return getWidth() * getHeight() / 2;
  }

  void showStyle() {
    System.out.println("Triangle is " + style);
  }
}

// A subclass of TwoDShape for rectangles.
class Rectangle extends TwoDShape {
  // A default constructor.
  Rectangle() {
    super();
  }
```

```
    // Constructor for Rectangle.
    Rectangle(double w, double h) {
      super(w, h, "rectangle"); // call superclass constructor
    }

    // Construct a square.
    Rectangle(double x) {
      super(x, "rectangle"); // call superclass constructor
    }

    // Construct an object from an object.
    Rectangle(Rectangle ob) {
      super(ob); // pass object to TwoDShape constructor
    }

    boolean isSquare() {
      if(getWidth() == getHeight()) return true;
      return false;
    }

    // Override area() for Rectangle.
    double area() {                                    Override area( ) for Rectangle.
      return getWidth() * getHeight();
    }
  }

  class DynShapes {
    public static void main(String args[]) {
      TwoDShape shapes[] = new TwoDShape[5];

      shapes[0] = new Triangle("right", 8.0, 12.0);
      shapes[1] = new Rectangle(10);
      shapes[2] = new Rectangle(10, 4);
      shapes[3] = new Triangle(7.0);
      shapes[4] = new TwoDShape(10, 20, "generic");
                                                      The proper version of area( )
                                                      is called for each shape.
      for(int i=0; i < shapes.length; i++) {
        System.out.println("object is " + shapes[i].getName());
        System.out.println("Area is " + shapes[i].area());
```

```
    System.out.println();
  }
 }
}
```

The output from the program is shown here:

```
object is triangle
Area is 48.0

object is rectangle
Area is 100.0

object is rectangle
Area is 40.0

object is triangle
Area is 24.5

object is generic
area() must be overridden
Area is 0.0
```

Let's examine this program closely. First, as explained, **area( )** is now part of the **TwoDShape** class and is overridden by **Triangle** and **Rectangle**. Inside **TwoDShape**, **area( )** is given a placeholder implementation that simply informs the user that this method must be overridden by a subclass. Each override of **area( )** supplies an implementation that is suitable for the type of object encapsulated by the subclass. Thus, if you were to implement an ellipse class, for example, then **area( )** would need to compute the **area( )** of an ellipse.

There is one other important feature in the preceding program. Notice in **main( )** that **shapes** is declared as an array of **TwoDShape** objects. However, the elements of this array are assigned **Triangle**, **Rectangle**, and **TwoDShape** references. This is valid because, as explained, a superclass reference can refer to a subclass object. The program then cycles through the array, displaying information about each object. Although quite simple, this illustrates the power of both inheritance and method overriding. The type of object referred to by a superclass reference variable is determined at run time and acted on accordingly. If an object is derived from **TwoDShape**, then its area can be obtained by calling **area( )**. The interface to this operation is the same no matter what type of shape is being used.

Progress Check

1. What is method overriding?

2. Why is method overriding important?

3. When an overridden method is called through a superclass reference, which version of the method is executed?

CRITICAL SKILL

7.9 Using Abstract Classes

Sometimes you will want to create a superclass that defines only a generalized form that will be shared by all of its subclasses, leaving it to each subclass to fill in the details. Such a class determines the nature of the methods that the subclasses must implement but does not, itself, provide an implementation of one or more of these methods. One way this situation can occur is when a superclass is unable to create a meaningful implementation for a method. This is the case with the version of **TwoDShape** used in the preceding example. The definition of **area( )** is simply a placeholder. It will not compute and display the area of any type of object.

As you will see as you create your own class libraries, it is not uncommon for a method to have no meaningful definition in the context of its superclass. You can handle this situation in two ways. One way, as shown in the previous example, is to simply have it report a warning message. While this approach can be useful in certain situations—such as debugging—it is not usually appropriate. You may have methods which must be overridden by the subclass in order for the subclass to have any meaning. Consider the class **Triangle**. It is incomplete if **area( )** is not defined. In this case, you want some way to ensure that a subclass does, indeed, override all necessary methods. Java's solution to this problem is the *abstract method*.

An abstract method is created by specifying the **abstract** type modifier. An abstract method contains no body and is, therefore, not implemented by the superclass. Thus, a subclass must override it—it cannot simply use the version defined in the superclass. To declare an abstract method, use this general form:

abstract *type name(parameter-list)*;

As you can see, no method body is present. The **abstract** modifier can be used only on normal methods. It cannot be applied to **static** methods or to constructors.

---

1. Method overriding occurs when a subclass defines a method that has the same signature as a method in its superclass.

2. Overridden methods allow Java to support run-time polymorphism.

3. The version of an overridden method that is executed is determined by the type of the object being referred to at the time of the call. Thus, this determination is made at run time.

A class that contains one or more abstract methods must also be declared as abstract by preceding its **class** declaration with the **abstract** specifier. Since an abstract class does not define a complete implementation, there can be no objects of an abstract class. Thus, attempting to create an object of an abstract class by using **new** will result in a compile-time error.

When a subclass inherits an abstract class, it must implement all of the abstract methods in the superclass. If it doesn't, then the subclass must also be specified as **abstract**. Thus, the **abstract** attribute is inherited until such time as a complete implementation is achieved.

Using an abstract class, you can improve the **TwoDShape** class. Since there is no meaningful concept of area for an undefined two-dimensional figure, the following version of the preceding program declares **area( )** as **abstract** inside **TwoDShape**, and **TwoDShape** as **abstract**. This, of course, means that all classes derived from **TwoDShape** must override **area( )**.

```
// Create an abstract class.
abstract class TwoDShape {          ← TwoDShape is now abstract.
  private double width;
  private double height;
  private String name;

  // A default constructor.
  TwoDShape() {
    width = height = 0.0;
    name = "null";
  }

  // Parameterized constructor.
  TwoDShape(double w, double h, String n) {
    width = w;
    height = h;
    name = n;
  }

  // Construct object with equal width and height.
  TwoDShape(double x, String n) {
    width = height = x;
    name = n;
  }

  // Construct an object from an object.
  TwoDShape(TwoDShape ob) {
    width = ob.width;
    height = ob.height;
    name = ob.name;
  }
```

```
    // Accessor methods for width and height.
    double getWidth() { return width; }
    double getHeight() { return height; }
    void setWidth(double w) { width = w; }
    void setHeight(double h) { height = h; }

    String getName() { return name; }

    void showDim() {
      System.out.println("Width and height are " +
                          width + " and " + height);
    }

    // Now, area() is abstract.
    abstract double area();  ◄──────── Make area( ) into an
}                                       abstract method.

// A subclass of TwoDShape for triangles.
class Triangle extends TwoDShape {
  private String style;

  // A default constructor.
  Triangle() {
    super();
    style = "null";
  }

  // Constructor for Triangle.
  Triangle(String s, double w, double h) {
    super(w, h, "triangle");

    style = s;
  }

  // Construct an isosceles triangle.
  Triangle(double x) {
    super(x, "triangle"); // call superclass constructor

    style = "isosceles";
  }

  // Construct an object from an object.
  Triangle(Triangle ob) {
    super(ob); // pass object to TwoDShape constructor
    style = ob.style;
  }
```

```
  double area() {
    return getWidth() * getHeight() / 2;
  }

  void showStyle() {
    System.out.println("Triangle is " + style);
  }
}

// A subclass of TwoDShape for rectangles.
class Rectangle extends TwoDShape {
  // A default constructor.
  Rectangle() {
    super();
  }

  // Constructor for Rectangle.
  Rectangle(double w, double h) {
    super(w, h, "rectangle"); // call superclass constructor
  }

  // Construct a square.
  Rectangle(double x) {
    super(x, "rectangle"); // call superclass constructor
  }

  // Construct an object from an object.
  Rectangle(Rectangle ob) {
    super(ob); // pass object to TwoDShape constructor
  }

  boolean isSquare() {
    if(getWidth() == getHeight()) return true;
    return false;
  }

  double area() {
    return getWidth() * getHeight();
  }
}

class AbsShape {
  public static void main(String args[]) {
    TwoDShape shapes[] = new TwoDShape[4];
```

```
shapes[0] = new Triangle("right", 8.0, 12.0);
shapes[1] = new Rectangle(10);
shapes[2] = new Rectangle(10, 4);
shapes[3] = new Triangle(7.0);

for(int i=0; i < shapes.length; i++) {
  System.out.println("object is " +
                         shapes[i].getName());
  System.out.println("Area is " + shapes[i].area());

  System.out.println();
  }
 }
}
```

As the program illustrates, all subclasses of **TwoDShape** *must* override **area( )**. To prove this to yourself, try creating a subclass that does not override **area( )**. You will receive a compile-time error. Of course, it is still possible to create an object reference of type **TwoDShape**, which the program does. However, it is no longer possible to declare objects of type **TwoDShape**. Because of this, in **main( )** the **shapes** array has been shortened to 4, and a **TwoDShape** object is no longer created.

One last point: notice that **TwoDShape** still includes the **showDim( )** and **getName( )** methods and that these are not modified by **abstract**. It is perfectly acceptable—indeed, quite common—for an abstract class to contain concrete methods which a subclass is free to use as is. Only those methods declared as **abstract** need be overridden by subclasses.

Progress Check

1. What is an abstract method? How is one created?

2. What is an abstract class?

3. Can an object of an abstract class be instantiated?

---

1. An abstract method is a method without a body. Thus it consists of a return type, name, and parameter list and is preceded by the keyword **abstract**.

2. An abstract class contains at least one abstract method.

3. No.

CRITICAL SKILL
7.10 Using final

As powerful and useful as method overriding and inheritance are, sometimes you will want to prevent them. For example, you might have a class that encapsulates control of some hardware device. Further, this class might offer the user the ability to initialize the device, making use of private, proprietary information. In this case, you don't want users of your class to be able to override the initialization method. Whatever the reason, in Java it is easy to prevent a method from being overridden or a class from being inherited by using the keyword **final**.

final Prevents Overriding

To prevent a method from being overridden, specify **final** as a modifier at the start of its declaration. Methods declared as **final** cannot be overridden. The following fragment illustrates **final**:

```
class A {
  final void meth() {
    System.out.println("This is a final method.");
  }
}

class B extends A {
  void meth() { // ERROR! Can't override.
    System.out.println("Illegal!");
  }
}
```

Because **meth( )** is declared as **final**, it cannot be overridden in **B**. If you attempt to do so, a compile-time error will result.

final Prevents Inheritance

You can prevent a class from being inherited by preceding its declaration with **final**. Declaring a class as **final** implicitly declares all of its methods as **final**, too. As you might expect, it is illegal to declare a class as both **abstract** and **final** since an abstract class is incomplete by itself and relies upon its subclasses to provide complete implementations.

Here is an example of a **final** class:

```
final class A {
  // ...
}
```

```
// The following class is illegal.
class B extends A { // ERROR! Can't subclass A
  // ...
}
```

As the comments imply, it is illegal for **B** to inherit **A** since **A** is declared as **final**.

Using final with Data Members

In addition to the uses of **final** just shown, **final** can also be applied to variables to create what amounts to named constants. If you precede a class variable's name with **final**, its value cannot be changed throughout the lifetime of your program. You can, of course, give that variable an initial value. For example, in Module 6 a simple error-management class called **ErrorMsg** was shown. That class mapped a human-readable string to an error code. Here, that original class is improved by the addition of **final** constants which stand for the errors. Now, instead of passing **getErrorMsg( )** a number such as 2, you can pass the named integer constant **DISKERR**.

```
// Return a String object.
class ErrorMsg {
  // Error codes.
  final int OUTERR   = 0;
  final int INERR    = 1;  ◄─────── Declare final constants.
  final int DISKERR  = 2;
  final int INDEXERR = 3;

  String msgs[] = {
    "Output Error",
    "Input Error",
    "Disk Full",
    "Index Out-Of-Bounds"
  };

  // Return the error message.
  String getErrorMsg(int i) {
    if(i >=0 & i < msgs.length)
      return msgs[i];
    else
      return "Invalid Error Code";
  }
}
```

```
class FinalD {
  public static void main(String args[]) {
    ErrorMsg err = new ErrorMsg();                        Use final constants.

    System.out.println(err.getErrorMsg(err.OUTERR));
    System.out.println(err.getErrorMsg(err.DISKERR));
  }
}
```

Notice how the **final** constants are used in **main( )**. Since they are members of the **ErrorMsg** class, they must be accessed via an object of that class. Of course, they can also be inherited by subclasses and accessed directly inside those subclasses.

As a point of style, many Java programmers use uppercase identifiers for **final** constants, as does the preceding example. But this is not a hard and fast rule.

Ask the Expert

Q: Can final **variables be made** static?

A: Yes. Doing so allows you to refer to the constant through its class name rather than through an object. For example, if the constants in **ErrorMsg** were modified by **static**, then the **println( )** statements in **main( )** could look like this:

```
System.out.println(err.getErrorMsg(ErrorMsg.OUTERR));
System.out.println(err.getErrorMsg(ErrorMsg.DISKERR));
```

Progress Check

1. How do you prevent a method from being overridden?

2. If a class is declared as **final**, can it be inherited?

---

1. Precede its declaration with the keyword **final**.

2. No.

CRITICAL SKILL
7.11 The Object Class

Java defines one special class called **Object** that is an implicit superclass of all other classes. In other words, all other classes are subclasses of **Object**. This means that a reference variable of type **Object** can refer to an object of any other class. Also, since arrays are implemented as classes, a variable of type **Object** can also refer to any array.

Object defines the following methods, which means that they are available in every object.

Method	Purpose
Object clone( )	Creates a new object that is the same as the object being cloned.
boolean equals(Object *object*)	Determines whether one object is equal to another.
void finalize( )	Called before an unused object is recycled.
Class<? extends Object> getClass( )	Obtains the class of an object at run time.
int hashCode( )	Returns the hash code associated with the invoking object.
void notify( )	Resumes execution of a thread waiting on the invoking object.
void notifyAll( )	Resumes execution of all threads waiting on the invoking object.
String toString( )	Returns a string that describes the object.
void wait( ) void wait(long *milliseconds*) void wait(long *milliseconds*, int *nanoseconds*)	Waits on another thread of execution.

The methods **getClass( )**, **notify( )**, **notifyAll( )**, and **wait( )** are declared as **final**. You can override the others. Several of these methods are described later in this book. However, notice two methods now: **equals( )** and **toString( )**. The **equals( )** method compares two objects. It returns **true** if the objects are equivalent, and **false** otherwise. The **toString( )** method returns a string that contains a description of the object on which it is called. Also, this method is automatically called when an object is output using **println( )**. Many classes override this method. Doing so allows them to tailor a description specifically for the types of objects that they create.

One last point: notice the unusual syntax in the return type for **getClass( )**. This is a *generic type*. Generic types are a recent (and powerful) addition to Java that enables the type of data used by a class or method to be specified as a parameter. Generic types are discussed in Module 13.

✓ Module 7 Mastery Check

1. Does a superclass have access to the members of a subclass? Does a subclass have access to the members of a superclass?

2. Create a subclass of **TwoDShape** called **Circle**. Include an **area( )** method that computes the area of the circle and a constructor that uses **super** to initialize the **TwoDShape** portion.

3. How do you prevent a subclass from having access to a member of a superclass?

4. Describe the purpose and use of both versions of **super**.

5. Given the following hierarchy:

```
class Alpha { ...

class Beta extends Alpha { ...

Class Gamma extends Beta { ...
```

In what order are the constructors for these classes called when a **Gamma** object is instantiated?

6. A superclass reference can refer to a subclass object. Explain why this is important as it relates to method overriding.

7. What is an abstract class?

8. How do you prevent a method from being overridden? How do you prevent a class from being inherited?

9. Explain how inheritance, method overriding, and abstract classes are used to support polymorphism.

10. What class is a superclass of every other class?

11. A class that contains at least one abstract method must, itself, be declared abstract. True or False?

12. What keyword is used to create a named constant?

Module 8

Packages and Interfaces

This module examines two of Java's most innovative features: packages and interfaces. *Packages* are groups of related classes. Packages help organize your code and provide another layer of encapsulation. An *interface* defines a set of methods that will be implemented by a class. An interface does not, itself, implement any method. It is a purely logical construct. Packages and interfaces give you greater control over the organization of your program.

CRITICAL SKILL
8.1 Packages

In programming, it is often helpful to group related pieces of a program together. In Java, this is accomplished by using a package. A package serves two purposes. First, it provides a mechanism by which related pieces of a program can be organized as a unit. Classes defined within a package must be accessed through their package name. Thus, a package provides a way to name a collection of classes. Second, a package participates in Java's access control mechanism. Classes defined within a package can be made private to that package and not accessible by code outside the package. Thus, the package provides a means by which classes can be encapsulated. Let's examine each feature a bit more closely.

In general, when you name a class, you are allocating a name from the *namespace*. A namespace defines a declarative region. In Java, no two classes can use the same name from the same namespace. Thus, within a given namespace, each class name must be unique. The examples shown in the preceding modules have all used the default or global namespace. While this is fine for short sample programs, it becomes a problem as programs grow and the default namespace becomes crowded. In large programs, finding unique names for each class can be difficult. Furthermore, you must avoid name collisions with code created by other programmers working on the same project, and with Java's library. The solution to these problems is the package because it gives you a way to partition the namespace. When a class is defined within a package, the name of that package is attached to each class, thus avoiding name collisions with other classes that have the same name, but are in other packages.

Since a package usually contains related classes, Java defines special access rights to code within a package. In a package, you can define code that is accessible by other code within the same package but not by code outside the package. This enables you to create self-contained groups of related classes that keep their operation private.

Defining a Package

All classes in Java belong to some package. When no **package** statement is specified, the default (or global) package is used. Furthermore, the default package has no name, which makes the default package transparent. This is why you haven't had to worry about packages before now. While the default package is fine for short, sample programs, it is inadequate for real applications. Most of the time, you will define one or more packages for your code.

To create a package, put a **package** command at the top of a Java source file. The classes declared within that file will then belong to the specified package. Since a package defines a namespace, the names of the classes that you put into the file become part of that package's namespace.

This is the general form of the **package** statement:

package *pkg*;

Here, *pkg* is the name of the package. For example, the following statement creates a package called **Project1**.

```
package Project1;
```

Java uses the file system to manage packages, with each package stored in its own directory. For example, the **.class** files for any classes you declare to be part of **Project1** must be stored in a directory called **Project1**.

Like the rest of Java, package names are case sensitive. This means that the directory in which a package is stored must be precisely the same as the package name. If you have trouble trying the examples in this module, remember to check your package and directory names carefully.

More than one file can include the same **package** statement. The **package** statement simply specifies to which package the classes defined in a file belong. It does not exclude other classes in other files from being part of that same package. Most real-world packages are spread across many files.

You can create a hierarchy of packages. To do so, simply separate each package name from the one above it by use of a period. The general form of a multileveled package statement is shown here:

package *pack1.pack2.pack3...packN*;

Of course, you must create directories that support the package hierarchy that you create. For example,

```
package X.Y.Z;
```

must be stored in .../X/Y/Z, where ... specifies the path to the specified directories.

Finding Packages and CLASSPATH

As just explained, packages are mirrored by directories. This raises an important question: How does the Java run-time system know where to look for packages that you create? The answer has three parts. First, by default, the Java run-time system uses the current working directory as its starting point. Thus, if your package is in a subdirectory of the current directory, it will be found. Second, you can specify a directory path or paths by setting the **CLASSPATH** environmental variable. Third, you can use the **-classpath** option with **java** and **javac** to specify the path to your classes.

For example, consider the following package specification:

```
package MyPack
```

In order for a program to find **MyPack,** one of three things must be true: The program can be executed from a directory immediately above **MyPack**, or **CLASSPATH** must be set to include the path to **MyPack**, or the **-classpath** option must specify the path to **MyPack** when the program is run via **java**.

The easiest way to try the examples shown in this book is to simply create the package directories below your current development directory, put the **.class** files into the appropriate directories, and then execute the programs from the development directory. This is the approach used by the following examples.

One last point: To avoid problems, it is best to keep all **.java** and **.class** files associated with a package in that package's directory.

A Short Package Example

Keeping the preceding discussion in mind, try this short package example. It creates a simple book database that is contained within a package called **BookPack**.

```
// A short package demonstration.
package BookPack;          ──────────── This file is part of the BookPack package.

class Book {  ◄──────────── Thus, Book is part of BookPack.
  private String title;
  private String author;
  private int pubDate;

  Book(String t, String a, int d) {
    title = t;
    author = a;
    pubDate = d;
  }
```

```
  void show() {
    System.out.println(title);
    System.out.println(author);
    System.out.println(pubDate);
    System.out.println();
  }
}
```

BookDemo is also part of **BookPack**.

```
class BookDemo {
  public static void main(String args[]) {
    Book books[] = new Book[5];

    books[0] = new Book("Java: A Beginner's Guide",
                        "Schildt", 2007);
    books[1] = new Book("Java: The Complete Reference",
                        "Schildt", 2007);
    books[2] = new Book("The Art of Java",
                        "Schildt and Holmes", 2003);
    books[3] = new Book("Red Storm Rising",
                        "Clancy", 1986);
    books[4] = new Book("On the Road",
                        "Kerouac", 1955);

    for(int i=0; i < books.length; i++) books[i].show();
  }
}
```

Call this file **BookDemo.java** and put it in a directory called **BookPack**.

Next, compile the file. Make sure that the resulting **.class** file is also in the **BookPack** directory. Then try executing the class, using the following command line:

```
java BookPack.BookDemo
```

Remember, you will need to be in the directory above **BookPack** when you execute this command. (Or, use one of the other two options described in the preceding section to specify the path to **BookPack**.)

As explained, **BookDemo** and **Book** are now part of the package **BookPack**. This means that **BookDemo** cannot be executed by itself. That is, you cannot use this command line:

```
java BookDemo
```

Instead, **BookDemo** must be qualified with its package name.

Progress Check

1. What is a package?

2. Show how to declare a package called **ToolPack**.

3. What is **CLASSPATH**?

Packages and Member Access

The preceding modules have introduced the fundamentals of access control, including the **private** and **public** specifiers, but they have not told the entire story. The reason for this is that packages also participate in Java's access control mechanism, and a complete discussion had to wait until packages were covered.

The visibility of an element is determined by its access specification—**private**, **public**, **protected**, or default—and the package in which it resides. Thus, the visibility of an element is determined by its visibility within a class and its visibility within a package. This multilayered approach to access control supports a rich assortment of access privileges. Table 8-1 summarizes the various access levels. Let's examine each access option individually.

If a member of a class has no explicit access specifier, then it is visible within its package but not outside its package. Therefore, you will use the default access specification for elements that you want to keep private to a package but public within that package.

Members explicitly declared **public** are visible everywhere, including different classes and different packages. There is no restriction on their use or access.

A **private** member is accessible only to the other members of its class. A **private** member is unaffected by its membership in a package.

A member specified as **protected** is accessible within its package and to all subclasses, including subclasses in other packages.

Table 8-1 applies only to members of classes. A top-level class has only two possible access levels: default and public. When a class is declared as **public**, it is accessible by any other code. If a class has default access, it can be accessed only by other code within its same package. Also, a class that is declared **public** must reside in a file by the same name.

---

1. A package is a container for classes. It performs both an organization and an encapsulation role.
2. `package ToolPack;`
3. **CLASSPATH** is the environmental variable that specifies the path to classes.

	Private Member	Default Member	Protected Member	Public Member
Visible within same class	Yes	Yes	Yes	Yes
Visible within same package by subclass	No	Yes	Yes	Yes
Visible within same package by non-subclass	No	Yes	Yes	Yes
Visible within different package by subclass	No	No	Yes	Yes
Visible within different package by non-subclass	No	No	No	Yes

Table 8-1 Class Member Access

Progress Check

1. If a class member has default access inside a package, is that member accessible by other packages?

2. What does **protected** do?

3. A **private** member can be accessed by subclasses within its packages. True or False?

A Package Access Example

In the **package** example shown earlier, both **Book** and **BookDemo** were in the same package, so there was no problem with **BookDemo** using **Book** because the default access privilege grants all members of the same package access. However, if **Book** were in one package and

1. No.

2. It allows a member to be accessible by other code in its package and by all subclasses, no matter what package the subclass is in.

3. False.

BookDemo were in another, the situation would be different. In this case, access to **Book** would be denied. To make **Book** available to other packages, you must make three changes. First, **Book** needs to be declared **public**. This makes **Book** visible outside of **BookPack**. Second, its constructor must be made **public**, and finally its **show( )** method needs to be **public**. This allows them to be visible outside of **BookPack**, too. Thus, to make **Book** usable by other packages, it must be recoded as shown here.

```
// Book recoded for public access.
package BookPack;

public class Book {          Book and its members must be public
  private String title;      in order to be used by other packages.
  private String author;
  private int pubDate;

  // Now public.
  public Book(String t, String a, int d) {
    title = t;
    author = a;
    pubDate = d;
  }

  // Now public.
  public void show() {
    System.out.println(title);
    System.out.println(author);
    System.out.println(pubDate);
    System.out.println();
  }
}
```

To use **Book** from another package, either you must use the **import** statement described in the next section, or you must fully qualify its name to include its full package specification. For example, here is a class called **UseBook**, which is contained in the **BookPackB** package. It fully qualifies **Book** in order to use it.

```
// This class is in package BookPackB.
package BookPackB;

// Use the Book Class from BookPack.          Qualify Book with its
class UseBook {                               package name: BookPack.
  public static void main(String args[]) {
    BookPack.Book books[] = new BookPack.Book[5];
```

```
      books[0] = new BookPack.Book("Java: A Beginner's Guide",
                         "Schildt", 2007);
      books[1] = new BookPack.Book("Java: The Complete Reference",
                         "Schildt", 2007);
      books[2] = new BookPack.Book("The Art of Java",
                         "Schildt and Holmes", 2003);
      books[3] = new BookPack.Book("Red Storm Rising",
                         "Clancy", 1986);
      books[4] = new BookPack.Book("On the Road",
                         "Kerouac", 1955);

      for(int i=0; i < books.length; i++) books[i].show();
   }
}
```

Notice how every use of **Book** is preceded with the **BookPack** qualifier. Without this specification, **Book** would not be found when you tried to compile **UseBook**.

CRITICAL SKILL
8.3 # Understanding Protected Members

Newcomers to Java are sometimes confused by the meaning and use of **protected**. As explained, the **protected** specifier creates a member that is accessible within its package and to subclasses in other packages. Thus, a **protected** member is available for all subclasses to use but is still protected from arbitrary access by code outside its package.

To better understand the effects of **protected**, let's work through an example. First, change the **Book** class so that its instance variables are **protected**, as shown here.

```
// Make the instance variables in Book protected.
package BookPack;

public class Book {
  // these are now protected
  protected String title;
  protected String author;   ─These are now protected.
  protected int pubDate;

  public Book(String t, String a, int d) {
    title = t;
    author = a;
    pubDate = d;
  }
```

```
    public void show() {
      System.out.println(title);
      System.out.println(author);
      System.out.println(pubDate);
      System.out.println();
    }
}
```

Next, create a subclass of **Book**, called **ExtBook**, and a class called **ProtectDemo** that uses **ExtBook**. **ExtBook** adds a field that stores the name of the publisher and several accessor methods. Both of these classes will be in their own package called **BookPackB**. They are shown here.

```
// Demonstrate Protected.
package BookPackB;

class ExtBook extends BookPack.Book {
  private String publisher;

  public ExtBook(String t, String a, int d, String p) {
    super(t, a, d);
    publisher = p;
  }

  public void show() {
    super.show();
    System.out.println(publisher);
    System.out.println();
  }

  public String getPublisher() { return publisher; }
  public void setPublisher(String p) { publisher = p; }

  /* These are OK because subclass can access
     a protected member. */
  public String getTitle() { return title; }
  public void setTitle(String t) { title = t; }
  public String getAuthor() { return author; }          ◄─── Access to **Book**'s members
  public void setAuthor(String a) { author = a; }            is allowed for subclasses.
  public int getPubDate() { return pubDate; }
  public void setPubDate(int d) { pubDate = d; }
}
```

```
class ProtectDemo {
  public static void main(String args[]) {
    ExtBook books[] = new ExtBook[5];

    books[0] = new ExtBook("Java: A Beginner's Guide",
                    "Schildt", 2007, "Osborne/McGraw-Hill");
    books[1] = new ExtBook("Java: The Complete Reference",
                    "Schildt", 2007, "Osborne/McGraw-Hill");
    books[2] = new ExtBook("The Art of Java",
                    "Schildt and Holmes", 2003,
                    "Osborne/McGraw-Hill");
    books[3] = new ExtBook("Red Storm Rising",
                    "Clancy", 1986, "Putnam");
    books[4] = new ExtBook("On the Road",
                    "Kerouac", 1955, "Viking");

    for(int i=0; i < books.length; i++) books[i].show();

    // Find books by author
    System.out.println("Showing all books by Schildt.");
    for(int i=0; i < books.length; i++)
      if(books[i].getAuthor() == "Schildt")
        System.out.println(books[i].getTitle());

//    books[0].title = "test title"; // Error - not accessible
  }
}
```

Access to **protected** field not allowed by non-subclass.

Look first at the code inside **ExtBook**. Because **ExtBook** extends **Book**, it has access to the **protected** members of **Book** even though **ExtBook** is in a different package. Thus, it can access **title**, **author**, and **pubDate** directly, as it does in the accessor methods it creates for those variables. However, in **ProtectDemo**, access to these variables is denied because **ProtectDemo** is not a subclass of **Book**. For example, if you remove the comment symbol from the following line, the program will not compile.

```
//    books[0].title = "test title"; // Error - not accessible
```

CRITICAL SKILL

8.4 Importing Packages

When you use a class from another package, you can fully qualify the name of the class with the name of its package, as the preceding examples have done. However, such an approach could easily become tiresome and awkward, especially if the classes you are qualifying are

Ask the Expert

Q: I know that C++ also includes an access specifier called protected. Is it similar to Java's?

A: Similar, but not the same. In C++, **protected** creates a member that can be accessed by subclasses but is otherwise private. In Java, **protected** creates a member that can be accessed by any code within its package but only by subclasses outside of its package. You need to be careful of this difference when porting code between C++ and Java.

deeply nested in a package hierarchy. Since Java was invented by programmers for programmers—and programmers don't like tedious constructs—it should come as no surprise that a more convenient method exists for using the contents of packages: the **import** statement. Using **import** you can bring one or more members of a package into view. This allows you to use those members directly, without explicit package qualification.

Here is the general form of the **import** statement:

import *pkg.classname*;

Here, *pkg* is the name of the package, which can include its full path, and *classname* is the name of the class being imported. If you want to import the entire contents of a package, use an asterisk (*) for the class name. Here are examples of both forms:

```
import MyPack.MyClass
import MyPack.*;
```

In the first case, the **MyClass** class is imported from **MyPack**. In the second, all of the classes in **MyPack** are imported. In a Java source file, **import** statements occur immediately following the **package** statement (if it exists) and before any class definitions.

You can use **import** to bring the **BookPack** package into view so that the **Book** class can be used without qualification. To do so, simply add this **import** statement to the top of any file that uses **Book**.

```
import BookPack.*;
```

For example, here is the **UseBook** class recoded to use **import**.

```
// Demonstrate import.
package BookPackB;
import BookPack.*;                          Import BookPack.

// Use the Book Class from BookPack.
class UseBook {
  public static void main(String args[]) {
    Book books[] = new Book[5];             Now, you can refer to Book
                                            directly, without qualification.
    books[0] = new Book("Java: A Beginner's Guide",
                        "Schildt", 2007);
    books[1] = new Book("Java: The Complete Reference",
                        "Schildt", 2007);
    books[2] = new Book("The Art of Java",
                        "Schildt and Holmes", 2003);
    books[3] = new Book("Red Storm Rising",
                        "Clancy", 1986);
    books[4] = new Book("On the Road",
                        "Kerouac", 1955);

    for(int i=0; i < books.length; i++) books[i].show();
  }
}
```

Notice that you no longer need to qualify **Book** with its package name.

Ask the Expert

Q: Does importing a package have an impact on the performance of my program?

A: Yes and no! Importing a package can create a small amount of overhead during compilation, but it has no impact on performance at run time.

CRITICAL SKILL
8.5 # Java's Class Library
Is Contained in Packages

As explained earlier in this book, Java defines a large number of standard classes that are available to all programs. This class library is often referred to as the Java API (Application Programming Interface). The Java API is stored in packages. At the top of the package hierarchy is **java**. Descending from **java** are several subpackages, including these:

Subpackage	Description
java.lang	Contains a large number of general-purpose classes
java.io	Contains the I/O classes
java.net	Contains those classes that support networking
java.applet	Contains classes for creating applets
java.awt	Contains classes that support the Abstract Window Toolkit

Since the beginning of this book, you have been using **java.lang**. It contains, among several others, the **System** class, which you have been using when performing output using **println( )**. The **java.lang** package is unique because it is imported automatically into every Java program. This is why you did not have to import **java.lang** in the preceding sample programs. However, you must explicitly import the other packages. We will be examining several packages in subsequent modules.

Progress Check

1. How do you include another package in a source file?

2. Show how to include all of the classes in a package called **ToolPack**.

3. Do you need to include **java.lang** explicitly?

---

1. Use the **import** statement.
2. `import ToolPack.*;`
3. No.

CRITICAL SKILL

8.6 Interfaces

In object-oriented programming, it is sometimes helpful to define what a class must do but not how it will do it. You have already seen an example of this: the abstract method. An abstract method defines the signature for a method but provides no implementation. A subclass must provide its own implementation of each abstract method defined by its superclass. Thus, an abstract method specifies the *interface* to the method but not the *implementation*. While abstract classes and methods are useful, it is possible to take this concept a step further. In Java, you can fully separate a class' interface from its implementation by using the keyword **interface**.

Interfaces are syntactically similar to abstract classes. However, in an interface, no method can include a body. That is, an interface provides no implementation whatsoever. It specifies what must be done, but not how. Once an interface is defined, any number of classes can implement it. Also, one class can implement any number of interfaces.

To implement an interface, a class must provide bodies (implementations) for the methods described by the interface. Each class is free to determine the details of its own implementation. Thus, two classes might implement the same interface in different ways, but each class still supports the same set of methods. Thus, code that has knowledge of the interface can use objects of either class since the interface to those objects is the same. By providing the **interface** keyword, Java allows you to fully utilize the "one interface, multiple methods" aspect of polymorphism.

Here is the general form of an interface:

```
access interface name {
  ret-type method-name1(param-list);
  ret-type method-name2(param-list);
  type var1 = value;
  type var2 = value;
  // ...
  ret-type method-nameN(param-list);
  type varN = value;
}
```

Here, *access* is either **public** or not used. When no access specifier is included, then default access results, and the interface is available only to other members of its package. When it is declared as **public**, the interface can be used by any other code. (When an **interface** is declared **public**, it must be in a file of the same name.) *name* is the name of the interface and can be any valid identifier.

Methods are declared using only their return type and signature. They are, essentially, abstract methods. As explained, in an **interface**, no method can have an implementation.

Thus, each class that includes an **interface** must implement all of the methods. In an interface, methods are implicitly **public**.

Variables declared in an **interface** are not instance variables. Instead, they are implicitly **public**, **final**, and **static** and must be initialized. Thus, they are essentially constants.

Here is an example of an **interface** definition. It specifies the interface to a class that generates a series of numbers.

```
public interface Series {
  int getNext(); // return next number in series
  void reset(); // restart
  void setStart(int x); // set starting value
}
```

This interface is declared **public** so that it can be implemented by code in any package.

CRITICAL SKILL
8.7

Implementing Interfaces

Once an **interface** has been defined, one or more classes can implement that interface. To implement an interface, include the **implements** clause in a class definition and then create the methods defined by the interface. The general form of a class that includes the **implements** clause looks like this:

class *classname* extends *superclass* implements *interface* {
   // class-body
}

To implement more than one interface, the interfaces are separated with a comma. Of course, the **extends** clause is optional.

The methods that implement an interface must be declared **public**. Also, the type signature of the implementing method must match exactly the type signature specified in the **interface** definition.

Here is an example that implements the **Series** interface shown earlier. It creates a class called **ByTwos**, which generates a series of numbers, each two greater than the previous one.

```
// Implement Series.
class ByTwos implements Series {
  int start;
  int val;               Implement the Series interface.

  ByTwos() {
    start = 0;
```

```
      val = 0;
    }

    public int getNext() {
      val += 2;
      return val;
    }

    public void reset() {
      start = 0;
      val = 0;
    }

    public void setStart(int x) {
      start = x;
      val = x;
    }
}
```

Notice that the methods **getNext( )**, **reset( )**, and **setStart( )** are declared using the **public** access specifier. This is necessary. Whenever you implement a method defined by an interface, it must be implemented as **public** because all members of an interface are implicitly **public**.

Here is a class that demonstrates **ByTwos**.

```
class SeriesDemo {
  public static void main(String args[]) {
    ByTwos ob = new ByTwos();

    for(int i=0; i < 5; i++)
      System.out.println("Next value is " +
                         ob.getNext());

    System.out.println("\nResetting");
    ob.reset();
    for(int i=0; i < 5; i++)
      System.out.println("Next value is " +
                         ob.getNext());

    System.out.println("\nStarting at 100");
    ob.setStart(100);
    for(int i=0; i < 5; i++)
      System.out.println("Next value is " +
                         ob.getNext());
  }
}
```

The output from this program is shown here.

```
Next value is 2
Next value is 4
Next value is 6
Next value is 8
Next value is 10

Resetting
Next value is 2
Next value is 4
Next value is 6
Next value is 8
Next value is 10

Starting at 100
Next value is 102
Next value is 104
Next value is 106
Next value is 108
Next value is 110
```

It is both permissible and common for classes that implement interfaces to define additional members of their own. For example, the following version of **ByTwos** adds the method **getPrevious( )**, which returns the previous value.

```
// Implement Series and add getPrevious().
class ByTwos implements Series {
  int start;
  int val;
  int prev;

  ByTwos() {
    start = 0;
    val = 0;
    prev = -2;
  }

  public int getNext() {
    prev = val;
    val += 2;
    return val;
  }

  public void reset() {
    start = 0;
```

```
      val = 0;
      prev = -2;
    }

  public void setStart(int x) {
      start = x;
      val = x;
      prev = x - 2;
    }

  int getPrevious() {          ◄──────── Add a method not defined by Series.
      return prev;
    }
}
```

Notice that the addition of **getPrevious( )** required a change to the implementations of the methods
defined by **Series**. However, since the interface to those methods stays the same, the change is
seamless and does not break preexisting code. This is one of the advantages of interfaces.

As explained, any number of classes can implement an **interface**. For example, here is
a class called **ByThrees** that generates a series that consists of multiples of three.

```
// Implement Series.
class ByThrees implements Series {  ◄──────── Implement Series a different way.
  int start;
  int val;

  ByThrees() {
    start = 0;
    val = 0;
  }

  public int getNext() {
    val += 3;
    return val;
  }

  public void reset() {
    start = 0;
    val = 0;
  }

  public void setStart(int x) {
    start = x;
    val = x;
  }
}
```

One more point: If a class includes an interface but does not fully implement the methods defined by that interface, then that class must be declared as **abstract**. No objects of such a class can be created, but it can be used as an abstract superclass, allowing subclasses to provide the complete implementation.

Using Interface References

You might be somewhat surprised to learn that you can declare a reference variable of an interface type. In other words, you can create an interface reference variable. Such a variable can refer to any object that implements its interface. When you call a method on an object through an interface reference, it is the version of the method implemented by the object that is executed. This process is similar to using a superclass reference to access a subclass object, as described in Module 7.

The following example illustrates this process. It uses the same interface reference variable to call methods on objects of both **ByTwos** and **ByThrees**.

```
// Demonstrate interface references.

class ByTwos implements Series {
  int start;
  int val;

  ByTwos() {
    start = 0;
    val = 0;
  }

  public int getNext() {
    val += 2;
    return val;
  }

  public void reset() {
    start = 0;
    val = 0;
  }

  public void setStart(int x) {
    start = x;
    val = x;
  }
}
```

```
class ByThrees implements Series {
  int start;
  int val;

  ByThrees() {
    start = 0;
    val = 0;
  }

  public int getNext() {
    val += 3;
    return val;
  }

  public void reset() {
    start = 0;
    val = 0;
  }

  public void setStart(int x) {
    start = x;
    val = x;
  }
}

class SeriesDemo2 {
  public static void main(String args[]) {
    ByTwos twoOb = new ByTwos();
    ByThrees threeOb = new ByThrees();
    Series ob;

    for(int i=0; i < 5; i++) {
      ob = twoOb;
      System.out.println("Next ByTwos value is " +
                          ob.getNext());
      ob = threeOb;
      System.out.println("Next ByThrees value is " +
                          ob.getNext());
    }
  }
}
```

Access an object via an interface reference.

In **main( )**, **ob** is declared to be a reference to a **Series** interface. This means that it can be used to store references to any object that implements **Series**. In this case, it is used to refer to **twoOb** and **threeOb**, which are objects of type **ByTwos** and **ByThrees**, respectively, which both implement **Series**. An interface reference variable has knowledge only of the methods declared by its **interface** declaration. Thus, **ob** could not be used to access any other variables or methods that might be supported by the object.

Progress Check

1. What is an interface? What keyword is used to define one?

2. What is **implements** for?

3. Can an interface reference variable refer to an object that implements that interface?

Project 8-1 Creating a Queue Interface

ICharQ.java
IQDemo.java

To see the power of interfaces in action, we will look at a practical example. In earlier modules, you developed a class called **Queue** that implemented a simple fixed-size queue for characters. However, there are many ways to implement a queue. For example, the queue can be of a fixed size or it can be "growable." The queue can be linear, in which case it can be used up, or it can be circular, in which case elements can be put in as long as elements are being taken off. The queue can also be held in an array, a linked list, a binary tree, and so on. No matter how the queue is implemented, the interface to the queue remains the same, and the methods **put( )** and **get( )** define the interface to the queue independently of the details of the implementation. Because the interface to a queue is separate from its implementation, it is easy to define a queue interface, leaving it to each implementation to define the specifics.

In this project, you will create an interface for a character queue and three implementations. All three implementations will use an array to store the characters. One queue will be the fixed-size, linear queue developed earlier. Another will be a circular queue. In a circular queue, when the end of the underlying array is encountered, the get and put indices automatically loop back to the start. Thus, any number of items can be stored in a circular queue as long as items are also being taken out. The final implementation creates a dynamic queue, which grows as necessary when its size is exceeded.

---

1. An interface defines the methods that a class must implement but defines no implementation of its own.
It is defined by the keyword **interface**.

2. To implement an interface, include that interface in a class by using the **implements** keyword.

3. Yes.

Step by Step

1. Create a file called **ICharQ.java** and put into that file the following interface definition.

```
// A character queue interface.
public interface ICharQ {
  // Put a character into the queue.
  void put(char ch);

  // Get a character from the queue.
  char get();
}
```

As you can see, this interface is very simple, consisting of only two methods. Each class that implements **ICharQ** will need to implement these methods.

2. Create a file called **IQDemo.java**.

3. Begin creating **IQDemo.java** by adding the **FixedQueue** class shown here:

```
// A fixed-size queue class for characters.
class FixedQueue implements ICharQ {
  private char q[]; // this array holds the queue
  private int putloc, getloc; // the put and get indices

  // Construct an empty queue given its size.
  public FixedQueue(int size) {
    q = new char[size+1]; // allocate memory for queue
    putloc = getloc = 0;
  }

  // Put a character into the queue.
  public void put(char ch) {
    if(putloc==q.length-1) {
      System.out.println(" - Queue is full.");
      return;
    }

    putloc++;
    q[putloc] = ch;
  }

  // Get a character from the queue.
  public char get() {
    if(getloc == putloc) {
      System.out.println(" - Queue is empty.");
      return (char) 0;
```

(continued)

```
      }

      getloc++;
      return q[getloc];
    }
  }
```

This implementation of **ICharQ** is adapted from the **Queue** class shown in Module 5 and should already be familiar to you.

4. To **IQDemo.java** add the **CircularQueue** class shown here. It implements a circular queue for characters.

```
// A circular queue.
class CircularQueue implements ICharQ {
  private char q[]; // this array holds the queue
  private int putloc, getloc; // the put and get indices

  // Construct an empty queue given its size.
  public CircularQueue(int size) {
    q = new char[size+1]; // allocate memory for queue
    putloc = getloc = 0;
  }

  // Put a character into the queue.
  public void put(char ch) {
    /* Queue is full if either putloc is one less than
       getloc, or if putloc is at the end of the array
       and getloc is at the beginning. */
    if(putloc+1==getloc |
        ((putloc==q.length-1) & (getloc==0))) {
      System.out.println(" - Queue is full.");
      return;
    }

    putloc++;
    if(putloc==q.length) putloc = 0; // loop back
    q[putloc] = ch;
  }

  // Get a character from the queue.
  public char get() {
    if(getloc == putloc) {
      System.out.println(" - Queue is empty.");
      return (char) 0;
    }

    getloc++;
    if(getloc==q.length) getloc = 0; // loop back
```

8

Packages and Interfaces

```
    return q[getloc];
  }
}
```

The circular queue works by reusing space in the array that is freed when elements are retrieved. Thus, it can store an unlimited number of elements as long as elements are also being removed. While conceptually simple—just reset the appropriate index to zero when the end of the array is reached—the boundary conditions are a bit confusing at first. In a circular queue, the queue is full not when the end of the underlying array is reached, but rather when storing an item would cause an unretrieved item to be overwritten. Thus, **put( )** must check several conditions in order to determine if the queue is full. As the comments suggest, the queue is full when either **putloc** is one less than **getloc**, or if **putloc** is at the end of the array and **getloc** is at the beginning. As before, the queue is empty when **getloc** and **putloc** are equal.

5. Put into **IQDemo.java** the **DynQueue** class shown next. It implements a "growable" queue that expands its size when space is exhausted.

```
// A dynamic queue.
class DynQueue implements ICharQ {
  private char q[]; // this array holds the queue
  private int putloc, getloc; // the put and get indices

  // Construct an empty queue given its size.
  public DynQueue(int size) {
    q = new char[size+1]; // allocate memory for queue
    putloc = getloc = 0;
  }

  // Put a character into the queue.
  public void put(char ch) {
    if(putloc==q.length-1) {
      // increase queue size
      char t[] = new char[q.length * 2];

      // copy elements into new queue
      for(int i=0; i < q.length; i++)
        t[i] = q[i];

      q = t;
    }

    putloc++;
    q[putloc] = ch;
  }

  // Get a character from the queue.
```

Project
8-1

Creating a Queue Interface

(continued)

```
   public char get() {
     if(getloc == putloc) {
       System.out.println(" - Queue is empty.");
       return (char) 0;
     }

     getloc++;
     return q[getloc];
   }
 }
```

In this queue implementation, when the queue is full, an attempt to store another element causes a new underlying array to be allocated that is twice as large as the original, the current contents of the queue are copied into this array, and a reference to the new array is stored in **q**.

6. To demonstrate the three **ICharQ** implementations, enter the following class into **IQDemo.java**. It uses an **ICharQ** reference to access all three queues.

```
// Demonstrate the ICharQ interface.
class IQDemo {
  public static void main(String args[]) {
    FixedQueue q1 = new FixedQueue(10);
    DynQueue q2 = new DynQueue(5);
    CircularQueue q3 = new CircularQueue(10);

    ICharQ iQ;

    char ch;
    int i;

    iQ = q1;
    // Put some characters into fixed queue.
    for(i=0; i < 10; i++)
      iQ.put((char) ('A' + i));

    // Show the queue.
    System.out.print("Contents of fixed queue: ");
    for(i=0; i < 10; i++) {
      ch = iQ.get();
      System.out.print(ch);
    }
    System.out.println();

    iQ = q2;
    // Put some characters into dynamic queue.
    for(i=0; i < 10; i++)
      iQ.put((char) ('Z' - i));
```

```
// Show the queue.
System.out.print("Contents of dynamic queue: ");
for(i=0; i < 10; i++) {
  ch = iQ.get();
  System.out.print(ch);
}

System.out.println();

iQ = q3;
// Put some characters into circular queue.
for(i=0; i < 10; i++)
  iQ.put((char) ('A' + i));

// Show the queue.
System.out.print("Contents of circular queue: ");
for(i=0; i < 10; i++) {
  ch = iQ.get();
  System.out.print(ch);
}

System.out.println();

// Put more characters into circular queue.
for(i=10; i < 20; i++)
  iQ.put((char) ('A' + i));

// Show the queue.
System.out.print("Contents of circular queue: ");
for(i=0; i < 10; i++) {
  ch = iQ.get();
  System.out.print(ch);
}

System.out.println("\nStore and consume from" +
                   " circular queue.");

// Use and consume from circular queue.
for(i=0; i < 20; i++) {
  iQ.put((char) ('A' + i));
  ch = iQ.get();
  System.out.print(ch);
}

  }
}
```

(continued)

7. The output from this program is shown here.

```
Contents of fixed queue: ABCDEFGHIJ
Contents of dynamic queue: ZYXWVUTSRQ
Contents of circular queue: ABCDEFGHIJ
Contents of circular queue: KLMNOPQRST
Store and consume from circular queue.
ABCDEFGHIJKLMNOPQRST
```

8. Here are some things to try on your own. Create a circular version of **DynQueue**. Add a **reset( )** method to **ICharQ** which resets the queue. Create a **static** method that copies the contents of one type of queue into another.

Variables in Interfaces

As mentioned, variables can be declared in an interface, but they are implicitly **public**, **static**, and **final**. At first glance, you might think that there would be very limited use for such variables, but the opposite is true. Large programs typically make use of several constant values that describe such things as array size, various limits, special values, and the like. Since a large program is typically held in a number of separate source files, there needs to be a convenient way to make these constants available to each file. In Java, interface variables offer a solution.

To define a set of shared constants, simply create an **interface** that contains only these constants, without any methods. Each file that needs access to the constants simply "implements" the interface. This brings the constants into view. Here is a simple example.

```
// An interface that contains constants.
interface IConst {
  int MIN = 0;
  int MAX = 10;                              ⎤
  String ERRORMSG = "Boundary Error";        ⎦ These are constants.
}

class IConstD implements IConst {
  public static void main(String args[]) {
    int nums[] = new int[MAX];

    for(int i=MIN; i < 11; i++) {
      if(i >= MAX) System.out.println(ERRORMSG);
      else {
        nums[i] = i;
        System.out.print(nums[i] + " ");
      }
    }
  }
}
```

Ask the Expert

Q: When I convert a C++ program to Java, how do I handle #define statements in a C++-style header file?

A: Java's answer to the header files and **#define**s found in C++ is the interface and interface variables. To port a header file, simply perform a one-to-one translation.

CRITICAL SKILL
8.10 Interfaces Can Be Extended

One interface can inherit another by use of the keyword **extends**. The syntax is the same as for inheriting classes. When a class implements an interface that inherits another interface, it must provide implementations for all methods defined within the interface inheritance chain. Following is an example:

```
// One interface can extend another.
interface A {
  void meth1();
  void meth2();
}

// B now includes meth1() and meth2() - it adds meth3().
interface B extends A {
  void meth3();
}                          B inherits A.

// This class must implement all of A and B
class MyClass implements B {
  public void meth1() {
    System.out.println("Implement meth1().");
  }

  public void meth2() {
    System.out.println("Implement meth2().");
  }

  public void meth3() {
    System.out.println("Implement meth3().");
```

```
    }
}

class IFExtend {
  public static void main(String arg[]) {
    MyClass ob = new MyClass();

    ob.meth1();
    ob.meth2();
    ob.meth3();
  }
}
```

As an experiment, you might try removing the implementation for **meth1( )** in **MyClass**. This will cause a compile-time error. As stated earlier, any class that implements an interface must implement all methods defined by that interface, including any that are inherited from other interfaces.

Although the examples we've included in this book do not make frequent use of packages or interfaces, both of these tools are an important part of the Java programming environment. Virtually all real programs and applets that you write in Java will be contained within packages. A number will probably implement interfaces as well. It is important, therefore, that you be comfortable with their usage.

✓ Module 8 Mastery Check

1. Using the code from Project 8-1, put the **ICharQ** interface and its three implementations into a package called **QPack**. Keeping the queue demonstration class **IQDemo** in the default package, show how to import and use the classes in **QPack**.

2. What is a namespace? Why is it important that Java allows you to partition the namespace?

3. Packages are stored in _____.

4. Explain the difference between **protected** and default access.

5. Explain the two ways that the members of a package can be used by other packages.

6. "One interface, multiple methods" is a key tenet of Java. What feature best exemplifies it?

7. How many classes can implement an interface? How many interfaces can a class implement?

8. Can interfaces be extended?

9. Create an interface for the **Vehicle** class from Module 7. Call the interface **IVehicle**.

10. Variables declared in an interface are implicitly **static** and **final**. What good are they?

11. A package is, in essence, a container for classes. True or False?

12. What standard Java package is automatically imported into a program?

Module 9

Exception Handling

This module discusses exception handling. An exception is an error that occurs at run time. Using Java's exception handling subsystem you can, in a structured and controlled manner, handle run-time errors. Although most modern programming languages offer some form of exception handling, Java's support for it is cleaner and more flexible than most others.

A principal advantage of exception handling is that it automates much of the error handling code that previously had to be entered "by hand" into any large program. For example, in some computer languages, error codes are returned when a method fails, and these values must be checked manually, each time the method is called. This approach is both tedious and error-prone. Exception handling streamlines error handling by allowing your program to define a block of code, called an *exception handler,* that is executed automatically when an error occurs. It is not necessary to manually check the success or failure of each specific operation or method call. If an error occurs, it will be processed by the exception handler.

Another reason that exception handling is important is that Java defines standard exceptions for common program errors, such as divide-by-zero or file-not-found. To respond to these errors, your program must watch for and handle these exceptions. Also, Java's API library makes extensive use of exceptions.

In the final analysis, to be a successful Java programmer means that you are fully capable of navigating Java's exception handling subsystem.

CRITICAL SKILL
9.1 The Exception Hierarchy

In Java, all exceptions are represented by classes. All exception classes are derived from a class called **Throwable**. Thus, when an exception occurs in a program, an object of some type of exception class is generated. There are two direct subclasses of **Throwable**: **Exception** and **Error**. Exceptions of type **Error** are related to errors that occur in the Java virtual machine itself, and not in your program. These types of exceptions are beyond your control, and your program will not usually deal with them. Thus, these types of exceptions are not described here.

Errors that result from program activity are represented by subclasses of **Exception**. For example, divide-by-zero, array boundary, and file errors fall into this category. In general, your program should handle exceptions of these types. An important subclass of **Exception** is **RuntimeException**, which is used to represent various common types of run-time errors.

CRITICAL SKILL
9.2 Exception Handling Fundamentals

Java exception handling is managed via five keywords: **try**, **catch**, **throw**, **throws**, and **finally**. They form an interrelated subsystem in which the use of one implies the use of another.

Throughout the course of this module, each keyword is examined in detail. However, it is useful at the outset to have a general understanding of the role each plays in exception handling. Briefly, here is how they work.

Program statements that you want to monitor for exceptions are contained within a **try** block. If an exception occurs within the **try** block, it is *thrown*. Your code can catch this exception using **catch** and handle it in some rational manner. System-generated exceptions are automatically thrown by the Java run-time system. To manually throw an exception, use the keyword **throw**. In some cases, an exception that is thrown out of a method must be specified as such by a **throws** clause. Any code that absolutely must be executed upon exiting from a **try** block is put in a **finally** block.

Ask the Expert

Q: **Just to be sure, could you review the conditions that cause an exception to be generated?**

A: Exceptions are generated in three different ways. First, the Java Virtual Machine can generate an exception in response to some internal error which is beyond your control. Normally, your program won't handle these types of exceptions. Second, standard exceptions, such as those corresponding to divide-by-zero or array index out-of-bounds, are generated by errors in program code. You need to handle these exceptions. Third, you can manually generate an exception by using the **throw** statement. No matter how an exception is generated, it is handled in the same way.

Using try and catch

At the core of exception handling are **try** and **catch**. These keywords work together; you can't have a **catch** without a **try**. Here is the general form of the **try/catch** exception handling blocks:

```
try {
  // block of code to monitor for errors
}

catch (ExcepType1 exOb) {
  // handler for ExcepType1
}
```

```
catch (ExcepType2 exOb) {
  // handler for ExcepType2
}
    .
    .
    .
```

Here, *ExcepType* is the type of exception that has occurred. When an exception is thrown, it is caught by its corresponding **catch** statement, which then processes the exception. As the general form shows, there can be more than one **catch** statement associated with a **try**. The type of the exception determines which **catch** statement is executed. That is, if the exception type specified by a **catch** statement matches that of the exception, then that **catch** statement is executed (and all others are bypassed). When an exception is caught, *exOb* will receive its value.

Here is an important point: If no exception is thrown, then a **try** block ends normally, and all of its **catch** statements are bypassed. Execution resumes with the first statement following the last **catch**. Thus, **catch** statements are executed only if an exception is thrown.

A Simple Exception Example

Here is a simple example that illustrates how to watch for and catch an exception. As you know, it is an error to attempt to index an array beyond its boundaries. When this occurs, the JVM throws an **ArrayIndexOutOfBoundsException**. The following program purposely generates such an exception and then catches it.

```
// Demonstrate exception handling.
class ExcDemo1 {
  public static void main(String args[]) {
    int nums[] = new int[4];

    try {                    ◄─────── Create a try block.
      System.out.println("Before exception is generated.");

      // Generate an index out-of-bounds exception.
      nums[7] = 10;  ◄──────────────────────────  Attempt to index past
      System.out.println("this won't be displayed");    nums boundary.
    }
    catch (ArrayIndexOutOfBoundsException exc) {  ◄─────── Catch array boundary
      // catch the exception                               errors.
      System.out.println("Index out-of-bounds!");
    }
    System.out.println("After catch statement.");
  }
}
```

This program displays the following output:

```
Before exception is generated.
Index out-of-bounds!
After catch statement.
```

Although quite short, the preceding program illustrates several key points about exception handling. First, the code that you want to monitor for errors is contained within a **try** block. Second, when an exception occurs (in this case, because of the attempt to index **nums** beyond its bounds), the exception is thrown out of the **try** block and caught by the **catch** statement. At this point, control passes to the **catch**, and the **try** block is terminated. That is, **catch** is *not* called. Rather, program execution is transferred to it. Thus, the **println( )** statement following the out-of-bounds index will never execute. After the **catch** statement executes, program control continues with the statements following the **catch**. Thus, it is the job of your exception handler to remedy the problem that caused the exception so that program execution can continue normally.

Remember, if no exception is thrown by a **try** block, no **catch** statements will be executed and program control resumes after the **catch** statement. To confirm this, in the preceding program, change the line

```
nums[7] = 10;
```

to

```
nums[0] = 10;
```

Now, no exception is generated, and the **catch** block is not executed.

It is important to understand that all code within a **try** block is monitored for exceptions. This includes exceptions that might be generated by a method called from within the **try** block. An exception thrown by a method called from within a **try** block can be caught by the **catch** statements associated with that **try** block—assuming, of course, that the method did not catch the exception itself. For example, this is a valid program:

```
/* An exception can be generated by one
   method and caught by another. */

class ExcTest {
  // Generate an exception.
  static void genException() {
    int nums[] = new int[4];

    System.out.println("Before exception is generated.");

    // generate an index out-of-bounds exception
```

```
      nums[7] = 10;              ←——————————————— Exception generated here.
      System.out.println("this won't be displayed");
   }
}

class ExcDemo2 {
  public static void main(String args[]) {

    try {
      ExcTest.genException();                    Exception caught here.
    }
    catch (ArrayIndexOutOfBoundsException exc) { ←——————┐
      // catch the exception
      System.out.println("Index out-of-bounds!");
    }
    System.out.println("After catch statement.");
  }
}
```

This program produces the following output, which is the same as that produced by the first version of the program shown earlier.

```
Before exception is generated.
Index out-of-bounds!
After catch statement.
```

Since **genException( )** is called from within a **try** block, the exception that it generates (and does not catch) is caught by the **catch** in **main( )**. Understand, however, that if **genException( )** had caught the exception itself, it never would have been passed back to **main( )**.

Progress Check

1. What is an exception?

2. Code monitored for exceptions must be part of what statement?

3. What does **catch** do? After a **catch** executes, what happens to the flow of execution?

---

1. An exception is a run-time error.

2. To monitor code for exceptions, it must be part of a **try** block.

3. The **catch** statement receives exceptions. A **catch** statement is not called; thus execution does not return to the point at which the exception was generated. Rather, execution continues on after the **catch** block.

CRITICAL SKILL

9.3 The Consequences of an Uncaught Exception

Catching one of Java's standard exceptions, as the preceding program does, has a side benefit: It prevents abnormal program termination. When an exception is thrown, it must be caught by some piece of code, somewhere. In general, if your program does not catch an exception, then it will be caught by the JVM. The trouble is that the JVM's default exception handler terminates execution and displays a stack trace and error message. For example, in this version of the preceding example, the index out-of-bounds exception is not caught by the program.

```
// Let JVM handle the error.
class NotHandled {
  public static void main(String args[]) {
    int nums[] = new int[4];

    System.out.println("Before exception is generated.");

    // generate an index out-of-bounds exception
    nums[7] = 10;
  }
}
```

When the array index error occurs, execution is halted, and the following error message is displayed.

```
Exception in thread "main" java.lang.ArrayIndexOutOfBoundsException: 7
        at NotHandled.main(NotHandled.java:9)
```

While such a message is useful for you while debugging, it would not be something that you would want others to see, to say the least! This is why it is important for your program to handle exceptions itself, rather than rely upon the JVM.

As mentioned earlier, the type of the exception must match the type specified in a **catch** statement. If it doesn't, the exception won't be caught. For example, the following program tries to catch an array boundary error with a **catch** statement for an **ArithmeticException** (another of Java's built-in exceptions). When the array boundary is overrun, an **ArrayIndexOutOfBoundsException** is generated, but it won't be caught by the **catch** statement. This results in abnormal program termination.

```
// This won't work!
class ExcTypeMismatch {
  public static void main(String args[]) {
```

```
int nums[] = new int[4];                         This throws an
                                                 ArrayIndexOutOfBoundsException.
try {
  System.out.println("Before exception is generated.");

  // generate an index out-of-bounds exception
  nums[7] = 10;
  System.out.println("this won't be displayed");
}

/* Can't catch an array boundary error with an
   ArithmeticException. */
catch (ArithmeticException exc) {                This tries to catch it with an
  // catch the exception                         ArithmeticException.
  System.out.println("Index out-of-bounds!");
}
System.out.println("After catch statement.");
  }
}
```

The output is shown here.

```
Before exception is generated.
Exception in thread "main" java.lang.ArrayIndexOutOfBoundsException: 7
        at ExcTypeMismatch.main(ExcTypeMismatch.java:10)
```

As the output demonstrates, a **catch** for **ArithmeticException** won't catch an **ArrayIndexOutOfBoundsException**.

Exceptions Enable You to Handle Errors Gracefully

One of the key benefits of exception handling is that it enables your program to respond to an error and then continue running. For example, consider the following example that divides the elements of one array by the elements of another. If a division by zero occurs, an **ArithmeticException** is generated. In the program, this exception is handled by reporting the error and then continuing with execution. Thus, attempting to divide by zero does not cause an abrupt run-time error resulting in the termination of the program. Instead, it is handled gracefully, allowing program execution to continue.

```
// Handle error gracefully and continue.
class ExcDemo3 {
  public static void main(String args[]) {
    int numer[] = { 4, 8, 16, 32, 64, 128 };
    int denom[] = { 2, 0, 4, 4, 0, 8 };
```

```
for(int i=0; i<numer.length; i++) {
  try {
    System.out.println(numer[i] + " / " +
                       denom[i] + " is " +
                       numer[i]/denom[i]);
  }
  catch (ArithmeticException exc) {
    // catch the exception
    System.out.println("Can't divide by Zero!");
  }
}
}
}
```

The output from the program is shown here.

```
4 / 2 is 2
Can't divide by Zero!
16 / 4 is 4
32 / 4 is 8
Can't divide by Zero!
128 / 8 is 16
```

This example makes another important point: Once an exception has been handled, it is removed from the system. Therefore, in the program, each pass through the loop enters the **try** block anew; any prior exceptions have been handled. This enables your program to handle repeated errors.

Progress Check

1. Does the exception type in a **catch** statement matter?

2. What happens if an exception is not caught?

3. When an exception occurs, what should your program do?

1. The type of exception in a **catch** must match the type of exception that you want to catch.

2. An uncaught exception ultimately leads to abnormal program termination.

3. A program should handle exceptions in a rational, graceful manner, eliminating the cause of the exception if possible and then continuing.

Using Multiple catch Statements

As stated earlier, you can associate more than one **catch** statement with a **try**. In fact, it is common to do so. However, each **catch** must catch a different type of exception. For example, the program shown here catches both array boundary and divide-by-zero errors.

```java
// Use multiple catch statements.
class ExcDemo4 {
  public static void main(String args[]) {
    // Here, numer is longer than denom.
    int numer[] = { 4, 8, 16, 32, 64, 128, 256, 512 };
    int denom[] = { 2, 0, 4, 4, 0, 8 };

    for(int i=0; i<numer.length; i++) {
      try {
        System.out.println(numer[i] + " / " +
                           denom[i] + " is " +
                           numer[i]/denom[i]);
      }
      catch (ArithmeticException exc) {              ◄──────────── Multiple catch statements
        // catch the exception
        System.out.println("Can't divide by Zero!");
      }
      catch (ArrayIndexOutOfBoundsException exc) {  ◄──
        // catch the exception
        System.out.println("No matching element found.");
      }
    }
  }
}
```

This program produces the following output:

```
4 / 2 is 2
Can't divide by Zero!
16 / 4 is 4
32 / 4 is 8
Can't divide by Zero!
128 / 8 is 16
No matching element found.
No matching element found.
```

As the output confirms, each **catch** statement responds only to its own type of exception.

In general, **catch** expressions are checked in the order in which they occur in a program. Only a matching statement is executed. All other **catch** blocks are ignored.

CRITICAL SKILL
9.5 Catching Subclass Exceptions

There is one important point about multiple **catch** statements that relates to subclasses. A **catch** clause for a superclass will also match any of its subclasses. For example, since the superclass of all exceptions is **Throwable**, to catch all possible exceptions, catch **Throwable**. If you want to catch exceptions of both a superclass type and a subclass type, put the subclass first in the **catch** sequence. If you don't, then the superclass **catch** will also catch all derived classes. This rule is self-enforcing because putting the superclass first causes unreachable code to be created, since the subclass **catch** clause can never execute. In Java, unreachable code is an error.

For example, consider the following program.

```
// Subclasses must precede superclasses in catch statements.
class ExcDemo5 {
  public static void main(String args[]) {
    // Here, numer is longer than denom.
    int numer[] = { 4, 8, 16, 32, 64, 128, 256, 512 };
    int denom[] = { 2, 0, 4, 4, 0, 8 };

    for(int i=0; i<numer.length; i++) {
      try {
        System.out.println(numer[i] + " / " +
                           denom[i] + " is " +
                           numer[i]/denom[i]);
      }
      catch (ArrayIndexOutOfBoundsException exc) {      ←——— Catch subclass
        // catch the exception
        System.out.println("No matching element found.");
      }
      catch (Throwable exc) {      ←——————————————— Catch superclass
        System.out.println("Some exception occurred.");
      }
    }
  }
}
```

The output from the program is shown here.

```
4 / 2 is 2
Some exception occurred.
16 / 4 is 4
32 / 4 is 8
Some exception occurred.
128 / 8 is 16
No matching element found.
No matching element found.
```

In this case, **catch(Throwable)** catches all exceptions except for **ArrayIndexOutOfBounds-Exception**.

The issue of catching subclass exceptions becomes more important when you create exceptions of your own.

Ask the Expert

Q: Why would I want to catch superclass exceptions?

A: There are, of course, a variety of reasons. Here are a couple. First, if you add a **catch** clause that catches exceptions of type **Exception**, then you have effectively added a "catch all" clause to your exception handler that deals with all program-related exceptions. Such a "catch all" clause might be useful in a situation in which abnormal program termination must be avoided no matter what occurs. Second, in some situations, an entire category of exceptions can be handled by the same clause. Catching the superclass of these exceptions allows you to handle all without duplicated code.

CRITICAL SKILL
9.6 Try Blocks Can Be Nested

One **try** block can be nested within another. An exception generated within the inner **try** block that is not caught by a **catch** associated with that **try** is propagated to the outer **try** block. For example, here the **ArrayIndexOutOfBoundsException** is not caught by the inner **catch**, but by the outer **catch**.

```
// Use a nested try block.
class NestTrys {
  public static void main(String args[]) {
    // Here, numer is longer than denom.
    int numer[] = { 4, 8, 16, 32, 64, 128, 256, 512 };
    int denom[] = { 2, 0, 4, 4, 0, 8 };

    try { // outer try  ◄─────────────────── Nested try blocks
      for(int i=0; i<numer.length; i++) {
        try { // nested try  ◄───────────────
          System.out.println(numer[i] + " / " +
                             denom[i] + " is " +
                             numer[i]/denom[i]);
        }
        catch (ArithmeticException exc) {
          // catch the exception
```

```
        System.out.println("Can't divide by Zero!");
      }
    }
  }
  catch (ArrayIndexOutOfBoundsException exc) {
    // catch the exception
    System.out.println("No matching element found.");
    System.out.println("Fatal error - program terminated.");
  }
 }
}
```

The output from the program is shown here.

```
4 / 2 is 2
Can't divide by Zero!
16 / 4 is 4
32 / 4 is 8
Can't divide by Zero!
128 / 8 is 16
No matching element found.
Fatal error - program terminated.
```

In this example, an exception that can be handled by the inner **try**—in this case, a divide-by-zero error—allows the program to continue. However, an array boundary error is caught by the outer **try**, which causes the program to terminate.

Although certainly not the only reason for nested **try** statements, the preceding program makes an important point that can be generalized. Often nested **try** blocks are used to allow different categories of errors to be handled in different ways. Some types of errors are catastrophic and cannot be fixed. Some are minor and can be handled immediately. Many programmers use an outer **try** block to catch the most severe errors, allowing inner **try** blocks to handle less serious ones.

Progress Check

1. Can one **try** block be used to handle two or more different types of exceptions?

2. Can a **catch** statement for a superclass exception also catch subclasses of that superclass?

3. In nested **try** blocks, what happens to an exception that is not caught by the inner block?

---

1. Yes.

2. Yes.

3. An exception not caught by an inner **try/catch** block moves outward to the enclosing **try** block.

Throwing an Exception

The preceding examples have been catching exceptions generated automatically by the JVM. However, it is possible to manually throw an exception by using the **throw** statement. Its general form is shown here.

throw *exceptOb*;

Here, *exceptOb* must be an object of an exception class derived from **Throwable**.

Here is an example that illustrates the **throw** statement by manually throwing an **ArithmeticException**.

```
// Manually throw an exception.
class ThrowDemo {
  public static void main(String args[]) {
    try {
      System.out.println("Before throw.");
      throw new ArithmeticException();  ←——————— Throw an exception.
    }
    catch (ArithmeticException exc) {
      // catch the exception
      System.out.println("Exception caught.");
    }
    System.out.println("After try/catch block.");
  }
}
```

The output from the program is shown here.

```
Before throw.
Exception caught.
After try/catch block.
```

Notice how the **ArithmeticException** was created using **new** in the **throw** statement. Remember, **throw** throws an object. Thus, you must create an object for it to throw. That is, you can't just throw a type.

Rethrowing an Exception

An exception caught by one **catch** statement can be rethrown so that it can be caught by an outer **catch**. The most likely reason for rethrowing this way is to allow multiple handlers access to the exception. For example, perhaps one exception handler manages one aspect of an exception, and a second handler copes with another aspect. Remember, when you rethrow an

Ask the Expert

Q: Why would I want to manually throw an exception?

A: Most often, the exceptions that you will throw will be instances of exception classes that you created. As you will see later in this module, creating your own exception classes allows you to handle errors in your code as part of your program's overall exception handling strategy.

exception, it will not be recaught by the same **catch** statement. It will propagate to the next **catch** statement.

The following program illustrates rethrowing an exception.

```java
// Rethrow an exception.
class Rethrow {
  public static void genException() {
    // here, numer is longer than denom
    int numer[] = { 4, 8, 16, 32, 64, 128, 256, 512 };
    int denom[] = { 2, 0, 4, 4, 0, 8 };

    for(int i=0; i<numer.length; i++) {
      try {
        System.out.println(numer[i] + " / " +
                           denom[i] + " is " +
                           numer[i]/denom[i]);
      }
      catch (ArithmeticException exc) {
        // catch the exception
        System.out.println("Can't divide by Zero!");
      }
      catch (ArrayIndexOutOfBoundsException exc) {
        // catch the exception
        System.out.println("No matching element found.");
        throw exc; // rethrow the exception
      }
    }
  }
}
```

Rethrow the exception.

```java
class RethrowDemo {
  public static void main(String args[]) {
    try {
      Rethrow.genException();
```

```
      }
      catch(ArrayIndexOutOfBoundsException exc) {  ◄──── Catch rethrown exception.
        // recatch exception
        System.out.println("Fatal error - " +
                           "program terminated.");
      }
    }
  }
}
```

In this program, divide-by-zero errors are handled locally, by **genException( )**, but an array boundary error is rethrown. In this case, it is caught by **main( )**.

Progress Check

1. What does **throw** do?

2. Does **throw** throw types or objects?

3. Can an exception be rethrown after it is caught?

Up to this point, we have been catching exceptions, but we haven't been doing anything with the exception object itself. As the preceding examples all show, a **catch** clause specifies an exception type and a parameter. The parameter receives the exception object. Since all exceptions are subclasses of **Throwable**, all exceptions support the methods defined by **Throwable**. Several commonly used ones are shown in Table 9-1.

Of the methods defined by **Throwable**, the two of greatest interest are **printStackTrace( )** and **toString( )**. You can display the standard error message plus a record of the method calls that lead up to the exception by calling **printStackTrace( )**. You can use **toString( )** to retrieve the standard error message. The **toString( )** method is also called when an exception is used as an argument to **println( )**. The following program demonstrates these methods.

---

1. **throw** generates an exception.
2. **throw** throws objects. These objects must be instances of valid exception classes, of course.
3. Yes.

Method	Description
Throwable fillInStackTrace( )	Returns a **Throwable** object that contains a completed stack trace. This object can be rethrown.
String getLocalizedMessage( )	Returns a localized description of the exception.
String getMessage( )	Returns a description of the exception.
void printStackTrace( )	Displays the stack trace.
void printStackTrace(PrintStream *stream*)	Sends the stack trace to the specified stream.
void printStackTrace(PrintWriter *stream*)	Sends the stack trace to the specified stream.
String toString( )	Returns a **String** object containing a complete description of the exception. This method is called by **println( )** when outputting a **Throwable** object.

Table 9-1 Commonly Used Methods Defined by **Throwable**

```
// Using the Throwable methods.

class ExcTest {
  static void genException() {
    int nums[] = new int[4];

    System.out.println("Before exception is generated.");

    // generate an index out-of-bounds exception
    nums[7] = 10;
    System.out.println("this won't be displayed");
  }
}

class UseThrowableMethods {
  public static void main(String args[]) {

    try {
      ExcTest.genException();
    }
    catch (ArrayIndexOutOfBoundsException exc) {
      // catch the exception
      System.out.println("Standard message is: ");
      System.out.println(exc);
      System.out.println("\nStack trace: ");
      exc.printStackTrace();
    }
```

```
          System.out.println("After catch statement.");
     }
   }
}
```

The output from this program is shown here.

```
Before exception is generated.
Standard message is:
java.lang.ArrayIndexOutOfBoundsException: 7

Stack trace:
java.lang.ArrayIndexOutOfBoundsException: 7
     at ExcTest.genException(UseThrowableMethods.java:10)
     at UseThrowableMethods.main(UseThrowableMethods.java:19)
After catch statement.
```

CRITICAL SKILL
9.9 Using finally

Sometimes you will want to define a block of code that will execute when a **try/catch** block is left. For example, an exception might cause an error that terminates the current method, causing its premature return. However, that method may have opened a file or a network connection that needs to be closed. Such types of circumstances are common in programming, and Java provides a convenient way to handle them: **finally**.

To specify a block of code to execute when a **try/catch** block is exited, include a **finally** block at the end of a **try/catch** sequence. The general form of a **try/catch** that includes **finally** is shown here.

```
try {
 // block of code to monitor for errors
}

catch (ExcepType1 exOb) {
 // handler for ExcepType1
}

catch (ExcepType2 exOb) {
 // handler for ExcepType2
}

//...
finally {
 // finally code
}
```

The **finally** block will be executed whenever execution leaves a **try/catch** block, no matter what conditions cause it. That is, whether the **try** block ends normally, or because of an exception, the last code executed is that defined by **finally**. The **finally** block is also executed if any code within the **try** block or any of its **catch** statements return from the method.

Here is an example of **finally**.

```
// Use finally.
class UseFinally {
  public static void genException(int what) {
    int t;
    int nums[] = new int[2];

    System.out.println("Receiving " + what);
    try {
      switch(what) {
        case 0:
          t = 10 / what; // generate div-by-zero error
          break;
        case 1:
          nums[4] = 4; // generate array index error.
          break;
        case 2:
          return; // return from try block
      }
    }
    catch (ArithmeticException exc) {
      // catch the exception
      System.out.println("Can't divide by Zero!");
      return; // return from catch
    }
    catch (ArrayIndexOutOfBoundsException exc) {
      // catch the exception
      System.out.println("No matching element found.");
    }
    finally {                                                   This is executed on way out
      System.out.println("Leaving try.");                      of try/catch blocks.
    }
  }
}

class FinallyDemo {
  public static void main(String args[]) {

    for(int i=0; i < 3; i++) {
      UseFinally.genException(i);
      System.out.println();
```

```
      }
    }
  }
```

Here is the output produced by the program.

```
Receiving 0
Can't divide by Zero!
Leaving try.

Receiving 1
No matching element found.
Leaving try.

Receiving 2
Leaving try.
```

As the output shows, no matter how the **try** block is exited, the **finally** block is executed.

Progress Check

1. Exception classes are subclasses of what class?

2. When is the code within a **finally** block executed?

3. How can you display a stack trace of the events leading up to an exception?

CRITICAL SKILL
9.10 Using throws

In some cases, if a method generates an exception that it does not handle, it must declare that exception in a **throws** clause. Here is the general form of a method that includes a **throws** clause.

ret-type methName(param-list) throws *except-list* {
   // body
}

Here, *except-list* is a comma-separated list of exceptions that the method might throw outside of itself.

You might be wondering why you did not need to specify a **throws** clause for some of the preceding examples, which threw exceptions outside of methods. The answer is that exceptions

---

1. **Throwable**.
2. A **finally** block is the last thing executed when a **try/catch** block is exited.
3. To print a stack trace, call **printStackTrace( )**, which is defined by **Throwable**.

that are subclasses of **Error** or **RuntimeException** don't need to be specified in a **throws** list. Java simply assumes that a method may throw one. All other types of exceptions *do* need to be declared. Failure to do so causes a compile-time error.

Actually, you saw an example of a **throws** clause earlier in this book. As you will recall, when performing keyboard input, you needed to add the clause

```
throws java.io.IOException
```

to **main( )**. Now you can understand why. An input statement might generate an **IOException**, and at that time, we weren't able to handle that exception. Thus, such an exception would be thrown out of **main( )** and needed to be specified as such. Now that you know about exceptions, you can easily handle **IOException**.

Let's look at an example that handles **IOException**. It creates a method called **prompt( )**, which displays a prompting message and then reads a character from the keyboard. Since input is being performed, an **IOException** might occur. However, the **prompt( )** method does not handle **IOException** itself. Instead, it uses a **throws** clause, which means that the calling method must handle it. In this example, the calling method is **main( )**, and it deals with the error.

```
// Use throws.
class ThrowsDemo {
  public static char prompt(String str)
    throws java.io.IOException {          ◄──────────── Notice the throws clause.

    System.out.print(str + ": ");
    return (char) System.in.read();
  }

  public static void main(String args[]) {
    char ch;

    try {
      ch = prompt("Enter a letter");  ◄──   Since prompt( ) might throw an
    }                                       exception, a call to it must be
    catch(java.io.IOException exc) {        enclosed within a try block.
      System.out.println("I/O exception occurred.");
      ch = 'X';
    }

    System.out.println("You pressed " + ch);
  }
}
```

On a related point, notice that **IOException** is fully qualified by its package name **java.io**. As you will learn in Module 10, Java's I/O system is contained in the **java.io** package. Thus, the **IOException** is also contained there. It would also have been possible to import **java.io** and then refer to **IOException** directly.

CRITICAL SKILL
9.11 Java's Built-in Exceptions

Inside the standard package **java.lang**, Java defines several exception classes. A few have been used by the preceding examples. The most general of these exceptions are subclasses of the standard type **RuntimeException**. Since **java.lang** is implicitly imported into all Java programs, most exceptions derived from **RuntimeException** are automatically available. Furthermore, they need not be included in any method's **throws** list. In the language of Java, these are called *unchecked exceptions* because the compiler does not check to see if a method handles or throws these exceptions. The unchecked exceptions defined in **java.lang** are listed in Table 9-2. Table 9-3 lists those exceptions defined by **java.lang** that must be included in a method's **throws** list if that method can generate one of these exceptions and does not handle it, itself. These are called *checked exceptions*. Java defines several other types of exceptions that relate to its various class libraries, such as **IOException** mentioned earlier.

Exception	Meaning
ArithmeticException	Arithmetic error, such as divide-by-zero.
ArrayIndexOutOfBoundsException	Array index is out-of-bounds.
ArrayStoreException	Assignment to an array element of an incompatible type.
ClassCastException	Invalid cast.
EnumConstNotPresentException	An attempt is made to use an undefined enumeration value.
IllegalArgumentException	Illegal argument used to invoke a method.
IllegalMonitorStateException	Illegal monitor operation, such as waiting on an unlocked thread.
IllegalStateException	Environment or application is in incorrect state.
IllegalThreadStateException	Requested operation not compatible with current thread state.
IndexOutOfBoundsException	Some type of index is out-of-bounds.
NegativeArraySizeException	Array created with a negative size.
NullPointerException	Invalid use of a null reference.
NumberFormatException	Invalid conversion of a string to a numeric format.
SecurityException	Attempt to violate security.
StringIndexOutOfBounds	Attempt to index outside the bounds of a string.
TypeNotPresentException	Type not found.
UnsupportedOperationException	An unsupported operation was encountered.

Table 9-2 The Unchecked Exceptions Defined in **java.lang**

Exception	Meaning
ClassNotFoundException	Class not found.
CloneNotSupportedException	Attempt to clone an object that does not implement the **Cloneable** interface.
IllegalAccessException	Access to a class is denied.
InstantiationException	Attempt to create an object of an abstract class or interface.
InterruptedException	One thread has been interrupted by another thread.
NoSuchFieldException	A requested field does not exist.
NoSuchMethodException	A requested method does not exist.

Table 9-3 The Checked Exceptions Defined in **java.lang**

Ask the Expert

Q: I have heard that Java supports something called *chained exceptions*. What are they?

A: Chained exceptions are a relatively recent addition to Java. The chained exception feature allows you to specify one exception as the underlying cause of another. For example, imagine a situation in which a method throws an **ArithmeticException** because of an attempt to divide by zero. However, the actual cause of the problem was that an I/O error occurred, which caused the divisor to be set improperly. Although the method must certainly throw an **ArithmeticException**, since that is the error that occurred, you might also want to let the calling code know that the underlying cause was an I/O error. Chained exceptions let you handle this, and any other situation, in which layers of exceptions exist.

To allow chained exceptions, two constructors and two methods were added to **Throwable**. The constructors are shown here:

Throwable(Throwable *causeExc*)

Throwable(String *msg*, Throwable *causeExc*)

In the first form, *causeExc* is the exception that causes the current exception. That is, *causeExc* is the underlying reason that an exception occurred. The second form allows you to specify a description at the same time that you specify a cause exception. These

(continued)

two constructors have also been added to the **Error**, **Exception**, and **RuntimeException** classes.

The chained exception methods added to **Throwable** are **getCause( )** and **initCause( )**. These methods are shown here:

Throwable getCause( )

Throwable initCause(Throwable *causeExc*)

The **getCause( )** method returns the exception that underlies the current exception. If there is no underlying exception, **null** is returned. The **initCause( )** method associates *causeExc* with the invoking exception and returns a reference to the exception. Thus, you can associate a cause with an exception after the exception has been created. In general, **initCause( )** is used to set a cause for legacy exception classes that don't support the two additional constructors described earlier.

Chained exceptions are not something that every program will need. However, in cases in which knowledge of an underlying cause is useful, they offer an elegant solution.

Progress Check

1. What is **throws** used for?

2. What is the difference between checked and unchecked exceptions?

3. If a method generates an exception that it handles, must it include a **throws** clause for the exception?

CRITICAL SKILL
9.12 Creating Exception Subclasses

Although Java's built-in exceptions handle most common errors, Java's exception handling mechanism is not limited to these errors. In fact, part of the power of Java's approach to exceptions is its ability to handle exceptions that you create which correspond to errors in your own code. Creating an exception is easy. Just define a subclass of **Exception** (which is, of

---

1. When a method generates an exception that it does not handle, it must state this fact using a **throws** clause.
2. No **throws** clause is needed for unchecked exceptions.
3. No. A **throws** clause is needed only when the method does not handle the exception.

course, a subclass of **Throwable**). Your subclasses don't need to actually implement anything—it is their existence in the type system that allows you to use them as exceptions.

The **Exception** class does not define any methods of its own. It does, of course, inherit those methods provided by **Throwable**. Thus, all exceptions, including those that you create, have the methods defined by **Throwable** available to them. Of course, you can override one or more of these methods in exception subclasses that you create.

Here is an example that creates an exception called **NonIntResultException**, which is generated when the result of dividing two integer values produces a result with a fractional component. **NonIntResultException** has two fields which hold the integer values, a constructor and an override of the **toString( )** method, allowing the description of the exception to be displayed using **println( )**.

```
// Use a custom exception.

// Create an exception.
class NonIntResultException extends Exception {
  int n;
  int d;

  NonIntResultException(int i, int j) {
    n = i;
    d = j;
  }

  public String toString() {
    return "Result of " + n + " / " + d +
           " is non-integer.";
  }
}

class CustomExceptDemo {
  public static void main(String args[]) {

    // Here, numer contains some odd values.
    int numer[] = { 4, 8, 15, 32, 64, 127, 256, 512 };
    int denom[] = { 2, 0, 4, 4, 0, 8 };
    for(int i=0; i<numer.length; i++) {
      try {
        if((numer[i]%2) != 0)
          throw new
            NonIntResultException(numer[i], denom[i]);

        System.out.println(numer[i] + " / " +
                    denom[i] + " is " +
                    numer[i]/denom[i]);
```

```
        }
        catch (ArithmeticException exc) {
          // catch the exception
          System.out.println("Can't divide by Zero!");
        }
        catch (ArrayIndexOutOfBoundsException exc) {
          // catch the exception
          System.out.println("No matching element found.");
        }
        catch (NonIntResultException exc) {
          System.out.println(exc);
        }
      }
    }
}
```

The output from the program is shown here.

```
4 / 2 is 2
Can't divide by Zero!
Result of 15 / 4 is non-integer.
32 / 4 is 8
Can't divide by Zero!
Result of 127 / 8 is non-integer.
No matching element found.
No matching element found.
```

Ask the Expert

Q: When should I use exception handling in a program? When should I create my own custom exception classes?

A: Since the Java API makes extensive use of exceptions to report errors, nearly all real-world programs will make use of exception handling. This is the part of exception handling that most new Java programmers find easy. It is harder to decide when and how to use your own custom-made exceptions. In general, errors can be reported in two ways: return values and exceptions. When is one approach better than the other? Simply put, in Java, exception handling should be the norm. Certainly returning an error code is a valid alternative in some cases, but exceptions provide a more powerful, structured way to handle errors. They are the way professional Java programmers handle errors in their code.

Project 9-1   Adding Exceptions to the Queue Class

`QExcDemo.java`

In this project, you will create two exception classes that can be used by the queue classes developed by Project 8-1. They will indicate the queue-full and queue-empty error conditions. These exceptions can be thrown by the **put( )** and **get( )** methods, respectively. For the sake of simplicity, this project will add these exceptions to the **FixedQueue** class, but you can easily incorporate them into the other queue classes from Project 8-1.

Step by Step

1. Create a file called **QExcDemo.java**.

2. Into **QExcDemo.java**, define the following exceptions.

```
/*
    Project 9-1

    Add exception handling to the queue classes.
*/

// An exception for queue-full errors.
class QueueFullException extends Exception {
  int size;

  QueueFullException(int s) { size = s; }

  public String toString() {
   return "\nQueue is full. Maximum size is " +
          size;
  }
}

// An exception for queue-empty errors.
class QueueEmptyException extends Exception {

  public String toString() {
   return "\nQueue is empty.";
  }
}
```

A **QueueFullException** is generated when an attempt is made to store an item in an already full queue. A **QueueEmptyException** is generated when an attempt is made to remove an element from an empty queue.

(continued)

3. Modify the **FixedQueue** class so that it throws exceptions when an error occurs, as shown here. Add it to **QExcDemo.java**.

```java
// A fixed-size queue class for characters that uses exceptions.
class FixedQueue implements ICharQ {
  private char q[]; // this array holds the queue
  private int putloc, getloc; // the put and get indices

  // Construct an empty queue given its size.
  public FixedQueue(int size) {
    q = new char[size+1]; // allocate memory for queue
    putloc = getloc = 0;
  }

  // Put a character into the queue.
  public void put(char ch)
    throws QueueFullException {

    if(putloc==q.length-1)
      throw new QueueFullException(q.length-1);

    putloc++;
    q[putloc] = ch;
  }

  // Get a character from the queue.
  public char get()
    throws QueueEmptyException {

    if(getloc == putloc)
      throw new QueueEmptyException();

    getloc++;
    return q[getloc];
  }
}
```

Notice that two steps are required to add exceptions to **FixedQueue**. First, **get( )** and **put( )** must have a **throws** clause added to their declarations. Second, when an error occurs, these methods throw an exception. Using exceptions allows the calling code to handle the error in a rational fashion. You might recall that the previous versions simply reported the error. Throwing an exception is a much better approach.

4. To try the updated **FixedQueue** class, add the **QExcDemo** class shown here to **QExcDemo.java**.

```
// Demonstrate the queue exceptions.
class QExcDemo {
  public static void main(String args[]) {
    FixedQueue q = new FixedQueue(10);
    char ch;
    int i;

    try {
      // overrun the queue
      for(i=0; i < 11; i++) {
        System.out.print("Attempting to store : " +
                         (char) ('A' + i));
        q.put((char) ('A' + i));
        System.out.println(" - OK");
      }
      System.out.println();
    }
    catch (QueueFullException exc) {
      System.out.println(exc);
    }
    System.out.println();

    try {
      // over-empty the queue
      for(i=0; i < 11; i++) {
        System.out.print("Getting next char: ");
        ch = q.get();
        System.out.println(ch);
      }
    }
    catch (QueueEmptyException exc) {
      System.out.println(exc);
    }
  }
}
```

5. Since **FixedQueue** implements the **ICharQ** interface, which defines the two queue methods **get( )** and **put( )**, **ICharQ** will need to be changed to reflect the **throws** clause. Here is the updated **ICharQ** interface. Remember, this must be in a file by itself called **ICharQ.java**.

```
// A character queue interface that throws exceptions.
public interface ICharQ {
  // Put a character into the queue.
  void put(char ch) throws QueueFullException;
```

(continued)

```
    // Get a character from the queue.
    char get() throws QueueEmptyException;
}
```

6. Now, compile the updated **IQChar.java** file. Then, compile **QExcDemo.java**. Finally, run **QExcDemo**. You will see the following output.

```
Attempting to store : A - OK
Attempting to store : B - OK
Attempting to store : C - OK
Attempting to store : D - OK
Attempting to store : E - OK
Attempting to store : F - OK
Attempting to store : G - OK
Attempting to store : H - OK
Attempting to store : I - OK
Attempting to store : J - OK
Attempting to store : K
Queue is full. Maximum size is 10

Getting next char: A
Getting next char: B
Getting next char: C
Getting next char: D
Getting next char: E
Getting next char: F
Getting next char: G
Getting next char: H
Getting next char: I
Getting next char: J
Getting next char:
Queue is empty.
```

✓ Module 9 Mastery Check

1. What class is at the top of the exception hierarchy?

2. Briefly explain how to use **try** and **catch**.

3. What is wrong with this fragment?

```
// ...
vals[18] = 10;
catch (ArrayIndexOutOfBoundsException exc) {
  // handle error
}
```

4. What happens if an exception is not caught?

5. What is wrong with this fragment?

```
class A extends Exception { ...

class B extends A { ...

// ...

try {
  // ...
}
catch (A exc) { ... }
catch (B exc) { ... }
```

6. Can an inner **catch** rethrow an exception to an outer **catch**?

7. The **finally** block is the last bit of code executed before your program ends. True or False? Explain your answer.

8. What type of exceptions must be explicitly declared in a **throws** clause of a method?

9. What is wrong with this fragment?

```
class MyClass { // ... }
// ...
throw new MyClass();
```

10. In question 3 of the Mastery Check in Module 6, you created a **Stack** class. Add custom exceptions to your class that report stack full and stack empty conditions.

11. What are the three ways that an exception can be generated?

12. What are the two direct subclasses of **Throwable**?

Module 10

Using I/O

Since the beginning of this book, you have been using parts of the Java I/O system, such as **println( )**. However, you have been doing so without much formal explanation. Because the Java I/O system is based upon a hierarchy of classes, it was not possible to present its theory and details without first discussing classes, inheritance, and exceptions. Now it is time to examine Java's approach to I/O in detail.

Be forewarned, Java's I/O system is quite large, containing many classes, interfaces, and methods. Part of the reason for its size is that Java defines two complete I/O systems: one for byte I/O and the other for character I/O. It won't be possible to discuss every aspect of Java's I/O here. (An entire book could easily be dedicated to Java's I/O system!) This module will, however, introduce you to the most important and commonly used features. Fortunately, Java's I/O system is cohesive and consistent; once you understand its fundamentals, the rest of the I/O system is easy to master.

Before we begin, an important point needs to be made. The I/O classes described in this module support text-based console I/O and file I/O. They are not used to create graphical user interfaces (GUIs). Thus, you will not use them to create windowed applications, for example. However, Java *does* include substantial support for building graphical user interfaces. The basics of GUI programming are found in Module 14, where the applets are introduced, and Module 15, which offers an introduction to Swing. (Swing is Java's modern GUI toolkit.)

CRITICAL SKILL

10.1 Java's I/O Is Built upon Streams

Java programs perform I/O through streams. A *stream* is an abstraction that either produces or consumes information. A stream is linked to a physical device by the Java I/O system. All streams behave in the same manner, even if the actual physical devices they are linked to differ. Thus, the same I/O classes and methods can be applied to any type of device. For example, the same methods that you use to write to the console can also be used to write to a disk file. Java implements streams within class hierarchies defined in the **java.io** package.

CRITICAL SKILL

10.2 Byte Streams and Character Streams

Modern versions of Java define two types of streams: byte and character. (The original version of Java defined only the byte stream, but character streams were quickly added.) Byte streams provide a convenient means for handling input and output of bytes. They are used, for example, when reading or writing binary data. They are especially helpful when working with files. Character streams are designed for handling the input and output of characters. They use Unicode and, therefore, can be internationalized. Also, in some cases, character streams are more efficient than byte streams.

The fact that Java defines two different types of streams makes the I/O system quite large because two separate sets of class hierarchies (one for bytes, one for characters) is needed. The sheer number of I/O classes can make the I/O system appear more intimidating than it actually is. Just remember, for the most part, the functionality of byte streams is paralleled by that of the character streams.

One other point: at the lowest level, all I/O is still byte-oriented. The character-based streams simply provide a convenient and efficient means for handling characters.

CRITICAL SKILL
10.3 The Byte Stream Classes

Byte streams are defined by using two class hierarchies. At the top of these are two abstract classes: **InputStream** and **OutputStream**. **InputStream** defines the characteristics common to byte input streams and **OutputStream** describes the behavior of byte output streams.

From **InputStream** and **OutputStream** are created several concrete subclasses that offer varying functionality and handle the details of reading and writing to various devices, such as disk files. The byte stream classes are shown in Table 10-1. Don't be overwhelmed by the number of different classes. Once you can use one byte stream, the others are easy to master.

CRITICAL SKILL
10.4 The Character Stream Classes

Character streams are defined by using two class hierarchies topped by these two abstract classes: **Reader** and **Writer**. **Reader** is used for input, and **Writer** is used for output. Concrete classes derived from **Reader** and **Writer** operate on Unicode character streams.

From **Reader** and **Writer** are derived several concrete subclasses that handle various I/O situations. In general, the character-based classes parallel the byte-based classes. The character stream classes are shown in Table 10-2.

CRITICAL SKILL
10.5 The Predefined Streams

As you know, all Java programs automatically import the **java.lang** package. This package defines a class called **System**, which encapsulates several aspects of the run-time environment. Among other things, it contains three predefined stream variables, called **in**, **out**, and **err**. These fields are declared as **public**, **final**, and **static** within **System**. This means that they can be used by any other part of your program and without reference to a specific **System** object.

System.out refers to the standard output stream. By default, this is the console. **System.in** refers to standard input, which is by default the keyboard. **System.err** refers to the standard

Byte Stream Class	Meaning
BufferedInputStream	Buffered input stream
BufferedOutputStream	Buffered output stream
ByteArrayInputStream	Input stream that reads from a byte array
ByteArrayOutputStream	Output stream that writes to a byte array
DataInputStream	An input stream that contains methods for reading the Java standard data types
DataOutputStream	An output stream that contains methods for writing the Java standard data types
FileInputStream	Input stream that reads from a file
FileOutputStream	Output stream that writes to a file
FilterInputStream	Implements **InputStream**
FilterOutputStream	Implements **OutputStream**
InputStream	Abstract class that describes stream input
ObjectInputStream	Input stream for objects
ObjectOutputStream	Output stream for objects
OutputStream	Abstract class that describes stream output
PipedInputStream	Input pipe
PipedOutputStream	Output pipe
PrintStream	Output stream that contains **print( )** and **println( )**
PushbackInputStream	Input stream that allows bytes to be returned to the stream
RandomAccessFile	Supports random access file I/O
SequenceInputStream	Input stream that is a combination of two or more input streams that will be read sequentially, one after the other

Table 10-1 The Byte Stream Classes

error stream, which is also the console by default. However, these streams can be redirected to any compatible I/O device.

System.in is an object of type **InputStream**; **System.out** and **System.err** are objects of type **PrintStream**. These are byte streams, even though they are typically used to read and write characters from and to the console. The reason they are byte and not character streams is that the predefined streams were part of the original specification for Java, which did not include the character streams. As you will see, it is possible to wrap these within character-based streams if desired.

Character Stream Class	Meaning
BufferedReader	Buffered input character stream
BufferedWriter	Buffered output character stream
CharArrayReader	Input stream that reads from a character array
CharArrayWriter	Output stream that writes to a character array
FileReader	Input stream that reads from a file
FileWriter	Output stream that writes to a file
FilterReader	Filtered reader
FilterWriter	Filtered writer
InputStreamReader	Input stream that translates bytes to characters
LineNumberReader	Input stream that counts lines
OutputStreamWriter	Output stream that translates characters to bytes
PipedReader	Input pipe
PipedWriter	Output pipe
PrintWriter	Output stream that contains **print( )** and **println( )**
PushbackReader	Input stream that allows characters to be returned to the input stream
Reader	Abstract class that describes character stream input
StringReader	Input stream that reads from a string
StringWriter	Output stream that writes to a string
Writer	Abstract class that describes character stream output

Table 10-2 The Character Stream I/O Classes

Progress Check

1. What is a stream?

2. What types of streams does Java define?

3. What are the built-in streams?

---

1. A stream is an abstraction that either produces or consumes information.
2. Java defines both byte and character streams.
3. **System.in**, **System.out**, and **System.err**.

Using the Byte Streams

We will begin our examination of Java's I/O with the byte streams. As explained, at the top of the byte stream hierarchy are the **InputStream** and **OutputStream** classes. Table 10-3 shows the methods in **InputStream**, and Table 10-4 shows the methods in **OutputStream**. In general, the methods in **InputStream** and **OutputStream** can throw an **IOException** on error. The methods defined by these two abstract classes are available to all of their subclasses. Thus, they form a minimal set of I/O functions that all byte streams will have.

Reading Console Input

Originally, the only way to perform console input was to use a byte stream, and much Java code still uses the byte streams exclusively. Today, you can use byte or character streams. For commercial code, the preferred method of reading console input is to use a character-oriented

Method	Description
int available( )	Returns the number of bytes of input currently available for reading.
void close( )	Closes the input source. Further read attempts will generate an **IOException**.
void mark(int *numBytes*)	Places a mark at the current point in the input stream that will remain valid until *numBytes* bytes are read.
boolean markSupported( )	Returns **true** if **mark( )/reset( )** are supported by the invoking stream.
int read( )	Returns an integer representation of the next available byte of input. −1 is returned when the end of the file is encountered.
int read(byte *buffer*[ ])	Attempts to read up to *buffer.length* bytes into *buffer* and returns the actual number of bytes that were successfully read. −1 is returned when the end of the file is encountered.
int read(byte *buffer*[ ], int *offset*, int *numBytes*)	Attempts to read up to *numBytes* bytes into *buffer* starting at *buffer*[*offset*], returning the number of bytes successfully read. −1 is returned when the end of the file is encountered.
void reset( )	Resets the input pointer to the previously set mark.
long skip(long *numBytes*)	Ignores (that is, skips) *numBytes* bytes of input, returning the number of bytes actually ignored.

Table 10-3 The Methods Defined by **InputStream**

Method	Description
void close( )	Closes the output stream. Further write attempts will generate an **IOException**.
void flush( )	Finalizes the output state so that any buffers are cleared. That is, it flushes the output buffers.
void write(int *b*)	Writes a single byte to an output stream. Note that the parameter is an **int**, which allows you to call **write** with expressions without having to cast them back to **byte**.
void write(byte *buffer*[ ])	Writes a complete array of bytes to an output stream.
void write(byte *buffer*[ ], int *offset*, int *numBytes*)	Writes a subrange of *numBytes* bytes from the array *buffer*, beginning at *buffer*[*offset*].

Table 10-4 The Methods Defined by **OutputStream**

stream. Doing so makes your program easier to internationalize and easier to maintain. It is also more convenient to operate directly on characters rather than converting back and forth between characters and bytes. However, for sample programs, simple utility programs for your own use, and applications that deal with raw keyboard input, using the byte streams is acceptable. For this reason, console I/O using byte streams is examined here.

Because **System.in** is an instance of **InputStream**, you automatically have access to the methods defined by **InputStream**. Unfortunately, **InputStream** defines only one input method, **read( )**, which reads bytes. There are three versions of **read( )**, which are shown here:

int read( ) throws IOException

int read(byte *data*[ ]) throws IOException

int read(byte *data*[ ], int *start*, int *max*) throws IOException

In Module 3 you saw how to use the first version of **read( )** to read a single character from the keyboard (from **System.in**). It returns −1 when the end of the stream is encountered. The second version reads bytes from the input stream and puts them into *data* until either the array is full, the end of stream is reached, or an error occurs. It returns the number of bytes read, or −1 when the end of the stream is encountered. The third version reads input into *data* beginning at the location specified by *start*. Up to *max* bytes are stored. It returns the number of bytes read, or −1 when the end of the stream is reached. All throw an **IOException** when an error occurs. When reading from **System.in**, pressing ENTER generates an end-of-stream condition.

Here is a program that demonstrates reading an array of bytes from **System.in**. Notice that any I/O exceptions that might be generated are simply thrown out of **main( )**. Such an approach is common when reading from the console, but you can handle these types of errors yourself, if you choose.

```java
// Read an array of bytes from the keyboard.

import java.io.*;

class ReadBytes {
  public static void main(String args[])
    throws IOException {
      byte data[] = new byte[10];

      System.out.println("Enter some characters.");
      System.in.read(data);                          Read an array of bytes
      System.out.print("You entered: ");             from the keyboard.
      for(int i=0; i < data.length; i++)
         System.out.print((char) data[i]);
  }
}
```

Here is a sample run:

```
Enter some characters.
Read Bytes
You entered: Read Bytes
```

Writing Console Output

As is the case with console input, Java originally provided only byte streams for console output. Java 1.1 added character streams. For the most portable code, character streams are recommended. Because **System.out** is a byte stream, however, byte-based console output is still widely used. In fact, all of the programs in this book up to this point have used it! Thus, it is examined here.

Console output is most easily accomplished with **print( )** and **println( )**, with which you are already familiar. These methods are defined by the class **PrintStream** (which is the type of the object referenced by **System.out**). Even though **System.out** is a byte stream, it is still acceptable to use this stream for simple console output.

Since **PrintStream** is an output stream derived from **OutputStream**, it also implements the low-level method **write( )**. Thus, it is possible to write to the console by using **write( )**. The simplest form of **write( )** defined by **PrintStream** is shown here:

void write(int *byteval*)

This method writes the byte specified by *byteval* to the file. Although *byteval* is declared as an integer, only the low-order 8 bits are written. Here is a short example that uses **write( )** to output the character "X" followed by a new line:

```
// Demonstrate System.out.write().
class WriteDemo {
  public static void main(String args[]) {
    int b;

    b = 'X';
    System.out.write(b); ◄──────── Write a byte to the screen.
    System.out.write('\n');
  }
}
```

You will not often use **write( )** to perform console output (although it might be useful in some situations), since **print( )** and **println( )** are substantially easier to use.

PrintStream supplies two additional output methods: **printf( )** and **format( )**. Both give you detailed control over the precise format of data that you output. For example, you can specify the number of decimal places displayed, a minimum field width, or the format of a negative value. Although we won't be using these methods in the examples in this book, they are features that you will want to look into as you advance in your knowledge of Java.

Progress Check

1. What method is used to read a byte from **System.in**?

2. Other than **print( )** and **println( )**, what method can be used to write to **System.out**?

CRITICAL SKILL
10.7 Reading and Writing Files Using Byte Streams

Java provides a number of classes and methods that allow you to read and write files. Of course, the most common types of files are disk files. In Java, all files are byte-oriented, and Java provides methods to read and write bytes from and to a file. Thus, reading and writing

---

1. To read a byte, call **read( )**.
2. You can write to **System.out** by calling **write( )**.

files using byte streams is very common. However, Java allows you to wrap a byte-oriented file stream within a character-based object, which is shown later in this module.

To create a byte stream linked to a file, use **FileInputStream** or **FileOutputStream**. To open a file, simply create an object of one of these classes, specifying the name of the file as an argument to the constructor. Once the file is open, you can read from or write to it.

Inputting from a File

A file is opened for input by creating a **FileInputStream** object. Here is its most commonly used constructor.

FileInputStream(String *fileName*) throws FileNotFoundException

Here, *fileName* specifies the name of the file you want to open. If the file does not exist, then **FileNotFoundException** is thrown.

To read from a file, you can use **read( )**. The version that we will use is shown here:

int read( ) throws IOException

Each time it is called, **read( )** reads a single byte from the file and returns it as an integer value. It returns –1 when the end of the file is encountered. It throws an **IOException** when an error occurs. Thus, this version of **read( )** is the same as the one used to read from the console.

When you are done with a file, you should close it by calling **close( )**. Its general form is shown here.

void close( ) throws IOException

Closing a file releases the system resources allocated to the file, allowing them to be used by another file.

The following program uses **read( )** to input and display the contents of a text file, the name of which is specified as a command-line argument. Notice how the **try/catch** blocks handle I/O errors.

```
/* Display a text file.

   To use this program, specify the name
   of the file that you want to see.
   For example, to see a file called TEST.TXT,
   use the following command line.

   java ShowFile TEST.TXT
*/

import java.io.*;

class ShowFile {
```

```
public static void main(String args[])
{
  int i;
  FileInputStream fin;

  // First make sure that a file has been specified.
  if(args.length != 1) {
    System.out.println("Usage: ShowFile File");
    return;
  }

  try {
    fin = new FileInputStream(args[0]);  ←————— Open the file.
  } catch(FileNotFoundException exc) {
    System.out.println("File Not Found");
    return;
  }

  try {
    // read bytes until EOF is encountered
    do {
      i = fin.read();  ←————— Read from the file.
      if(i != -1) System.out.print((char) i);
    } while(i != -1);  ←————————— When i equals –1, the end of
  } catch(IOException exc) {           the file has been reached.
    System.out.println("Error reading file.");
  }

  try {
    fin.close();  ←————— Close the file.
  } catch(IOException exc) {
    System.out.println("Error closing file.");
  }

}
}
```

Ask the Expert

Q: I noticed that read( ) returns –1 when the end of the file has been reached, but that it does not have a special return value for a file error. Why not?

A: In Java, errors are handled by exceptions. Thus, if **read( )**, or any other I/O method, returns a value, it means that no error has occurred. This is a much cleaner way than handling I/O errors by using special error codes.

Writing to a File

To open a file for output, create a **FileOutputStream** object. Here are its two most commonly used constructors.

FileOutputStream(String *fileName*) throws FileNotFoundException

FileOutputStream(String *fileName,* boolean *append*)
    throws FileNotFoundException

If the file cannot be created, then **FileNotFoundException** is thrown. In the first form, when an output file is opened, any preexisting file by the same name is destroyed. In the second form, if *append* is **true**, then output is appended to the end of the file. Otherwise, the file is overwritten.

To write to a file, you will use the **write( )** method. Its simplest form is shown here:

void write(int *byteval*) throws IOException

This method writes the byte specified by *byteval* to the file. Although *byteval* is declared as an integer, only the low-order 8 bits are written to the file. If an error occurs during writing, an **IOException** is thrown.

As you may know, when file output is performed, that output often is not immediately written to the actual physical device. Instead, output is buffered until a sizable chunk of data can be written all at once. This improves the efficiency of the system. For example, disk files are organized by sectors, which might be anywhere from 128 bytes long on up. Output is usually buffered until an entire sector can be written all at once. However, if you want to cause data to be written to the physical device whether or not the buffer is full, you can call **flush( )**, shown here.

void flush( ) throws IOException

An exception is thrown on failure.

Once you are done with an output file, you must close it using **close( )**, shown here:

void close( ) throws IOException

Closing a file releases the system resources allocated to the file, allowing them to be used by another file. It also ensures that any output remaining in a disk buffer is actually written to the disk.

The following example copies a text file. The names of the source and destination files are specified on the command line.

```
/* Copy a text file.

   To use this program, specify the name
   of the source file and the destination file.
   For example, to copy a file called FIRST.TXT
   to a file called SECOND.TXT, use the following
```

```
   command line.

   java CopyFile FIRST.TXT SECOND.TXT
*/

import java.io.*;

class CopyFile {
  public static void main(String args[])
  {
    int i;
    FileInputStream fin;
    FileOutputStream fout;

    // First make sure that both files have been specified.
    if(args.length !=2 ) {
      System.out.println("Usage: CopyFile From To");
      return;
    }

    // open input file
    try {
      fin = new FileInputStream(args[0]);
    } catch(FileNotFoundException exc) {
      System.out.println("Input File Not Found");
      return;
    }

    // open output file
    try {
      fout = new FileOutputStream(args[1]);
    } catch(FileNotFoundException exc) {
      System.out.println("Error Opening Output File");

      // Close the open input file.
      try {
        fin.close();
      } catch(IOException exc2) {
        System.out.println("Error closing input file.");
      }
      return;
    }

    // Copy File
    try {
      do {
        i = fin.read();          ◄──────────── Read bytes from one file and
        if(i != -1) fout.write(i);  ◄──── write them to another.
```

```
      } while(i != -1);
   } catch(IOException exc) {
     System.out.println("File Error");
   }

   try {
     fin.close();
   } catch(IOException exc) {
     System.out.println("Error closing input file.");
   }

   try {
     fout.close();
   } catch(IOException exc) {
     System.out.println("Error closing output file.");
   }

  }
}
```

Progress Check

1. What does **read( )** return when the end of the file is reached?

2. What does **flush( )** do?

CRITICAL SKILL
10.8 Reading and Writing Binary Data

So far, we have just been reading and writing bytes containing ASCII characters, but it is possible—indeed, common—to read and write other types of data. For example, you might want to create a file that contains **int**s, **double**s, or **short**s. To read and write binary values of the Java primitive types, you will use **DataInputStream** and **DataOutputStream**.

DataOutputStream implements the **DataOutput** interface. This interface defines methods that write all of Java's primitive types to a file. It is important to understand that this data is written using its internal, binary format, not its human-readable text form. The most commonly used output methods for Java's primitive types are shown in Table 10-5. Each throws an **IOException** on failure.

1. A −1 is returned by **read( )** when the end of the file is encountered.
2. A call to **flush( )** causes any buffered output to be physically written to the storage device.

Output Method	Purpose
void writeBoolean(boolean *val*)	Writes the **boolean** specified by *val*.
void writeByte(int *val*)	Writes the low-order byte specified by *val*.
void writeChar(int *val*)	Writes the value specified by *val* as a character.
void writeDouble(double *val*)	Writes the **double** specified by *val*.
void writeFloat(float *val*)	Writes the **float** specified by *val*.
void writeInt(int *val*)	Writes the **int** specified by *val*.
void writeLong(long *val*)	Writes the **long** specified by *val*.
void writeShort(int *val*)	Writes the value specified by *val* as a **short**.

Table 10-5 Commonly Used Output Methods Defined by **DataOutputStream**

Here is the constructor for **DataOutputStream**. Notice that it is built upon an instance of **OutputStream**.

DataOutputStream(OutputStream *outputStream*)

Here, *outputStream* is the stream to which data is written. To write output to a file, you can use the object created by **FileOutputStream** for this parameter.

DataInputStream implements the **DataInput** interface, which provides methods for reading all of Java's primitive types. These methods are shown in Table 10-6, and each can throw an **IOException**. **DataInputStream** uses an **InputStream** instance as its foundation, overlaying it with methods that read the various Java data types. Remember that **DataInputStream** reads data in its binary format, not its human-readable form. The constructor for **DataInputStream** is shown here.

DataInputStream(InputStream *inputStream*)

Input Method	Purpose
boolean readBoolean( )	Reads a **boolean**
byte readByte( )	Reads a **byte**
char readChar( )	Reads a **char**
double readDouble( )	Reads a **double**
float readFloat( )	Reads a **float**
int readInt( )	Reads an **int**
long readLong( )	Reads a **long**
short readShort( )	Reads a **short**

Table 10-6 Commonly Used Input Methods Defined by **DataInputStream**

Here, *inputStream* is the stream that is linked to the instance of **DataInputStream** being created. To read input from a file, you can use the object created by **FileInputStream** for this parameter.

Here is a program that demonstrates **DataOutputStream** and **DataInputStream**. It writes and then reads back various types of data to and from a file.

```java
// Write and then read back binary data.
import java.io.*;

class RWData {
  public static void main(String args[])
    {

    DataOutputStream dataOut;
    DataInputStream dataIn;

    int i = 10;
    double d = 1023.56;
    boolean b = true;

    try {
      dataOut = new
        DataOutputStream(new FileOutputStream("testdata"));
    }
    catch(IOException exc) {
      System.out.println("Cannot open output file.");
      return;
    }

    try {
      System.out.println("Writing " + i);
      dataOut.writeInt(i);

      System.out.println("Writing " + d);
      dataOut.writeDouble(d);

      System.out.println("Writing " + b);
      dataOut.writeBoolean(b);

      System.out.println("Writing " + 12.2 * 7.4);
      dataOut.writeDouble(12.2 * 7.4);

    }
    catch(IOException exc) {
      System.out.println("Write error.");
    }

    try {
      dataOut.close();
```

Write binary data.

```
  } catch(IOException exc) {
    System.out.println("Error closing output file.");
    return;
  }

  System.out.println();

  // Now, read them back.
  try {
    dataIn = new
      DataInputStream(new FileInputStream("testdata"));
  }
  catch(IOException exc) {
    System.out.println("Cannot open input file.");
    return;
  }

  try {
    i = dataIn.readInt();
    System.out.println("Reading " + i);

    d = dataIn.readDouble();
    System.out.println("Reading " + d);

    b = dataIn.readBoolean();
    System.out.println("Reading " + b);

    d = dataIn.readDouble();
    System.out.println("Reading " + d);
  }
  catch(IOException exc) {
    System.out.println("Read error.");
  }

  try {
    dataIn.close();
  } catch(IOException exc) {
    System.out.println("Error closing input file.");
  }

  }
}
```

Read binary data.

The output from the program is shown here.

```
Writing 10
Writing 1023.56
Writing true
Writing 90.28
```

```
Reading 10
Reading 1023.56
Reading true
Reading 90.28
```

Progress Check

1. To write binary data, what type of stream should you use?

2. What method do you call to write a **double**?

3. What method do you call to read a **short**?

Project 10-1 A File Comparison Utility

CompFiles.java

This project develops a simple, yet useful file comparison utility. It works by opening both files to be compared and then reading and comparing each corresponding set of bytes. If a mismatch is found, the files differ. If the end of each file is reached at the same time and if no mismatches have been found, then the files are the same.

Step by Step

1. Create a file called **CompFiles.java**.

2. Into **CompFiles.java**, add the following program.

```
/*
    Project 10-1

    Compare two files.

    To use this program, specify the names
    of the files to be compared on the command line.

    java CompFile FIRST.TXT SECOND.TXT
*/

import java.io.*;

class CompFiles {
```

---

1. To write binary data, use **DataOutputStream**.
2. To write a **double**, call **writeDouble( )**.
3. To read a **short**, call **readShort( )**.

```java
public static void main(String args[])
{
  int i=0, j=0;
  FileInputStream f1;
  FileInputStream f2;

  // First make sure that both files have been specified.
  if(args.length !=2 ) {
    System.out.println("Usage: CompFile f1 f2");
    return;
  }

  // open first file
  try {
    f1 = new FileInputStream(args[0]);
  } catch(FileNotFoundException exc) {
    System.out.println(args[0] + " File Not Found");
    return;
  }

  // open second file
  try {
    f2 = new FileInputStream(args[1]);
  } catch(FileNotFoundException exc) {
    System.out.println(args[1] + " File Not Found");

    // Close the first file if the second file
    // cannot be opened.
    try {
      f1.close();
    } catch(IOException exc2) {
      System.out.println("Cannot close " + args[0]);
    }
    return;
  }

  // Compare files.
  try {
    do {
      i = f1.read();
      j = f2.read();
      if(i != j) break;
    } while(i != -1 && j != -1);

    if(i != j)
      System.out.println("Files differ.");
    else
```

(continued)

```
        System.out.println("Files are the same.");
    } catch(IOException exc) {
      System.out.println("File Error");
    }

    try {
      f1.close();
    } catch(IOException exc) {
      System.out.println("Error closing " + args[0]);
    }

    try {
      f2.close();
    } catch(IOException exc) {
      System.out.println("Error closing " + args[1]);
    }

  }
}
```

3. To try **CompFiles**, first copy **CompFiles.java** to a file called **temp**. Then, try this command line

```
java CompFiles CompFiles.java temp
```

The program will report that the files are the same. Next, compare **CompFiles.java** to **CopyFile.java** (shown earlier) using this command line:

```
java CompFiles CompFiles.java CopyFile.java
```

These files differ and **CompFiles** will report this fact.

4. On your own, try enhancing **CompFiles** with various options. For example, add an option that ignores the case of letters. Another idea is to have **CompFiles** display the position within the file where the files differ.

CRITICAL SKILL
10.9 Random Access Files

Up to this point, we have been using *sequential files*, which are files that are accessed in a strictly linear fashion, one byte after another. However, Java also allows you to access the contents of a file in random order. To do this you will use **RandomAccessFile**, which encapsulates a random-access file. **RandomAccessFile** is not derived from **InputStream** or **OutputStream**. Instead, it implements the interfaces **DataInput** and **DataOutput**, which define the basic I/O methods. It also supports positioning requests—that is, you can position the *file pointer* within the file. The constructor that we will be using is shown here.

RandomAccessFile(String *fileName*, String *access*)
    throws FileNotFoundException

Here, the name of the file is passed in *fileName* and *access* determines what type of file access is permitted. If it is "r", the file can be read but not written. If it is "rw", the file is opened in read-write mode.

    The method **seek( )**, shown here, is used to set the current position of the file pointer within the file:

void seek(long *newPos*) throws IOException

Here, *newPos* specifies the new position, in bytes, of the file pointer from the beginning of the file. After a call to **seek( )**, the next read or write operation will occur at the new file position.
    RandomAccessFile implements the **read( )** and **write( )** methods. It also implements the **DataInput** and **DataOuput** interfaces, which means that methods to read and write the primitive types, such as **readInt( )** and **writeDouble( )**, are available.
    Here is an example that demonstrates random access I/O. It writes six **double**s to a file and then reads them back in nonsequential order.

```
// Demonstrate random access files.
import java.io.*;

class RandomAccessDemo {
  public static void main(String args[])
  {

    double data[] = { 19.4, 10.1, 123.54, 33.0, 87.9, 74.25 };
    double d;
    RandomAccessFile raf;
                                                    Open random access file.
    try {
      raf = new RandomAccessFile("random.dat", "rw");  ←──────┘
    }
    catch(FileNotFoundException exc) {
      System.out.println("Cannot open file.");
      return ;
    }

    try {
      // Write values to the file.
      for(int i=0; i < data.length; i++) {
        raf.writeDouble(data[i]);
      }
```

```
            // Now, read back specific values
            raf.seek(0); // seek to first double     ◄────── Use seek( ) to set the file
            d = raf.readDouble();                             pointer.
            System.out.println("First value is " + d);

            raf.seek(8); // seek to second double
            d = raf.readDouble();
            System.out.println("Second value is " + d);

            raf.seek(8 * 3); // seek to fourth double
            d = raf.readDouble();
            System.out.println("Fourth value is " + d);

            System.out.println();

            // Now, read every other value.
            System.out.println("Here is every other value: ");
            for(int i=0; i < data.length; i+=2) {
                raf.seek(8 * i); // seek to ith double
                d = raf.readDouble();
                System.out.print(d + " ");
            }
        }
        catch(IOException exc) {
            System.out.println("File error.");
        }

        try {
            raf.close();
        } catch(IOException exc) {
            System.out.println("Error closing file.");
        }
    }
}
```

The output from the program is shown here.

```
First value is 19.4
Second value is 10.1
Fourth value is 33.0

Here is every other value:
19.4 123.54 87.9
```

Notice how each value is located. Since each double value is 8 bytes long, each value starts on an 8-byte boundary. Thus, the first value is located at zero, the second begins at byte 8, the third starts at byte 16, and so on. Thus, to read the fourth value, the program seeks to location 24.

Progress Check

1. What class do you use to create a random access file?

2. How do you position the file pointer?

Ask the Expert

Q: In looking through the documentation provided by the JDK, I noticed a new class called Console. **Is this a class that I can use to perform console-based I/O?**

A: The short answer is Yes. The **Console** class was added by Java SE 6 and it is used to read from and write to the console. **Console** is primarily a convenience class because most of its functionality is available through **System.in** and **System.out**. However, its use can simplify some types of console interactions, especially when reading strings from the console.

Console supplies no constructors. Instead, a **Console** object is obtained by calling **System.console( )**, which was also added by Java SE 6. It is shown here.

static Console console( )

If a console is available, then a reference to it is returned. Otherwise, null is returned. A console may not be available in all cases, such as when a program runs as a background task. Therefore, if null is returned, no console I/O is possible.

Console defines several methods that perform I/O, such as **readLine( )** and **printf( )**. It also defines a method called **readPassword( )**, which can be used to obtain a password. It lets your application read a password without echoing what is typed. You can also obtain a reference to the **Reader** and the **Writer** that is attached to the console. In general, **Console** is a class that you may find useful for some types of applications.

---

1. To create a random access file, use **RandomAccessFile**.
2. To position the file pointer, use **seek( )**.

CRITICAL SKILL

10.10 Using Java's Character-Based Streams

As the preceding sections have shown, Java's byte streams are both powerful and flexible. However, they are not the ideal way to handle character-based I/O. For this purpose, Java defines the character stream classes. At the top of the character stream hierarchy are the abstract classes **Reader** and **Writer**. Table 10-7 shows the methods in **Reader**, and Table 10-8 shows the methods in **Writer**. Most of the methods can throw an **IOException** on error. The methods defined by these two abstract classes are available to all of their subclasses. Thus, they form a minimal set of I/O functions that all character streams will have.

Method	Description
abstract void close( )	Closes the input source. Further read attempts will generate an **IOException**.
void mark(int *numChars*)	Places a mark at the current point in the input stream that will remain valid until *numChars* characters are read.
boolean markSupported( )	Returns **true** if **mark( )**/**reset( )** are supported on this stream.
int read( )	Returns an integer representation of the next available character from the invoking input stream. −1 is returned when the end of the file is encountered.
int read(char *buffer*[ ])	Attempts to read up to *buffer.length* characters into *buffer* and returns the actual number of characters that were successfully read. −1 is returned when the end of the file is encountered.
abstract int read(char *buffer*[ ], int *offset*, int *numChars*)	Attempts to read up to *numChars* characters into *buffer* starting at *buffer*[*offset*], returning the number of characters successfully read. −1 is returned when the end of the file is encountered.
int read(CharBuffer *buffer*)	Attempts to fill the buffer specified by *buffer*, returning the number of characters successfully read. −1 is returned when the end of the file is encountered. **CharBuffer** is a class that encapsulates a sequence of characters, such as a string.
boolean ready( )	Returns **true** if the next input request will not wait. Otherwise, it returns **false**.
void reset( )	Resets the input pointer to the previously set mark.
long skip(long *numChars*)	Skips over *numChars* characters of input, returning the number of characters actually skipped.

Table 10-7 The Methods Defined by **Reader**

Method	Description
Writer append(char *ch*)	Appends *ch* to the end of the invoking output stream. Returns a reference to the invoking stream.
Writer append(CharSequence *chars*)	Appends *chars* to the end of the invoking output stream. Returns a reference to the invoking stream. **CharSequence** is an interface that defines read-only operations on a sequence of characters.
Writer append(CharSequence *chars*, int *begin*, int *end*)	Appends the sequence of *chars* starting at *begin* and stopping with *end* to the end of the invoking output stream. Returns a reference to the invoking stream. **CharSequence** is an interface that defines read-only operations on a sequence of characters.
abstract void close( )	Closes the output stream. Further write attempts will generate an **IOException**.
abstract void flush( )	Finalizes the output state so that any buffers are cleared. That is, it flushes the output buffers.
void write(int *ch*)	Writes a single character to the invoking output stream. Note that the parameter is an **int**, which allows you to call **write** with expressions without having to cast them back to **char**.
void write(char *buffer*[ ])	Writes a complete array of characters to the invoking output stream.
abstract void write(char *buffer*[ ], int *offset*, int *numChars*)	Writes a subrange of *numChars* characters from the array *buffer*, beginning at *buffer*[*offset*] to the invoking output stream.
void write(String *str*)	Writes *str* to the invoking output stream.
void write(String *str*, int *offset*, int *numChars*)	Writes a subrange of *numChars* characters from the array *str*, beginning at the specified *offset*.

Table 10-8 The Methods Defined by **Writer**

Console Input Using Character Streams

For code that will be internationalized, inputting from the console using Java's character-based streams is a better, more convenient way to read characters from the keyboard than is using the byte streams. However, since **System.in** is a byte stream, you will need to wrap **System.in** inside some type of **Reader**. The best class for reading console input is **BufferedReader**, which supports a buffered input stream. However, you cannot construct a **BufferedReader** directly from **System.in**. Instead, you must first convert it into a character stream. To do this, you will use **InputStreamReader**, which converts bytes to characters. To obtain an **InputStreamReader** object that is linked to **System.in**, use the constructor shown next.

InputStreamReader(InputStream *inputStream*)

Since **System.in** refers to an object of type **InputStream**, it can be used for *inputStream*.

Next, using the object produced by **InputStreamReader**, construct a **BufferedReader** using the constructor shown here:

BufferedReader(Reader *inputReader*)

Here, *inputReader* is the stream that is linked to the instance of **BufferedReader** being created. Putting it all together, the following line of code creates a **BufferedReader** that is connected to the keyboard.

```
BufferedReader br = new BufferedReader(new
                    InputStreamReader(System.in));
```

After this statement executes, **br** will be a character-based stream that is linked to the console through **System.in**.

Reading Characters

Characters can be read from **System.in** using the **read( )** method defined by **BufferedReader** in much the same way as they were read using byte streams. Here are three versions of **read( )** defined by **BufferedReader**.

int read( ) throws IOException

int read(char *data*[ ]) throws IOException

int read(char *data*[ ], int *start*, int *max*) throws IOException

The first version of **read( )** reads a single Unicode character. It returns –1 when the end of the stream is reached. The second version reads characters from the input stream and puts them into *data* until either the array is full, the end of file is reached, or an error occurs. It returns the number of characters read or –1 at the end of the stream. The third version reads input into *data* beginning at the location specified by *start*. Up to *max* characters are stored. It returns the number of characters read or –1 when the end of the stream is encountered. All throw an **IOException** on error. When reading from **System.in**, pressing ENTER generates an end-of-stream condition.

The following program demonstrates **read( )** by reading characters from the console until the user types a period. Notice that any I/O exceptions that might be generated are simply thrown out of **main( )**. As mentioned earlier in this module, such an approach is common when reading from the console. Of course, you can handle these types of errors under program control, if you choose.

```
// Use a BufferedReader to read characters from the console.
import java.io.*;
```

```
class ReadChars {
  public static void main(String args[])
    throws IOException
  {
    char c;
    BufferedReader br = new
            BufferedReader(new
                    InputStreamReader(System.in));

    System.out.println("Enter characters, period to quit.");

    // read characters
    do {
      c = (char) br.read();
      System.out.println(c);
    } while(c != '.');
  }
}
```

Create **BufferedReader** linked to **System.in**.

Here is a sample run.

```
Enter characters, period to quit.
One Two.
O
n
e

T
w
o
.
```

Reading Strings

To read a string from the keyboard, use the version of **readLine( )** that is a member of the **BufferedReader** class. Its general form is shown here:

String readLine( ) throws IOException

It returns a **String** object that contains the characters read. It returns null if an attempt is made to read when at the end of the stream.

The following program demonstrates **BufferedReader** and the **readLine( )** method. The program reads and displays lines of text until you enter the word "stop".

```
// Read a string from console using a BufferedReader.
import java.io.*;
```

```
class ReadLines {
  public static void main(String args[])
    throws IOException
  {
    // create a BufferedReader using System.in
    BufferedReader br = new BufferedReader(new
                            InputStreamReader(System.in));
    String str;

    System.out.println("Enter lines of text.");
    System.out.println("Enter 'stop' to quit.");
    do {
      str = br.readLine();
      System.out.println(str);
    } while(!str.equals("stop"));
  }
}
```

Use **readLine( )** from **BufferedReader** to read a line of text.

Console Output Using Character Streams

While it is still permissible to use **System.out** to write to the console under Java, its use is recommended mostly for debugging purposes or for sample programs such as those found in this book. For real-world programs, the preferred method of writing to the console when using Java is through a **PrintWriter** stream. **PrintWriter** is one of the character-based classes. As explained, using a character-based class for console output makes it easier to internationalize your program.

PrintWriter defines several constructors. The one we will use is shown here:

PrintWriter(OutputStream *outputStream*, boolean *flushOnNewline*)

Here, *outputStream* is an object of type **OutputStream** and *flushOnNewline* controls whether Java flushes the output stream every time a **println( )** method is called. If *flushOnNewline* is **true**, flushing automatically takes place. If **false**, flushing is not automatic.

PrintWriter supports the **print( )** and **println( )** methods for all types including **Object**. Thus, you can use these methods in just the same way as they have been used with **System.out**. If an argument is not a primitive type, the **PrintWriter** methods will call the object's **toString( )** method and then print out the result.

To write to the console using a **PrintWriter**, specify **System.out** for the output stream and flush the stream after each call to **println( )**. For example, this line of code creates a **PrintWriter** that is connected to console output.

PrintWriter pw = new PrintWriter(System.out, true);

The following application illustrates using a **PrintWriter** to handle console output.

```
// Demonstrate PrintWriter.
import java.io.*;                          Create a PrintWriter linked
                                           to System.out.

public class PrintWriterDemo {
  public static void main(String args[]) {
    PrintWriter pw = new PrintWriter(System.out, true);
    int i = 10;
    double d = 123.65;

    pw.println("Using a PrintWriter.");
    pw.println(i);
    pw.println(d);

    pw.println(i + " + " + d + " is " + (i+d));
  }
}
```

The output from this program is:

```
Using a PrintWriter.
10
123.65
10 + 123.65 is 133.65
```

Remember that there is nothing wrong with using **System.out** to write simple text output to the console when you are learning Java or debugging your programs. However, using a **PrintWriter** will make your real-world applications easier to internationalize. Since no advantage is to be gained by using a **PrintWriter** in the sample programs shown in this book, for convenience we will continue to use **System.out** to write to the console.

Progress Check

1. What classes top the character-based stream classes?

2. To read from the console, you will open what type of reader?

3. To write to the console, you will open what type of writer?

---

1. At the top of the character-based stream classes are **Reader** and **Writer**.
2. To read from the console, open a **BufferedReader**.
3. To write to the console, open a **PrintWriter**.

File I/O Using Character Streams

Although byte-oriented file handling is the most common, it is possible to use character-based streams for this purpose. The advantage to the character streams is that they operate directly on Unicode characters. Thus, if you want to store Unicode text, the character streams are certainly your best option. In general, to perform character-based file I/O, you will use the **FileReader** and **FileWriter** classes.

Using a FileWriter

FileWriter creates a **Writer** that you can use to write to a file. Its most commonly used constructors are shown here:

FileWriter(String *fileName*) throws IOException

FileWriter(String *fileName,* boolean *append*) throws IOException

Here, *fileName* is the full path name of a file. If *append* is **true**, then output is appended to the end of the file. Otherwise, the file is overwritten. Either throws an **IOException** on failure. **FileWriter** is derived from **OutputStreamWriter** and **Writer**. Thus, it has access to the methods defined by these classes.

Here is a simple key-to-disk utility that reads lines of text entered at the keyboard and writes them to a file called "test.txt." Text is read until the user enters the word "stop." It uses a **FileWriter** to output to the file.

```
/* A simple key-to-disk utility that
   demonstrates a FileWriter. */

import java.io.*;

class KtoD {
  public static void main(String args[])
  {

    String str;
    FileWriter fw;
    BufferedReader br =
           new BufferedReader(
                new InputStreamReader(System.in));

    try {
      fw = new FileWriter("test.txt");          ◄──────── Create a FileWriter.
    }
    catch(IOException exc) {
      System.out.println("Cannot open file.");
```

```
      return ;
    }

    System.out.println("Enter text ('stop' to quit).");

    try {
      do {
        System.out.print(": ");
        str = br.readLine();

        if(str.compareTo("stop") == 0) break;

        str = str + "\r\n"; // add newline
        fw.write(str);   ←─────────────────── Write strings to the file.
        } while(str.compareTo("stop") != 0);
    } catch(IOException exc) {
      System.out.println("Error writing to file.");
    }

    try {
      fw.close();
    } catch(IOException exc) {
      System.out.println("Error closing file.");
    }

  }
}
```

Using a FileReader

The **FileReader** class creates a **Reader** that you can use to read the contents of a file. Its most commonly used constructor is shown here:

FileReader(String *fileName*) throws FileNotFoundException

Here, *fileName* is the full path name of a file. It throws a **FileNotFoundException** if the file does not exist. **FileReader** is derived from **InputStreamReader** and **Reader**. Thus, it has access to the methods defined by these classes.

The following program creates a simple disk-to-screen utility that reads a text file called "test.txt" and displays its contents on the screen. Thus, it is the complement of the key-to-disk utility shown in the previous section.

```
/* A simple disk-to-screen utility that
   demonstrates a FileReader. */

import java.io.*;

class DtoS {
```

```
public static void main(String args[]) {
  String s;
  FileReader fr;
  BufferedReader br;

  try {
    fr = new FileReader("test.txt");
    br = new BufferedReader(fr);
  } catch(FileNotFoundException exc) {
    System.out.println("Cannot open input file.");
    return;
  }

  try {
    while((s = br.readLine()) != null) {        ← Read lines from the file and
      System.out.println(s);                       display them on the screen.
    }
  } catch(IOException exc) {
    System.out.println("Error reading file.");
  }

  try {
    fr.close();
  } catch(IOException exc) {
    System.out.println("Error closing file.");
  }

  }
}
```

In this example, notice that the **FileReader** is wrapped in a **BufferedReader**. This gives it access to **readLine( )**.

Progress Check

1. What class is used to read characters from a file?

2. What class is used to write characters to a file?

---

1. To read characters, use a **FileReader**.
2. To write characters, use a **FileWriter**.

Ask the Expert

Q: I have heard about another I/O package called NIO. Can you tell me about it?

A: Called the *new I/O APIs*, NIO is one of the more interesting additions that Sun made to Java a few years ago because it supports a channel-based approach to I/O operations. The new I/O classes are contained in **java.nio** and its subordinate packages, such as **java.nio.channels** and **java.nio.charset**.

The new I/O system is built on two foundational items: *buffers* and *channels*. A buffer holds data. A channel represents an open connection to an I/O device, such as a file or a socket. In general, to use the new I/O system, you obtain a channel to an I/O device and a buffer to hold data. You then operate on the buffer, inputting or outputting data as needed.

Two other entities used by NIO are charsets and selectors. A *charset* defines the way that bytes are mapped to characters. You can encode a sequence of characters into bytes using an *encoder*. You can decode a sequence of bytes into characters using a *decoder*. A *selector* supports key-based, non-blocking, multiplexed I/O. In other words, selectors enable you to perform I/O through multiple channels. Selectors are most applicable to socket-backed channels.

It is important to understand that the new I/O subsystem is not intended to replace the I/O classes found in **java.io**, which are discussed in this module. Instead, the NIO classes are designed to supplement the standard I/O system, offering an alternative approach, which can be beneficial in some circumstances.

CRITICAL SKILL
10.12 Using Java's Type Wrappers to Convert Numeric Strings

Before leaving the topic of I/O, we will examine a technique useful when reading numeric strings. As you know, Java's **println( )** method provides a convenient way to output various types of data to the console, including numeric values of the built-in types, such as **int** and **double**. Thus, **println( )** automatically converts numeric values into their human-readable form. However, Java does not provide a parallel input method that reads and converts strings containing numeric values into their internal, binary format. For example, there is no version of **read( )** that reads a string such as "100" and then automatically converts it into its corresponding binary value that is able to be stored in an **int** variable. Instead, Java provides various other ways to accomplish this task. Perhaps the easiest is to use one of Java's *type wrappers*.

Java's type wrappers are classes that encapsulate, or *wrap*, the primitive types. Type wrappers are needed because the primitive types are not objects. This limits their use to some extent. For example, a primitive type cannot be passed by reference. To address this kind of need, Java provides classes that correspond to each of the primitive types.

The type wrappers are **Double, Float, Long, Integer, Short, Byte, Character,** and **Boolean**. These classes offer a wide array of methods that allow you to fully integrate the primitive types into Java's object hierarchy. As a side benefit, the numeric wrappers also define methods that convert a numeric string into its corresponding binary equivalent. These conversion methods are shown here. Each returns a binary value that corresponds to the string.

Wrapper	Conversion Method
Double	static double parseDouble(String *str*) throws NumberFormatException
Float	static float parseFloat(String *str*) throws NumberFormatException
Long	static long parseLong(String *str*) throws NumberFormatException
Integer	static int parseInt(String *str*) throws NumberFormatException
Short	static short parseShort(String *str*) throws NumberFormatException
Byte	static byte parseByte(String *str*) throws NumberFormatException

The integer wrappers also offer a second parsing method that allows you to specify the radix.

The parsing methods give us an easy way to convert a numeric value, read as a string from the keyboard or a text file, into its proper internal format. For example, the following program demonstrates **parseInt( )** and **parseDouble( )**. It averages a list of numbers entered by the user. It first asks the user for the number of values to be averaged. It then reads that number using **readLine( )** and uses **parseInt( )** to convert the string into an integer. Next, it inputs the values, using **parseDouble( )** to convert the strings into their **double** equivalents.

```java
/* This program averages a list of numbers entered
   by the user. */

import java.io.*;

class AvgNums {
  public static void main(String args[])
    throws IOException
  {
    // create a BufferedReader using System.in
    BufferedReader br = new
      BufferedReader(new InputStreamReader(System.in));
    String str;
    int n;
    double sum = 0.0;
    double avg, t;

    System.out.print("How many numbers will you enter: ");
    str = br.readLine();
    try {
      n = Integer.parseInt(str); //              Convert string to int.
    }
```

```
    catch(NumberFormatException exc) {
      System.out.println("Invalid format");
      n = 0;
    }

    System.out.println("Enter " + n + " values.");
    for(int i=0; i < n ; i++)  {
      System.out.print(": ");
      str = br.readLine();
      try {
        t = Double.parseDouble(str);  ←──────── Convert string to double.
      } catch(NumberFormatException exc) {
        System.out.println("Invalid format");
        t = 0.0;
      }
      sum += t;
    }
    avg = sum / n;
    System.out.println("Average is " + avg);
  }
}
```

Here is a sample run.

```
How many numbers will you enter: 5
Enter 5 values.
: 1.1
: 2.2
: 3.3
: 4.4
: 5.5
Average is 3.3
```

Ask the Expert

Q: What else can the primitive type wrapper classes do?

A: The primitive type wrappers provide a number of methods that help integrate the primitive types into the object hierarchy. For example, various storage mechanisms provided by the Java library, including maps, lists, and sets, work only with objects. Thus, to store an **int**, for example, in a list, it must be wrapped in an object. Also, all type wrappers have a method called **compareTo( )**, which compares the value contained within the wrapper; **equals( )**, which tests two values for equality; and methods that return the value of the object in various forms. The topic of type wrappers is taken up again in Module 12, when autoboxing is discussed.

Project 10-2 Creating a Disk-Based Help System

FileHelp.java

In Project 4-1 you created a **Help** class that displayed information about Java's control statements. In that implementation, the help information was stored within the class itself, and the user selected help from a menu of numbered options. Although this approach was fully functional, it is certainly not the ideal way of creating a Help system. For example, to add to or change the help information, the source code of the program needed to be modified. Also, the selection of the topic by number rather than by name is tedious, and is not suitable for long lists of topics. Here, we will remedy these shortcomings by creating a disk-based Help system.

The disk-based Help system stores help information in a help file. The help file is a standard text file that can be changed or expanded at will, without changing the Help program. The user obtains help about a topic by typing in its name. The Help system searches the help file for the topic. If it is found, information about the topic is displayed.

Step by Step

1. Create the help file that will be used by the Help system. The help file is a standard text file that is organized like this:

   #topic-name1
   topic info

   #topic-name2
   topic info

   .

   .

   .

   #topic-nameN
   topic info

   The name of each topic must be preceded by a #, and the topic name must be on a line of its own. Preceding each topic name with a # allows the program to quickly find the start of each topic. After the topic name are any number of information lines about the topic. However, there must be a blank line between the end of one topic's information and the start of the next topic. Also, there must be no trailing spaces at the end of any lines.

   Here is a simple help file that you can use to try the disk-based Help system. It stores information about Java's control statements.

   ```
   #if
   if(condition) statement;
   else statement;
   ```

```
#switch
switch(expression) {
  case constant:
    statement sequence
    break;
    // ...
  }

#for
for(init; condition; iteration) statement;

#while
while(condition) statement;

#do
do {
  statement;
} while (condition);

#break
break; or break label;

#continue
continue; or continue label;
```

Call this file **helpfile.txt**.

2. Create a file called **FileHelp.java**.

3. Begin creating the new **Help** class with these lines of code.

```
class Help {
  String helpfile; // name of help file

  Help(String fname) {
    helpfile = fname;
  }
```

The name of the help file is passed to the **Help** constructor and stored in the instance variable **helpfile**. Since each instance of **Help** will have its own copy of **helpfile**, each instance can use a different file. Thus, you can create different sets of help files for different sets of topics.

4. Add the **helpon( )** method shown here to the **Help** class. This method retrieves help on the specified topic.

```
// Display help on a topic.
boolean helpon(String what) {
```

(continued)

```
FileReader fr;
BufferedReader helpRdr;
int ch;
String topic, info;

try {
  fr = new FileReader(helpfile);
  helpRdr = new BufferedReader(fr);
}
catch(FileNotFoundException exc) {
  System.out.println("Help file not found.");
  return false;
}

try {
  do {
    // read characters until a # is found
    ch = helpRdr.read();

    // now, see if topics match
    if(ch == '#') {
      topic = helpRdr.readLine();
      if(what.compareTo(topic) == 0) { // found topic
        do {
          info = helpRdr.readLine();
          if(info != null) System.out.println(info);
        } while((info != null) &&
                (info.compareTo("") != 0));
        return true;
      }
    }
  } while(ch != -1);
}
catch(IOException exc) {
  System.out.println("File error.");
  try {
    helpRdr.close();
  }
  catch(IOException exc2) {
    System.out.println("Error closing file.");
  }
  return false;
}
try {
  helpRdr.close();
}
```

```
catch(IOException exc) {
    System.out.println("Error closing file.");
}
return false; // topic not found
}
```

The first thing to notice is that **helpon( )** handles all possible I/O exceptions itself and does not include a **throws** clause. By handling its own exceptions, it prevents this burden from being passed on to all code that uses it. Thus, other code can simply call **helpon( )** without having to wrap that call in a **try/catch** block.

The help file is opened using a **FileReader** that is wrapped in a **BufferedReader**. Since the help file contains text, using a character stream allows the Help system to be more efficiently internationalized.

The **helpon( )** method works like this. A string containing the name of the topic is passed in the **what** parameter. The help file is then opened. Then, the file is searched, looking for a match between **what** and a topic in the file. Remember, in the file, each topic is preceded by a #, so the search loop scans the file for #s. When it finds one, it then checks to see if the topic following that # matches the one passed in **what**. If it does, the information associated with that topic is displayed. If a match is found, **helpon( )** returns **true**. Otherwise, it returns **false**.

5. The **Help** class also provides a method called **getSelection( )**. It prompts the user for a topic and returns the topic string entered by the user.

```
// Get a Help topic.
String getSelection() {
    String topic = "";

    BufferedReader br = new BufferedReader(
                new InputStreamReader(System.in));

    System.out.print("Enter topic: ");
    try {
        topic = br.readLine();
    }
    catch(IOException exc) {
        System.out.println("Error reading console.");
    }
    return topic;
}
```

This method creates a **BufferedReader** attached to **System.in**. It then prompts for the name of a topic, reads the topic, and returns it to the caller.

(continued)

6. The entire disk-based Help system is shown here.

```
/*
   Project 10-2

   A help program that uses a disk file
   to store help information.
*/

import java.io.*;

/* The Help class opens a help file,
   searches for a topic, and then displays
   the information associated with that topic.
   Notice that it handles all I/O exceptions
   itself, avoiding the need for calling
   code to do so. */
class Help {
  String helpfile; // name of help file

  Help(String fname) {
    helpfile = fname;
  }

  // Display help on a topic.
  boolean helpon(String what) {
    FileReader fr;
    BufferedReader helpRdr;
    int ch;
    String topic, info;

    try {
      fr = new FileReader(helpfile);
      helpRdr = new BufferedReader(fr);
    }
    catch(FileNotFoundException exc) {
      System.out.println("Help file not found.");
      return false;
    }

    try {
      do {
        // read characters until a # is found
        ch = helpRdr.read();

        // now, see if topics match
        if(ch == '#') {
          topic = helpRdr.readLine();
```

```
            if(what.compareTo(topic) == 0) { // found topic
              do {
                info = helpRdr.readLine();
                if(info != null) System.out.println(info);
              } while((info != null) &&
                      (info.compareTo("") != 0));
              return true;
            }
          }
        } while(ch != -1);
      }
      catch(IOException exc) {
        System.out.println("File error.");
        try {
          helpRdr.close();
        }
        catch(IOException exc2) {
          System.out.println("Error closing file.");
        }
        return false;
      }
      try {
        helpRdr.close();
      }
      catch(IOException exc) {
        System.out.println("Error closing file.");
      }
      return false; // topic not found
    }

    // Get a Help topic.
    String getSelection() {
      String topic = "";

      BufferedReader br = new BufferedReader(
                 new InputStreamReader(System.in));

      System.out.print("Enter topic: ");
      try {
        topic = br.readLine();
      }
      catch(IOException exc) {
        System.out.println("Error reading console.");
      }
      return topic;
    }
  }
```

```
// Demonstrate the file-based Help system.
class FileHelp {
  public static void main(String args[]) {
    Help hlpobj = new Help("helpfile.txt");
    String topic;

    System.out.println("Try the help system. " +
                       "Enter 'stop' to end.");
    do {
      topic = hlpobj.getSelection();

      if(!hlpobj.helpon(topic))
        System.out.println("Topic not found.\n");

    } while(topic.compareTo("stop") != 0);
  }
}
```

Module 10 Mastery Check

1. Why does Java define both byte and character streams?

2. Even though console input and output is text-based, why does Java still use byte streams for this purpose?

3. Show how to open a file for reading bytes.

4. Show how to open a file for reading characters.

5. Show how to open a file for random access I/O.

6. How can you convert a numeric string such as "123.23" into its binary equivalent?

7. Write a program that copies a text file. In the process, have it convert all spaces into hyphens. Use the byte stream file classes.

8. Rewrite the program described in question 7 so that it uses the character stream classes.

9. What type of stream is **System.in**?

10. What does the **read( )** method of **InputStream** return when the end of the stream is reached?

11. What type of stream is used to read binary data?

12. **Reader** and **Writer** are at the top of the _____ class hierarchies.

Module 11

Multithreaded Programming

Although Java contains many innovative features, one of its most exciting is its built-in support for *multithreaded programming.* A multithreaded program contains two or more parts that can run concurrently. Each part of such a program is called a *thread,* and each thread defines a separate path of execution. Thus, multithreading is a specialized form of multitasking.

CRITICAL SKILL
11.1
Multithreading Fundamentals

There are two distinct types of multitasking: process-based and thread-based. It is important to understand the difference between the two. A process is, in essence, a program that is executing. Thus, *process-based* multitasking is the feature that allows your computer to run two or more programs concurrently. For example, it is process-based multitasking that allows you to run the Java compiler at the same time you are using a text editor or browsing the Internet. In process-based multitasking, a program is the smallest unit of code that can be dispatched by the scheduler.

In a *thread-based* multitasking environment, the thread is the smallest unit of dispatchable code. This means that a single program can perform two or more tasks at once. For instance, a text editor can be formatting text at the same time that it is printing, as long as these two actions are being performed by two separate threads. Although Java programs make use of process-based multitasking environments, process-based multitasking is not under the control of Java. Multithreaded multitasking is.

The principal advantage of multithreading is that it enables you to write very efficient programs because it lets you utilize the idle time that is present in most programs. As you probably know, most I/O devices, whether they be network ports, disk drives, or the keyboard, are much slower than the CPU. Thus, a program will often spend a majority of its execution time waiting to send or receive information to or from a device. By using multithreading, your program can execute another task during this idle time. For example, while one part of your program is sending a file over the Internet, another part can be reading keyboard input, and still another can be buffering the next block of data to send.

A thread can be in one of several states. It can be *running.* It can be *ready to run* as soon as it gets CPU time. A running thread can be *suspended,* which is a temporary halt to its execution. It can later be *resumed.* A thread can be *blocked* when waiting for a resource. A thread can be *terminated*, in which case its execution ends and cannot be resumed.

Along with thread-based multitasking comes the need for a special type of feature called *synchronization*, which allows the execution of threads to be coordinated in certain well-defined ways. Java has a complete subsystem devoted to synchronization, and its key features are also described here.

If you have programmed for operating systems such as Windows, then you are already familiar with multithreaded programming. However, the fact that Java manages threads through language elements makes multithreading especially convenient. Many of the details are handled for you.

CRITICAL SKILL
11.2 The Thread Class and Runnable Interface

Java's multithreading system is built upon the **Thread** class and its companion interface, **Runnable**. Both are packaged in **java.lang**. **Thread** encapsulates a thread of execution. To create a new thread, your program will either extend **Thread** or implement the **Runnable** interface.

The **Thread** class defines several methods that help manage threads. Here are some of the more commonly used ones (we will be looking at these more closely as they are used):

Method	Meaning
final String getName( )	Obtains a thread's name.
final int getPriority( )	Obtains a thread's priority.
final boolean isAlive( )	Determines whether a thread is still running.
final void join( )	Waits for a thread to terminate.
void run( )	Entry point for the thread.
static void sleep(long *milliseconds*)	Suspends a thread for a specified period of milliseconds.
void start( )	Starts a thread by calling its **run( )** method.

All processes have at least one thread of execution, which is usually called the *main thread*, because it is the one that is executed when your program begins. Thus, the main thread is the thread that all of the preceding example programs in the book have been using. From the main thread, you can create other threads.

Progress Check

1. What is the difference between process-based multitasking and thread-based multitasking?

2. In what states can a thread exist?

3. What class encapsulates a thread?

---

1. Process-based multitasking is used to run two or more programs concurrently. Thread-based multitasking, called *multithreading*, is used to run pieces of one program concurrently.

2. The thread states are *running*, *ready-to-run*, *suspended*, *blocked*, and *terminated*. When a suspended thread is restarted, it is said to be *resumed*.

3. **Thread**.

Creating a Thread

You create a thread by instantiating an object of type **Thread**. The **Thread** class encapsulates an object that is runnable. As mentioned, Java defines two ways in which you can create a runnable object:

- You can implement the **Runnable** interface.

- You can extend the **Thread** class.

Most of the examples in this module will use the approach that implements **Runnable**. However, Project 11-1 shows how to implement a thread by extending **Thread**. Remember: Both approaches still use the **Thread** class to instantiate, access, and control the thread. The only difference is how a thread-enabled class is created.

The **Runnable** interface abstracts a unit of executable code. You can construct a thread on any object that implements the **Runnable** interface. **Runnable** defines only one method called **run( )**, which is declared like this:

```
public void run( )
```

Inside **run( )**, you will define the code that constitutes the new thread. It is important to understand that **run( )** can call other methods, use other classes, and declare variables just like the main thread. The only difference is that **run( )** establishes the entry point for another, concurrent thread of execution within your program. This thread will end when **run( )** returns.

After you have created a class that implements **Runnable**, you will instantiate an object of type **Thread** on an object of that class. **Thread** defines several constructors. The one that we will use first is shown here:

Thread(Runnable *threadOb*)

In this constructor, *threadOb* is an instance of a class that implements the **Runnable** interface. This defines where execution of the thread will begin.

Once created, the new thread will not start running until you call its **start( )** method, which is declared within **Thread**. In essence, **start( )** executes a call to **run( )**. The **start( )** method is shown here:

void start( )

Here is an example that creates a new thread and starts it running:

```
// Create a thread by implementing Runnable.

class MyThread implements Runnable {    ◀─────────
```

Objects of **MyThread** can be run in their own threads because **MyThread** implements **Runnable**.

```java
    int count;
    String thrdName;

    MyThread(String name) {
      count = 0;
      thrdName = name;
    }

    // Entry point of thread.
    public void run() {    ◄─────────────────── Threads start executing here.
      System.out.println(thrdName + " starting.");
      try {
        do {
          Thread.sleep(500);
          System.out.println("In " + thrdName +
                             ", count is " + count);
          count++;
        } while(count < 10);
      }
      catch(InterruptedException exc) {
        System.out.println(thrdName + " interrupted.");
      }
      System.out.println(thrdName + " terminating.");
    }
}

class UseThreads {
  public static void main(String args[]) {
    System.out.println("Main thread starting.");

    // First, construct a MyThread object.
    MyThread mt = new MyThread("Child #1");    ◄─────── Create a runnable object.

    // Next, construct a thread from that object.
    Thread newThrd = new Thread(mt);    ◄─────────── Construct a thread on that object.

    // Finally, start execution of the thread.
    newThrd.start();    ◄────────────────────────── Start running the thread.

    do {
      System.out.print(".");
      try {
        Thread.sleep(100);
      }
      catch(InterruptedException exc) {
        System.out.println("Main thread interrupted.");
```

```
      }
    } while (mt.count != 10);

    System.out.println("Main thread ending.");
  }
}
```

Let's look closely at this program. First, **MyThread** implements **Runnable**. This means that an object of type **MyThread** is suitable for use as a thread and can be passed to the **Thread** constructor.

Inside **run( )**, a loop is established that counts from 0 to 9. Notice the call to **sleep( )**. The **sleep( )** method causes the thread from which it is called to suspend execution for the specified period of milliseconds. Its general form is shown here:

static void sleep(long *milliseconds*) throws InterruptedException

The number of milliseconds to suspend is specified in *milliseconds*. This method can throw an **InterruptedException**. Thus, calls to it must be wrapped in a **try** block. The **sleep( )** method also has a second form, which allows you to specify the period in terms of milliseconds and nanoseconds if you need that level of precision.

Inside **main( )**, a new **Thread** object is created by the following sequence of statements:

```
// First, construct a MyThread object.
MyThread mt = new MyThread("Child #1");

// Next, construct a thread from that object.
Thread newThrd = new Thread(mt);

// Finally, start execution of the thread.
newThrd.start();
```

As the comments suggest, first an object of **MyThread** is created. This object is then used to construct a **Thread** object. This is possible because **MyThread** implements **Runnable**. Finally, execution of the new thread is started by calling **start( )**. This causes the child thread's **run( )** method to begin. After calling **start( )**, execution returns to **main( )**, and it enters **main( )**'s **do** loop. Both threads continue running, sharing the CPU, until their loops finish. The output produced by this program is as follows. Because of differences between computing environments, the precise output that you see may differ from that shown here.

```
Main thread starting.
.Child #1 starting.
....In Child #1, count is 0
.....In Child #1, count is 1
.....In Child #1, count is 2
```

```
.....In Child #1, count is 3
.....In Child #1, count is 4
.....In Child #1, count is 5
.....In Child #1, count is 6
.....In Child #1, count is 7
.....In Child #1, count is 8
.....In Child #1, count is 9
Child #1 terminating.
Main thread ending.
```

In a multithreaded program, you often will want the main thread to be the last thread to finish running. As a general rule, a program continues to run until all of its threads have ended. Thus, having the main thread finish last is not a requirement. It is, however, good practice to follow—especially when you are first learning about multithreaded programs. The preceding program ensures that the main thread will finish last, because the **do** loop stops when **count** equals 10. Since **count** will equal 10 only after **newThrd** has terminated, the main thread finishes last. Later in this module, you will see a better way for one thread to wait until another finishes.

Some Simple Improvements

While the preceding program is perfectly valid, some simple improvements can be made that will make it more efficient and easier to use. First, it is possible to have a thread begin execution as soon as it is created. In the case of **MyThread**, this is done by instantiating a **Thread** object inside **MyThread**'s constructor. Second, there is no need for **MyThread** to store the name of the thread since it is possible to give a name to a thread when it is created. To do so, use this version of **Thread**'s constructor.

Thread(Runnable *threadOb*, String *name*)

Here, *name* becomes the name of the thread.

Ask the Expert

Q: Why do you recommend that the main thread be the last to finish?

A: In older Java run-time systems, if the main thread finished before a child thread had completed, there was a possibility that the Java run-time system would "hang." This problem is not exhibited by the modern Java run-time systems to which this author has access. However, since this behavior was exhibited by some older Java run-time systems, it seems better to be safe rather than sorry since you don't always know the environment in which your program may run. The main thread is also a convenient place to perform the orderly shutdown of your program, such as the closing of files. Therefore, it often just makes sense for it to finish last. Fortunately, it is trivially easy for the main thread to wait until the child threads have completed.

You can obtain the name of a thread by calling **getName( )** defined by **Thread**. Its general form is shown here:

final String getName( )

Although not needed by the following program, you can set the name of a thread after it is created by using **setName( )**, which is shown here:

final void setName(String *threadName*)

Here, *threadName* specifies the name of the thread.

Here is the improved version of the preceding program:

```
// Improved MyThread.

class MyThread implements Runnable {
  int count;
  Thread thrd;   ◄──────── A reference to the thread is stored in thrd.

  // Construct a new thread.
  MyThread(String name) {
    thrd = new Thread(this, name);   ◄──── The thread is named when it is created.
    count = 0;
    thrd.start(); // start the thread   ◄──────── Begin executing the thread.
  }

  // Begin execution of new thread.
  public void run() {
    System.out.println(thrd.getName() + " starting.");
    try {
      do {
        Thread.sleep(500);
        System.out.println("In " + thrd.getName() +
                          ", count is " + count);
        count++;
      } while(count < 10);
    }
    catch(InterruptedException exc) {
      System.out.println(thrd.getName() + " interrupted.");
    }
    System.out.println(thrd.getName() + " terminating.");
  }
}

class UseThreadsImproved {
  public static void main(String args[]) {
```

```
      System.out.println("Main thread starting.");

      MyThread mt = new MyThread("Child #1");
      do {                          Now the thread starts when it is created.
        System.out.print(".");
        try {
          Thread.sleep(100);
        }
        catch(InterruptedException exc) {
          System.out.println("Main thread interrupted.");
        }
      } while (mt.count != 10);

      System.out.println("Main thread ending.");
    }
}
```

This version produces the same output as before. Notice that the thread is stored in **thrd** inside **MyThread**.

Progress Check

1. In what two ways can you create a class that can act as a thread?

2. What is the purpose of the **run( )** method defined by **Runnable**?

3. What does the **start( )** method defined by **Thread** do?

Project 11-1 Extending Thread

`ExtendThread.java`

Implementing **Runnable** is one way to create a class that can instantiate thread objects. Extending **Thread** is the other. In this project, you will see how to extend **Thread** by creating a program functionally identical to the **UseThreadsImproved** program.

(continued)

1. To create a thread, either implement **Runnable** or extend **Thread**.
2. The **run( )** method is the entry point to a thread.
3. The **start( )** method starts the execution of a thread.

When a class extends **Thread**, it must override the **run( )** method, which is the entry point for the new thread. It must also call **start( )** to begin execution of the new thread. It is possible to override other **Thread** methods, but doing so is not required.

Step by Step

1. Create a file called **ExtendThread.java**. Into this file, copy the code from the second threading example (**UseThreadsImproved.java**).

2. Change the declaration of **MyThread** so that it extends **Thread** rather than implementing **Runnable**, as shown here.

```
class MyThread extends Thread {
```

3. Remove this line:

```
Thread thrd;
```

The **thrd** variable is no longer needed since **MyThread** includes an instance of **Thread** and can refer to itself.

4. Change the **MyThread** constructor so that it looks like this:

```
// Construct a new thread.
MyThread(String name) {
  super(name); // name thread
  count = 0;
  start(); // start the thread
}
```

As you can see, first **super** is used to call this version of **Thread**'s constructor:

Thread(String *name*);

Here, *name* is the name of the thread.

5. Change **run( )** so it calls **getName( )** directly, without qualifying it with the **thrd** variable. It should look like this:

```
// Begin execution of new thread.
public void run() {
  System.out.println(getName() + " starting.");
  try {
    do {
      Thread.sleep(500);
      System.out.println("In " + getName() +
                         ", count is " + count);
```

```
      count++;
    } while(count < 10);
  }
  catch(InterruptedException exc) {
    System.out.println(getName() + " interrupted.");
  }
  System.out.println(getName() + " terminating.");
}
```

6. Here is the completed program that now extends **Thread** rather than implementing **Runnable**. The output is the same as before.

```
/*
   Project 11-1

   Extend Thread.
*/
class MyThread extends Thread {
  int count;

  // Construct a new thread.
  MyThread(String name) {
    super(name); // name thread
    count = 0;
    start(); // start the thread
  }

  // Begin execution of new thread.
  public void run() {
    System.out.println(getName() + " starting.");
    try {
      do {
        Thread.sleep(500);
        System.out.println("In " + getName() +
                            ", count is " + count);
        count++;
      } while(count < 10);
    }
    catch(InterruptedException exc) {
      System.out.println(getName() + " interrupted.");
    }
    System.out.println(getName() + " terminating.");
  }
}

class ExtendThread {
```

(continued)

```
      public static void main(String args[]) {
        System.out.println("Main thread starting.");

        MyThread mt = new MyThread("Child #1");

        do {
          System.out.print(".");
          try {
            Thread.sleep(100);
          }
          catch(InterruptedException exc) {
            System.out.println("Main thread interrupted.");
          }
        } while (mt.count != 10);

        System.out.println("Main thread ending.");
      }
    }
```

CRITICAL SKILL
11.4 Creating Multiple Threads

The preceding examples have created only one child thread. However, your program can spawn as many threads as it needs. For example, the following program creates three child threads:

```
// Create multiple threads.

class MyThread implements Runnable {
  int count;
  Thread thrd;

  // Construct a new thread.
  MyThread(String name) {
    thrd = new Thread(this, name);
    count = 0;
    thrd.start(); // start the thread
  }

  // Begin execution of new thread.
  public void run() {
    System.out.println(thrd.getName() + " starting.");
    try {
      do {
        Thread.sleep(500);
        System.out.println("In " + thrd.getName() +
                           ", count is " + count);
```

```
        count++;
      } while(count < 10);
    }
    catch(InterruptedException exc) {
      System.out.println(thrd.getName() + " interrupted.");
    }
    System.out.println(thrd.getName() + " terminating.");
  }
}

class MoreThreads {
  public static void main(String args[]) {
    System.out.println("Main thread starting.");

    MyThread mt1 = new MyThread("Child #1");
    MyThread mt2 = new MyThread("Child #2");  ◄──────── Create and start executing
    MyThread mt3 = new MyThread("Child #3");                three threads.

    do {
      System.out.print(".");
      try {
        Thread.sleep(100);
      }
      catch(InterruptedException exc) {
        System.out.println("Main thread interrupted.");
      }
    } while (mt1.count < 10 ||
             mt2.count < 10 ||
             mt3.count < 10);

    System.out.println("Main thread ending.");
  }
}
```

Ask the Expert

Q: **Why does Java have two ways to create child threads (by extending** Thread **or implementing** Runnable**) and which approach is better?**

A: The **Thread** class defines several methods that can be overridden by a derived class. Of these methods, the only one that *must* be overridden is **run( )**. This is, of course, the same method required when you implement **Runnable**. Some Java programmers feel that classes should be extended only when they are being enhanced or modified in some way. So, if you will not be overriding any of **Thread**'s other methods, it is probably best to simply implement **Runnable**. This is, of course, up to you.

Sample output from this program follows.

```
Main thread starting.
.Child #1 starting.
Child #2 starting.
Child #3 starting.
.....In Child #1, count is 0
In Child #2, count is 0
In Child #3, count is 0
.....In Child #1, count is 1
In Child #2, count is 1
In Child #3, count is 1
.....In Child #1, count is 2
In Child #2, count is 2
In Child #3, count is 2
.....In Child #1, count is 3
In Child #2, count is 3
In Child #3, count is 3
.....In Child #1, count is 4
In Child #2, count is 4
In Child #3, count is 4
.....In Child #1, count is 5
In Child #2, count is 5
In Child #3, count is 5
.....In Child #1, count is 6
In Child #2, count is 6
In Child #3, count is 6
.....In Child #1, count is 7
In Child #2, count is 7
In Child #3, count is 7
.....In Child #1, count is 8
In Child #2, count is 8
In Child #3, count is 8
.....In Child #1, count is 9
Child #1 terminating.
In Child #2, count is 9
Child #2 terminating.
In Child #3, count is 9
Child #3 terminating.
Main thread ending.
```

As you can see, once started, all three child threads share the CPU. Notice that the threads are started in the order in which they are created. However, this may not always be the case. Java is free to schedule the execution of threads in its own way. Of course, because of differences in timing or environment, the precise output from the program may differ, so don't be surprised if you see slightly different results when you try the program.

CRITICAL SKILL
11.5 Determining When a Thread Ends

It is often useful to know when a thread has ended. In the preceding examples, we accomplished this by watching the **count** variable, but this is, of course, hardly a satisfactory or generalizable solution. Fortunately, **Thread** provides two means by which you can determine if a thread has ended. First, you can call **isAlive( )** on the thread. Its general form is shown here:

final boolean isAlive( )

The **isAlive( )** method returns **true** if the thread upon which it is called is still running. It returns **false** otherwise. To try **isAlive( )**, substitute this version of **MoreThreads** for the one shown in the preceding program.

```
// Use isAlive().
class MoreThreads {
  public static void main(String args[]) {
    System.out.println("Main thread starting.");

    MyThread mt1 = new MyThread("Child #1");
    MyThread mt2 = new MyThread("Child #2");
    MyThread mt3 = new MyThread("Child #3");

    do {
      System.out.print(".");
      try {
        Thread.sleep(100);
      }
      catch(InterruptedException exc) {
        System.out.println("Main thread interrupted.");
      }
    } while (mt1.thrd.isAlive() ||
             mt2.thrd.isAlive() ||   ←——— This waits until all threads terminate.
             mt3.thrd.isAlive());

    System.out.println("Main thread ending.");
  }
}
```

This version produces the same output as before. The only difference is that it uses **isAlive( )** to wait for the child threads to terminate.

Another way to wait for a thread to finish is to call **join( )**, shown here:

final void join( ) throws InterruptedException

This method waits until the thread on which it is called terminates. Its name comes from the concept of the calling thread waiting until the specified thread *joins* it. Additional forms of **join( )** allow you to specify a maximum amount of time that you want to wait for the specified thread to terminate.

Here is a program that uses **join( )** to ensure that the main thread is the last to stop.

```
// Use join().

class MyThread implements Runnable {
  int count;
  Thread thrd;

  // Construct a new thread.
  MyThread(String name) {
    thrd = new Thread(this, name);
    count = 0;
    thrd.start(); // start the thread
  }

  // Begin execution of new thread.
  public void run() {
    System.out.println(thrd.getName() + " starting.");
    try {
      do {
        Thread.sleep(500);
        System.out.println("In " + thrd.getName() +
                           ", count is " + count);
        count++;
      } while(count < 10);
    }
    catch(InterruptedException exc) {
      System.out.println(thrd.getName() + " interrupted.");
    }
    System.out.println(thrd.getName() + " terminating.");
  }
}

class JoinThreads {
  public static void main(String args[]) {
    System.out.println("Main thread starting.");

    MyThread mt1 = new MyThread("Child #1");
    MyThread mt2 = new MyThread("Child #2");
    MyThread mt3 = new MyThread("Child #3");
```

```
    try {
      mt1.thrd.join();
      System.out.println("Child #1 joined.");
      mt2.thrd.join();
      System.out.println("Child #2 joined.");
      mt3.thrd.join();
      System.out.println("Child #3 joined.");
    }
    catch(InterruptedException exc) {
      System.out.println("Main thread interrupted.");
    }

    System.out.println("Main thread ending.");
  }
}
```

Wait until the specified thread ends.

Sample output from this program is shown here. Remember that when you try the program, your precise output may vary slightly.

```
Main thread starting.
Child #1 starting.
Child #2 starting.
Child #3 starting.
In Child #2, count is 0
In Child #1, count is 0
In Child #3, count is 0
In Child #2, count is 1
In Child #3, count is 1
In Child #1, count is 1
In Child #2, count is 2
In Child #1, count is 2
In Child #3, count is 2
In Child #2, count is 3
In Child #3, count is 3
In Child #1, count is 3
In Child #3, count is 4
In Child #2, count is 4
In Child #1, count is 4
In Child #3, count is 5
In Child #1, count is 5
In Child #2, count is 5
In Child #3, count is 6
In Child #2, count is 6
In Child #1, count is 6
In Child #3, count is 7
In Child #1, count is 7
```

```
In Child #2, count is 7
In Child #3, count is 8
In Child #2, count is 8
In Child #1, count is 8
In Child #3, count is 9
Child #3 terminating.
In Child #2, count is 9
Child #2 terminating.
In Child #1, count is 9
Child #1 terminating.
Child #1 joined.
Child #2 joined.
Child #3 joined.
Main thread ending.
```

As you can see, after the calls to **join( )** return, the threads have stopped executing.

Progress Check

1. What are the two ways in which you can determine whether a thread has ended?

2. Explain **join( )**.

Thread Priorities

Each thread has associated with it a priority setting. A thread's priority determines, in part, how much CPU time a thread receives relative to the other active threads. In general, low-priority threads receive little. High-priority threads receive a lot. As you might expect, how much CPU time a thread receives has profound impact on its execution characteristics and its interaction with other threads currently executing in the system.

It is important to understand that factors other than a thread's priority also affect how much CPU time a thread receives. For example, if a high-priority thread is waiting on some resource, perhaps for keyboard input, then it will be blocked, and a lower priority thread will run. However, when that high-priority thread gains access to the resource, it can preempt the low-priority thread and resume execution. Another factor that affects the scheduling of threads

---

1. To determine whether a thread has ended, you can call **isAlive( )** or use **join( )** to wait for the thread to join the calling thread.

2. The **join( )** method suspends execution of the calling thread until the thread on which **join( )** is called, ends.

is the way the operating system implements multitasking. (See "Ask the Expert," at the end of this section.) Thus, just because you give one thread a high priority and another a low priority does not necessarily mean that one thread will run faster or more often than the other. It's just that the high-priority thread has greater potential access to the CPU.

When a child thread is started, its priority setting is equal to that of its parent thread. You can change a thread's priority by calling **setPriority( )**, which is a member of **Thread**. This is its general form:

final void setPriority(int *level*)

Here, *level* specifies the new priority setting for the calling thread. The value of *level* must be within the range **MIN_PRIORITY** and **MAX_PRIORITY**. Currently, these values are 1 and 10, respectively. To return a thread to default priority, specify **NORM_PRIORITY**, which is currently 5. These priorities are defined as **static final** variables within **Thread**.

You can obtain the current priority setting by calling the **getPriority( )** method of **Thread**, shown here:

final int getPriority( )

The following example demonstrates two threads at different priorities. The threads are created as instances of **Priority**. The **run( )** method contains a loop that counts the number of iterations. The loop stops when either the count reaches 10,000,000 or the static variable **stop** is **true**. Initially, **stop** is set to **false**, but the first thread to finish counting sets **stop** to **true**. This causes the second thread to terminate with its next time slice. Each time through the loop the string in **currentName** is checked against the name of the executing thread. If they don't match, it means that a task-switch occurred. Each time a task-switch happens, the name of the new thread is displayed, and **currentName** is given the name of the new thread. This allows you to watch how often each thread has access to the CPU. After both threads stop, the number of iterations for each loop is displayed.

```
// Demonstrate thread priorities.

class Priority implements Runnable {
  int count;
  Thread thrd;

  static boolean stop = false;
  static String currentName;

  /* Construct a new thread. Notice that this
     constructor does not actually start the
     threads running. */
```

```
    Priority(String name) {
      thrd = new Thread(this, name);
      count = 0;
      currentName = name;
    }

    // Begin execution of new thread.
    public void run() {
      System.out.println(thrd.getName() + " starting.");
      do {
        count++;

        if(currentName.compareTo(thrd.getName()) != 0) {
          currentName = thrd.getName();
          System.out.println("In " + currentName);
        }

      } while(stop == false && count < 10000000);
      stop = true;

      System.out.println("\n" + thrd.getName() +
                         " terminating.");
    }
  }

  class PriorityDemo {
    public static void main(String args[]) {
      Priority mt1 = new Priority("High Priority");
      Priority mt2 = new Priority("Low Priority");

      // set the priorities
      mt1.thrd.setPriority(Thread.NORM_PRIORITY+2);
      mt2.thrd.setPriority(Thread.NORM_PRIORITY-2);

      // start the threads
      mt1.thrd.start();
      mt2.thrd.start();

      try {
        mt1.thrd.join();
        mt2.thrd.join();
      }
      catch(InterruptedException exc) {
        System.out.println("Main thread interrupted.");
      }
```

← The first thread to 10,000,000 stops all threads.

← Give **mt1** a higher priority than **mt2**.

```
        System.out.println("\nHigh priority thread counted to " +
                           mt1.count);
        System.out.println("Low priority thread counted to " +
                           mt2.count);
    }
}
```

Here is a sample run.

```
High Priority starting.
In High Priority
Low Priority starting.
In Low Priority
In High Priority

High Priority terminating.

Low Priority terminating.

High priority thread counted to 10000000
Low priority thread counted to 8183
```

In this run, the high-priority thread got a vast majority of the CPU time. Of course, the exact output produced by this program will depend upon the speed of your CPU, the operating system you are using, and the number of other tasks running in the system.

Ask the Expert

Q: Does the operating system's implementation of multitasking affect how much CPU time a thread receives?

A: Aside from a thread's priority setting, the most important factor affecting thread execution is the way the operating system implements multitasking and scheduling. Some operating systems use preemptive multitasking in which each thread receives a time slice, at least occasionally. Other systems use nonpreemptive scheduling in which one thread must yield execution before another thread will execute. In nonpreemptive systems, it is easy for one thread to dominate, preventing others from running.

Synchronization

When using multiple threads, it is sometimes necessary to coordinate the activities of two or more. The process by which this is achieved is called *synchronization*. The most common reason for synchronization is when two or more threads need access to a shared resource that can be used by only one thread at a time. For example, when one thread is writing to a file, a second thread must be prevented from doing so at the same time. Another reason for synchronization is when one thread is waiting for an event that is caused by another thread. In this case, there must be some means by which the first thread is held in a suspended state until the event has occurred. Then, the waiting thread must resume execution.

Key to synchronization in Java is the concept of the *monitor*, which controls access to an object. A monitor works by implementing the concept of a *lock*. When an object is locked by one thread, no other thread can gain access to the object. When the thread exits, the object is unlocked and is available for use by another thread.

All objects in Java have a monitor. This feature is built into the Java language, itself. Thus, all objects can be synchronized. Synchronization is supported by the keyword **synchronized** and a few well-defined methods that all objects have. Since synchronization was designed into Java from the start, it is much easier to use than you might first expect. In fact, for many programs, the synchronization of objects is almost transparent.

There are two ways that you can synchronize your code. Both involve the use of the **synchronized** keyword, and both are examined here.

Using Synchronized Methods

You can synchronize access to a method by modifying it with the **synchronized** keyword. When that method is called, the calling thread enters the object's monitor, which then locks the object. While locked, no other thread can enter the method, or enter any other synchronized method defined by the object. When the thread returns from the method, the monitor unlocks the object, allowing it to be used by the next thread. Thus, synchronization is achieved with virtually no programming effort on your part.

The following program demonstrates synchronization by controlling access to a method called **sumArray( )**, which sums the elements of an integer array.

```
// Use synchronize to control access.

class SumArray {
  private int sum;

  synchronized int sumArray(int nums[]) {   ◄——— sumArray( ) is synchronized.
```

```
      sum = 0; // reset sum

    for(int i=0; i<nums.length; i++) {
      sum += nums[i];
      System.out.println("Running total for " +
              Thread.currentThread().getName() +
              " is " + sum);
      try {
        Thread.sleep(10); // allow task-switch
      }
      catch(InterruptedException exc) {
        System.out.println("Main thread interrupted.");
      }
    }
    return sum;
  }
}

class MyThread implements Runnable {
  Thread thrd;
  static SumArray sa = new SumArray();
  int a[];
  int answer;

  // Construct a new thread.
  MyThread(String name, int nums[]) {
    thrd = new Thread(this, name);
    a = nums;
    thrd.start(); // start the thread
  }

  // Begin execution of new thread.
  public void run() {
    int sum;

    System.out.println(thrd.getName() + " starting.");

    answer = sa.sumArray(a);
    System.out.println("Sum for " + thrd.getName() +
                    " is " + answer);

    System.out.println(thrd.getName() + " terminating.");
  }
}

class Sync {
  public static void main(String args[]) {
```

```
    int a[] = {1, 2, 3, 4, 5};

    MyThread mt1 = new MyThread("Child #1", a);
    MyThread mt2 = new MyThread("Child #2", a);
  }
}
```

The output from the program is shown here. (The precise output may differ on your computer.)

```
Child #1 starting.
Running total for Child #1 is 1
Child #2 starting.
Running total for Child #1 is 3
Running total for Child #1 is 6
Running total for Child #1 is 10
Running total for Child #1 is 15
Sum for Child #1 is 15
Child #1 terminating.
Running total for Child #2 is 1
Running total for Child #2 is 3
Running total for Child #2 is 6
Running total for Child #2 is 10
Running total for Child #2 is 15
Sum for Child #2 is 15
Child #2 terminating.
```

Let's examine this program in detail. The program creates three classes. The first is **SumArray**. It contains the method **sumArray( )**, which sums an integer array. The second class is **MyThread**, which uses a **static** object of type **SumArray** to obtain the sum of an integer array. This object is called **sa** and because it is **static**, there is only one copy of it that is shared by all instances of **MyThread**. Finally, the class **Sync** creates two threads and has each compute the sum of an integer array.

Inside **sumArray( )**, **sleep( )** is called to purposely allow a task switch to occur, if one can—but it can't. Because **sumArray( )** is synchronized, it can be used by only one thread at a time. Thus, when the second child thread begins execution, it does not enter **sumArray( )** until after the first child thread is done with it. This ensures that the correct result is produced.

To fully understand the effects of **synchronized**, try removing it from the declaration of **sumArray( )**. After doing this, **sumArray( )** is no longer synchronized, and any number of threads may use it concurrently. The problem with this is that the running total is stored in **sum**, which will be changed by each thread that calls **sumArray( )** through the **static** object **sa**. Thus, when two threads call **sa.sumArray( )** at the same time, incorrect results are produced because **sum** reflects the summation of both threads, mixed together. For example, here is sample output from the program after **synchronized** has been removed from **sumArray( )**'s declaration. (The precise output may differ on your computer.)

```
Child #1 starting.
Running total for Child #1 is 1
Child #2 starting.
Running total for Child #2 is 1
Running total for Child #1 is 3
Running total for Child #2 is 5
Running total for Child #2 is 8
Running total for Child #1 is 11
Running total for Child #2 is 15
Running total for Child #1 is 19
Running total for Child #2 is 24
Sum for Child #2 is 24
Child #2 terminating.
Running total for Child #1 is 29
Sum for Child #1 is 29
Child #1 terminating.
```

As the output shows, both child threads are calling **sa.sumArray( )** concurrently, and the value of **sum** is corrupted.

Before moving on, let's review the key points of a synchronized method:

● A synchronized method is created by preceding its declaration with **synchronized**.

● For any given object, once a synchronized method has been called, the object is locked and no synchronized methods on the same object can be used by another thread of execution.

● Other threads trying to call an in-use synchronized object will enter a wait state until the object is unlocked.

● When a thread leaves the synchronized method, the object is unlocked.

CRITICAL SKILL
11.9 The synchronized Statement

Although creating **synchronized** methods within classes that you create is an easy and effective means of achieving synchronization, it will not work in all cases. For example, you might want to synchronize access to some method that is not modified by **synchronized**. This can occur because you want to use a class that was not created by you but by a third party, and you do not have access to the source code. Thus, it is not possible for you to add **synchronized** to the appropriate methods within the class. How can access to an object of this class be synchronized? Fortunately, the solution to this problem is quite easy: You simply put calls to the methods defined by this class inside a **synchronized** block.

This is the general form of a **synchronized** block:

```
synchronized(objref) {
  // statements to be synchronized
}
```

Here, *objref* is a reference to the object being synchronized. Once a synchronized block has been entered, no other thread can call a synchronized method on *objref* until the block has been exited.

For example, another way to synchronize calls to **sumArray( )** is to call it from within a synchronized block, as shown in this version of the program.

```
// Use a synchronized block to control access to SumArray.
class SumArray {
  private int sum;

  int sumArray(int nums[]) {          Here, sumArray( ) is
    sum = 0; // reset sum            not synchronized.

    for(int i=0; i<nums.length; i++) {
      sum += nums[i];
      System.out.println("Running total for " +
              Thread.currentThread().getName() +
              " is " + sum);
      try {
        Thread.sleep(10); // allow task-switch
      }
      catch(InterruptedException exc) {
        System.out.println("Main thread interrupted.");
      }
    }
    return sum;
  }
}

class MyThread implements Runnable {
  Thread thrd;
  static SumArray sa = new SumArray();
  int a[];
  int answer;
```

```
   // Construct a new thread.
   MyThread(String name, int nums[]) {
     thrd = new Thread(this, name);
     a = nums;
     thrd.start(); // start the thread
   }

   // Begin execution of new thread.
   public void run() {
     int sum;

     System.out.println(thrd.getName() + " starting.");

     // synchronize calls to sumArray()
     synchronized(sa) {
       answer = sa.sumArray(a);
     }
     System.out.println("Sum for " + thrd.getName() +
                        " is " + answer);

     System.out.println(thrd.getName() + " terminating.");
   }
}

class Sync {
  public static void main(String args[]) {
    int a[] = {1, 2, 3, 4, 5};

    MyThread mt1 = new MyThread("Child #1", a);
    MyThread mt2 = new MyThread("Child #2", a);

    try {
      mt1.thrd.join();
      mt2.thrd.join();
    } catch(InterruptedException exc) {
      System.out.println("Main thread interrupted.");
    }
  }
}
```

Here, calls to **sumArray( )** on **sa** are synchronized.

This version produces the same, correct output as the one shown earlier that uses a synchronized method.

Progress Check

1. How do you set a thread's priority?

2. How do you restrict access to an object to one thread at a time?

3. The **synchronized** keyword can be used to modify a method or to create a _____ block.

CRITICAL SKILL
11.10 # Thread Communication Using notify( ), wait( ), and notifyAll( )

Consider the following situation. A thread called T is executing inside a synchronized method and needs access to a resource called R that is temporarily unavailable. What should T do? If T enters some form of polling loop that waits for R, T ties up the object, preventing other threads' access to it. This is a less than optimal solution because it partially defeats the advantages of programming for a multithreaded environment. A better solution is to have T temporarily relinquish control of the object, allowing another thread to run. When R becomes available, T can be notified and resume execution. Such an approach relies upon some form of interthread communication in which one thread can notify another that it is blocked and be notified that it can resume execution. Java supports interthread communication with the **wait( )**, **notify( )**, and **notifyAll( )** methods.

The **wait( )**, **notify( )**, and **notifyAll( )** methods are part of all objects because they are implemented by the **Object** class. These methods can only be called from within a **synchronized** context. Here is how they are used. When a thread is temporarily blocked from running, it calls **wait( )**. This causes the thread to go to sleep and the monitor for that object to be released, allowing another thread to use the object. At a later point, the sleeping thread is awakened when some other thread enters the same monitor and calls **notify( )**, or **notifyAll( )**.

Following are the various forms of **wait( )** defined by **Object**.

final void wait( ) throws InterruptedException

final void wait(long *millis*) throws InterruptedException

final void wait(long *millis,* int *nanos*) throws InterruptedException

---

1. To set a thread's priority, call **setPriority( )**.
2. To restrict access to an object to one thread at a time, use the **synchronized** keyword.
3. synchronized

The first form waits until notified. The second form waits until notified or until the specified period of milliseconds has expired. The third form allows you to specify the wait period in terms of nanoseconds.

Here are the general forms for **notify( )** and **notifyAll( )**.

final void notify( )

final void notifyAll( )

A call to **notify( )** resumes one waiting thread. A call to **notifyAll( )** notifies all threads, with the highest priority thread gaining access to the object.

Before looking at an example that uses **wait( )**, an important point needs to be made. Although **wait( )** normally waits until **notify( )** or **notifyAll( )** is called, there is a possibility that in very rare cases the waiting thread could be awakened due to a *spurious wakeup*. The conditions that lead to a spurious wakeup are complex and beyond the scope of this book. However, Sun recommends that because of the remote possibility of a spurious wakeup, calls to **wait( )** should take place within a loop that checks the condition on which the thread is waiting. The following example shows this technique.

An Example That Uses wait( ) and notify( )

To understand the need for and the application of **wait( )** and **notify( )**, we will create a program that simulates the ticking of a clock by displaying the words "tick" and "tock" on the screen. To accomplish this, we will create a class called **TickTock** that contains two methods: **tick( )** and **tock( )**. The **tick( )** method displays the word "Tick", and **tock( )** displays "Tock". To run the clock, two threads are created, one that calls **tick( )** and one that calls **tock( )**. The goal is to make the two threads execute in a way that the output from the program displays a consistent "Tick Tock"—that is, a repeated pattern of one tick followed by one tock.

```
// Use wait() and notify() to create a ticking clock.

class TickTock {

  String state; // contains the state of the clock

  synchronized void tick(boolean running) {
    if(!running) { // stop the clock
      state = "ticked";
      notify(); // notify any waiting threads
      return;
    }

    System.out.print("Tick ");

    state = "ticked"; // set the current state to ticked
```

```
    notify(); // let tock() run  ◄──────── tick() notifies tock().
    try {
      while(!state.equals("tocked"))
        wait(); // wait for tock() to complete  ◄──────── tick() waits for tock().
    }
    catch(InterruptedException exc) {
      System.out.println("Thread interrupted.");
    }
  }

  synchronized void tock(boolean running) {
    if(!running) { // stop the clock
      state = "tocked";
      notify(); // notify any waiting threads
      return;
    }

    System.out.println("Tock");

    state = "tocked"; // set the current state to tocked

    notify(); // let tick() run  ◄──────── tock() notifies tick().
    try {
      while(!state.equals("ticked"))
        wait(); // wait for tick to complete  ◄──────── tock() waits for tick().
    }
    catch(InterruptedException exc) {
      System.out.println("Thread interrupted.");
    }
  }
}

class MyThread implements Runnable {
  Thread thrd;
  TickTock ttOb;

  // Construct a new thread.
  MyThread(String name, TickTock tt) {
    thrd = new Thread(this, name);
    ttOb = tt;
    thrd.start(); // start the thread
  }

  // Begin execution of new thread.
  public void run() {

    if(thrd.getName().compareTo("Tick") == 0) {
      for(int i=0; i<5; i++) ttOb.tick(true);
```

```
        ttOb.tick(false);
      }
      else {
        for(int i=0; i<5; i++) ttOb.tock(true);
        ttOb.tock(false);
      }
    }
  }
}

class ThreadCom {
  public static void main(String args[]) {
    TickTock tt = new TickTock();
    MyThread mt1 = new MyThread("Tick", tt);
    MyThread mt2 = new MyThread("Tock", tt);

    try {
      mt1.thrd.join();
      mt2.thrd.join();
    } catch(InterruptedException exc) {
      System.out.println("Main thread interrupted.");
    }
  }
}
```

Here is the output produced by the program:

```
Tick Tock
Tick Tock
Tick Tock
Tick Tock
Tick Tock
```

Let's take a close look at this program. The heart of the clock is the **TickTock** class. It contains two methods, **tick( )** and **tock( )**, which communicate with each other to ensure that a Tick is always followed by a Tock, which is always followed by a Tick, and so on. Notice the **state** field. When the clock is running, **state** will hold either the string "ticked" or "tocked", which indicates the current state of the clock. In **main( )**, a **TickTock** object called **tt** is created, and this object is used to start two threads of execution.

The threads are based on objects of type **MyThread**. The **MyThread** constructor is passed two arguments. The first becomes the name of the thread. This will be either "Tick" or "Tock". The second is a reference to the **TickTock** object, which is **tt** in this case. Inside the **run( )** method of **MyThread**, if the name of the thread is "Tick", then calls to **tick( )** are made. If the name of the thread is "Tock", then the **tock( )** method is called. Five calls that pass **true** as an argument are made to each method. The clock runs as long as **true** is passed. A final call that passes **false** to each method stops the clock.

The most important part of the program is found in the **tick( )** and **tock( )** methods of
TickTock. We will begin with the **tick( )** method, which, for convenience, is shown here.

```
synchronized void tick(boolean running) {
  if(!running) { // stop the clock
    state = "ticked";
    notify(); // notify any waiting threads
    return;
  }

  System.out.print("Tick ");

  state = "ticked"; // set the current state to ticked

  notify(); // let tock() run
  try {
    while(!state.equals("tocked"))
      wait(); // wait for tock() to complete
  }
  catch(InterruptedException exc) {
    System.out.println("Thread interrupted.");
  }
}
```

First, notice that **tick( )** is modified by **synchronized**. Remember, **wait( )** and **notify( )**
apply only to synchronized methods. The method begins by checking the value of the
running parameter. This parameter is used to provide a clean shutdown of the clock. If
it is **false**, then the clock has been stopped. If this is the case, **state** is set to "ticked" and
a call to **notify( )** is made to enable any waiting thread to run. We will return to this point
in a moment.

Assuming that the clock is running when **tick( )** executes, the word "Tick" is displayed,
state is set to "ticked", and then a call to **notify( )** takes place. The call to **notify( )** allows a
thread waiting on the same object to run. Next, **wait( )** is called within a **while** loop. The call
to **wait( )** causes **tick( )** to suspend until another thread calls **notify( )**. Therefore, the loop will
not iterate until another thread calls **notify( )** on the same object. As a result, when **tick( )** is
called, it displays one "Tick", lets another thread run, and then suspends.

The **while** loop that calls **wait( )** checks the value of **state**, waiting for it to equal "tocked",
which will be the case only after the **tock( )** method executes. As explained, using a **while** loop
to check this condition prevents a spurious wakeup from incorrectly restarting the thread. If
state does not equal "tocked" when **wait( )** returns, it means that a spurious wakeup occurred,
and **wait( )** is simply called again.

The **tock( )** method is an exact copy of **tick( )** except that it displays "Tock" and sets **state** to "tocked". Thus, when entered, it displays "Tock", calls **notify( )**, and then waits. When viewed as a pair, a call to **tick( )** can only be followed by a call to **tock( )**, which can only be followed by a call to **tick( )**, and so on. Therefore, the two methods are mutually synchronized.

The reason for the call to **notify( )** when the clock is stopped is to allow a final call to **wait( )** to succeed. Remember, both **tick( )** and **tock( )** execute a call to **wait( )** after displaying their message. The problem is that when the clock is stopped, one of the methods will still be waiting. Thus, a final call to **notify( )** is required in order for the waiting method to run. As an experiment, try removing this call to **notify( )** and watch what happens. As you will see, the program will "hang," and you will need to press CONTROL-C to exit. The reason for this is that when the final call to **tock( )** calls **wait( )**, there is no corresponding call to **notify( )** that lets **tock( )** conclude. Thus, **tock( )** just sits there, waiting forever.

Before moving on, if you have any doubt that the calls to **wait( )** and **notify( )** are actually needed to make the "clock" run right, substitute this version of **TickTock** into the preceding program. It has all calls to **wait( )** and **notify( )** removed.

```
// No calls to wait() or notify().
class TickTock {

  String state; // contains the state of the clock

  synchronized void tick(boolean running) {
    if(!running) { // stop the clock
      state = "ticked";
      return;
    }

    System.out.print("Tick ");

    state = "ticked"; // set the current state to ticked
  }

  synchronized void tock(boolean running) {
    if(!running) { // stop the clock
      state = "tocked";
      return;
    }

    System.out.println("Tock");

    state = "tocked"; // set the current state to tocked
  }
}
```

After the substitution, the output produced by the program will look like this:

```
Tick Tick Tick Tick Tick Tock
Tock
Tock
Tock
Tock
```

Clearly, the **tick( )** and **tock( )** methods are no longer working together!

Progress Check

1. What methods support interthread communication?

2. Do all objects support interthread communication?

3. What happens when **wait( )** is called?

Ask the Expert

Q: I have heard the term *deadlock* applied to misbehaving multithreaded programs. What is it, and how can I avoid it?

A: Deadlock is, as the name implies, a situation in which one thread is waiting for another thread to do something, but that other thread is waiting on the first. Thus, both threads are suspended, waiting on each other, and neither executes. This situation is analogous to two overly polite people, both insisting that the other step through a door first!

Avoiding deadlock seems easy, but it's not. For example, deadlock can occur in roundabout ways. The cause of the deadlock often is not readily understood just by looking at the source code to the program because concurrently executing threads can interact in complex ways at run time. To avoid deadlock, careful programming and thorough testing is required. Remember, if a multithreaded program occasionally "hangs," deadlock is the likely cause.

---

1. The interthread communication methods are **wait( )**, **notify( )**, and **notifyAll( )**.

2. Yes, all objects support interthread communication because this support is part of **Object**.

3. When **wait( )** is called, the calling thread relinquishes control of the object and suspends until it receives a notification.

CRITICAL SKILL

Suspending, Resuming, and Stopping Threads

It is sometimes useful to suspend execution of a thread. For example, a separate thread can be used to display the time of day. If the user does not desire a clock, then its thread can be suspended. Whatever the case, it is a simple matter to suspend a thread. Once suspended, it is also a simple matter to restart the thread.

The mechanisms to suspend, stop, and resume threads differ between early versions of Java and more modern versions, beginning with Java 2. Prior to Java 2, a program used **suspend( )**, **resume( )**, and **stop( )**, which are methods defined by **Thread**, to pause, restart, and stop the execution of a thread. They have the following forms:

final void resume( )

final void suspend( )

final void stop( )

While these methods seem to be a perfectly reasonable and convenient approach to managing the execution of threads, they must no longer be used. Here's why. The **suspend( )** method of the **Thread** class was deprecated by Java 2. This was done because **suspend( )** can sometimes cause serious problems that involve deadlock. The **resume( )** method is also deprecated. It does not cause problems but cannot be used without the **suspend( )** method as its counterpart. The **stop( )** method of the **Thread** class was also deprecated by Java 2. This was done because this method too can sometimes cause serious problems.

Since you cannot now use the **suspend( )**, **resume( )**, or **stop( )** methods to control a thread, you might at first be thinking that there is no way to pause, restart, or terminate a thread. But, fortunately, this is not true. Instead, a thread must be designed so that the **run( )** method periodically checks to determine if that thread should suspend, resume, or stop its own execution. Typically, this is accomplished by establishing two flag variables: one for suspend and resume, and one for stop. For suspend and resume, as long as the flag is set to "running," the **run( )** method must continue to let the thread execute. If this variable is set to "suspend," the thread must pause. For the stop flag, if it is set to "stop," the thread must terminate.

The following example shows one way to implement your own versions of **suspend( )**, **resume( )**, and **stop( )**.

```
// Suspending, resuming, and stopping a thread.

class MyThread implements Runnable {
  Thread thrd;
```

```
    volatile boolean suspended;  ←——— Suspends thread when true.
    volatile boolean stopped;  ←——— Stops thread when true.

MyThread(String name) {
  thrd = new Thread(this, name);
  suspended = false;
  stopped = false;
  thrd.start();
}

// This is the entry point for thread.
public void run() {
  System.out.println(thrd.getName() + " starting.");
  try {
    for(int i = 1; i < 1000; i++) {
      System.out.print(i + " ");
      if((i%10)==0) {
        System.out.println();
        Thread.sleep(250);
      }

      // Use synchronized block to check suspended and stopped.
      synchronized(this) {  ←
        while(suspended) {
          wait();                    This synchronized block checks
        }                            suspended and stopped.
        if(stopped) break;
      }
    }
  } catch (InterruptedException exc) {
    System.out.println(thrd.getName() + " interrupted.");
  }
  System.out.println(thrd.getName() + " exiting.");
}

// Stop the thread.
synchronized void mystop() {
  stopped = true;

 // The following lets a suspended thread be stopped.
  suspended = false;
  notify();
}

// Suspend the thread.
synchronized void mysuspend() {
  suspended = true;
}
```

```java
    // Resume the thread.
    synchronized void myresume() {
      suspended = false;
      notify();
    }
}

class Suspend {
  public static void main(String args[]) {
    MyThread ob1 = new MyThread("My Thread");

    try {
      Thread.sleep(1000); // let ob1 thread start executing

      ob1.mysuspend();
      System.out.println("Suspending thread.");
      Thread.sleep(1000);

      ob1.myresume();
      System.out.println("Resuming thread.");
      Thread.sleep(1000);


      ob1.mysuspend();
      System.out.println("Suspending thread.");
      Thread.sleep(1000);

      ob1.myresume();
      System.out.println("Resuming thread.");
      Thread.sleep(1000);

      ob1.mysuspend();
      System.out.println("Stopping thread.");
      ob1.mystop();
    } catch (InterruptedException e) {
      System.out.println("Main thread Interrupted");
    }

    // wait for thread to finish
    try {
      ob1.thrd.join();
    } catch (InterruptedException e) {
      System.out.println("Main thread Interrupted");
    }

    System.out.println("Main thread exiting.");
  }
}
```

Sample output from this program is shown here. (Your output may differ slightly.)

```
My Thread starting.
1 2 3 4 5 6 7 8 9 10
11 12 13 14 15 16 17 18 19 20
21 22 23 24 25 26 27 28 29 30
31 32 33 34 35 36 37 38 39 40
Suspending thread.
Resuming thread.
41 42 43 44 45 46 47 48 49 50
51 52 53 54 55 56 57 58 59 60
61 62 63 64 65 66 67 68 69 70
71 72 73 74 75 76 77 78 79 80
Suspending thread.
Resuming thread.
81 82 83 84 85 86 87 88 89 90
91 92 93 94 95 96 97 98 99 100
101 102 103 104 105 106 107 108 109 110
111 112 113 114 115 116 117 118 119 120
Stopping thread.
My Thread exiting.
Main thread exiting.
```

Here is how the program works. The thread class **MyThread** defines two Boolean variables, **suspended** and **stopped**, which govern the suspension and termination of a thread. Both are initialized to **false** by the constructor. The **run( )** method contains a **synchronized** statement block that checks **suspended**. If that variable is **true**, the **wait( )** method is invoked to suspend the execution of the thread. To suspend execution of the thread, call **mysuspend( )**, which sets **suspended** to **true**. To resume execution, call **myresume( )**, which sets **suspended** to **false** and invokes **notify( )** to restart the thread.

Ask the Expert

Q: Multithreading seems like a great way to improve the efficiency of my programs. Can you give me any tips on effectively using it?

A: The key to effectively utilizing multithreading is to think concurrently rather than serially. For example, when you have two subsystems within a program that are fully independent of each other, consider making them into individual threads. A word of caution is in order, however. If you create too many threads, you can actually degrade the performance of your program rather than enhance it. Remember, overhead is associated with context switching. If you create too many threads, more CPU time will be spent changing contexts than in executing your program!

To stop the thread, call **mystop( )**, which sets **stopped** to **true**. In addition, **mystop( )** sets **suspended** to **false** and then calls **notify( )**. These steps are necessary to stop a suspended thread.

One other note about the preceding program. Notice that **suspended** and **stopped** are preceded by the keyword **volatile**. The **volatile** modifier is another of Java's keywords, and is discussed in Module 14. Briefly, it tells the compiler that a variable can be changed unexpectedly by other parts of your program, such as another thread.

Project 11-2   Using the Main Thread

`UseMain.java`

All Java programs have at least one thread of execution, called the *main thread*, which is given to the program automatically when it begins running. So far, we have been taking the main thread for granted. In this project, you will see that the main thread can be handled just like all other threads.

Step by Step

1. Create a file called **UseMain.java**.

2. To access the main thread, you must obtain a **Thread** object that refers to it. You do this by calling the **currentThread( )** method, which is a **static** member of **Thread**. Its general form is shown here:

   static Thread currentThread( )

   This method returns a reference to the thread in which it is called. Therefore, if you call **currentThread( )** while execution is inside the main thread, you will obtain a reference to the main thread. Once you have this reference, you can control the main thread just like any other thread.

3. Enter the following program into the file. It obtains a reference to the main thread, and then gets and sets the main thread's name and priority.

```
/*
   Project 11-2

   Controlling the main thread.
*/

class UseMain {
  public static void main(String args[]) {
    Thread thrd;
```

(continued)

```
    // Get the main thread.
    thrd = Thread.currentThread();

    // Display main thread's name.
    System.out.println("Main thread is called: " +
                        thrd.getName());

    // Display main thread's priority.
    System.out.println("Priority: " +
                        thrd.getPriority());

    System.out.println();

    // Set the name and priority.
    System.out.println("Setting name and priority.\n");
    thrd.setName("Thread #1");
    thrd.setPriority(Thread.NORM_PRIORITY+3);

    System.out.println("Main thread is now called: " +
                        thrd.getName());

    System.out.println("Priority is now: " +
                        thrd.getPriority());
  }
}
```

4. The output from the program is shown here.

```
Main thread is called: main
Priority: 5

Setting name and priority.

Main thread is now called: Thread #1
Priority is now: 8
```

5. You need to be careful about what operations you perform on the main thread. For example, if you add the following code to the end of **main( )**, the program will never terminate because it will be waiting for the main thread to end!

```
try {
   thrd.join();
} catch(InterruptedException exc) {
  System.out.println("Interrupted");
}
```

Module 11 Mastery Check

1. Why does Java's multithreading capability enable you to write more efficient programs?

2. Multithreading is supported by the _____ class and the _____ interface.

3. When creating a runnable object, why might you want to extend **Thread** rather than implement **Runnable**?

4. Show how to use **join( )** to wait for a thread object called **MyThrd** to end.

5. Show how to set a thread called **MyThrd** to three levels above normal priority.

6. What is the effect of adding the **synchronized** keyword to a method?

7. The **wait( )** and **notify( )** methods are used to perform _____.

8. Change the **TickTock** class so that it actually keeps time. That is, have each tick take one half second, and each tock take one half second. Thus, each tick-tock will take one second. (Don't worry about the time it takes to switch tasks, etc.)

9. Why can't you use **suspend( )**, **resume( )**, and **stop( )** for new programs?

10. What method defined by **Thread** obtains the name of a thread?

11. What does **isAlive( )** return?

12. On your own, try adding synchronization to the **Queue** class developed in previous modules so that it is safe for multithreaded use.

Module 12

Enumerations, Autoboxing, and Static Import

449

In late 2004 a major change took place in the Java language. These changes were part of the J2SE 5 (JDK 5) release. Prior to J2SE 5, the Java language (that is, its keywords, syntax, and semantics) was essentially the same as the original version of Java. Earlier revisions had added a few new features, but none had fundamentally changed the language. However, the release of J2SE 5 was very different. It included several very significant new features that profoundly altered the character and scope of Java. They are shown here:

- Generics

- Enumerations

- Autoboxing/unboxing

- The enhanced **for** loop

- Variable-length arguments (varargs)

- Static Import

- Annotations (Metadata)

Features such as enumerations and autoboxing/unboxing answer long-standing needs. Others, such as generics and annotations, broke new ground. In both cases, these new features have fundamentally recast Java, and their effects continue to be felt in the latest version: Java SE 6. Because the existing base of Java code is so large, don't be surprised if you often see code that does not make use of them. However, these changes significantly impact the way that new Java code is written. They are features that all Java programmers should master.

Two of these new features, the enhanced **for** loop and varargs, have already been discussed. This module examines in detail enumerations, autoboxing, and static import. An overview of annotations ends the module. Module 13 discusses generics.

CAUTION

If you are using an older version of Java that predates the J2SE 5 release, you will not be able to use the features described here and in Module 13.

CRITICAL SKILL
12.1 Enumerations

Although the enumeration is a common programming feature that is found in many other computer languages, it was not part of the original specification for Java. One reason for this is that the enumeration is technically a convenience, rather than a necessity. However, over the years, many programmers have wanted Java to support enumerations because they offer an elegant, structured solution to a variety of programming tasks. This request was granted by the release of J2SE 5, which added enumerations to Java.

In its simplest form, an *enumeration* is a list of named constants that define a new data type. An object of an enumeration type can hold only the values that are defined by the list. Thus, an enumeration gives you a way to precisely define a new type of data that has a fixed number of valid values.

Enumerations are common in everyday life. For example, an enumeration of the coins used in the United States is penny, nickel, dime, quarter, half-dollar, and dollar. An enumeration of the months in the year consists of the names January through December. An enumeration of the days of the week is Sunday, Monday, Tuesday, Wednesday, Thursday, Friday, and Saturday.

From a programming perspective, enumerations are useful whenever you need to define a set of values that represent a collection of items. For example, you might use an enumeration to represent a set of status codes, such as success, waiting, failed, and retrying, which indicate the progress of some action. In the past, such values were defined as **final** variables, but enumerations offer a much more structured approach.

Enumeration Fundamentals

An enumeration is created using the **enum** keyword. For example, here is a simple enumeration that lists various forms of transportation:

```
// An enumeration of transportation.
enum Transport {
  CAR, TRUCK, AIRPLANE, TRAIN, BOAT
}
```

The identifiers **CAR**, **TRUCK**, and so on, are called *enumeration constants*. Each is implicitly declared as a public, static member of **Transport**. Furthermore, the enumeration constants' type is the type of the enumeration in which the constants are declared, which is **Transport** in this case. Thus, in the language of Java, these constants are called *self-typed*, where "self" refers to the enclosing enumeration.

Once you have defined an enumeration, you can create a variable of that type. However, even though enumerations define a class type, you do not instantiate an **enum** using **new**. Instead, you declare and use an enumeration variable in much the same way that you do one of the primitive types. For example, this declares **tp** as a variable of enumeration type **Transport**:

```
Transport tp;
```

Because **tp** is of type **Transport**, the only values that it can be assigned are those defined by the enumeration. For example, this assigns **tp** the value **AIRPLANE**:

```
tp = Transport.AIRPLANE;
```

Notice that the symbol **AIRPLANE** is qualified by **Transport**.

Two enumeration constants can be compared for equality by using the == relational operator. For example, this statement compares the value in **tp** with the **TRAIN** constant:

```
if(tp == Transport.TRAIN) // ...
```

An enumeration value can also be used to control a **switch** statement. Of course, all of the **case** statements must use constants from the same **enum** as that used by the **switch** expression. For example, this **switch** is perfectly valid:

```
// Use an enum to control a switch statement.
switch(tp) {
  case CAR:
    // ...
  case TRUCK:
    // ...
```

Notice that in the **case** statements, the names of the enumeration constants are used without being qualified by their enumeration type name. That is, **TRUCK**, not **Transport.TRUCK**, is used. This is because the type of the enumeration in the **switch** expression has already implicitly specified the **enum** type of the **case** constants. There is no need to qualify the constants in the **case** statements with their **enum** type name. In fact, attempting to do so will cause a compilation error.

When an enumeration constant is displayed, such as in a **println( )** statement, its name is output. For example, given this statement:

```
System.out.println(Transport.BOAT);
```

the name **BOAT** is displayed.

The following program puts together all of the pieces and demonstrates the **Transport** enumeration.

```
// An enumeration of Transport varieties.
enum Transport {
  CAR, TRUCK, AIRPLANE, TRAIN, BOAT    ◄──────── Declare an enumeration.
}

class EnumDemo {
  public static void main(String args[])
  {
    Transport tp;   ◄──────── Declare a Transport reference.

    tp = Transport.AIRPLANE;   ◄──────── Assign tp the constant AIRPLANE.

    // Output an enum value.
```

```
      System.out.println("Value of tp: " + tp);
      System.out.println();

      tp = Transport.TRAIN;

      // Compare two enum values.
      if(tp == Transport.TRAIN)
        System.out.println("tp contains TRAIN.\n");

      // Use an enum to control a switch statement.
      switch(tp) {
        case CAR:
          System.out.println("A car carries people.");
          break;
        case TRUCK:
          System.out.println("A truck carries freight.");
          break;
        case AIRPLANE:
          System.out.println("An airplane flies.");
          break;
        case TRAIN:
          System.out.println("A train runs on rails.");
          break;
        case BOAT:
          System.out.println("A boat sails on water.");
          break;
      }
    }
  }
}
```

Compare two **Transport** objects for equality.

Use an enumeration to control a **switch** statement.

The output from the program is shown here:

```
Value of tp: AIRPLANE

tp contains TRAIN.

A train runs on rails.
```

Before moving on, it's necessary to make one stylistic point. The constants in **Transport** use uppercase. (Thus, **CAR**, not **car**, is used.) However, the use of uppercase is not required. In other words, there is no rule that requires enumeration constants to be in uppercase. Because enumerations often replace **final** variables, which have traditionally used uppercase, some programmers believe that uppercasing enumeration constants is also appropriate. There are, of course, other viewpoints and styles. The examples in this book will use uppercase for enumeration constants, for consistency.

Progress Check

1. An enumeration defines a list of _____ constants.

2. What keyword declares an enumeration?

3. Given

   ```
   enum Directions {
     LEFT, RIGHT, UP, DOWN
   }
   ```

   What is the data type of **UP**?

CRITICAL SKILL
12.2 # Java Enumerations Are Class Types

Although the preceding examples show the mechanics of creating and using an enumeration, they don't show all of its capabilities. Unlike the way enumerations are implemented in many other languages, *Java implements enumerations as class types*. Although you don't instantiate an **enum** using **new**, it otherwise acts much like other classes. The fact that **enum** defines a class enables the Java enumeration to have powers that enumerations in other languages do not. For example, you can give it constructors, add instance variables and methods, and even implement interfaces.

CRITICAL SKILL
12.3 # The values( ) and valueOf( ) Methods

All enumerations automatically have two predefined methods: **values( )** and **valueOf( )**. Their general forms are shown here:

public static *enum-type*[ ] values( )

public static *enum-type* valueOf(String *str*)

The **values( )** method returns an array that contains a list of the enumeration constants. The **valueOf( )** method returns the enumeration constant whose value corresponds to the string passed in *str*. In both cases, *enum-type* is the type of the enumeration. For

1. named

2. **enum**

3. The data type of **UP** is **Directions** because enumerated constants are self-typed.

example, in the case of the **Transport** enumeration shown earlier, the return type of **Transport.valueOf("TRAIN")** is **Transport**. The value returned is **TRAIN**.

The following program demonstrates the **values( )** and **valueOf( )** methods.

```
// Use the built-in enumeration methods.

// An enumeration of Transport varieties.
enum Transport {
  CAR, TRUCK, AIRPLANE, TRAIN, BOAT
}

class EnumDemo2 {
  public static void main(String args[])
  {
    Transport tp;

    System.out.println("Here are all Transport constants");

    // use values()
    Transport allTransports[] = Transport.values();   ⟵┐
    for(Transport t : allTransports)                      Obtain an array of **Transport** constants.
      System.out.println(t);

    System.out.println();

    // use valueOf()
    tp = Transport.valueOf("AIRPLANE");   ⟵──── Obtain the constant with
    System.out.println("tp contains " + tp);         the name **AIRPLANE**.

  }
}
```

The output from the program is shown here:

```
Here are all Transport constants
CAR
TRUCK
AIRPLANE
TRAIN
BOAT

tp contains AIRPLANE
```

Notice that this program uses a for-each style **for** loop to cycle through the array of constants obtained by calling **values( )**. For the sake of illustration, the variable **allTransports** was created and assigned a reference to the enumeration array. However, this step is not necessary because the **for** could have been written as shown here, eliminating the need for the **allTransports** variable:

```
for(Transport t : Transport.values())
  System.out.println(t);
```

Now, notice how the value corresponding to the name **AIRPLANE** was obtained by calling **valueOf( )**:

```
tp = Transport.valueOf("AIRPLANE");
```

As explained, **valueOf( )** returns the enumeration value associated with the name of the constant represented as a string.

CRITICAL SKILL
12.4 # Constructors, Methods, Instance Variables, and Enumerations

It is important to understand that each enumeration constant is an object of its enumeration type. Thus, an enumeration can define constructors, add methods, and have instance variables. When you define a constructor for an **enum**, the constructor is called when each enumeration constant is created. Each enumeration constant can call any method defined by the enumeration. Each enumeration constant has its own copy of any instance variables defined by the enumeration. The following version of **Transport** illustrates the use of a constructor, an instance variable, and a method. It gives each type of transportation a typical speed.

```
// Use an enum constructor, instance variable, and method.
enum Transport {                                    Notice the
  CAR(65), TRUCK(55), AIRPLANE(600), TRAIN(70), BOAT(22); ←— initialization
                                                    values.
  private int speed; // typical speed of each transport ←┐
                                                    Add an instance variable.
  // Constructor
  Transport(int s) { speed = s; } ←———————— Add a constructor.

  int getSpeed() { return speed; } ←———————— Add a method.
}

class EnumDemo3 {
  public static void main(String args[])
  {
    Transport tp;
```

```
        // Display speed of an airplane.
        System.out.println("Typical speed for an airplane is " +
                        Transport.AIRPLANE.getSpeed() +
                        " miles per hour.\n");

        // Display all Transports and speeds.
        System.out.println("All Transport speeds: ");
        for(Transport t : Transport.values())
          System.out.println(t + " typical speed is " +
                        t.getSpeed() +
                        " miles per hour.");

    }
}
```

Obtain the speed by calling **getSpeed( )**.

The output is shown here:

```
Typical speed for an airplane is 600 miles per hour.

All Transport speeds:
CAR typical speed is 65 miles per hour.
TRUCK typical speed is 55 miles per hour.
AIRPLANE typical speed is 600 miles per hour.
TRAIN typical speed is 70 miles per hour.
BOAT typical speed is 22 miles per hour.
```

This version of **Transport** adds three things. The first is the instance variable **speed**, which is used to hold the speed of each kind of transport. The second is the **Transport** constructor, which is passed the speed of a transport. The third is the method **getSpeed( )**, which returns the value of **Speed**.

When the variable **tp** is declared in **main( )**, the constructor for **Transport** is called once for each constant that is specified. Notice how the arguments to the constructor are specified, by putting them inside parentheses, after each constant, as shown here:

```
CAR(65), TRUCK(55), AIRPLANE(600), TRAIN(70), BOAT(22);
```

These values are passed to the **s** parameter of **Transport( )**, which then assigns this value to **speed**. There is something else to notice about the list of enumeration constants: it is terminated by a semicolon. That is, the last constant, **BOAT**, is followed by a semicolon. When an enumeration contains other members, the enumeration list must end in a semicolon.

Because each enumeration constant has its own copy of **speed**, you can obtain the speed of a specified type of transport by calling **getSpeed( )**. For example, in **main( )** the speed of an airplane is obtained by the following call:

```
Transport.AIRPLANE.getSpeed()
```

Ask the Expert

Q: Now that enumerations are part of Java, should I avoid the use of final **variables?**

A: No. Enumerations are appropriate when you are working with lists of items that must be represented by identifiers. A **final** variable is appropriate when you have a constant value, such as an array size, that will be used in many places. Thus, each has its own use. The advantage of enumerations is that now final variables don't have to be pressed into service for a job for which they are not ideally suited.

The speed of each transport is obtained by cycling through the enumeration using a **for** loop. Because there is a copy of **speed** for each enumeration constant, the value associated with one constant is separate and distinct from the value associated with another constant. This is a powerful concept, which is available only when enumerations are implemented as classes, as Java does.

Although the preceding example contains only one constructor, an **enum** can offer two or more overloaded forms, just as can any other class.

Two Important Restrictions

There are two restrictions that apply to enumerations. First, an enumeration can't inherit another class. Second, an **enum** cannot be a superclass. This means that an **enum** can't be extended. Otherwise, **enum** acts much like any other class type. The key is to remember that each of the enumeration constants is an object of the class in which it is defined.

CRITICAL SKILL
12.5 Enumerations Inherit Enum

Although you can't inherit a superclass when declaring an **enum**, all enumerations automatically inherit one: **java.lang.Enum**. This class defines several methods that are available for use by all enumerations. Most often you won't need to use these methods, but there are two that you may occasionally employ: **ordinal( )** and **compareTo( )**.

The **ordinal( )** method obtains a value that indicates an enumeration constant's position in the list of constants. This is called its *ordinal value*. The **ordinal( )** method is shown here:

final int ordinal( )

It returns the ordinal value of the invoking constant. Ordinal values begin at zero. Thus, in the **Transport** enumeration, **CAR** has an ordinal value of zero, **TRUCK** has an ordinal value of 1, **AIRPLANE** has an ordinal value of 2, and so on.

You can compare the ordinal value of two constants of the same enumeration by using the **compareTo( )** method. It has this general form:

final int compareTo(*enum-type e*)

Here, *enum-type* is the type of the enumeration and *e* is the constant being compared to the invoking constant. Remember, both the invoking constant and *e* must be of the same enumeration. If the invoking constant has an ordinal value less than *e*'s, then **compareTo( )** returns a negative value. If the two ordinal values are the same, then zero is returned. If the invoking constant has an ordinal value greater than *e*'s, then a positive value is returned.

The following program demonstrates **ordinal( )** and **compareTo( )**.

```
// Demonstrate ordinal() and compareTo().

// An enumeration of Transport varieties.
enum Transport {
  CAR, TRUCK, AIRPLANE, TRAIN, BOAT
}

class EnumDemo4 {
  public static void main(String args[])
  {
    Transport tp, tp2, tp3;

    // Obtain all ordinal values using ordinal().
    System.out.println("Here are all Transport constants" +
                       " and their ordinal values: ");
    for(Transport t : Transport.values())
      System.out.println(t + " " + t.ordinal());    ◄──── Obtain ordinal values.

    tp = Transport.AIRPLANE;
    tp2 = Transport.TRAIN;
    tp3 = Transport.AIRPLANE;

    System.out.println();
                                        Compare ordinal values.
    // Demonstrate compareTo()             │
    if(tp.compareTo(tp2) < 0) ◄───────────┘
      System.out.println(tp + " comes before " + tp2);

    if(tp.compareTo(tp2) > 0)
```

```
      System.out.println(tp2 + " comes before " + tp);

    if(tp.compareTo(tp3) == 0)
      System.out.println(tp + " equals " + tp3);
  }
}
```

The output from the program is shown here:

```
Here are all Transport constants and their ordinal values:
CAR 0
TRUCK 1
AIRPLANE 2
TRAIN 3
BOAT 4

AIRPLANE comes before TRAIN
AIRPLANE equals AIRPLANE
```

Progress Check

1. What does **values( )** return?

2. Can an enumeration have a constructor?

3. What is the ordinal value of an enumeration constant?

Project 12-1 A Computer-Controlled Traffic Light

TrafficLightDemo.java   Enumerations are particularly useful when your program needs a set of constants, but the actual values of the constants are arbitrary, as long as all differ. This type of situation comes up quite often when programming. One common instance involves handling the states in which some device can exist. For example, imagine that you are writing a program that controls a traffic light. Your traffic light code must automatically cycle through the light's three states: green, yellow, and red. It also must enable other code to know the current color of the light and let the color of the light be

---

1. The **values( )** method returns an array that contains a list of all the constants defined by the invoking enumeration.

2. Yes.

3. The ordinal value of an enumeration constant describes its position in the list of constants, with the first constant having the ordinal value of zero.

set to a known initial value. This means that the three states must be represented in some way. Although it would be possible to represent these three states by integer values (for example, the values 1, 2, and 3) or by strings (such as "red", "green", and "yellow"), an enumeration offers a much better approach. Using an enumeration results in code that is more efficient than if strings represented the states and more structured than if integers represented the states.

In this project, you will create a simulation of an automated traffic light, as just described. This project not only demonstrates an enumeration in action, it also shows another example of multithreading and synchronization.

Step by Step

1. Create a file called **TrafficLightDemo.java**.

2. Begin by defining an enumeration called **TrafficLightColor** that represents the three states of the light, as shown here:

```
// An enumeration of the colors of a traffic light.
enum TrafficLightColor {
  RED, GREEN, YELLOW
}
```

Whenever the color of the light is needed, its enumeration value is used.

3. Next, begin defining **TrafficLightSimulator**, as shown next. **TrafficLightSimulator** is the class that encapsulates the traffic light simulation.

```
// A computerized traffic light.
class TrafficLightSimulator implements Runnable {
  private Thread thrd; // holds the thread that runs the simulation
  private TrafficLightColor tlc; // holds the current traffic light color
  boolean stop = false; // set to true to stop the simulation
  boolean changed = false; // true when the light has changed

  TrafficLightSimulator(TrafficLightColor init) {
    tlc = init;

    thrd = new Thread(this);
    thrd.start();
  }

  TrafficLightSimulator() {
    tlc = TrafficLightColor.RED;

    thrd = new Thread(this);
    thrd.start();
  }
```

(continued)

Notice that **TrafficLightSimulator** implements **Runnable**. This is necessary because a separate thread is used to run each traffic light. This thread will cycle through the colors. Two constructors are created. The first lets you specify the initial light color. The second defaults to red. Both start a new thread to run the light.

Now look at the instance variables. A reference to the traffic light thread is stored in **thrd**. The current traffic light color is stored in **tlc**. The **stop** variable is used to stop the simulation. It is initially set to false. The light will run until this variable is set to true. The **changed** variable is **true** when the light has changed.

4. Next, add the **run( )** method, shown here, which begins running the traffic light.

```
// Start up the light.
public void run() {
  while(!stop) {

    try {
      switch(tlc) {
        case GREEN:
          Thread.sleep(10000); // green for 10 seconds
          break;
        case YELLOW:
          Thread.sleep(2000);  // yellow for 2 seconds
          break;
        case RED:
          Thread.sleep(12000); // red for 12 seconds
          break;
      }
    } catch(InterruptedException exc) {
      System.out.println(exc);
    }
    changeColor();
  }
}
```

This method cycles the light through the colors. First, it sleeps an appropriate amount of time, based on the current color. Then, it calls **changeColor( )** to change to the next color in the sequence.

5. Now, add the **changeColor( )** method, as shown here:

```
// Change color.
synchronized void changeColor() {

  switch(tlc) {
    case RED:
      tlc = TrafficLightColor.GREEN;
```

```
      break;
    case YELLOW:
      tlc = TrafficLightColor.RED;
      break;
    case GREEN:
      tlc = TrafficLightColor.YELLOW;
  }

  changed = true;
  notify(); // signal that the light has changed
}
```

The **switch** statement examines the color currently stored in **tlc** and then assigns the next color in the sequence. Notice that this method is synchronized. This is necessary because it calls **notify( )** to signal that a color change has taken place. (Recall that **notify( )** can be called only from a synchronized context.)

6. The next method is **waitForChange( )**, which waits until the color of the light is changed.

```
// Wait until a light change occurs.
synchronized void waitForChange() {
  try {
    while(!changed)
      wait(); // wait for light to change
    changed = false;
  } catch(InterruptedException exc) {
    System.out.println(exc);
  }
}
```

This method simply calls **wait( )**. This call won't return until **changeColor( )** executes a call to **notify( )**. Thus, **waitForChange( )** won't return until the color has changed.

7. Finally, add the methods **getColor( )**, which returns the current light color, and **cancel( )**, which stops the traffic light thread by setting **stop** to true. These methods are shown here:

```
// Return current color.
TrafficLightColor getColor() {
  return tlc;
}

// Stop the traffic light.
void cancel() {
  stop = true;
}
```

(continued)

8. Here is all the code assembled into a complete program that demonstrates the traffic light:

```
// A simulation of a traffic light that uses
// an enumeration to describe the light's color.

// An enumeration of the colors of a traffic light.
enum TrafficLightColor {
  RED, GREEN, YELLOW
}

// A computerized traffic light.
class TrafficLightSimulator implements Runnable {
  private Thread thrd; // holds the thread that runs the simulation
  private TrafficLightColor tlc; // holds the current traffic light color
  boolean stop = false; // set to true to stop the simulation
  boolean changed = false; // true when the light has changed

  TrafficLightSimulator(TrafficLightColor init) {
    tlc = init;

    thrd = new Thread(this);
    thrd.start();
  }

  TrafficLightSimulator() {
    tlc = TrafficLightColor.RED;

    thrd = new Thread(this);
    thrd.start();
  }

  // Start up the light.
  public void run() {
    while(!stop) {

      try {
        switch(tlc) {
          case GREEN:
            Thread.sleep(10000); // green for 10 seconds
            break;
          case YELLOW:
            Thread.sleep(2000);  // yellow for 2 seconds
            break;
          case RED:
            Thread.sleep(12000); // red for 12 seconds
            break;
        }
      } catch(InterruptedException exc) {
        System.out.println(exc);
      }
      changeColor();
    }
```

```
  }

  // Change color.
  synchronized void changeColor() {

    switch(tlc) {
      case RED:
        tlc = TrafficLightColor.GREEN;
        break;
      case YELLOW:
        tlc = TrafficLightColor.RED;
        break;
      case GREEN:
        tlc = TrafficLightColor.YELLOW;
    }

    changed = true;
    notify(); // signal that the light has changed
  }

  // Wait until a light change occurs.
  synchronized void waitForChange() {
    try {
      while(!changed)
        wait(); // wait for light to change
      changed = false;
    } catch(InterruptedException exc) {
      System.out.println(exc);
    }
  }

  // Return current color.
  TrafficLightColor getColor() {
    return tlc;
  }

  // Stop the traffic light.
  void cancel() {
    stop = true;
  }
}

class TrafficLightDemo {
  public static void main(String args[]) {
    TrafficLightSimulator tl =
      new TrafficLightSimulator(TrafficLightColor.GREEN);

    for(int i=0; i < 9; i++) {
      System.out.println(tl.getColor());
      tl.waitForChange();
```

(continued)

```
    }

    tl.cancel();
  }
}
```

The following output is produced. As you can see, the traffic light cycles through the colors in order of green, yellow, and red:

```
GREEN
YELLOW
RED
GREEN
YELLOW
RED
GREEN
YELLOW
RED
```

In the program, notice how the use of the enumeration simplifies and adds structure to the code that needs to know the state of the traffic light. Because the light can have only three states (red, green, or yellow), the use of an enumeration ensures that only these values are valid, thus preventing accidental misuse.

9. It is possible to improve the preceding program by taking advantage of the class capabilities of an enumeration. For example, by adding a constructor, instance variable, and method to **TrafficLightColor**, you can substantially improve the preceding programming. This improvement is left as an exercise. See Mastery Check, question 4.

Autoboxing

With the release of J2SE 5, Java added two features that were long desired by Java programmers: *autoboxing* and *auto-unboxing*. Autoboxing/unboxing greatly simplifies and streamlines code that must convert primitive types into objects, and vice versa. Because such situations are found frequently in Java code, the benefits of autoboxing/unboxing affect nearly all Java programmers. As you will see in Module 13, autoboxing/unboxing contributes greatly to the usability of another new feature: generics. The addition of autoboxing/unboxing subtly changes the relationship between objects and the primitive types. These changes are more profound than the conceptual simplicity of autoboxing/unboxing might at first suggest. Their effects are widely felt throughout the Java language.

Autoboxing/unboxing is directly related to Java's type wrappers, and to the way that values are moved into and out of an instance of a wrapper. For this reason, we will begin with an overview of the type wrappers and the process of manually boxing and unboxing values.

CRITICAL SKILL
12.6 Type Wrappers

As you know, Java uses primitive types, such as **int** or **double**, to hold the basic data types supported by the language. Primitive types, rather than objects, are used for these quantities for the sake of performance. Using objects for these basic types would add an unacceptable overhead to even the simplest of calculations. Thus, the primitive types are not part of the object hierarchy, and they do not inherit **Object**.

Despite the performance benefit offered by the primitive types, there are times when you will need an object representation. For example, you can't pass a primitive type by reference to a method. Also, many of the standard data structures implemented by Java operate on objects, which means that you can't use these data structures to store primitive types. To handle these (and other) situations, Java provides *type wrappers*, which are classes that encapsulate a primitive type within an object. The type wrapper classes were introduced briefly in Module 10. Here, we will look at them more closely.

The type wrappers are **Double**, **Float**, **Long**, **Integer**, **Short**, **Byte**, **Character**, and **Boolean**, which are packaged in **java.lang**. These classes offer a wide array of methods that allow you to fully integrate the primitive types into Java's object hierarchy.

By far, the most commonly used type wrappers are those that represent numeric values. These are **Byte**, **Short**, **Integer**, **Long**, **Float**, and **Double**. All of the numeric type wrappers inherit the abstract class **Number**. **Number** declares methods that return the value of an object in each of the different numeric types. These methods are shown here:

byte byteValue( )

double doubleValue( )

float floatValue( )

int intValue( )

long longValue( )

short shortValue( )

For example, **doubleValue( )** returns the value of an object as a **double**, **floatValue( )** returns the value as a **float**, and so on. These methods are implemented by each of the numeric type wrappers.

All of the numeric type wrappers define constructors that allow an object to be constructed from a given value, or a string representation of that value. For example, here are the constructors defined for **Integer** and **Double**:

Integer(int *num*)

Integer(String *str*)

Double(double *num*)

Double(String *str*)

If *str* does not contain a valid numeric value, then a **NumberFormatException** is thrown.

All of the type wrappers override **toString( )**. It returns the human-readable form of the value contained within the wrapper. This allows you to output the value by passing a type wrapper object to **println( )**, for example, without having to convert it into its primitive type.

The process of encapsulating a value within an object is called *boxing*. Prior to J2SE 5, all boxing took place manually, with the programmer explicitly constructing an instance of a wrapper with the desired value. For example, this line manually boxes the value 100 into an **Integer**:

```
Integer iOb = new Integer(100);
```

In this example, a new **Integer** object with the value 100 is explicitly created and a reference to this object is assigned to **iOb**.

The process of extracting a value from a type wrapper is called *unboxing*. Again, prior to J2SE 5, all unboxing also took place manually, with the programmer explicitly calling a method on the wrapper to obtain its value. For example, this manually unboxes the value in **iOb** into an **int**.

```
int i = iOb.intValue();
```

Here, **intValue( )** returns the value encapsulated within **iOb** as an **int**.

The following program demonstrates the preceding concepts.

```
// Demonstrate manual boxing and unboxing with a type wrapper.
class Wrap {
  public static void main(String args[]) {

    Integer iOb = new Integer(100);  ←——————— Manually box the value 100.

    int i = iOb.intValue();  ←——————— Manually unbox the value in iOb.
```

```
    System.out.println(i + " " + iOb); // displays 100 100
  }
}
```

This program wraps the integer value 100 inside an **Integer** object called **iOb**. The program then obtains this value by calling **intValue( )** and stores the result in **i**. Finally, it displays the values of **i** and **iOb**, both of which are 100.

The same general procedure used by the preceding example to manually box and unbox values has been employed since the original version of Java. Although this approach to boxing and unboxing works, it is both tedious and error-prone because it requires the programmer to manually create the appropriate object to wrap a value and to explicitly obtain the proper primitive type when its value is needed. Fortunately, autoboxing/unboxing fundamentally improves on these essential procedures.

CRITICAL SKILL
12.7

Autoboxing Fundamentals

Autoboxing is the process by which a primitive type is automatically encapsulated (boxed) into its equivalent type wrapper whenever an object of that type is needed. There is no need to explicitly construct an object. Auto-unboxing is the process by which the value of a boxed object is automatically extracted (unboxed) from a type wrapper when its value is needed. There is no need to call a method such as **intValue( )** or **doubleValue( )**.

The addition of autoboxing and auto-unboxing greatly streamlines the coding of several algorithms, removing the tedium of manually boxing and unboxing values. It also helps prevent errors. With autoboxing it is not necessary to manually construct an object in order to wrap a primitive type. You need only assign that value to a type-wrapper reference. Java automatically constructs the object for you. For example, here is the modern way to construct an **Integer** object that has the value 100:

```
Integer iOb = 100; // autobox an int
```

Notice that no object is explicitly created through the use of **new**. Java handles this for you, automatically.

To unbox an object, simply assign that object reference to a primitive-type variable. For example, to unbox **iOb**, you can use this line:

```
int i = iOb; // auto-unbox
```

Java handles the details for you.

The following program demonstrates the preceding statements.

```
// Demonstrate autoboxing/unboxing.
class AutoBox {
```

```
public static void main(String args[]) {

  Integer iOb = 100; // autobox an int
                                              Autobox and then auto-
  int i = iOb; // auto-unbox                  unbox the value 100.

  System.out.println(i + " " + iOb);  // displays 100 100
}
}
```

Progress Check

1. What is the type wrapper for **double**?

2. When you box a primitive value, what happens?

3. Autoboxing is the feature that automatically boxes a primitive value into an object of its corresponding type wrapper. True or False?

Autoboxing and Methods

In addition to the simple case of assignments, autoboxing automatically occurs whenever a primitive type must be converted into an object, and auto-unboxing takes place whenever an object must be converted into a primitive type. Thus, autoboxing/unboxing might occur when an argument is passed to a method or when a value is returned by a method. For example, consider the following:

```
// Autoboxing/unboxing takes place with
// method parameters and return values.

class AutoBox2 {
  // This method has an Integer parameter.
  static void m(Integer v) {  ─────────── Receives an Integer.
    System.out.println("m() received " + v);
  }
```

---

1. **Double**

2. When a primitive value is boxed, its value is placed inside an object of its corresponding type wrapper.

3. True.

```
// This method returns an int.
static int m2() {                          Returns an int.
  return 10;
}
                                            Returns an Integer.
// This method returns an Integer.
static Integer m3() {
  return 99; // autoboxing 99 into an Integer.
}

public static void main(String args[]) {

  // Pass an int to m().  Because m() has an Integer
  // parameter, the int value passed is automatically boxed.
  m(199);

  // Here, iOb receives the int value returned by m2().
  // This value is automatically boxed so that it can be
  // assigned to iOb.
  Integer iOb = m2();
  System.out.println("Return value from m2() is " + iOb);

  // Next, m3() is called. It returns an Integer value
  // which is auto-unboxed into an int.
  int i = m3();
  System.out.println("Return value from m3() is " + i);

  // Next, Math.sqrt() is called with iOb as an argument.
  // In this case, iOb is auto-unboxed and its value promoted to
  // double, which is the type needed by sqrt().
  iOb = 100;
  System.out.println("Square root of iOb is " + Math.sqrt(iOb));
  }
}
```

This program displays the following result:

```
m() received 199
Return value from m2() is 10
Return value from m3() is 99
Square root of iOb is 10.0
```

In the program, notice that **m( )** specifies an **Integer** parameter. Inside **main( )**, **m( )** is passed the **int** value 199. Because **m( )** is expecting an **Integer**, this value is automatically boxed. Next, **m2( )** is called. It returns the **int** value 10. This **int** value is assigned to **iOb** in **main( )**. Because **iOb** is an **Integer**, the value returned by **m2( )** is autoboxed. Next, **m3( )** is called. It returns an **Integer** that is auto-unboxed into an **int**. Finally, **Math.sqrt( )** is called with **iOb** as an argument. In this case, **iOb** is auto-unboxed and its value promoted to **double**, since that is the type expected by **Math.sqrt( )**.

Autoboxing/Unboxing Occurs in Expressions

In general, autoboxing and unboxing take place whenever a conversion into an object or from an object is required. This applies to expressions. Within an expression, a numeric object is automatically unboxed. The outcome of the expression is reboxed, if necessary. For example, consider the following program.

```
// Autoboxing/unboxing occurs inside expressions.

class AutoBox3 {
  public static void main(String args[]) {

    Integer iOb, iOb2;
    int i;

    iOb = 99;
    System.out.println("Original value of iOb: " + iOb);

    // The following automatically unboxes iOb,
    // performs the increment, and then reboxes
    // the result back into iOb.
    ++iOb;
    System.out.println("After ++iOb: " + iOb);

    // Here, iOb is unboxed, its value is increased by 10,
    // and the result is boxed and stored back in iOb.
    iOb += 10;
    System.out.println("After iOb += 10: " + iOb);

    // Here, iOb is unboxed, the expression is
    // evaluated, and the result is reboxed and
    // assigned to iOb2.
    iOb2 = iOb + (iOb / 3);
    System.out.println("iOb2 after expression: " + iOb2);

    // The same expression is evaluated, but the
    // result is not reboxed.
    i = iOb + (iOb / 3);
```

Autoboxing/unboxing occurs in expressions.

```
        System.out.println("i after expression: " + i);
    }
}
```

The output is shown here:

```
Original value of iOb: 99
After ++iOb: 100
After iOb += 10: 110
iOb2 after expression: 146
i after expression: 146
```

In the program, pay special attention to this line:

```
++iOb;
```

This causes the value in **iOb** to be incremented. It works like this: **iOb** is unboxed, the value is incremented, and the result is reboxed.

Because of auto-unboxing, you can use integer numeric objects, such as an **Integer**, to control a **switch** statement. For example, consider this fragment:

```
Integer iOb = 2;

switch(iOb) {
  case 1: System.out.println("one");
    break;
  case 2: System.out.println("two");
    break;
  default: System.out.println("error");
}
```

When the **switch** expression is evaluated, **iOb** is unboxed and its **int** value is obtained.

As the examples in the program show, because of autoboxing/unboxing, using numeric objects in an expression is both intuitive and easy. In the past, such code would have involved casts and calls to methods such as **intValue( )**.

A Word of Warning

Now that Java includes autoboxing and auto-unboxing, one might be tempted to use objects such as **Integer** or **Double** exclusively, abandoning primitives altogether. For example, with autoboxing/unboxing it is possible to write code like this:

```
// A bad use of autoboxing/unboxing!
Double a, b, c;
```

```
a = 10.2;
b = 11.4;
c = 9.8;

Double avg = (a + b + c) / 3;
```

In this example, objects of type **Double** hold values, which are then averaged and the result assigned to another **Double** object. Although this code is technically correct and does, in fact, work properly, it is a very bad use of autoboxing/unboxing. It is far less efficient than the equivalent code written using the primitive type **double**. The reason is that each autobox and auto-unbox adds overhead that is not present if the primitive type is used.

In general, you should restrict your use of the type wrappers to only those cases in which an object representation of a primitive type is required. Autoboxing/unboxing was not added to Java as a "back door" way of eliminating the primitive types.

Progress Check

1. Will a primitive value be autoboxed when it is passed as an argument to a method that is expecting a type wrapper object?

2. Because of the limits imposed by the Java run-time system, autoboxing/unboxing will not occur on objects used in expressions. True or False?

3. Because of autoboxing/unboxing, you should use objects rather than primitive types for performing most arithmetic operations. True or False?

CRITICAL SKILL
12.10 Static Import

Beginning with J2SE 5, Java expanded the use of the **import** keyword so that it supports a new feature called *static import*. By following **import** with the keyword **static**, an **import** statement can be used to import the static members of a class or interface. When using static import, it is possible to refer to static members directly by their names, without having to qualify them with the name of their class. This simplifies and shortens the syntax required to use a static member.

---

1. Yes.
2. False.
3. False.

To understand the usefulness of static import, let's begin with an example that *does not* use it. The following program computes the solutions to a quadratic equation, which has this form:

$$ax^2 + bx + c = 0$$

The program uses two static methods from Java's built-in math class **Math**, which is part of **java.lang**. The first is **Math.pow( )**, which returns a value raised to a specified power. The second is **Math.sqrt( )**, which returns the square root of its argument.

```java
// Find the solutions to a quadratic equation.
class Quadratic {
  public static void main(String args[]) {

    // a, b, and c represent the coefficients in the
    // quadratic equation: ax² + bx + c = 0
    double a, b, c, x;

    // Solve 4x² + x - 3 = 0 for x.
    a = 4;
    b = 1;
    c = -3;

    // Find first solution.
    x = (-b + Math.sqrt(Math.pow(b, 2) - 4 * a * c)) / (2 * a);
    System.out.println("First solution: " + x);

    // Find second solution.
    x = (-b - Math.sqrt(Math.pow(b, 2) - 4 * a * c)) / (2 * a);
    System.out.println("Second solution: " + x);
  }
}
```

Because **pow( )** and **sqrt( )** are static methods, they must be called through the use of their class' name, **Math**. This results in a somewhat unwieldy expression:

```java
x = (-b + Math.sqrt(Math.pow(b, 2) - 4 * a * c)) / (2 * a);
```

Furthermore, having to specify the class name each time **pow( )** or **sqrt( )** (or any of Java's other math methods, such as **sin( )**, **cos( )**, and **tan( )**) are used, can become tedious.

You can eliminate the tedium of specifying the class name through the use of static import, as shown in the following version of the preceding program.

```java
// Use static import to bring sqrt() and pow() into view.
```

```
import static java.lang.Math.sqrt;
import static java.lang.Math.pow;
```

Use static import to bring **sqrt( )** and **pow( )** into view.

```
class Quadratic {
  public static void main(String args[]) {

    // a, b, and c represent the coefficients in the
    // quadratic equation: ax² + bx + c = 0
    double a, b, c, x;

    // Solve 4x² + x - 3 = 0 for x.
    a = 4;
    b = 1;
    c = -3;

    // Find first solution.
    x = (-b + sqrt(pow(b, 2) - 4 * a * c)) / (2 * a);
    System.out.println("First solution: " + x);

    // Find second solution.
    x = (-b - sqrt(pow(b, 2) - 4 * a * c)) / (2 * a);
    System.out.println("Second solution: " + x);
  }
}
```

In this version, the names **sqrt** and **pow** are brought into view by these static import statements:

```
import static java.lang.Math.sqrt;
import static java.lang.Math.pow;
```

After these statements, it is no longer necessary to qualify **sqrt( )** or **pow( )** with its class name. Therefore, the expression can more conveniently be specified, as shown here:

```
x = (-b + sqrt(pow(b, 2) - 4 * a * c)) / (2 * a);
```

As you can see, this form is considerably shorter and easier to read.

There are two general forms of the **import static** statement. The first, which is used by the preceding example, brings into view a single name. Its general form is shown here:

import static *pkg.type-name.static-member-name*;

Here, *type-name* is the name of a class or interface that contains the desired static member. Its full package name is specified by *pkg*. The name of the member is specified by *static-member-name*.

The second form of static import imports all static members. Its general form is shown here:

import static *pkg.type-name*.*;

If you will be using many static methods or fields defined by a class, then this form lets you bring them into view without having to specify each individually. Therefore, the preceding program could have used this single **import** statement to bring both **pow( )** and **sqrt( )** (and *all other* static members of **Math**) into view:

```
import static java.lang.Math.*;
```

Of course, static import is not limited just to the **Math** class or just to methods. For example, this brings the static field **System.out** into view:

```
import static java.lang.System.out;
```

After this statement, you can output to the console without having to qualify **out** with **System**, as shown here:

```
out.println("After importing System.out, you can use out directly.");
```

Whether importing **System.out** as just shown is a good idea is subject to debate. Although it does shorten the statement, it is no longer instantly clear to anyone reading the program that the **out** being referred to is **System.out**.

As convenient as static import can be, it is important not to abuse it. Remember, the reason that Java organizes its libraries into packages is to avoid namespace collisions. When you import static members, you are bringing those members into the global namespace. Thus, you are increasing the potential for namespace conflicts and the inadvertent hiding of other names. If you are using a static member once or twice in the program, it's best not to import it. Also, some static names, such as **System.out**, are so recognizable that you might not want to import them. Static import is designed for those situations in which you are using a static member repeatedly, such as when performing a series of mathematical computations. In essence, you should use, but not abuse, this feature.

Ask the Expert

Q: Using static import, can I import the static members of classes that I create?

A: Yes, you can use static import to import the static members of classes and interfaces you create. Doing so is especially convenient when you define several static members that are used frequently throughout a large program. For example, if a class defines a number of **static final** constants that define various limits, then using static import to bring them into view will save you a lot of tedious typing.

CRITICAL SKILL
12.11
Annotations (Metadata)

Of the new features added to Java by J2SE 5, annotations are the most innovative. This powerful facility enables you to embed supplemental information into a source file. This information, called an *annotation*, does not change the actions of a program. However, this information can be used by various tools, during both development and deployment. For example, an annotation might be processed by a source-code generator, by the compiler, or by a deployment tool. The term *metadata* is also used to refer to this feature, but the term annotation is the most descriptive, and more commonly used.

Annotation is a large and sophisticated topic, and it is far beyond scope of this book to cover it in detail. However, a brief overview is given here so that you will be familiar with the concept.

NOTE

A detailed discussion of metadata and annotations can be found in my book *Java: The Complete Reference, 7th Edition* (McGraw-Hill/Osborne, 2007).

An annotation is created through a mechanism based on the **interface**. Here is a simple example:

```
// A simple annotation type.
@interface MyAnno {
  String str();
  int val();
}
```

This declares an annotation called **MyAnno**. Notice the @ that precedes the keyword **interface**. This tells the compiler that an annotation type is being declared. Next, notice the two members **str( )** and **val( )**. All annotations consist solely of method declarations. However, you don't provide bodies for these methods. Instead, Java implements these methods. Moreover, the methods act much like fields.

All annotation types automatically extend the **Annotation** interface. Thus, **Annotation** is a super-interface of all annotations. It is declared within the **java.lang.annotation** package.

Once you have declared an annotation, you can use it to annotate a declaration. Any type of declaration can have an annotation associated with it. For example, classes, methods, fields, parameters, and **enum** constants can be annotated. Even an annotation can be annotated. In all cases, the annotation precedes the rest of the declaration.

When you apply an annotation, you give values to its members. For example, here is an example of **MyAnno** being applied to a method:

```
// Annotate a method.
@MyAnno(str = "Annotation Example", val = 100)
public static void myMeth() { // ...
```

This annotation is linked with the method **myMeth( )**. Look closely at the annotation syntax. The name of the annotation, preceded by an **@**, is followed by a parenthesized list of member initializations. To give a member a value, that member's name is assigned a value. Therefore, in the example, the string "Annotation Example" is assigned to the **str** member of **MyAnno**. Notice that no parentheses follow **str** in this assignment. When an annotation member is given a value, only its name is used. Thus, annotation members look like fields in this context.

Annotations that don't have parameters are called *marker annotations*. These are specified without passing any arguments and without using parentheses. Their sole purpose is to mark a declaration with some attribute.

Java defines many built-in annotations. Most are specialized, but seven are general purpose. Four are imported from **java.lang.annotation**: **@Retention**, **@Documented**, **@Target**, and **@Inherited**. Three, **@Override**, **@Deprecated**, and **@SuppressWarnings**, are included in **java.lang**. These are shown in Table 12-1.

Here is an example that uses **@Deprecated** to mark the **MyClass** class and the **getMsg( )** method. When you try to compile this program, warnings will report the use of these deprecated elements.

```
// An example that uses @Deprecated.

// Deprecate a class.
@Deprecated  ◄──────────────── Mark a class as deprecated.
class MyClass {
  private String msg;

  MyClass(String m) {
    msg = m;
```

```
    }

    // Deprecate a method within a class.
    @Deprecated ◄─────────────────┐
    String getMsg() {              │    Mark a method as deprecated.
      return msg;
    }

    // ...
  }

  class AnnoDemo {
    public static void main(String args[]) {
      MyClass myObj = new MyClass("test");

      System.out.println(myObj.getMsg());
    }
  }
```

Annotation	Description
@Retention	Specifies the retention policy that will be associated with the annotation. The retention policy determines how long an annotation is present during the compilation and deployment process.
@Documented	A marker annotation that tells a tool that an annotation is to be documented. It is designed to be used only as an annotation to an annotation declaration.
@Target	Specifies the types of declarations to which an annotation can be applied. It is designed to be used only as an annotation to another annotation. **@Target** takes one argument, which must be a constant from the **ElementType** enumeration, which defines various constants, such as **CONSTRUCTOR**, **FIELD**, and **METHOD**. The argument determines the types of declarations to which the annotation can be applied.
@Inherited	A marker annotation that causes the annotation for a superclass to be inherited by a subclass.
@Override	A method annotated with **@Override** must override a method from a superclass. If it doesn't, a compile-time error will result. It is used to ensure that a superclass method is actually overridden, and not simply overloaded. This is a marker annotation.
@Deprecated	A marker annotation that indicates that a declaration is obsolete and has been replaced by a newer form.
@SuppressWarnings	Specifies that one or more warnings that might be issued by the compiler are to be suppressed. The warnings to suppress are specified by name, in string form.

Table 12-1 The Built-in Annotations

Progress Check

1. Show the two forms of static import.

2. Show how to import **Thread**'s **sleep( )** method so that it can be used without being qualified by **Thread**.

3. Static import works with methods, but not variables. True or False?

4. An annotation begins with a/an _____.

Module 12 Mastery Check

1. Enumeration constants are said to be *self-typed*. What does this mean?

2. What class do all enumerations automatically inherit?

3. Given the following enumeration, write a program that uses **values( )** to show a list of the constants and their ordinal values.

```
enum Tools {
   SCREWDRIVER, WRENCH, HAMMER, PLIERS
}
```

4. The traffic light simulation developed in Project 12-1 can be improved with a few simple changes that take advantage of an enumeration's class features. In the version shown, the duration of each color was controlled by the **TrafficLightSimulator** class by hard-coding these values into the **run( )** method. Change this so that the duration of each color is stored by the constants in the **TrafficLightColor** enumeration. To do this, you will need to add a constructor, a private instance variable, and a method called **getDelay( )**. After making these changes, what improvements do you see? On your own, can you think of other improvements? (Hint: try using ordinal values to switch light colors rather than relying on a **switch** statement.)

5. Define boxing and unboxing. How does autoboxing/unboxing affect these actions?

---

1. import static *pkg.type-name.static-member-name*;
   import static *pkg.type-name*.*;
2. import static java.lang.Thread.sleep;
3. False.
4. **@**

6. Change the following fragment so that it uses autoboxing.

```
Short val = new Short(123);
```

7. In your own words, what does static import do?

8. What does this statement do?

```
import static java.lang.Integer.parseInt;
```

9. Is static import designed for special-case situations, or is it good practice to bring all static members of all classes into view?

10. An annotation is syntactically based on a/an _____ .

11. What is a marker annotation?

12. An annotation can be applied only to methods. True or False?

Module 13

Generics

As explained in Module 12, many new features were recently added to Java. All of these new features substantially enhanced and expanded the scope of the language, but the one that has the most profound impact is *generics* because its effects are felt throughout the entire Java language. For example, generics add a completely new syntax element and cause changes to many of the classes and methods in the core API. It is not an overstatement to say that the inclusion of generics has fundamentally reshaped the character of Java.

The topic of generics is quite large, and some of it is sufficiently advanced to be beyond the scope of this book. However, a basic understanding of generics is necessary for all Java programmers. At first glance, the generics syntax may look a bit intimidating, but don't worry. Generics are surprisingly simple to use. By the time you finish this module, you will have a grasp of the key concepts that underlie generics and sufficient knowledge to use generics effectively in your own programs.

CAUTION

If you are using an older version of Java that predates the J2SE 5 release, you will not be able to use generics.

CRITICAL SKILL
13.1 Generics Fundamentals

At its core, the term *generics* means *parameterized types*. Parameterized types are important because they enable you to create classes, interfaces, and methods in which the type of data upon which they operate is specified as a parameter. A class, interface, or method that operates on a type parameter is called *generic*, as in *generic class* or *generic method*.

A principal advantage of generic code is that it will automatically work with the type of data passed to its type parameter. Many algorithms are logically the same no matter what type of data they are being applied to. For example, a Quicksort is the same whether it is sorting items of type **Integer**, **String**, **Object**, or **Thread**. With generics, you can define an algorithm once, independently of any specific type of data, and then apply that algorithm to a wide variety of data types without any additional effort.

It is important to understand that Java has always given you the ability to create generalized classes, interfaces, and methods by operating through references of type **Object**. Because **Object** is the superclass of all other classes, an **Object** reference can refer to any type of object. Thus, in pre-generics code, generalized classes, interfaces, and methods used **Object** references to operate on various types of data. The problem was that they could not do so with *type safety* because casts were needed to explicitly convert from **Object** to the actual type of data being operated upon. Thus, it was possible to accidentally create type mismatches. Generics add the type safety that was lacking because they make these casts automatic and implicit. In short, generics expand your ability to reuse code and let you do so safely and reliably.

Ask the Expert

Q: I have heard that Java's generics are similar to templates in C++. Is this the case?

A: Java generics are similar to templates in C++. What Java calls a parameterized type, C++ calls a template. However, Java generics and C++ templates are not the same, and there are some fundamental differences between the two approaches to generic types. For the most part, Java's approach is simpler to use.

A word of warning: If you have a background in C++, it is important not to jump to conclusions about how generics work in Java. The two approaches to generic code differ in subtle but fundamental ways.

CRITICAL SKILL
13.2 A Simple Generics Example

Before discussing any more theory, it's best to look at a simple generics example. The following program defines two classes. The first is the generic class **Gen**, and the second is **GenDemo**, which uses **Gen**.

```java
// A simple generic class.
// Here, T is a type parameter that
// will be replaced by a real type
// when an object of type Gen is created.
class Gen<T> {          ←————————————————  Declare a generic class. T is the
  T ob; // declare an object of type T      generic type parameter.

  // Pass the constructor a reference to
  // an object of type T.
  Gen(T o) {
    ob = o;
  }

  // Return ob.
  T getob() {
    return ob;
  }

  // Show type of T.
  void showType() {
    System.out.println("Type of T is " +
                       ob.getClass().getName());
  }
}
```

```
// Demonstrate the generic class.
class GenDemo {
  public static void main(String args[]) {
    // Create a Gen reference for Integers.
    Gen<Integer> iOb;

    // Create a Gen<Integer> object and assign its
    // reference to iOb.  Notice the use of autoboxing
    // to encapsulate the value 88 within an Integer object.
    iOb = new Gen<Integer>(88);

    // Show the type of data used by iOb.
    iOb.showType();

    // Get the value in iOb. Notice that
    // no cast is needed.
    int v = iOb.getob();
    System.out.println("value: " + v);

    System.out.println();

    // Create a Gen object for Strings.
    Gen<String> strOb = new Gen<String>("Generics Test");

    // Show the type of data used by strOb.
    strOb.showType();

    // Get the value of strOb. Again, notice
    // that no cast is needed.
    String str = strOb.getob();
    System.out.println("value: " + str);
  }
}
```

Create a reference to an object of type **Gen<Integer>**.

Instantiate an object of type **Gen<Integer>**.

Create a reference and an object of type **Gen<String>**.

The output produced by the program is shown here:

```
Type of T is java.lang.Integer
value: 88

Type of T is java.lang.String
value: Generics Test
```

Let's examine this program carefully. First, notice how **Gen** is declared by the following line:

```
class Gen<T> {
```

Here, **T** is the name of a *type parameter*. This name is used as a placeholder for the actual type that will be passed to **Gen** when an object is created. Thus, **T** is used within **Gen** whenever the type parameter is needed. Notice that **T** is contained within < >. This syntax can be generalized. Whenever a type parameter is being declared, it is specified within angle brackets. Because **Gen** uses a type parameter, **Gen** is a generic class.

In the declaration of **Gen**, there is no special significance to the name **T**. Any valid identifier could have been used, but **T** is traditional. Furthermore, it is recommended that type parameter names be single-character, capital letters. Other commonly used type parameter names are **V** and **E**.

Next, **T** is used to declare an object called **ob**, as shown here:

```
T ob; // declare an object of type T
```

As explained, **T** is a placeholder for the actual type that will be specified when a **Gen** object is created. Thus, **ob** will be an object of the type passed to **T**. For example, if type **String** is passed to **T**, then in that instance, **ob** will be of type **String**.

Now consider **Gen**'s constructor:

```
Gen(T o) {
  ob = o;
}
```

Notice that its parameter, **o**, is of type **T**. This means that the actual type of **o** is determined by the type passed to **T** when a **Gen** object is created. Also, because both the parameter **o** and the member variable **ob** are of type **T**, they will both be of the same actual type when a **Gen** object is created.

The type parameter **T** can also be used to specify the return type of method, as is the case with the **getob( )** method, shown here:

```
T getob() {
  return ob;
}
```

Because **ob** is also of type **T**, its type is compatible with the return type specified by **getob( )**.

The **showType( )** method displays the type of **T**. It does this by calling **getName( )** on the **Class** object returned by the call to **getClass( )** on **ob**. We haven't used this feature before, so let's examine it closely. As you should recall from Module 7, the **Object** class defines the method **getClass( )**. Thus, **getClass( )** is a member of all class types. It returns a **Class** object that corresponds to the class type of the object on which it is called. **Class** is a class defined within **java.lang** that encapsulates information about a class. **Class** defines several methods that can be used to obtain information about a class at run time. Among these is the **getName( )** method, which returns a string representation of the class name.

The **GenDemo** class demonstrates the generic **Gen** class. It first creates a version of **Gen** for integers, as shown here:

```
Gen<Integer> iOb;
```

Look carefully at this declaration. First, notice that the type **Integer** is specified within the angle brackets after **Gen**. In this case, **Integer** is a *type argument* that is passed to **Gen**'s type parameter, **T**. This effectively creates a version of **Gen** in which all references to **T** are translated into references to **Integer**. Thus, for this declaration, **ob** is of type **Integer**, and the return type of **getob( )** is of type **Integer**.

Before moving on, it's necessary to state that the Java compiler does not actually create different versions of **Gen**, or of any other generic class. Although it's helpful to think in these terms, it is not what actually happens. Instead, the compiler removes all generic type information, substituting the necessary casts, to make your code *behave as if* a specific version of **Gen** was created. Thus, there is really only one version of **Gen** that actually exists in your program. The process of removing generic type information is called *erasure*, which is discussed later in this module.

The next line assigns to **iOb** a reference to an instance of an **Integer** version of the **Gen** class.

```
iOb = new Gen<Integer>(88);
```

Notice that when the **Gen** constructor is called, the type argument **Integer** is also specified. This is necessary because the type of the object (in this case **iOb**) to which the reference is being assigned is of type **Gen<Integer>**. Thus, the reference returned by **new** must also be of type **Gen<Integer>**. If it isn't, a compile-time error will result. For example, the following assignment will cause a compile-time error:

```
iOb = new Gen<Double>(88.0); // Error!
```

Because **iOb** is of type **Gen<Integer>**, it can't be used to refer to an object of **Gen<Double>**. This type checking is one of the main benefits of generics because it ensures type safety.

As the comments in the program state, the assignment

```
iOb = new Gen<Integer>(88);
```

makes use of autoboxing to encapsulate the value 88, which is an **int**, into an **Integer**. This works because **Gen<Integer>** creates a constructor that takes an **Integer** argument. Because an **Integer** is expected, Java will automatically box 88 inside one. Of course, the assignment could also have been written explicitly, like this:

```
iOb = new Gen<Integer>(new Integer(88));
```

However, there would be no benefit to using this version.

The program then displays the type of **ob** within **iOb**, which is **Integer**. Next, the program obtains the value of **ob** by use of the following line:

```
int v = iOb.getob();
```

Because the return type of **getob( )** is **T**, which was replaced by **Integer** when **iOb** was declared, the return type of **getob( )** is also **Integer**, which auto-unboxes into **int** when assigned to **v** (which is an **int**). Thus, there is no need to cast the return type of **getob( )** to **Integer**.

Next, **GenDemo** declares an object of type **Gen<String>**:

```
Gen<String> strOb = new Gen<String>("Generics Test");
```

Because the type argument is **String**, **String** is substituted for **T** inside **Gen**. This creates (conceptually) a **String** version of **Gen**, as the remaining lines in the program demonstrate.

Generics Work Only with Objects

When declaring an instance of a generic type, the type argument passed to the type parameter must be a class type. You cannot use a primitive type, such as **int** or **char**. For example, with **Gen**, it is possible to pass any class type to **T**, but you cannot pass a primitive type to **T**. Therefore, the following declaration is illegal:

```
Gen<int> strOb = new Gen<int>(53); // Error, can't use primitive type
```

Of course, not being able to specify a primitive type is not a serious restriction because you can use the type wrappers (as the preceding example did) to encapsulate a primitive type. Further, Java's autoboxing and auto-unboxing mechanism makes the use of the type wrapper transparent.

Generic Types Differ Based on Their Type Arguments

A key point to understand about generic types is that a reference of one specific version of a generic type is not type-compatible with another version of the same generic type. For example, assuming the program just shown, the following line of code is in error, and will not compile:

```
iOb = strOb; // Wrong!
```

Even though both **iOb** and **strOb** are of type **Gen<T>**, they are references to different types because their type parameters differ. This is part of the way that generics add type safety and prevent errors.

A Generic Class with Two Type Parameters

You can declare more than one type parameter in a generic type. To specify two or more type parameters, simply use a comma-separated list. For example, the following **TwoGen** class is a variation of the **Gen** class that has two type parameters.

```
// A simple generic class with two type
// parameters: T and V.
class TwoGen<T, V> {          Use two type parameters.
  T ob1;
  V ob2;

  // Pass the constructor references to
  // objects of type T and V.
  TwoGen(T o1, V o2) {
    ob1 = o1;
    ob2 = o2;
  }

  // Show types of T and V.
  void showTypes() {
    System.out.println("Type of T is " +
                       ob1.getClass().getName());

    System.out.println("Type of V is " +
                       ob2.getClass().getName());
  }

  T getob1() {
    return ob1;
  }

  V getob2() {
    return ob2;
  }
}

// Demonstrate TwoGen.
class SimpGen {
```

```
public static void main(String args[]) {          Here, Integer is passed to T,
                                                   and String is passed to V.
    TwoGen<Integer, String> tgObj = ◄──────────────┐
      new TwoGen<Integer, String>(88, "Generics");

    // Show the types.
    tgObj.showTypes();

    // Obtain and show values.
    int v = tgObj.getob1();
    System.out.println("value: " + v);

    String str = tgObj.getob2();
    System.out.println("value: " + str);
  }
}
```

The output from this program is shown here:

```
Type of T is java.lang.Integer
Type of V is java.lang.String
value: 88
value: Generics
```

Notice how **TwoGen** is declared:

```
class TwoGen<T, V> {
```

It specifies two type parameters, **T** and **V**, separated by a comma. Because it has two type parameters, two type arguments must be passed to **TwoGen** when an object is created, as shown next:

```
TwoGen<Integer, String> tgObj =
  new TwoGen<Integer, String>(88, "Generics");
```

In this case, **Integer** is substituted for **T**, and **String** is substituted for **V**.

Although the two type arguments differ in this example, it is possible for both types to be the same. For example, the following line of code is valid:

```
TwoGen<String, String> x = new TwoGen<String, String>("A", "B");
```

In this case, both **T** and **V** would be of type **String**. Of course, if the type arguments were always the same, then two type parameters would be unnecessary.

The General Form of a Generic Class

The generics syntax shown in the preceding examples can be generalized. Here is the syntax for declaring a generic class:

class *class-name<type-param-list>* { // ...

Here is the syntax for declaring a reference to a generics class:

class-name<type-arg-list> var-name =
    new *class-name<type-arg-list>(cons-arg-list)*;

Progress Check

1. The type of data operated upon by a generic class is passed to it through a/an _____

    _____.

2. Can a type parameter be passed a primitive type?

3. Assuming the **Gen** class shown in the preceding example, show how to declare a **Gen** reference that operates on data of type **Double**.

CRITICAL SKILL
13.3 Bounded Types

In the preceding examples, the type parameters could be replaced by any class type. This is fine for many purposes, but sometimes it is useful to limit the types that can be passed to a type parameter. For example, assume that you want to create a generic class that stores a numeric value and is capable of performing various mathematical functions, such as computing the reciprocal or obtaining the fractional component. Furthermore, you want to use the class to compute these quantities for any type of number, including integers, floats, and doubles. Thus, you want to specify the type of the numbers generically, using a type parameter. To create such a class, you might try something like this:

```
// NumericFns attempts (unsuccessfully) to create
// a generic class that can compute various
// numeric functions, such as the reciprocal or the
```

1. type parameter
2. No.
3. Gen<Double> d_ob;

```
// fractional component, given any type of number.
class NumericFns<T> {
  T num;

  // Pass the constructor a reference to
  // a numeric object.
  NumericFns(T n) {
    num = n;
  }

  // Return the reciprocal.
  double reciprocal() {
    return 1 / num.doubleValue(); // Error!
  }

  // Return the fractional component.
  double fraction() {
    return num.doubleValue() - num.intValue(); // Error!
  }

  // ...
}
```

Unfortunately, **NumericFns** will not compile as written because both methods will generate compile-time errors. First, examine the **reciprocal( )** method, which attempts to return the reciprocal of **num**. To do this, it must divide 1 by the value of **num**. The value of **num** is obtained by calling **doubleValue( )**, which obtains the **double** version of the numeric object stored in **num**. Because all numeric classes, such as **Integer** and **Double**, are subclasses of **Number**, and **Number** defines the **doubleValue( )** method, this method is available to all numeric wrapper classes. The trouble is that the compiler has no way to know that you are intending to create **NumericFns** objects using only numeric types. Thus, when you try to compile **NumericFns**, an error is reported that indicates that the **doubleValue( )** method is unknown. The same type of error occurs twice in **fraction( )**, which needs to call both **doubleValue( )** and **intValue( )**. Both calls result in error messages stating that these methods are unknown. To solve this problem, you need some way to tell the compiler that you intend to pass only numeric types to **T**. Furthermore, you need some way to *ensure* that *only* numeric types are actually passed.

To handle such situations, Java provides *bounded types*. When specifying a type parameter, you can create an upper bound that declares the superclass from which all type arguments must be derived. This is accomplished through the use of an **extends** clause when specifying the type parameter, as shown here:

<*T* extends *superclass*>

This specifies that *T* can only be replaced by *superclass*, or subclasses of *superclass*. Thus, *superclass* defines an inclusive, upper limit.

You can use an upper bound to fix the **NumericFns** class shown earlier by specifying **Number** as an upper bound, as shown here:

```
// In this version of NumericFns, the type argument
// for T must be either Number, or a class derived
// from Number.
class NumericFns<T extends Number> {        In this case, the type argument
  T num;                                     must be either Number or a
                                             subclass of Number.

  // Pass the constructor a reference to
  // a numeric object.
  NumericFns(T n) {
    num = n;
  }

  // Return the reciprocal.
  double reciprocal() {
    return 1 / num.doubleValue();
  }

  // Return the fractional component.
  double fraction() {
    return num.doubleValue() - num.intValue();
  }

  // ...
}

// Demonstrate NumericFns.
class BoundsDemo {
  public static void main(String args[]) {

    NumericFns<Integer> iOb =                    Integer is OK because it
                new NumericFns<Integer>(5);      is a subclass of Number.

    System.out.println("Reciprocal of iOb is " +
                iOb.reciprocal());
    System.out.println("Fractional component of iOb is " +
                iOb.fraction());

    System.out.println();

    NumericFns<Double> dOb =                    Double is also OK.
                new NumericFns<Double>(5.25);
```

```
    System.out.println("Reciprocal of dOb is " +
                          dOb.reciprocal());
    System.out.println("Fractional component of dOb is " +
                          dOb.fraction());


    // This won't compile because String is not a
    // subclass of Number.
//    NumericFns<String> strOb = new NumericFns<String>("Error");
  }
}
```

String is illegal because it is not a subclass of **Number**.

The output is shown here:

```
Reciprocal of iOb is 0.2
Fractional component of iOb is 0.0

Reciprocal of dOb is 0.19047619047619047
Fractional component of dOb is 0.25
```

Notice how **NumericFns** is now declared by this line:

```
class NumericFns<T extends Number> {
```

Because the type **T** is now bounded by **Number**, the Java compiler knows that all objects of type **T** can call **doubleValue( )** because it is a method declared by **Number**. This is, by itself, a major advantage. However, as an added bonus, the bounding of **T** also prevents nonnumeric **NumericFns** objects from being created. For example, if you try removing the comments from the lines at the end of the program, and then try re-compiling, you will receive compile-time errors because **String** is not a subclass of **Number**.

Bounded types are especially useful when you need to ensure that one type parameter is compatible with another. For example, consider the following class called **Pair**, which stores two objects that must be compatible with each other:

```
class Pair<T, V extends T> {
  T first;
  V second;

  Pair(T a, V b) {
    first = a;
    second = b;
  }

  // ...
}
```

Here, **V** must be either the same type as **T**, or a subclass of **T**.

Notice that **Pair** uses two type parameters, **T** and **V**, and that **V** extends **T**. This means that **V** will either be the same as **T** or a subclass of **T**. This ensures that the two arguments to **Pair**'s constructor will either be objects of the same type or of related types. For example, the following constructions are valid:

```
// This is OK because both T and V are Integer.
Pair<Integer, Integer> x = new Pair<Integer, Integer>(1, 2);

// This is OK because Integer is a subclass of Number.
Pair<Number, Integer> y = new Pair<Number, Integer>(10.4, 12);
```

However, the following is invalid:

```
// This causes an error because String is not
// a subclass of Number
Pair<Number, String> z = new Pair<Number, String>(10.4, "12");
```

In this case, **String** is not a subclass of **Number**, which violates the bound specified by **Pair**.

Progress Check

1. The keyword _____ specifies a bound for a type argument.

2. How do you declare a generic type **T** that must be a subclass of **Thread**?

3. Given

```
class X<T, V extends T> {
```

is the following declaration correct?

```
X<Integer, Double> x = new X<Integer, Double>(10, 1.1);
```

CRITICAL SKILL
13.4 Using Wildcard Arguments

As useful as type safety is, sometimes it can get in the way of perfectly acceptable constructs. For example, given the **NumericFns** class shown at the end of the preceding section, assume that you want to add a method called **absEqual( )** that returns true if two **NumericFns** objects

---

1. **extends**
2. T extends Thread
3. No, because **Double** is not a subclass of **Integer**.

contain the numbers whose absolute values are the same. Furthermore, you want this method to be able to work properly no matter what type of number each object holds. For example, if one object contains the **Double** value 1.25 and the other object contains the **Float** value −1.25, then **absEqual( )** would return true. One way to implement **absEqual( )** is to pass it a **NumericFns** argument, and then compare the absolute value of that argument against the absolute value of the invoking object, returning true only if the values are the same. For example, you want to be able to call **absEqual( )** as shown here:

```
NumericFns<Double> dOb = new NumericFns<Double>(1.25);
NumericFns<Float> fOb = new NumericFns<Float>(-1.25);

if(dOb.absEqual(fOb))
  System.out.println("Absolute values are the same.");
else
  System.out.println("Absolute values differ.");
```

At first, creating **absEqual( )** seems like an easy problem. Unfortunately, trouble starts as soon as you try to declare a parameter of type **NumericFns**. What type do you specify for **NumericFns'** type parameter? At first, you might think of a solution like this, in which **T** is used as the type parameter:

```
// This won't work!
// Determine if the absolute values of two objects are the same.
boolean absEqual(NumericFns<T> ob) {
  if(Math.abs(num.doubleValue()) ==
      Math.abs(ob.num.doubleValue())) return true;

  return false;
}
```

Here, the standard method **Math.abs( )** is used to obtain the absolute value of each number, and then the values are compared. The trouble with this attempt is that it will work only with other **NumericFns** objects whose type is the same as the invoking object. For example, if the invoking object is of type **NumericFns<Integer>**, then the parameter **ob** must also be of type **NumericFns<Integer>**. It can't be used to compare an object of type **NumericFns<Double>**, for example. Therefore, this approach does not yield a general (i.e., generic) solution.

To create a generic **absEqual( )** method, you must use another feature of Java generics: the *wildcard argument*. The wildcard argument is specified by the **?**, and it represents an unknown type. Using a wildcard, here is one way to write the **absEqual( )** method:

```
// Determine if the absolute values of two
// objects are the same.
boolean absEqual(NumericFns<?> ob) {          Notice the wildcard.
```

```
if(Math.abs(num.doubleValue()) ==
    Math.abs(ob.num.doubleValue())) return true;

    return false;
}
```

Here, **NumericFns<?>** matches any type of **NumericFns** object, allowing any two **NumericFns** objects to have their absolute values compared. The following program demonstrates this.

```
// Use a wildcard.
class NumericFns<T extends Number> {
  T num;

  // Pass the constructor a reference to
  // a numeric object.
  NumericFns(T n) {
    num = n;
  }

  // Return the reciprocal.
  double reciprocal() {
    return 1 / num.doubleValue();
  }

  // Return the fractional component.
  double fraction() {
    return num.doubleValue() - num.intValue();
  }

  // Determine if the absolute values of two
  // objects are the same.
  boolean absEqual(NumericFns<?> ob) {
    if(Math.abs(num.doubleValue()) ==
        Math.abs(ob.num.doubleValue())) return true;

    return false;
  }

  // ...
}

// Demonstrate a wildcard.
class WildcardDemo {
  public static void main(String args[]) {

    NumericFns<Integer> iOb =
                    new NumericFns<Integer>(6);
```

```
NumericFns<Double> dOb =
                  new NumericFns<Double>(-6.0);

NumericFns<Long> lOb =
                  new NumericFns<Long>(5L);

System.out.println("Testing iOb and dOb.");
if(iOb.absEqual(dOb))
  System.out.println("Absolute values are equal.");
else
  System.out.println("Absolute values differ.");

System.out.println();

System.out.println("Testing iOb and lOb.");
if(iOb.absEqual(lOb))
  System.out.println("Absolute values are equal.");
else
  System.out.println("Absolute values differ.");

  }
}
```

In this call, the wildcard type matches **Double**.

In this call, the wildcard matches **Long**.

The output is shown here:

```
Testing iOb and dOb.
Absolute values are equal.

Testing iOb and lOb.
Absolute values differ.
```

In the program, notice these two calls to **absEqual( )**:

```
if(iOb.absEqual(dOb))
```

```
if(iOb.absEqual(lOb))
```

In the first call, **iOb** is an object of type **NumericFns<Integer>** and **dOb** is an object of type **NumericFns<Double>**. However, through the use of a wildcard, it possible for **iOb** to pass **dOb** in the call to **absEqual( )**. The same applies to the second call, in which an object of type **NumericFns<Long>** is passed.

One last point: It is important to understand that the wildcard does not affect what type of **NumericFns** objects can be created. This is governed by the **extends** clause in the **NumericFns** declaration. The wildcard simply matches any *valid* **NumericFns** object.

CRITICAL SKILL

13.5 Bounded Wildcards

Wildcard arguments can be bounded in much the same way that a type parameter can be bounded. A bounded wildcard is especially important when you are creating a method that is designed to operate only on objects that are subclasses of a specific superclass. To understand why, let's work through a simple example. Consider the following set of classes:

```
class A {
  // ...
}

class B extends A {
  // ...
}

class C extends A {
  // ...
}

// Note that D does NOT extend A.
class D {
  // ...
}
```

Here, class **A** is extended by classes **B** and **C**, but not by **D**.

Next, consider the following very simple generic class:

```
// A simple generic class.
class Gen<T> {
  T ob;

  Gen(T o) {
    ob = o;
  }
}
```

Gen takes one type parameter, which specifies the type of object stored in **ob**. Because **T** is unbounded, the type of **T** is unrestricted. That is, **T** can be of any class type.

Now, suppose that you want to create a method that takes as an argument any type of **Gen** object so long as its type parameter is **A** or a subclass of **A**. In other words, you want to create a method that operates only on objects of **Gen**<*type*>, where *type* is either **A** or a subclass of

A. To accomplish this, you must use a bounded wildcard. For example, here is method called **test( )** that accepts as an argument only **Gen** objects whose type parameter is **A** or a subclass of **A**:

```
// Here, the ? will match A or any class type
// that extends A.
static void test(Gen<? extends A> o) {
  // ...
}
```

The following class demonstrates the types of **Gen** objects that can be passed to **test( )**.

```
class UseBoundedWildcard {
  // Here, the ? will match A or any class type
  // that extends A.
  static void test(Gen<? extends A> o) {  ◀——————— Use a bounded wildcard.
    // ...
  }

  public static void main(String args[]) {
    A a = new A();
    B b = new B();
    C c = new C();
    D d = new D();

    Gen<A> w = new Gen<A>(a);
    Gen<B> w2 = new Gen<B>(b);
    Gen<C> w3 = new Gen<C>(c);
    Gen<D> w4 = new Gen<D>(d);

    // These calls to test() are OK.
    test(w);   ⎤
    test(w2);  ⎬——————These are legal because w, w2, and w3 are subclasses of A.
    test(w3);  ⎦

    // Can't call test() with w4 because
    // it is not an object of a class that
    // inherits A.
//    test(w4); // Error!  ◀——————— This is illegal because w4 is not a subclass of A.
  }
}
```

In **main( )**, objects of type **A**, **B**, **C**, and **D** are created. These are then used to create four **Gen** objects, one for each type. Finally, four calls to **test( )** are made, with the last call commented out. The first three calls are valid because **w**, **w2**, and **w3** are **Gen** objects whose type is either **A** or a subclass of **A**. However, the last call to **test( )** is illegal because **w4** is an object of type **D**, which is not derived from **A**. Thus, the bounded wildcard in **test( )** will not accept **w4** as an argument.

In general, to establish an upper bound for a wildcard, use the following type of wildcard expression:

<? extends *superclass*>

where *superclass* is the name of the class that serves as the upper bound. Remember, this is an inclusive clause because the class forming the upper bound (specified by *superclass*) is also within bounds.

You can also specify a lower bound for a wildcard by adding a **super** clause to a wildcard declaration. Here is its general form:

<? super *subclass*>

In this case, only classes that are superclasses of *subclass* are acceptable arguments. This is an exclusive clause, because it will not match the class specified by *subclass*.

Progress Check

1. To specify a wildcard argument, use _____.

2. A wildcard argument matches any reference type. True or False?

3. Can a wildcard be bounded?

4. In this expression, what type of objects can be matched by the wildcard?

   ```
   void myMeth(XYZ<? extends Thread> trdOb) { // ...
   ```

1. ?
2. True.
3. Yes.
4. The wildcard can match any object that is of type **Thread** or a subclass of **Thread**.

Ask the Expert

Q: Can I cast one instance of a generic class into another?

A: Yes, you can cast one instance of a generic class into another, but only if the two are otherwise compatible and their type arguments are the same. For example, assume a generic class called **Gen** that is declared like this:

```
class Gen<T> { // ...
```

Next, assume that **x** is declared as shown here:

```
Gen<Integer> x = new Gen<Integer>();
```

Then, this cast is legal:

```
(Gen<Integer>) x // legal
```

because **x** is an instance of **Gen<Integer>**. But, this cast

```
(Gen<Long>) x // illegal
```

is not legal because **x** is not an instance of **Gen<Long>**.

CRITICAL SKILL
13.6 Generic Methods

As the preceding examples have shown, methods inside a generic class can make use of a class' type parameter and are, therefore, automatically generic relative to the type parameter. However, it is possible to declare a generic method that uses one or more type parameters of its own. Furthermore, it is possible to create a generic method that is enclosed within a nongeneric class.

The following program declares a nongeneric class called **GenericMethodDemo** and a static generic method within that class called **arraysEqual( )**. This method determines if two arrays contain the same elements, in the same order. It can be used to compare any two arrays as long as the arrays are of the same or compatible types.

```
// Demonstrate a simple generic method.
class GenericMethodDemo {

  // Determine if the contents of two arrays are the same.
```

```
static <T, V extends T> boolean arraysEqual(T[] x, V[] y) {
  // If array lengths differ, then the arrays differ.
  if(x.length != y.length) return false;                    A generic method.

  for(int i=0; i < x.length; i++)
    if(!x[i].equals(y[i])) return false; // arrays differ

  return true; // contents of arrays are equivalent
}

public static void main(String args[]) {

  Integer nums[] = { 1, 2, 3, 4, 5 };
  Integer nums2[] = { 1, 2, 3, 4, 5 };
  Integer nums3[] = { 1, 2, 7, 4, 5 };
  Integer nums4[] = { 1, 2, 7, 4, 5, 6 };

  if(arraysEqual(nums, nums))                   The type arguments for T and V
    System.out.println("nums equals nums");     are implicitly determined when
                                                the method is called.
  if(arraysEqual(nums, nums2))
    System.out.println("nums equals nums2");

  if(arraysEqual(nums, nums3))
    System.out.println("nums equals nums3");

  if(arraysEqual(nums, nums4))
    System.out.println("nums equals nums4");

  // Create an array of Doubles
  Double dvals[] = { 1.1, 2.2, 3.3, 4.4, 5.5 };

  // This won't compile because nums and dvals
  // are not of the same type.
//    if(arraysEqual(nums, dvals))
//      System.out.println("nums equals dvals");
  }
}
```

The output from the program is shown here:

```
nums equals nums
nums equals nums2
```

Let's examine **arraysEqual( )** closely. First, notice how it is declared by this line:

```
static <T, V extends T> boolean arraysEqual(T[] x, V[] y) {
```

The type parameters are declared *before* the return type of the method. Second, notice that the type **V** is upper-bounded by **T**. Thus, **V** must either be the same as type **T** or a subclass of **T**. This relationship enforces that **arraysEqual( )** can be called only with arguments that are compatible with each other. Also notice that **arraysEqual( )** is static, enabling it to be called independently of any object. Understand, though, that generic methods can be either static or nonstatic. There is no restriction in this regard.

Now, notice how **arraysEqual( )** is called within **main( )** by use of the normal call syntax, without the need to specify type arguments. This is because the types of the arguments are automatically discerned, and the types of **T** and **V** are adjusted accordingly. For example, in the first call:

```
if(arraysEqual(nums, nums))
```

the base type of the first argument is **Integer**, which causes **Integer** to be substituted for **T**. The base type of the second argument is also **Integer**, which makes **Integer** a substitute for **V**, too. Thus, the call to **arraysEqual( )** is legal, and the two arrays can be compared.

Now, notice the commented-out code, shown here:

```
//    if(arraysEqual(nums, dvals))
//        System.out.println("nums equals dvals");
```

If you remove the comments and then try to compile the program, you will receive an error. The reason is that the type parameter **V** is bounded by **T** in the **extends** clause in **V**'s declaration. This means that **V** must be either type **T** or a subclass of **T**. In this case, the first argument is of type **Integer**, making **T** into **Integer**, but the second argument is of type **Double**, which is not a subclass of **Integer**. This makes the call to **arraysEqual( )** illegal, and results in a compile-time type-mismatch error.

The syntax used to create **arraysEqual( )** can be generalized. Here is the syntax for a generic method:

<type-param-list> ret-type meth-name(param-list) { // ...

In all cases, *type-param-list* is a comma-separated list of type parameters. Notice that for a generic method, the type parameter list precedes the return type.

CRITICAL SKILL
13.7 Generic Constructors

A constructor can be generic, even if its class is not. For example, in the following program, the class **Summation** is not generic, but its constructor is.

```
// Use a generic constructor.
class Summation {
  private int sum;

  <T extends Number> Summation(T arg) {        ← A generic constructor
    sum = 0;

    for(int i=0; i <= arg.intValue(); i++)
      sum += i;
  }

  int getSum() {
    return sum;
  }
}

class GenConsDemo {
  public static void main(String args[]) {
    Summation ob = new Summation(4.0);

    System.out.println("Summation of 4.0 is " +
                        ob.getSum());
  }
}
```

The **Summation** class computes and encapsulates the summation of the numeric value passed to its constructor. Recall that the summation of N is the sum of all the whole numbers between 0 and N. Because **Summation( )** specifies a type parameter that is bounded by **Number**, a **Summation** object can be constructed using any numeric type, including **Integer**, **Float**, or **Double**. No matter what numeric type is used, its value is converted to **Integer** by calling **intValue( )**, and the summation is computed. Therefore, it is not necessary for the class **Summation** to be generic; only a generic constructor is needed.

Progress Check

1. Can a method or constructor be generic even if its class is not?

2. Show how to declare a generic method called **myMeth( )** that takes one generic type argument. Have it return an argument of that generic type.

CRITICAL SKILL
13.8 Generic Interfaces

In addition to generic classes and methods, you can also have generic interfaces. Generic interfaces are specified just like generic classes. Here is an example. It creates an interface called **Containment**, which can be implemented by classes that store one or more values. It declares a method called **contains( )** that determines if a specified value is contained by the invoking object.

```java
// A generic interface example.

// A generic containment interface.
// This interface implies that an implementing
// class contains one or more values.
interface Containment<T> {                          ←————————— A generic interface.
  // The contains() method tests if a
  // specific item is contained within
  // an object that implements Containment.
  boolean contains(T o);
}

// Implement Containment using an array to
// hold the values.
class MyClass<T> implements Containment<T> {   ←——— Any class that implements
  T[] arrayRef;                                      a generic interface must
                                                     itself be generic.
  MyClass(T[] o) {
    arrayRef = o;
  }
```

---

1. Yes.
2. `<T> T myMeth(T o)`

```
    // Implement Contains.
    public boolean contains(T o) {
      for(T x : arrayRef)
        if(x.equals(o)) return true;
      return false;
    }
  }

class GenIFDemo {
  public static void main(String args[]) {
    Integer x[] = { 1, 2, 3 };

    MyClass<Integer> ob = new MyClass<Integer>(x);

    if(ob.contains(2))
      System.out.println("2 is in ob");
    else
      System.out.println("2 is NOT in ob");

    if(ob.contains(5))
      System.out.println("5 is in ob");
    else
      System.out.println("5 is NOT in ob");

    // The following is illegal because ob
    // is an Integer Containment and 9.25 is
    // a Double value.
//    if(ob.contains(9.25)) // Illegal!
//       System.out.println("9.25 is in ob");

  }
}
```

The output is shown here:

```
2 is in ob
5 is NOT in ob
```

Although most aspects of this program should be easy to understand, a couple of key points need to be made. First, notice that **Containment** is declared like this:

```
interface Containment<T> {
```

In general, a generic interface is declared in the same way as a generic class. In this case, the type parameter **T** specifies the type of objects that are contained.

Next, **Containment** is implemented by **MyClass**. Notice the declaration of **MyClass**, shown here:

```
class MyClass<T> implements Containment<T> {
```

In general, if a class implements a generic interface, then that class must also be generic, at least to the extent that it takes a type parameter that is passed to the interface. For example, the following attempt to declare **MyClass** is in error:

```
class MyClass implements Containment<T> { // Wrong!
```

This declaration is wrong because **MyClass** does not declare a type parameter, which means that there is no way to pass one to **Containment**. In this case, the identifier **T** is simply unknown and the compiler reports an error. Of course, if a class implements a *specific type* of generic interface, such as shown here:

```
class MyClass implements Containment<Double> { // OK
```

then the implementing class does not need to be generic.

As you might expect, the type parameter(s) specified by a generic interface can be bounded. This lets you limit the type of data for which the interface can be implemented. For example, if you wanted to limit **Containment** to numeric types, then you could declare it like this:

```
interface Containment<T extends Number> {
```

Now, any implementing class must pass to **Containment** a type argument also having the same bound. For example, now **MyClass** must be declared as shown here:

```
class MyClass<T extends Number> implements Containment<T> {
```

Pay special attention to the way the type parameter **T** is declared by **MyClass** and then passed to **Containment**. Because **Containment** now requires a type that extends **Number**, the implementing class (**MyClass** in this case) must specify the same bound. Furthermore, once this bound has been established, there is no need to specify it again in the **implements** clause. In fact it would be wrong to do so. For example, this declaration is incorrect and won't compile:

```
// This is wrong!
class MyClass<T extends Number>
  implements Containment<T extends Number> { // Wrong!
```

Once the type parameter has been established, it is simply passed to the interface without further modification.

Here is the generalized syntax for a generic interface:

interface *interface-name<type-param-list>* { // ...

Here, *type-param-list* is a comma-separated list of type parameters. When a generic interface is implemented, you must specify the type arguments, as shown here:

class *class-name<type-param-list>*
   implements *interface-name<type-param-list>* {

Project 13-1   Create a Generic Queue

```
IGenQ.java
QExc.java
GenQueue.java
GenQDemo.java
```

One of the most powerful advantages that generics bring to programming is the ability to construct reliable, reusable code. As mentioned at the start of this module, many algorithms are the same no matter what type of data they are used on. For example, a queue works the same way whether that queue is for integers, strings, or **File** objects. Instead of creating a separate queue class for each type of object, you can craft a single, generic solution that can be used with any type of object. Thus, the development cycle of design, code, test, and debug occurs only once when you create a generic solution—not repeatedly, each time a queue is needed for a new data type.

In this project you will adapt the queue example that has been evolving since Project 5-2, making it generic. This project represents the final evolution of the queue. It includes a generic interface that defines the queue operations, two exception classes, and one queue implementation: a fixed-size queue. Of course, you can experiment with other types of generic queues, such as a generic dynamic queue or a generic circular queue. Just follow the lead of the example shown here.

This project also organizes the queue code into a set of separate files: one for the interface, one for the queue exceptions, one for the fixed-queue implementation, and one for the program that demonstrates it. This organization reflects the way that this project would normally be organized in the real world.

Step by Step

1. The first step in creating a generic queue is to create a generic interface that describes the queue's two operations: put and get. The generic version of the queue interface is called **IGenQ** and it is shown here. Put this interface into a file called **IGenQ.java**.

```
// A generic queue interface.
public interface IGenQ<T> {
  // Put an item into the queue.
  void put(T ch) throws QueueFullException;
```

```
  // Get an item from the queue.
  T get() throws QueueEmptyException;
}
```

Notice that the type of data stored by the queue is specified by the generic type parameter **T**.

2. Next, create a file called **QExc.java**. Add to that file these two queue exception classes:

```
// An exception for queue-full errors.
class QueueFullException extends Exception {
  int size;

  QueueFullException(int s) { size = s; }

  public String toString() {
   return "\nQueue is full. Maximum size is " +
        size;
  }
}

// An exception for queue-empty errors.
class QueueEmptyException extends Exception {

  public String toString() {
   return "\nQueue is empty.";
  }
}
```

These classes encapsulate the two queue errors: full or empty. They are not generic classes because they are the same no matter what type of data is stored in a queue.

3. Now, create a file called **GenQueue.java**. Into that file, put the following code, which implements a fixed-size queue:

```
// A generic, fixed-size queue class.
class GenQueue<T> implements IGenQ<T> {
  private T q[]; // this array holds the queue
  private int putloc, getloc; // the put and get indices

  // Construct an empty queue with the given array.
  public GenQueue(T[] aRef) {
    q = aRef;
    putloc = getloc = 0;
  }

  // Put an item into the queue.
  public void put(T obj)
    throws QueueFullException {
```

(continued)

```
    if(putloc==q.length-1)
      throw new QueueFullException(q.length-1);

    putloc++;
    q[putloc] = obj;
  }

  // Get a character from the queue.
  public T get()
    throws QueueEmptyException {

    if(getloc == putloc)
      throw new QueueEmptyException();

    getloc++;
    return q[getloc];
  }
}
```

GenQueue is a generic class with type parameter **T**, which specifies the type of data stored in the queue. Notice that **T** is also passed to the **IGenQ** interface.

Notice that the **GenQueue** constructor is passed a reference to an array that will be used to hold the queue. Thus, to construct a **GenQueue**, you will first create an array whose type is compatible with the objects that you will be storing in the queue and whose size is long enough to store the number of objects that will be placed in the queue. As the code is written, the array must be one longer than the number of items stored because the first location is unused.

For example, the following sequence shows how to create a queue that holds strings:

```
String strArray[] = new String[10];
GenQueue<String> strQ = new GenQueue<String>(strArray);
```

4. Create a file called **GenQDemo.java** and put the following code into it. This program demonstrates the generic queue.

```
/*
    Project 13-1

    Demonstrate a generic queue class.
*/
class GenQDemo {
  public static void main(String args[]) {
    // Create an integer queue.
    Integer iStore[] = new Integer[10];
    GenQueue<Integer> q = new GenQueue<Integer>(iStore);
```

```
Integer iVal;

System.out.println("Demonstrate a queue of Integers.");
try {
  for(int i=0; i < 5; i++) {
    System.out.println("Adding " + i + " to the q.");
    q.put(i); // add integer value to q

  }
}
catch (QueueFullException exc) {
  System.out.println(exc);
}
System.out.println();

try {
  for(int i=0; i < 5; i++) {
    System.out.print("Getting next Integer from q: ");
    iVal = q.get();
    System.out.println(iVal);
  }
}
catch (QueueEmptyException exc) {
  System.out.println(exc);
}

System.out.println();

// Create a Double queue.
Double dStore[] = new Double[10];
GenQueue<Double> q2 = new GenQueue<Double>(dStore);

Double dVal;

System.out.println("Demonstrate a queue of Doubles.");
try {
  for(int i=0; i < 5; i++) {
    System.out.println("Adding " + (double)i/2 +
                       " to the q2.");
    q2.put((double)i/2); // add double value to q2
  }
}
catch (QueueFullException exc) {
  System.out.println(exc);
}
```

(continued)

```
        System.out.println();

        try {
          for(int i=0; i < 5; i++) {
            System.out.print("Getting next Double from q2: ");
            dVal = q2.get();
            System.out.println(dVal);
          }
        }
        catch (QueueEmptyException exc) {
          System.out.println(exc);
        }
      }
    }
```

5. Compile the program and run it. You will see the output shown here:

```
Demonstrate a queue of Integers.
Adding 0 to the q.
Adding 1 to the q.
Adding 2 to the q.
Adding 3 to the q.
Adding 4 to the q.

Getting next Integer from q: 0
Getting next Integer from q: 1
Getting next Integer from q: 2
Getting next Integer from q: 3
Getting next Integer from q: 4

Demonstrate a queue of Doubles.
Adding 0.0 to the q2.
Adding 0.5 to the q2.
Adding 1.0 to the q2.
Adding 1.5 to the q2.
Adding 2.0 to the q2.

Getting next Double from q2: 0.0
Getting next Double from q2: 0.5
Getting next Double from q2: 1.0
Getting next Double from q2: 1.5
Getting next Double from q2: 2.0
```

6. On your own, try converting the **CircularQueue** and **DynQueue** classes from Project 8-1 into generic classes.

CRITICAL SKILL
13.9 Raw Types and Legacy Code

Because generics are a new feature, it was necessary for Java to provide some transition path from old, pre-generics code. At the time of this writing, there are still millions and millions of lines of pre-generics legacy code that must remain both functional and compatible with generics. This means that pre-generics code must be able to work with generics, and generic code must be able to work with pre-generics code.

To handle the transition to generics, Java allows a generic class to be used without any type arguments. This creates a *raw type* for the class. This raw type is compatible with legacy code, which has no knowledge of generics. The main drawback to using the raw type is that the type safety of generics is lost.

Here is an example that shows a raw type in action.

```java
// Demonstrate a raw type.
class Gen<T> {
  T ob; // declare an object of type T

  // Pass the constructor a reference to
  // an object of type T.
  Gen(T o) {
    ob = o;
  }

  // Return ob.
  T getob() {
    return ob;
  }
}

// Demonstrate raw type.
class RawDemo {
  public static void main(String args[]) {

    // Create a Gen object for Integers.
    Gen<Integer> iOb = new Gen<Integer>(88);

    // Create a Gen object for Strings.
    Gen<String> strOb = new Gen<String>("Generics Test");

    // Create a raw-type Gen object and give it
    // a Double value.
    Gen raw = new Gen(new Double(98.6));   ◄——————— When no type argument is
                                                    supplied, a raw type is created.
```

```
    // Cast here is necessary because type is unknown.
    double d = (Double) raw.getob();
    System.out.println("value: " + d);

    // The use of a raw type can lead to run-time
    // exceptions.  Here are some examples.

    // The following cast causes a run-time error!
//    int i = (Integer) raw.getob(); // run-time error

    // This assignment overrides type safety.
    strOb = raw; // OK, but potentially wrong          Raw types override
//    String str = strOb.getob(); // run-time error     type safety.

    // This assignment also overrides type safety.
    raw = iOb; // OK, but potentially wrong
//    d = (Double) raw.getob(); // run-time error
  }
}
```

This program contains several interesting things. First, a raw type of the generic **Gen** class is created by the following declaration:

```
Gen raw = new Gen(new Double(98.6));
```

Notice that no type arguments are specified. In essence, this creates a **Gen** object whose type **T** is replaced by **Object**.

A raw type is not type safe. Thus, a variable of a raw type can be assigned a reference to any type of **Gen** object. The reverse is also allowed, in which a variable of a specific **Gen** type can be assigned a reference to a raw **Gen** object. However, both operations are potentially unsafe because the type checking mechanism of generics is circumvented.

This lack of type safety is illustrated by the commented-out lines at the end of the program. Let's examine each case. First, consider the following situation:

```
//    int i = (Integer) raw.getob(); // run-time error
```

In this statement, the value of **ob** inside **raw** is obtained, and this value is cast to **Integer**. The trouble is that **raw** contains a **Double** value, not an integer value. However, this cannot be detected at compile time because the type of **raw** is unknown. Thus, this statement fails at run time.

The next sequence assigns to a **strOb** (a reference of type **Gen<String>**) a reference to a raw **Gen** object:

```
strOb = raw; // OK, but potentially wrong
//    String str = strOb.getob(); // run-time error
```

The assignment itself is syntactically correct, but questionable. Because **strOb** is of type **Gen<String>**, it is assumed to contain a **String**. However, after the assignment, the object referred to by **strOb** contains a **Double**. Thus, at run time, when an attempt is made to assign the contents of **strOb** to **str**, a run-time error results because **strOb** now contains a **Double**. Thus, the assignment of a raw reference to a generic reference bypasses the type-safety mechanism.

The following sequence inverts the preceding case:

```
    raw = iOb; // OK, but potentially wrong
//    d = (Double) raw.getob(); // run-time error
```

Here, a generic reference is assigned to a raw reference variable. Although this is syntactically correct, it can lead to problems, as illustrated by the second line. In this case, **raw** now refers to an object that contains an **Integer** object, but the cast assumes that it contains a **Double**. This error cannot be prevented at compile time. Rather, it causes a run-time error.

Because of the potential for danger inherent in raw types, **javac** displays _unchecked warnings_ when a raw type is used in a way that might jeopardize type safety. In the preceding program, these lines generate unchecked warnings:

```
Gen raw = new Gen(new Double(98.6));

strOb = raw; // OK, but potentially wrong
```

In the first line, it is the call to the **Gen** constructor without a type argument that causes the warning. In the second line, it is the assignment of a raw reference to a generic variable that generates the warning.

At first, you might think that this line should also generate an unchecked warning, but it does not:

```
raw = iOb; // OK, but potentially wrong
```

No compiler warning is issued because the assignment does not cause any _further_ loss of type safety than had already occurred when **raw** was created.

One final point: you should limit the use of raw types to those cases in which you must mix legacy code with newer, generic code. Raw types are simply a transitional feature and not something that should be used for new code.

Progress Check

1. If a generic interface is implemented by a class, that class must also be generic. True or False?

2. A type parameter in a generic interface cannot be bounded. True or False?

3. Given

```
class XYZ<T> { // ...
```

show how to declare an object called **ob** that is **XYZ**'s raw type.

CRITICAL SKILL
13.10 # Erasure

Usually, it is not necessary for the programmer to know the details about how the Java compiler transforms your source code into object code. However, in the case of generics, some general understanding of the process is important because it explains why the generic features work as they do—and why their behavior is sometimes a bit surprising. For this reason, a brief discussion of how generics are implemented in Java is in order.

An important constraint that governed the way generics were added to Java was the need for compatibility with previous versions of Java. Simply put: generic code had to be compatible with preexisting, nongeneric code. Thus, any changes to the syntax of the Java language, or to the JVM, had to avoid breaking older code. The way Java implements generics while satisfying this constraint is through the use of *erasure*.

In general, here is how erasure works. When your Java code is compiled, all generic type information is removed (erased). This means replacing type parameters with their bound type, which is **Object** if no explicit bound is specified, and then applying the appropriate casts (as determined by the type arguments) to maintain type compatibility with the types specified by the type arguments. The compiler also enforces this type compatibility. This approach to generics means that no type parameters exist at run time. They are simply a source-code mechanism.

To better understand how erasure works, consider the following two classes.

```
// Here, T is bound by Object by default.
class Gen<T> {
  T ob; // here, T will be replaced by Object
```

---

1. True.
2. False.
3. `XYZ ob = new XYZ();`

```
  Gen(T o) {
    ob = o;
  }

  // Return ob.
  T getob() {
    return ob;
  }
}

// Here, T is bound by String.
class GenStr<T extends String> {
  T str; // here, T will be replaced by String

  GenStr(T o) {
    str = o;
  }

  T getstr() { return str; }
}
```

After these two classes are compiled, the **T** in **Gen** will be replaced by **Object**. The **T** in **GenStr** will be replaced by **String**. Within the code for **Gen** and **GenStr**, implicit casts are employed to ensure proper typing. For example, this sequence

```
Gen<Integer> iOb = new Gen<Integer>(99);

int x = iOb.getob();
```

would be compiled as if it were written like this:

```
Gen iOb = new Gen(99);

int x = (Integer) iOb.getob();
```

Ambiguity Errors

The inclusion of generics gives rise to a new type of error that you must guard against:
ambiguity. Ambiguity errors occur when erasure causes two seemingly distinct generic

declarations to resolve to the same erased type, causing a conflict. Here is an example that involves method overloading:

```
// Ambiguity caused by erasure on
// overloaded methods.
class MyGenClass<T, V> {
  T ob1;
  V ob2;

  // ...

  // These two overloaded methods are ambiguous
  // and will not compile.
  void set(T o) {
    ob1 = o;
  }

  void set(V o) {
    ob2 = o;
  }
}
```

These two methods are inherently ambiguous.

Notice that **MyGenClass** declares two generic types: **T** and **V**. Inside **MyGenClass**, an attempt is made to overload **set( )** based on parameters of type **T** and **V**. This looks reasonable because **T** and **V** appear to be different types. However, there are two ambiguity problems here.

First, as **MyGenClass** is written there is no requirement that **T** and **V** actually be different types. For example, it is perfectly correct (in principle) to construct a **MyGenClass** object as shown here:

```
MyGenClass<String, String> obj = new MyGenClass<String, String>()
```

In this case, both **T** and **V** will be replaced by **String**. This makes both versions of **set( )** identical, which is, of course, an error.

Second, and more fundamental, is that the type erasure of **set( )** reduces both versions to the following:

```
void set(Object o) { // ...
```

Thus, the overloading of **set( )** as attempted in **MyGenClass** is inherently ambiguous. The solution in this case is to use two separate method names rather than trying to overload **set( )**.

Progress Check

1. Erasure _____ all type parameters, substituting their bound types and applying appropriate casts.

2. By default, the bound type of a type parameter is _____.

3. Ambiguity can occur when type erasure causes two seemingly different declarations to resolve to the same erased type. True or False?

CRITICAL SKILL
13.12 Some Generic Restrictions

There are a few restrictions that you need to keep in mind when using generics. They involve creating objects of a type parameter, static members, exceptions, and arrays. Each is examined here.

Type Parameters Can't Be Instantiated

It is not possible to create an instance of a type parameter. For example, consider this class:

```
// Can't create an instance of T.
class Gen<T> {
  T ob;
  Gen() {
    ob = new T(); // Illegal!!!
  }
}
```

Here, it is illegal to attempt to create an instance of **T**. The reason should be easy to understand: because **T** does not exist at run time, how would the compiler know what type of object to create? Remember, erasure removes all type parameters during the compilation process.

---

1. removes
2. **Object**
3. True.

Restrictions on Static Members

No **static** member can use a type parameter declared by the enclosing class. For example, all of the **static** members of this class are illegal:

```
class Wrong<T> {
  // Wrong, no static variables of type T.
  static T ob;

  // Wrong, no static method can use T.
  static T getob() {
    return ob;
  }

  // Wrong, no static method can access an object
  // of type T.
  static void showob() {
    System.out.println(ob);
  }
}
```

Although you can't declare **static** members that use a type parameter declared by the enclosing class, you *can* declare **static** generic methods, which define their own type parameters, as was done earlier in this chapter.

Generic Array Restrictions

There are two important generics restrictions that apply to arrays. First, you cannot instantiate an array whose base type is a type parameter. Second, you cannot create an array of type-specific generic references. The following short program shows both situations.

```
// Generics and arrays.
class Gen<T extends Number> {
  T ob;

  T vals[]; // OK

  Gen(T o, T[] nums) {
    ob = o;

    // This statement is illegal.
//  vals = new T[10]; // can't create an array of T

    // But, this statement is OK.
```

```
        vals = nums; // OK to assign reference to existent array
    }
}

class GenArrays {
  public static void main(String args[]) {
    Integer n[] = { 1, 2, 3, 4, 5 };

    Gen<Integer> iOb = new Gen<Integer>(50, n);

    // Can't create an array of type-specific generic references.
    // Gen<Integer> gens[] = new Gen<Integer>[10]; // Wrong!

    // This is OK.
    Gen<?> gens[] = new Gen<?>[10]; // OK

  }
}
```

As the program shows, it's valid to declare a reference to an array of type **T**, as this line does:

```
T vals[]; // OK
```

But, you cannot instantiate an array of **T**, as this commented-out line attempts:

```
// vals = new T[10]; // can't create an array of T
```

The reason you can't create an array of **T** is that **T** does not exist at run time, so there is no way for the compiler to know what type of array to actually create.

However, you can pass a reference to a type-compatible array to **Gen( )** when an object is created and assign that reference to **vals**, as the program does in this line:

```
vals = nums; // OK to assign reference to existent array
```

This works because the array passed to **Gen** has a known type, which will be the same type as **T** at the time of object creation.

Inside **main( )**, notice that you can't declare an array of references to a specific generic type. That is, this line

```
// Gen<Integer> gens[] = new Gen<Integer>[10]; // Wrong!
```

won't compile.

Generic Exception Restriction

A generic class cannot extend **Throwable**. This means that you cannot create generic exception classes.

Continuing Your Study of Generics

As mentioned at the start, this module gives you sufficient knowledge to use generics effectively in your own programs. However, there are many side issues and special cases that are not covered here. Readers especially interested in generics will want to learn about how generics affect class hierarchies, run-time type comparisons, and overriding, for example. Discussions of these and other topics are found in my book *Java: The Complete Reference, 7th Edition* (McGraw-Hill/Osborne, 2007).

Module 13 Mastery Check

1. Generics are an important addition to Java because they enable the creation of code that is
   A. Type-safe
   B. Reusable
   C. Reliable
   D. All of the above

2. Can a primitive type be used as a type argument?

3. Show how to declare a class called **FlightSched** that takes two generic parameters.

4. Beginning with your answer to question 3, change **FlightSched**'s second type parameter so that it must extend **Thread**.

5. Now, change **FlightSched** so that its second type parameter must be a subclass of its first type parameter.

6. As it relates to generics, what is the **?** and what does it do?

7. Can the wildcard argument be bounded?

8. A generic method called **MyGen( )** has one type parameter. Furthermore, **MyGen( )** has one parameter whose type is that of the type parameter. It also returns an object of that type parameter. Show how to declare **MyGen( )**.

9. Given this generic interface

```
interface IGenIF<T, V extends T> { // ...
```

show the declaration of a class called **MyClass** that implements **IGenIF**.

10. Given a generic class called **Counter<T>**, show how to create an object of its raw type.

11. Do type parameters exist at run time?

12. Convert your solution to question 10 of the Mastery Check for Module 9 so that it is generic. In the process, create a stack interface called **IGenStack** that generically defines the operations **push( )** and **pop( )**.

Module 14

Applets, Events, and Miscellaneous Topics

Teaching the elements of the Java language is the primary goal of this book, and in this regard, we are nearly finished. The preceding 13 modules have focused on the features of Java defined by the language, such as its keywords, syntax, block structure, type conversion rules, and so on. At this point, you have enough knowledge to write sophisticated, useful Java programs. However, there are two important parts of Java programming that are not defined by keywords, but by API classes and specialized techniques. These are applets and events.

Be forewarned: The topics of applets and event handling are very large. Full and detailed coverage of either is well beyond the scope of this book. Here you will learn their fundamentals and see several examples, but we will only scratch the surface. After finishing this module, however, you will have a foundation upon which to build your knowledge.

This module ends with a description of the remaining Java keywords, such as **instanceof** and **native**, that have not been described elsewhere in this book. These keywords are used for more advanced programming, but they are summarized here for completeness.

CRITICAL SKILL
14.1 Applet Basics

Applets differ from the type of programs shown in the preceding modules. As mentioned in Module 1, applets are small programs that are designed for transmission over the Internet and run within a browser. Because Java's virtual machine is in charge of executing all Java programs, including applets, applets offer a secure way to dynamically download and execute programs over the Web.

Before we begin, it is necessary to explain that there are two general varieties of applets: those based on the Abstract Window Toolkit (AWT) and those based on Swing. Both the AWT and Swing support the creation of a graphical user interface (GUI). The AWT is the original GUI toolkit and Swing is Java's lightweight alternative. This chapter describes AWT-based applets. (Swing is introduced in Module 15.) It is important to understand, however, that Swing-based applets are built upon the same basic architecture as AWT-based applets. Furthermore, Swing is built on top of the AWT. Therefore, the information and techniques presented here describe the foundation of applet programming and most of it applies to both types of applets.

Prior to discussing any theory or details, let's begin by examining a simple applet. It performs one function: It displays the string "Java makes applets easy." inside a window.

```
// A minimal applet.
import java.awt.*;              ◄──────────── Notice these import statements.
import java.applet.*;

public class SimpleApplet extends Applet {
  public void paint(Graphics g) {
    g.drawString("Java makes applets easy.", 20, 20);
  }                              ▲
}                               └──────────── This outputs to the
                                              applet's window.
```

This applet begins with two **import** statements. The first imports the Abstract Window Toolkit classes. Applets interact with the user (either directly or indirectly) through the AWT, not through the console-based I/O classes. The AWT contains support for a window-based, graphical user interface. As you might expect, it is quite large and sophisticated. A complete discussion of it would require a book of its own. Fortunately, since we will be creating only very simple applets, we will make only limited use of the AWT. The next **import** statement imports the **applet** package. This package contains the class **Applet**. Every applet that you create must be a subclass of **Applet**.

The next line in the program declares the class **SimpleApplet**. This class must be declared as **public** because it will be accessed by outside code.

Inside **SimpleApplet**, **paint( )** is declared. This method is defined by the AWT **Component** class (which is a superclass of **Applet**) and is overridden by the applet. **paint( )** is called each time the applet must redisplay its output. This can occur for several reasons. For example, the window in which the applet is running can be overwritten by another window and then uncovered. Or the applet window can be minimized and then restored. **paint( )** is also called when the applet begins execution. Whatever the cause, whenever the applet must redraw its output, **paint( )** is called. The **paint( )** method has one parameter of type **Graphics**. This parameter will contain the graphics context, which describes the graphics environment in which the applet is running. This context is used whenever output to the applet is required.

Inside **paint( )**, there is a call to **drawString( )**, which is a member of the **Graphics** class. This method outputs a string beginning at the specified X,Y location. It has the following general form:

void drawString(String *message*, int *x*, int *y*)

Here, *message* is the string to be output beginning at *x,y*. In a Java window, the upper-left corner is location 0,0. The call to **drawString( )** in the applet causes the message to be displayed beginning at location 20,20.

Notice that the applet does not have a **main( )** method. Unlike the programs shown earlier in this book, applets do not begin execution at **main( )**. In fact, most applets don't even have a **main( )** method. Instead, an applet begins execution when the name of its class is passed to a browser or other applet-enabled program.

After you have entered the source code for **SimpleApplet**, you compile in the same way that you have been compiling programs. However, running **SimpleApplet** involves a different process. There are two ways in which you can run an applet: inside a browser or with a special development tool that displays applets. The tool provided with the standard Java JDK is called **appletviewer**, and we will use it to run the applets developed in this module. Of course, you can also run them in your browser, but the **appletviewer** is much easier to use during development.

To execute an applet (in either a Web browser or the **appletviewer**), you need to write a short HTML text file that contains a tag that loads the applet. Currently, Sun recommends using the APPLET tag for this purpose. Here is the HTML file that will execute **SimpleApplet**:

```
<applet code="SimpleApplet" width=200 height=60>
</applet>
```

The **width** and **height** statements specify the dimensions of the display area used by the applet.

To execute **SimpleApplet** with an applet viewer, you will execute this HTML file. For example, if the preceding HTML file is called **StartApp.html**, then the following command line will run **SimpleApplet**:

```
C:\>appletviewer StartApp.html
```

Although there is nothing wrong with using a stand-alone HTML file to execute an applet, there is an easier way. Simply include a comment near the top of your applet's source code file that contains the APPLET tag. If you use this method, the **SimpleApplet** source file looks like this:

```
import java.awt.*;
import java.applet.*;                      ─── This HTML is used by appletviewer
/*                                              to run the applet.
<applet code="SimpleApplet" width=200 height=60>
</applet>
*/

public class SimpleApplet extends Applet {
  public void paint(Graphics g) {
    g.drawString("Java makes applets easy.", 20, 20);
  }
}
```

Now you can execute the applet by passing the name of its source file to **appletviewer**. For example, this command line will now display **SimpleApplet**.

```
C:>appletviewer SimpleApplet.java
```

The window produced by **SimpleApplet**, as displayed by **appletviewer**, is shown in the following illustration:

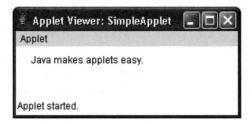

When using **appletviewer**, keep in mind that it provides the window frame. Applets run in a browser will not have a visible frame.

Let's review an applet's key points:

- All applets are subclasses of **Applet**.

- Applets do not need a **main( )** method.

- Applets must be run under an applet viewer or a Java-compatible browser.

- User I/O is not accomplished with Java's stream I/O classes. Instead, applets use the interface provided by the AWT (or by Swing).

Progress Check

1. What is an applet?

2. What method outputs to the applet's window?

3. What package must be included when creating an applet?

4. How are applets run?

---

1. An applet is a special type of Java program that is designed for transmission over the Internet and that runs inside a browser.

2. The **paint( )** method displays output in an applet's window.

3. The package **java.applet** must be included when creating an applet.

4. Applets are executed by a browser or by special tools, such as **appletviewer**.

Applet Organization and Essential Elements

Although the preceding applet is completely valid, such a simple applet is of little value. Before you can create useful applets, you need to know more about how applets are organized, what methods they use, and how they interact with the run-time system.

CRITICAL SKILL
14.2 The Applet Architecture

An applet is a GUI-based program. As such, its architecture is different from the console-based programs shown in the first part of this book. If you are familiar with GUI programming, you will be right at home writing applets. If not, then there are a few key concepts you must understand.

First, applets are event driven, and an applet resembles a set of interrupt service routines. Here is how the process works. An applet waits until an event occurs. The run-time system notifies the applet about an event by calling an event handler that has been provided by the applet. Once this happens, the applet must take appropriate action and then quickly return control to the system. This is a crucial point. For the most part, your applet should not enter a "mode" of operation, in which it maintains control for an extended period. Instead, it must perform specific actions in response to events and then return control to the run-time system. In those situations in which your applet needs to perform a repetitive task on its own (for example, displaying a scrolling message across its window), you must start an additional thread of execution.

Second, it is the user who initiates interaction with an applet—not the other way around. In a console-based program, when the program needs input, it will prompt the user and then call some input method. This is not the way it works in an applet. Instead, the user interacts with the applet as he or she wants, when he or she wants. These interactions are sent to the applet as events to which the applet must respond. For example, when the user clicks a mouse inside the applet's window, a mouse-clicked event is generated. If the user presses a key while the applet's window has input focus, a keypress event is generated. Applets can contain various controls, such as push buttons and check boxes. When the user interacts with one of these controls, an event is generated.

While the architecture of an applet is not as easy to understand as that of a console-based program, Java makes it as simple as possible. If you have written programs for Windows, you know how intimidating that environment can be. Fortunately, Java provides a much cleaner approach that is more quickly mastered.

CRITICAL SKILL
14.3 A Complete Applet Skeleton

Although **SimpleApplet** shown earlier is a real applet, it does not contain all of the elements required by most applets. Actually, all but the most trivial applets override a set of methods that provide the basic mechanism by which the browser or applet viewer interfaces to the applet and controls its execution. These lifecycle methods are **init( )**, **start( )**, **stop( )**, and **destroy( )** and they are defined by **Applet**. A fifth method, **paint( )**, is commonly overridden by AWT-based applets. It is inherited from the AWT **Component** class. Since default implementations for all of these methods are provided, applets do not need to override those methods they do not use. These five methods can be assembled into the skeleton shown here:

```
// An Applet skeleton.
import java.awt.*;
import java.applet.*;
/*
<applet code="AppletSkel" width=300 height=100>
</applet>
*/

public class AppletSkel extends Applet {
  // Called first.
  public void init() {
    // initialization
  }

  /* Called second, after init().  Also called whenever
     the applet is restarted. */
  public void start() {
    // start or resume execution
  }

  // Called when the applet is stopped.
  public void stop() {
    // suspends execution
  }

  /* Called when applet is terminated.  This is the last
     method executed. */
  public void destroy() {
    // perform shutdown activities
  }

  // Called when an applet's window must be restored.
  public void paint(Graphics g) {
    // redisplay contents of window
  }
}
```

Although this skeleton does not do anything, it can be compiled and run. Thus, it can be used as a starting point for applets that you create.

NOTE

Overriding **paint( )** applies mostly to AWT-based applets. Swing applets usually use a different painting mechanism.

Applet Initialization and Termination

It is important to understand the order in which the various methods shown in the skeleton are executed. When an applet begins, the following methods are called in this sequence:

1. init( )

2. start( )

3. paint( )

When an applet is terminated, the following sequence of method calls takes place:

1. stop( )

2. destroy( )

Let's look more closely at these methods.

The **init( )** method is the first method to be called. In **init( )** your applet will initialize variables and perform any other startup activities.

The **start( )** method is called after **init( )**. It is also called to restart an applet after it has been stopped, such as when the user returns to a previously displayed Web page that contains an applet. Thus, **start( )** might be called more than once during the life cycle of an applet.

The **paint( )** method is called each time your applet's output must be redrawn and was described earlier.

When the page containing your applet is left, the **stop( )** method is called. You will use **stop( )** to suspend any child threads created by the applet and to perform any other activities required to put the applet in a safe, idle state. Remember, a call to **stop( )** does not mean that the applet should be terminated because it might be restarted with a call to **start( )** if the user returns to the page.

The **destroy( )** method is called when the applet is no longer needed. It is used to perform any shutdown operations required of the applet.

Progress Check

1. What are the four lifecycle methods that most applets will override?

2. What must your applet do when **start( )** is called?

3. What must your applet do when **stop( )** is called?

CRITICAL SKILL

14.5 Requesting Repainting

As a general rule, an applet writes to its window only when its **paint( )** method is called by the run-time system. This raises an interesting question: How can the applet itself cause its window to be updated when its information changes? For example, if an applet is displaying a moving banner, what mechanism does the applet use to update the window each time this banner scrolls? Remember that one of the fundamental architectural constraints imposed on an applet is that it must quickly return control to the Java run-time system. It cannot create a loop inside **paint( )** that repeatedly scrolls the banner, for example. This would prevent control from passing back to the run-time system. Given this constraint, it may seem that output to your applet's window will be difficult at best. Fortunately, this is not the case. Whenever your applet needs to update the information displayed in its window, it simply calls **repaint( )**.

The **repaint( )** method is defined by the AWT's **Component** class. It causes the run-time system to execute a call to your applet's **paint( )** method. Thus, for another part of your applet to output to its window, simply store the output and then call **repaint( )**. This causes a call to **paint( )**, which can display the stored information. For example, if part of your applet needs to output a string, it can store this string in a **String** variable and then call **repaint( )**. Inside **paint( )**, you will output the string using **drawString( )**.

The simplest version of **repaint( )** is shown here:

void repaint( )

This version causes the entire window to be repainted.

Another version of **repaint( )** specifies a region that will be repainted:

void repaint(int *left*, int *top*, int *width*, int *height*)

1. The lifecycle methods are **init( )**, **start( )**, **stop( )**, and **destroy( )**.

2. When **start( )** is called, the applet must be started, or restarted.

3. When **stop( )** is called, the applet must be paused.

Ask the Expert

Q: **Is it possible for a method other than** paint( ) **or** update( ) **to output to an applet's window?**

A: Yes. To do so, you must obtain a graphics context by calling **getGraphics( )** (defined by **Component**) and then use this context to output to the window. However, for most applications, it is better and easier to route window output through **paint( )** and to call **repaint( )** when the contents of the window change.

Here, the coordinates of the upper-left corner of the region are specified by *left* and *top,* and the width and height of the region are passed in *width* and *height.* These dimensions are specified in pixels. You save time by specifying a region to repaint because window updates are costly in terms of time. If you only need to update a small portion of the window, it is more efficient to repaint only that region.

An example that demonstrates **repaint( )** is found in Project 14-1.

The update( ) Method

There is another method that relates to repainting called **update( )** that your applet may want to override. This method is defined by the **Component** class, and it is called when your applet has requested that a portion of its window be redrawn. The default version of **update( )** simply calls **paint( )**. However, you can override the **update( )** method so that it performs more subtle repainting, but this is an advanced technique that is beyond the scope of this book. Also, overriding **update( )** applies only to AWT-based applets.

Project 14-1 A Simple Banner Applet

Banner.java

To demonstrate **repaint( )**, a simple banner applet is presented. This applet scrolls a message, from right to left, across the applet's window. Since the scrolling of the message is a repetitive task, it is performed by a separate thread, created by the applet when it is initialized. Banners are popular Web features, and this project shows how to use a Java applet to create one.

Step by Step

1. Create a file called **Banner.java**.

2. Begin creating the banner applet with the following lines.

```
/*
   Project 14-1
```

```
   A simple banner applet.

   This applet creates a thread that scrolls
   the message contained in msg right to left
   across the applet's window.
*/
import java.awt.*;
import java.applet.*;
/*
<applet code="Banner" width=300 height=50>
</applet>
*/

public class Banner extends Applet implements Runnable {
  String msg = " Java Rules the Web ";
  Thread t;
  boolean stopFlag;

  // Initialize t to null.
  public void init() {
    t = null;
  }
```

Notice that **Banner** extends **Applet**, as expected, but it also implements **Runnable**. This is necessary since the applet will be creating a second thread of execution that will be used to scroll the banner. The message that will be scrolled in the banner is contained in the **String** variable **msg**. A reference to the thread that runs the applet is stored in **t**. The Boolean variable **stopFlag** is used to stop the applet. Inside **init( )**, the thread reference variable **t** is set to **null**.

3. Add the **start( )** method shown next.

```
// Start thread
public void start() {
  t = new Thread(this);
  stopFlag = false;
  t.start();
}
```

The run-time system calls **start( )** to start the applet running. Inside **start( )**, a new thread of execution is created and assigned to the **Thread** variable **t**. Then, **stopFlag** is set to **false**. Next, the thread is started by a call to **t.start( )**. Remember that **t.start( )** calls a method defined by **Thread**, which causes **run( )** to begin executing. It does not cause a call to the version of **start( )** defined by **Applet**. These are two separate methods.

(continued)

4. Add the **run( )** method, as shown here.

```
// Entry point for the thread that runs the banner.
public void run() {
  char ch;

  // Display banner
  for( ; ; ) {
    try {
      repaint();
      Thread.sleep(250);
      ch = msg.charAt(0);
      msg = msg.substring(1, msg.length());
      msg += ch;
      if(stopFlag)
        break;
    } catch(InterruptedException exc) {}
  }
}
```

In **run( )**, the characters in the string contained in **msg** are repeatedly rotated left. Between each rotation, a call to **repaint( )** is made. This eventually causes the **paint( )** method to be called, and the current contents of **msg** are displayed. Between each iteration, **run( )** sleeps for a quarter of a second. The net effect of **run( )** is that the contents of **msg** are scrolled right to left in a constantly moving display. The **stopFlag** variable is checked on each iteration. When it is **true**, the **run( )** method terminates.

5. Add the code for **stop( )** and **paint( )** as shown here.

```
// Pause the banner.
public void stop() {
  stopFlag = true;
  t = null;
}

// Display the banner.
public void paint(Graphics g) {
  g.drawString(msg, 50, 30);
}
```

If a browser is displaying the applet when a new page is viewed, the **stop( )** method is called, which sets **stopFlag** to **true**, causing **run( )** to terminate. It also sets **t** to **null**. Thus, there is no longer a reference to the **Thread** object, and it can be recycled the next time the garbage collector runs. This is the mechanism used to stop the thread when its page is no longer in view. When the applet is brought back into view, **start( )** is once again called, which starts a new thread to execute the banner.

6. The entire banner applet is shown here:

```
/*
   Project 14-1

   A simple banner applet.

   This applet creates a thread that scrolls
   the message contained in msg right to left
   across the applet's window.
*/
import java.awt.*;
import java.applet.*;
/*
<applet code="Banner" width=300 height=50>
</applet>
*/

public class Banner extends Applet implements Runnable {
  String msg = " Java Rules the Web ";
  Thread t;
  boolean stopFlag;

  // Initialize t to null.
  public void init() {
    t = null;
  }

  // Start thread
  public void start() {
    t = new Thread(this);
    stopFlag = false;
    t.start();
  }

  // Entry point for the thread that runs the banner.
  public void run() {
    char ch;

    // Display banner
    for( ; ; ) {
      try {
        repaint();
        Thread.sleep(250);
        ch = msg.charAt(0);
        msg = msg.substring(1, msg.length());
```

(continued)

```
        msg += ch;
        if(stopFlag)
          break;
      } catch(InterruptedException exc) {}
    }
  }

  // Pause the banner.
  public void stop() {
    stopFlag = true;
    t = null;
  }

  // Display the banner.
  public void paint(Graphics g) {
    g.drawString(msg, 50, 30);
  }
}
```

Sample output is shown here:

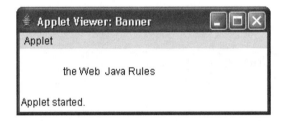

CRITICAL SKILL
14.6 Using the Status Window

In addition to displaying information in its window, an applet can also output a message to the status window of the browser or applet viewer on which it is running. To do so, call **showStatus( )**, which is defined by **Applet**, with the string that you want displayed. The general form of **showStatus( )** is shown here:

void showStatus(String *msg*)

Here, *msg* is the string to be displayed.

The status window is a good place to give the user feedback about what is occurring in the applet, suggest options, or possibly report some types of errors. The status window also makes an excellent debugging aid, because it gives you an easy way to output information about your applet.

The following applet demonstrates **showStatus( )**:

```
// Using the Status Window.
import java.awt.*;
import java.applet.*;
/*
<applet code="StatusWindow" width=300 height=50>
</applet>
*/

public class StatusWindow extends Applet{
  // Display msg in applet window.
  public void paint(Graphics g) {
    g.drawString("This is in the applet window.", 10, 20);
    showStatus("This is shown in the status window.");
  }
}
```

Sample output from this program is shown here:

 Passing Parameters to Applets

You can pass parameters to your applet. To do so, use the PARAM attribute of the APPLET tag, specifying the parameter's name and value. To retrieve a parameter, use the **getParameter( )** method, defined by **Applet**. Its general form is shown here:

String getParameter(String *paramName*)

Here, *paramName* is the name of the parameter. It returns the value of the specified parameter in the form of a **String** object. Thus, for numeric and **boolean** values, you will need to convert their string representations into their internal formats. If the specified parameter cannot be found, **null** is returned. Therefore, be sure to confirm that the value returned by **getParameter( )** is valid. Also, check any parameter that is converted into a numeric value, confirming that a valid conversion took place.

Here is an example that demonstrates passing parameters:

```
// Pass a parameter to an applet.
import java.awt.*;
import java.applet.*;

/*
```

(right margin, vertical) 14   Applets, Events, and Miscellaneous Topics

These HTML parameters are
passed to the applet.

```
<applet code="Param" width=300 height=80>
<param name=author value="Herb Schildt">
<param name=purpose value="Demonstrate Parameters">
<param name=version value=2>
</applet>
*/

public class Param extends Applet {
  String author;
  String purpose;
  int ver;

  public void start() {
    String temp;

    author = getParameter("author");
    if(author == null) author = "not found";

    purpose = getParameter("purpose");
    if(purpose == null) purpose = "not found";

    temp = getParameter("version");
    try {
      if(temp != null)
        ver = Integer.parseInt(temp);
      else
        ver = 0;
    } catch(NumberFormatException exc) {
      ver = -1; // error code
    }
  }

  public void paint(Graphics g) {
    g.drawString("Purpose: " + purpose, 10, 20);
    g.drawString("By: " + author, 10, 40);
    g.drawString("Version: " + ver, 10, 60);
  }
}
```

It is important to check that
the parameter exists!

It is also important to make sure
that numeric conversions succeed.

Sample output from this program is shown here:

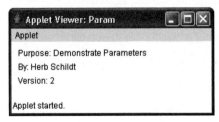

Progress Check

1. How do you cause an applet's **paint( )** method to be called?

2. Where does **showStatus( )** display a string?

3. What method is used to obtain a parameter specified in the APPLET tag?

CRITICAL SKILL
14.8 The Applet Class

As mentioned, all applets are subclasses of the **Applet** class. **Applet** inherits the following superclasses defined by the AWT: **Component**, **Container**, and **Panel**. Thus, an applet has access to the full functionality of the AWT.

In addition to the methods described in the preceding sections, **Applet** contains several others that give you detailed control over the execution of your applet. All of the methods defined by **Applet** are shown in Table 14-1.

Event Handling

In Java, GUI programs, such as applets, are event driven. Thus, event handling is at the core of successful GUI programming. Most events to which your program will respond are generated by the user. These events are passed to your program in a variety of ways, with the specific method depending upon the actual event. There are several types of events, including those generated by the mouse, the keyboard, and various controls, such as a push button. AWT-based events are supported by the **java.awt.event** package.

Before we start, it must be mentioned that it is not possible to fully discuss Java's event handling mechanism. Event handling is a large topic with many special features and attributes, and a complete discussion is well beyond the scope of this book. However, the overview presented here will help you get started.

---

1. To cause **paint( )** to be called, call **repaint( )**.
2. **showStatus( )** displays output in an applet's status window.
3. To obtain a parameter, call **getParameter( )**.

Method	Description
void destroy( )	Called by the browser just before an applet is terminated. Your applet will override this method if it needs to perform any cleanup prior to its destruction.
AccessibleContext getAccessibleContext( )	Returns the accessibility context for the invoking object.
AppletContext getAppletContext( )	Returns the context associated with the applet.
String getAppletInfo( )	Returns a string that describes the applet.
AudioClip getAudioClip(URL *url*)	Returns an **AudioClip** object that encapsulates the audio clip found at the location specified by *url*.
AudioClip getAudioClip(URL *url*, String *clipName*)	Returns an **AudioClip** object that encapsulates the audio clip found at the location specified by *url* and having the name specified by *clipName*.
URL getCodeBase( )	Returns the URL associated with the invoking applet.
URL getDocumentBase( )	Returns the URL of the HTML document that invokes the applet.
Image getImage(URL *url*)	Returns an **Image** object that encapsulates the image found at the location specified by *url*.
Image getImage(URL *url*, String *imageName*)	Returns an **Image** object that encapsulates the image found at the location specified by *url* and having the name specified by *imageName*.
Locale getLocale( )	Returns a **Locale** object that is used by various locale-sensitive classes and methods.
String getParameter(String *paramName*)	Returns the parameter associated with *paramName*. **null** is returned if the specified parameter is not found.
String[ ] [ ] getParameterInfo( )	Returns a **String** table that describes the parameters recognized by the applet. Each entry in the table must consist of three strings that contain the name of the parameter, a description of its type and/or range, and an explanation of its purpose.
void init( )	This method is called when an applet begins execution. It is the first method called for any applet.
boolean isActive( )	Returns **true** if the applet has been started. It returns **false** if the applet has been stopped.
static final AudioClip newAudioClip(URL *url*)	Returns an **AudioClip** object that encapsulates the audio clip found at the location specified by *url*. This method is similar to **getAudioClip( )** except that it is static and can be executed without the need for an **Applet** object.
void play(URL *url*)	If an audio clip is found at the location specified by *url*, the clip is played.

Table 14-1 The Methods Defined by **Applet**

Method	Description
void play(URL *url*, String *clipName*)	If an audio clip is found at the location specified by *url* with the name specified by *clipName*, the clip is played.
void resize(Dimension *dim*)	Resizes the applet according to the dimensions specified by *dim*. **Dimension** is a class stored inside **java.awt**. It contains two integer fields: **width** and **height**.
void resize(int *width*, int *height*)	Resizes the applet according to the dimensions specified by *width* and *height*.
final void setStub(AppletStub *stubObj*)	Makes *stubObj* the stub for the applet. This method is used by the run-time system and is not usually called by your applet. A *stub* is a small piece of code that provides the linkage between your applet and the browser.
void showStatus(String *str*)	Displays *str* in the status window of the browser or applet viewer. If the browser does not support a status window, then no action takes place.
void start( )	Called by the browser when an applet should start (or resume) execution. It is automatically called after **init( )** when an applet first begins.
void stop( )	Called by the browser to suspend execution of the applet. Once stopped, an applet is restarted when the browser calls **start( )**.

Table 14-1 The Methods Defined by **Applet** (continued)

CRITICAL SKILL
14.9 The Delegation Event Model

The modern approach to handling events is based on the *delegation event model*. The delegation event model defines standard and consistent mechanisms to generate and process events. Its concept is quite simple: a *source* generates an event and sends it to one or more *listeners*. In this scheme, the listener simply waits until it receives an event. Once received, the listener processes the event and then returns. The advantage of this design is that the logic that processes events is cleanly separated from the user interface logic that generates those events. A user interface element is able to "delegate" the processing of an event to a separate piece of code. In the delegation event model, listeners must register with a source in order to receive an event notification.

Events

In the delegation model, an event is an object that describes a state change in a source. It can be generated as a consequence of a person interacting with the elements in a graphical user interface, such as pressing a button, entering a character via the keyboard, selecting an item in a list, and clicking the mouse.

Event Sources

An event source is an object that generates an event. A source must register listeners in order for the listener to receive notifications about a specific type of event. Each type of event has its own registration method. Here is the general form:

public void add*Type*Listener(*Type*Listener *el*)

Here, *Type* is the name of the event, and *el* is a reference to the event listener. For example, the method that registers a keyboard event listener is called **addKeyListener( )**. The method that registers a mouse motion listener is called **addMouseMotionListener( )**. When an event occurs, all registered listeners are notified and receive a copy of the event object.

A source must also provide a method that allows a listener to unregister an interest in a specific type of event. The general form of such a method is this:

public void remove*Type*Listener(*Type*Listener *el*)

Here, *Type* is the name of the event, and *el* is a reference to the event listener. For example, to remove a keyboard listener, you would call **removeKeyListener( )**.

The methods that add or remove listeners are provided by the source that generates events. For example, the **Component** class provides methods to add and remove keyboard and mouse event listeners.

Event Listeners

A *listener* is an object that is notified when an event occurs. It has two major requirements. First, it must have been registered with one or more sources to receive notifications about specific types of events. Second, it must implement methods to receive and process these notifications.

The methods that receive and process AWT events are defined in a set of interfaces found in **java.awt.event**. For example, the **MouseMotionListener** interface defines methods that receive notifications when the mouse is dragged or moved. Any object may receive and process one or both of these events if it provides an implementation of this interface.

Event Classes

The classes that represent events are at the core of Java's event handling mechanism. At the root of the Java event class hierarchy is **EventObject**, which is in **java.util**. It is the superclass for all events. The class **AWTEvent**, defined within the **java.awt** package, is a subclass of

EventObject. It is the superclass (either directly or indirectly) for all AWT-based events used by the delegation event model.

The package **java.awt.event** defines several types of events that are generated by various user interface elements. Table 14-2 enumerates the most commonly used ones and provides a brief description of when they are generated.

Event Listener Interfaces

Event listeners receive event notifications. Listeners for AWT-based events are created by implementing one or more of the interfaces defined by the **java.awt.event** package. When an event occurs, the event source invokes the appropriate method defined by the listener and provides an event object as its argument. Table 14-3 lists commonly used listener interfaces and provides a brief description of the methods they define.

Event Class	Description
ActionEvent	Generated when a button is pressed, a list item is double-clicked, or a menu item is selected.
AdjustmentEvent	Generated when a scroll bar is manipulated.
ComponentEvent	Generated when a component is hidden, moved, resized, or becomes visible.
ContainerEvent	Generated when a component is added to or removed from a container.
FocusEvent	Generated when a component gains or loses keyboard focus.
InputEvent	Abstract superclass for all component input event classes.
ItemEvent	Generated when a check box or list item is clicked; also occurs when a choice selection is made or a checkable menu item is selected or deselected.
KeyEvent	Generated when input is received from the keyboard.
MouseEvent	Generated when the mouse is dragged or moved, clicked, pressed, or released; also generated when the mouse enters or exits a component.
TextEvent	Generated when the value of a text area or text field is changed.
WindowEvent	Generated when a window is activated, closed, deactivated, deiconified, iconified, opened, or quit.

Table 14-2 The Main Event Classes in **java.awt.event**

Interface	Description
ActionListener	Defines one method to receive action events. Action events are generated by such things as push buttons and menus.
AdjustmentListener	Defines one method to receive adjustment events, such as those produced by a scroll bar.
ComponentListener	Defines four methods to recognize when a component is hidden, moved, resized, or shown.
ContainerListener	Defines two methods to recognize when a component is added to or removed from a container.
FocusListener	Defines two methods to recognize when a component gains or loses keyboard focus.
ItemListener	Defines one method to recognize when the state of an item changes. An item event is generated by a check box, for example.
KeyListener	Defines three methods to recognize when a key is pressed, released, or typed.
MouseListener	Defines five methods to recognize when the mouse is clicked, enters a component, exits a component, is pressed, or is released.
MouseMotionListener	Defines two methods to recognize when the mouse is dragged or moved.
TextListener	Defines one method to recognize when a text value changes.
WindowListener	Defines seven methods to recognize when a window is activated, closed, deactivated, deiconified, iconified, opened, or quit.

Table 14-3 Common Event Listener Interfaces

Progress Check

1. Briefly explain the significance of **EventObject** and **AWTEvent**.

2. What is an event source? What is an event listener?

3. Listeners must be registered with a source in order to receive event notifications. True or False?

---

1. **EventObject** is a superclass of all events. **AWTEvent** is a superclass of all AWT events that are handled by the delegation event model.

2. An event source generates events. An event listener receives event notifications.

3. True.

CRITICAL SKILL
14.10 Using the Delegation Event Model

Now that you have had an overview of the delegation event model and its various components, it is time to see it in practice. Applet programming using the delegation event model is actually quite easy. Just follow these two steps:

1. Implement the appropriate interface in the listener so that it will receive the type of event desired.

2. Implement code to register and unregister (if necessary) the listener as a recipient for the event notifications.

Remember that a source may generate several types of events. Each event must be registered separately. Also, an object may register to receive several types of events, but it must implement all of the interfaces that are required to receive these events.

To see how the delegation model works in practice, we will look at an example that handles one of the most commonly used event generators: the mouse.

Handling Mouse Events

To handle mouse events, you must implement the **MouseListener** and the **MouseMotionListener** interfaces. The **MouseListener** interface defines five methods. If a mouse button is clicked, **mouseClicked( )** is invoked. When the mouse enters a component, the **mouseEntered( )** method is called. When it leaves, **mouseExited( )** is called. The **mousePressed( )** and **mouseReleased( )** methods are invoked when a mouse button is pressed and released, respectively. The general forms of these methods are shown here:

void mouseClicked(MouseEvent *me*)

void mouseEntered(MouseEvent *me*)

void mouseExited(MouseEvent *me*)

void mousePressed(MouseEvent *me*)

void mouseReleased(MouseEvent *me*)

The **MouseMotionListener** interface defines two methods. The **mouseDragged( )** method is called multiple times as the mouse is dragged. The **mouseMoved( )** method is called multiple times as the mouse is moved. Their general forms are shown here:

void mouseDragged(MouseEvent *me*)

void mouseMoved(MouseEvent *me*)

The **MouseEvent** object passed in *me* describes the event. **MouseEvent** defines a number of methods that you can use to get information about what happened. Probably the most commonly used methods in **MouseEvent** are **getX( )** and **getY( )**. These return the X and Y coordinates of the mouse (relative to the window) when the event occurred. Their forms are shown here:

int getX( )

int getY( )

The next example will use these methods to display the current location of the mouse.

Ask the Expert

Q: You state that the getX( ) and getY( ) methods defined by MouseEvent return the window-relative coordinates of the mouse. Are there methods that return its screen-relative (that is, absolute) location?

A: Yes. With the release of Java SE 6, **MouseEvent** now defines methods that obtain the X and Y coordinates of the mouse relative to the screen. They are shown here.

int getXOnScreen( )

int getYOnScreen( )

You might find it interesting to experiment with these methods by substituting them for **getX( )** and **getY( )** in the **MouseEvents** applet shown next.

A Simple Mouse Event Applet

The following applet demonstrates handling mouse events. It displays the current coordinates of the mouse in the applet's status window. Each time a button is pressed, the word "Down" is displayed at the location of the mouse pointer. Each time the button is released, the word "Up" is shown. If a button is clicked, the message "Mouse clicked" is displayed in the upper-left corner of the applet display area.

As the mouse enters or exits the applet window, a message is displayed in the upper-left corner of the applet display area. When dragging the mouse, a * is shown, which tracks with the mouse pointer as it is dragged. Notice that the two variables, **mouseX** and **mouseY**, store the location of the mouse when a mouse pressed, released, or dragged event occurs. These coordinates are then used by **paint( )** to display output at the point of these occurrences.

```
// Demonstrate the mouse event handlers.
import java.awt.*;
```

```
import java.awt.event.*;
import java.applet.*;
/*
  <applet code="MouseEvents" width=300 height=100>
  </applet>
*/

public class MouseEvents extends Applet
  implements MouseListener, MouseMotionListener {

  String msg = "";
  int mouseX = 0, mouseY = 0; // coordinates of mouse

  public void init() {
    addMouseListener(this);
    addMouseMotionListener(this);
  }

  // Handle mouse clicked.
  public void mouseClicked(MouseEvent me) {
    mouseX = 0;
    mouseY = 10;
    msg = "Mouse clicked.";
    repaint();
  }

  // Handle mouse entered.
  public void mouseEntered(MouseEvent me) {
    mouseX = 0;
    mouseY = 10;
    msg = "Mouse entered.";
    repaint();
  }

  // Handle mouse exited.
  public void mouseExited(MouseEvent me) {
    mouseX = 0;
    mouseY = 10;
    msg = "Mouse exited.";
    repaint();
  }

  // Handle button pressed.
  public void mousePressed(MouseEvent me) {
    // save coordinates
    mouseX = me.getX();
    mouseY = me.getY();
```

Register this class as a listener for mouse events.

This, and the other event handlers, respond to mouse events.

```
    msg = "Down";
    repaint();
  }

  // Handle button released.
  public void mouseReleased(MouseEvent me) {
    // save coordinates
    mouseX = me.getX();
    mouseY = me.getY();
    msg = "Up";
    repaint();
  }

  // Handle mouse dragged.
  public void mouseDragged(MouseEvent me) {
    // save coordinates
    mouseX = me.getX();
    mouseY = me.getY();
    msg = "*";
    showStatus("Dragging mouse at " + mouseX + ", " + mouseY);
    repaint();
  }

  // Handle mouse moved.
  public void mouseMoved(MouseEvent me) {
    // show status
    showStatus("Moving mouse at " + me.getX() + ", " +
               me.getY());
  }

  // Display msg in applet window at current X,Y location.
  public void paint(Graphics g) {
    g.drawString(msg, mouseX, mouseY);
  }
}
```

Sample output from this program is shown here:

Let's look closely at this example. The **MouseEvents** class extends **Applet** and implements both the **MouseListener** and **MouseMotionListener** interfaces. These two interfaces contain methods that receive and process the various types of mouse events. Notice that the applet is both the source and the listener for these events. This works because **Component**, which supplies the **addMouseListener( )** and **addMouseMotionListener( )** methods, is a superclass of **Applet**. Being both the source and the listener for events is a common situation for applets.

Inside **init( )**, the applet registers itself as a listener for mouse events. This is done by using **addMouseListener( )** and **addMouseMotionListener( )**, which are members of **Component**. They are shown here:

void addMouseListener(MouseListener *ml*)

void addMouseMotionListener(MouseMotionListener *mml*)

Here, *ml* is a reference to the object receiving mouse events, and *mml* is a reference to the object receiving mouse motion events. In this program, the same object is used for both.

The applet then implements all of the methods defined by the **MouseListener** and **MouseMotionListener** interfaces. These are the event handlers for the various mouse events. Each method handles its event and then returns.

CRITICAL SKILL
14.11 More Java Keywords

Before concluding this module, a few more Java keywords need to be briefly discussed:

- **transient**
- **volatile**
- **instanceof**
- **native**
- **strictfp**
- **assert**

These keywords are used in programs more advanced than those found in this book. However, an overview of each is presented so that you will know their purpose.

The transient and volatile Modifiers

The **transient** and **volatile** keywords are type modifiers that handle somewhat specialized situations. When an instance variable is declared as **transient**, then its value need not persist when an object is stored. Thus, a **transient** field is one that does not affect the state of an object.

The **volatile** modifier was mentioned briefly in Module 11 but warrants a closer look. Modifying a variable with **volatile** tells the compiler that the variable can be changed unexpectedly by other parts of your program. As you saw in Module 11, one of these situations involves multithreaded programs. In a multithreaded program, sometimes two or more threads will share the same variable. For efficiency considerations, each thread can keep its own, private copy of such a shared variable. The real (or *master*) copy of the variable is updated at various times, such as when a **synchronized** method is entered. While this approach works fine, there may be times when it is inappropriate. In some cases, all that really matters is that the master copy of a variable always reflects the current state. To ensure this, simply specify the variable as **volatile**. Doing so tells the compiler that it must always keep any private copies up to date with the master copy and vice versa. Also, accesses to the master variable must be executed in the precise order in which they are executed on any private copy.

instanceof

Sometimes it is useful to know the type of an object during run time. For example, you might have one thread of execution that generates various types of objects and another thread that processes these objects. In this situation, it might be useful for the processing thread to know the type of each object when it receives it. Another situation in which knowledge of an object's type at run time is important involves casting. In Java, an invalid cast causes a run-time error. Many invalid casts can be caught at compile time. However, casts involving class hierarchies can produce invalid casts that can only be detected at run time. Because a superclass reference can refer to subclass objects, it is not always possible to know at compile time whether or not a cast involving a superclass reference is valid. The **instanceof** keyword addresses these types of situations.

The **instanceof** operator has this general form:

objref instanceof *type*

Here, *objref* is a reference to an instance of a class, and *type* is a class or interface type. If *objref* is of the specified type or can be cast into the specified type, then the **instanceof** operator evaluates to **true**. Otherwise, its result is **false**. Thus, **instanceof** is the means by which your program can obtain run-time type information about an object.

strictfp

One of the more esoteric keywords is **strictfp**. With the creation of Java 2, the floating-point computation model was relaxed slightly. Specifically, the new model does not require the truncation of certain intermediate values that occur during a computation. This prevents overflow or underflow in some cases. By modifying a class or a method with **strictfp**, you ensure that floating-point calculations (and thus all truncations) take place precisely as they did in earlier versions of Java. When a class is modified by **strictfp**, all of the methods in the class are also **strictfp** automatically.

assert

The **assert** keyword is used during program development to create an *assertion*, which is a condition that is expected to be true during the execution of the program. For example, you might have a method that should always return a positive integer value. You might test this by asserting that the return value is greater than zero using an **assert** statement. At run time, if the condition actually is true, no other action takes place. However, if the condition is false, then an **AssertionError** is thrown. Assertions are often used during testing to verify that some expected condition is actually met. They are not usually used for released code.

The **assert** keyword has two forms. The first is shown here:

assert *condition*;

Here, *condition* is an expression that must evaluate to a Boolean result. If the result is true, then the assertion is true and no other action takes place. If the condition is false, then the assertion fails and a default **AssertionError** object is thrown. For example,

```
assert n > 0;
```

If **n** is less than or equal to zero, then an **AssertionError** is thrown. Otherwise, no action takes place.

The second form of **assert** is shown here:

assert *condition* : *expr*;

In this version, *expr* is a value that is passed to the **AssertionError** constructor. This value is converted to its string format and displayed if an assertion fails. Typically, you will specify a string for *expr*, but any non-**void** expression is allowed as long as it defines a reasonable string conversion.

To enable assertion checking at run time, you must specify the **-ea** option. For example, to enable assertions for **Sample**, execute it using this line:

```
java -ea Sample
```

Assertions are quite useful during development because they streamline the type of error checking that is common during testing. But be careful—you must not rely on an assertion to perform any action actually required by the program. The reason is that normally, released code will be run with assertions disabled and the expression in an assertion will not be evaluated.

Native Methods

Although rare, there may occasionally be times when you will want to call a subroutine that is written in a language other than Java. Typically, such a subroutine will exist as executable code for the CPU and environment in which you are working—that is, native code. For example, you may wish to call a native code subroutine in order to achieve faster execution time. Or you may want to use a specialized, third-party library, such as a statistical package. However, since Java programs are compiled to bytecode, which is then interpreted (or compiled on the fly) by the Java run-time system, it would seem impossible to call a native code subroutine from within your Java program. Fortunately, this conclusion is false. Java provides the **native** keyword, which is used to declare native code methods. Once declared, these methods can be called from inside your Java program just as you call any other Java method.

To declare a native method, precede the method with the **native** modifier, but do not define any body for the method. For example:

```
public native int meth() ;
```

Once you have declared a native method, you must provide the native method and follow a rather complex series of steps in order to link it with your Java code.

Ask the Expert

Q: While we are on the subject of keywords, I have a question about this. I have occasionally noticed a form of this that takes parentheses. For example,

```
this(x);
```

Can you tell me what this does?

A: The form of **this** that you refer to enables one constructor to invoke another constructor within the same class. The general form of this use of **this** is shown here:

this(*arg-list*)

When **this( )** is executed, the overloaded constructor that matches the parameter list specified by *arg-list* is executed first. Then, if there are any statements inside the original constructor, they are executed. The call to **this( )** must be the first statement within the constructor. Here is a simple example.

```
class MyClass {
  int a;
  int b;

  // Initialize a and b individually.
  MyClass(int i, int j) {
    a = i;
    b = j;
  }
```

(continued)

```
  // Use this() to initialize a and b to the same value.
  MyClass(int i) {
    this(i, i); // invokes MyClass(i, i)
  }
}
```

In **MyClass**, only the first constructor actually assigns a value to **a** and **b**. The second constructor simply invokes the first. Therefore, when this statement executes:

```
MyClass mc = new MyClass(8);
```

The call to **MyClass(8)** causes **this(8, 8)** to be executed, which translates into a call to **MyClass(8, 8)**.

Invoking overloaded constructors through **this( )** can be useful because it can prevent the unnecessary duplication of code. However, you need to be careful. Constructors that call **this( )** will execute a bit slower than those that contain all of their initialization code in-line. This is because the call and return mechanism used when the second constructor is invoked adds overhead. Remember that object creation affects all users of your class. If your class will be used to create large numbers of objects, then you must carefully balance the benefits of smaller code against the increased time it takes to create an object. As you gain more experience with Java, you will find these types of decisions easier to make.

There are two restrictions you need to keep in mind when using **this( )**. First, you cannot use any instance variable of the constructor's class in a call to **this( )**. Second, you cannot use **super( )** and **this( )** in the same constructor because each must be the first statement in the constructor.

✓ Module 14 Mastery Check

1. What method is called when an applet first begins running? What method is called when an applet is removed from the system?

2. Explain why an applet must use multithreading if it needs to run continually.

3. Enhance Project 14-1 so that it displays the string passed to it as a parameter. Add a second parameter that specifies the time delay (in milliseconds) between each rotation.

4. Extra challenge: Create an applet that displays the current time, updated once per second. To accomplish this, you will need to do a little research. Here is a hint to help you get started: One way to obtain the current time is to use a **Calendar** object, which is part of

the **java.util** package. (Remember, Sun provides online documentation for all of Java's standard classes.) You should now be at the point where you can examine the **Calendar** class on your own and use its methods to solve this problem.

5. Briefly explain Java's delegation event model.

6. Must an event listener register itself with a source?

7. Extra challenge: Another of Java's display methods is **drawLine( )**. It draws a line in the currently selected color between two points. It is part of the **Graphics** class. Using **drawLine( )**, write a program that tracks mouse movement. If the button is pressed, have the program draw a continuous line until the mouse button is released.

8. Briefly describe the **assert** keyword.

9. Give one reason why a native method might be useful to some types of programs.

Module 15

Introducing Swing

With the exception of the applet examples shown in Module 14, all of the programs in this book have been console-based. This means that they do not make use of a graphical user interface (GUI). While console-based programs are excellent for teaching the basics of Java and for some types of programs, most real-world applications will be GUI-based. Therefore, to conclude this book, this module introduces Java's modern GUI toolkit: Swing.

Swing is a collection of classes and interfaces that define the look and feel of the modern Java GUI. Swing offers a rich set of visual components, such as buttons, text fields, scroll bars, check boxes, trees, and tables, that can be tailored to fit any need. By using Swing, you give your applications the kind of up-to-date interface that users have come to expect.

It is important to state at the outset that Swing is a very large topic that requires an entire book of its own. This module can only scratch its surface. However, the material presented here will give you a general understanding of Swing, including its history, basic concepts, and design philosophy. It then introduces five commonly used Swing components: the label, push button, text field, check box, and list. The module ends by showing how to create a Swing-based applet. Although this module describes only a small part of Swing's features, after completing it, you will be able to begin writing simple GUI-based programs. You will also have a foundation upon which to continue your study of Swing.

NOTE

For a comprehensive introduction to Swing, see my book *Swing: A Beginner's Guide* published by McGraw-Hill/Osborne, 2007.

CRITICAL SKILL
15.1 The Origins and Design Philosophy of Swing

Swing did not exist in the early days of Java. Rather, it was a response to deficiencies present in Java's original GUI subsystem: the Abstract Window Toolkit (AWT). The AWT defines a basic set of components that support a usable, but limited graphical interface. One reason for the limited nature of the AWT is that it translates its various visual components into their corresponding, platform-specific equivalents, or *peers*. This means that the look and feel of an AWT component is defined by the platform, not by Java. Because the AWT components use native code resources, they are referred to as *heavyweight*.

The use of native peers led to several problems. First, because of differences between operating systems, a component might look, or even act, differently on different platforms. This potential variability threatened the overarching philosophy of Java: write once, run anywhere. Second, the look and feel of each component was fixed (because it is defined by the platform) and could not be (easily) changed. Third, the use of heavyweight components caused some frustrating restrictions. For example, a heavyweight component is always rectangular and opaque.

Not long after Java's original release, it became apparent that the limitations and restrictions present in the AWT were sufficiently serious that a better approach was needed. The solution was Swing. Introduced in 1997, Swing was included as part of the Java Foundation Classes (JFC). Swing was initially available for use with Java 1.1 as a separate library. However, beginning with Java 1.2, Swing (and the rest of JFC) was fully integrated into Java.

Swing addresses the limitations associated with the AWT's components through the use of two key features: *lightweight components* and a *pluggable look and feel*. Although they are largely transparent to the programmer, these two features are at the foundation of Swing's design philosophy and the reason for much of its power and flexibility. Let's look at each.

With very few exceptions, Swing components are *lightweight*. This means that a component is written entirely in Java. They do not rely on platform-specific peers. Lightweight components have some important advantages, including efficiency and flexibility. For example, a lightweight component can be transparent, which enables non-rectangular shapes. Furthermore, because lightweight components do not translate into platform-specific peers, the look and feel of each component is determined by Swing, not by the underlying operating system. This means that each component will work in a consistent manner across all platforms.

Because each Swing component is rendered by Java code rather than by platform-specific peers, it is possible to separate the look and feel of a component from the logic of the component, and this is what Swing does. Separating out the look and feel provides a significant advantage: it becomes possible to change the way that a component is rendered without affecting any of its other aspects. In other words, it is possible to "plug in" a new look and feel for any given component without creating any side effects in the code that uses that component.

Java provides look-and-feels, such as metal and Motif, that are available to all Swing users. The metal look and feel is also called the *Java look and feel*. It is a platform-independent look and feel that is available in all Java execution environments. It is also the default look and feel. For this reason, the default Java look and feel (metal) is used by the examples in this module.

Swing's pluggable look and feel is made possible because Swing uses a modified version of the classic *model-view-controller (MVC)* architecture. In MVC terminology, the *model* corresponds to the state information associated with the component. For example, in the case of a check box, the model contains a field that indicates if the box is checked or unchecked. The *view* determines how the component is displayed on the screen, including any aspects of the view that are affected by the current state of the model. The *controller* determines how the component reacts to the user. For example, when the user clicks a check box, the controller reacts by changing the model to reflect the user's choice (checked or unchecked). This then results in the view being updated. By separating a component into a model, a view, and a controller, the specific implementation of each can be changed without affecting the other two. For instance, different view implementations can render the same component in different ways without affecting the model or the controller.

Ask the Expert

Q: You say that Swing defines the look and feel of the modern Java GUI. Does this mean that Swing replaces the AWT?

A: No, Swing does not replace the AWT. Rather, Swing builds upon the foundation provided by the AWT. Thus, the AWT is still a crucial part of Java. Swing also uses the same event handling mechanism as the AWT (which was described in Module 14). Although knowledge of the AWT is not required by this module, you need a solid understanding of its structure and features if you seek full Swing mastery.

Although the MVC architecture and the principles behind it are conceptually sound, the high level of separation between the view and the controller was not beneficial for Swing components. Instead, Swing uses a modified version of MVC that combines the view and the controller into a single logical entity called the *UI delegate*. For this reason, Swing's approach is called either the *model-delegate* architecture or the *separable model* architecture. Therefore, although Swing's component architecture is based on MVC, it does not use a classical implementation of it. Although you won't work directly with models or UI delegates in this module, they are, nevertheless, present behind the scene.

As you work through this module, you will see that even though Swing embodies very sophisticated design concepts, it is easy to use. In fact, one could argue that Swing's ease of use is its most important advantage. Simply stated, Swing makes manageable the often difficult task of developing your program's user interface. This lets you concentrate on the GUI, itself, rather than on implementation details.

Progress Check

1. A lightweight component is written in highly optimized machine code. True or False?

2. What feature enables the look and feel of a Swing component to be changed?

3. Does Swing use a standard implementation of the MVC architecture?

---

1. False
2. Pluggable look and feel
3. No, Swing uses a modified approach called model-delegate or separable model.

CRITICAL SKILL
15.2 Components and Containers

A Swing GUI consists of two key items: *components* and *containers*. However, this distinction is mostly conceptual because all containers are also components. The difference between the two is found in their intended purpose: As the term is commonly used, a component is an independent visual control, such as a push button or text field. A container holds a group of components. Thus, a container is a special type of component that is designed to hold other components. Furthermore, in order for a component to be displayed, it must be held within a container. Thus, all Swing GUIs will have at least one container. Because containers are components, a container can also hold other containers. This enables Swing to define what is called a *containment hierarchy*, at the top of which must be a *top-level container*.

Components

In general, Swing components are derived from the **JComponent** class. (The only exceptions to this are the four top-level containers, described in the next section.) **JComponent** provides the functionality that is common to all components. For example, **JComponent** supports the pluggable look and feel. **JComponent** inherits the AWT classes **Container** and **Component**. Thus, a Swing component is built on and compatible with an AWT component.

All of Swing's components are represented by classes defined within the package **javax.swing**. The following table shows the class names for Swing components (including those used as containers).

JApplet	JButton	JCheckBox	JCheckBoxMenuItem
JColorChooser	JComboBox	JComponent	JDesktopPane
JDialog	JEditorPane	JFileChooser	JFormattedTextField
JFrame	JInternalFrame	JLabel	JLayeredPane
JList	JMenu	JMenuBar	JMenuItem
JOptionPane	JPanel	JPasswordField	JPopupMenu
JProgressBar	JRadioButton	JRadioButtonMenuItem	JRootPane
JScrollBar	JScrollPane	JSeparator	JSlider
JSpinner	JSplitPane	JTabbedPane	JTable
JTextArea	JTextField	JTextPane	JTogglebutton
JToolBar	JToolTip	JTree	JViewport
JWindow			

Notice that all component classes begin with the letter **J**. For example, the class for a label is **JLabel**, the class for a push button is **JButton**, and the class for a check box is **JCheckBox**.

As mentioned at the start of this module, it is not possible to examine all of Swing's components in this book. (Indeed, complete coverage of Swing's component set requires a complete book of its own.) However, this module will introduce five of the most commonly used components: **JLabel**, **JButton**, **JTextField**, **JCheckBox**, and **JList**. Once you understand the basic operation of these components, it will be easy for you to learn to use the others.

Containers

Swing defines two types of containers. The first are top-level containers: **JFrame**, **JApplet**, **JWindow**, and **JDialog**. These containers do not inherit **JComponent**. They do, however, inherit the AWT classes **Component** and **Container**. Unlike Swing's other components, which are lightweight, the top-level containers are heavyweight. This makes the top-level containers a special case in the Swing component library.

As the name implies, a top-level container must be at the top of a containment hierarchy. A top-level container is not contained within any other container. Furthermore, every containment hierarchy must begin with a top-level container. The one most commonly used for applications is **JFrame**. The one used for applets is **JApplet**.

The second type of container supported by Swing is the lightweight container. Lightweight containers *do* inherit **JComponent**. Examples of lightweight containers are **JPanel**, **JScrollPane**, and **JRootPane**. Lightweight containers are often used to collectively organize and manage groups of related components because a lightweight container can be contained within another container. Thus, you can use lightweight containers to create subgroups of related controls that are contained within an outer container.

The Top-Level Container Panes

Each top-level container defines a set of *panes*. At the top of the hierarchy is an instance of **JRootPane**. **JRootPane** is a lightweight container whose purpose is to manage the other panes. It also helps manage the optional menu bar. The panes that compose the root pane are called the *glass pane*, the *content pane*, and the *layered pane*.

The glass pane is the top-level pane. It sits above and completely covers all other panes. The glass pane enables you to manage mouse events that affect the entire container (rather than an individual control) or to paint over any other component, for example. In most cases, you won't need to use the glass pane directly. The layered pane allows components to be given a depth value. This value determines which component overlays another. (Thus, the layered pane lets you specify a Z-order for a component, although this is not something that you will usually need to do.) The layered pane holds the content pane and the (optional) menu bar.

Although the glass pane and the layered panes are integral to the operation of a top-level container and serve important purposes, much of what they provide occurs behind the scene.

The pane with which your application will interact the most is the content pane, because this is the pane to which you will add visual components. In other words, when you add a component, such as a button, to a top-level container, you will add it to the content pane. Therefore, the content pane holds the components that the user interacts with. By default, the content pane is an opaque instance of **JPanel** (which is one of Swing's lightweight containers).

**CRITICAL SKILL
15.3** Layout Managers

Before you begin writing a Swing program, there is one more thing that you need to be aware of: the *layout manager*. The layout manager controls the position of components within a container. Java offers several layout managers. Most are provided by the AWT (within **java.awt**), but Swing adds a few of its own. All layout managers are instances of a class that implements the **LayoutManager** interface. (Some will also implement the **LayoutManager2** interface.) Here is a list of a few of the layout managers available to the Swing programmer.

FlowLayout	A simple layout that positions components left-to-right, top-to-bottom. (Positions components right-to-left for some cultural settings.)
BorderLayout	Positions components within the center or the borders of the container. This is the default layout for a content pane.
GridLayout	Lays out components within a grid.
GridBagLayout	Lays out different size components within a flexible grid.
BoxLayout	Lays out components vertically or horizontally within a box.
SpringLayout	Lays out components subject to a set of constraints.

Frankly, the topic of layout managers is quite large, and it is not possible to examine it in detail in this book. Fortunately, this module uses only two layout managers—**BorderLayout** and **FlowLayout**—and both are very easy to use.

BorderLayout is the default layout manager for the content pane. It implements a layout style that defines five locations to which a component can be added. The first is the center. The other four are the sides (i.e., borders), which are called north, south, east, and west. By default, when you add a component to the content pane, you are adding the component to the center. To add a component to one of the other regions, specify its name.

Although a border layout is useful is some situations, often another, more flexible layout manager is needed. One of the simplest is **FlowLayout**. A flow layout lays out components one row at a time, top to bottom. When one row is full, layout advances to the next row. Although this scheme gives you little control over the placement of components, it is quite simple to use. However, be aware that if you resize the frame, the position of the components will change.

Progress Check

1. A container holds one or more components. True or False?

2. **JFrame** is a _____weight component.

3. To what pane are components added?

4. What function does a layout manager perform?

A First Simple Swing Program

Swing programs differ from the console-based programs shown earlier in this book. They also differ from the AWT-based applets shown in Module 14. Not only do Swing programs use the Swing component set to handle user interaction, but they also have special requirements that relate to threading. The best way to understand the structure of a Swing program is to work through an example. There are two types of Java programs in which Swing is typically used. The first is a desktop application. The second is the applet. This section shows how to create a Swing application. The creation of a Swing applet is described later in this module.

Although quite short, the following program shows one way to write a Swing application. In the process it demonstrates several key features of Swing. It uses two Swing components: **JFrame** and **JLabel**. **JFrame** is the top-level container that is commonly used for Swing applications. **JLabel** is the Swing component that creates a label, which is a component that displays information. The label is Swing's simplest component because it is passive. That is, a label does not respond to user input. It just displays output. The program uses a **JFrame** container to hold an instance of a **JLabel**. The label displays a short text message.

---

1. True

2. Heavy

3. The content pane

4. A layout manager positions components within a container.

```
// A simple Swing program.

import javax.swing.*;          ◄─────────── Swing programs must import javax.swing.

class SwingDemo {

  SwingDemo() {
                                                        Create a container.
    // Create a new JFrame container.
    JFrame jfrm = new JFrame("A Simple Swing Application");  ◄──┘

    // Give the frame an initial size.
    jfrm.setSize(275, 100);     ◄─────────── Set the dimensions of the frame.

    // Terminate the program when the user closes the application.
    jfrm.setDefaultCloseOperation(JFrame.EXIT_ON_CLOSE);  ◄─── Terminate
                                                             on close.
    // Create a text-based label.
    JLabel jlab = new JLabel(" Swing defines the modern Java GUI.");◄─┐

                                                       Create a swing label.

    // Add the label to the content pane.
    jfrm.add(jlab);     ◄─────────── Add the label to the content pane.

    // Display the frame.
    jfrm.setVisible(true);    ◄─────────── Make the frame visible.
  }

  public static void main(String args[]) {
    // Create the frame on the event dispatching thread.
    SwingUtilities.invokeLater(new Runnable() {
      public void run() {
        new SwingDemo();    ◄─────────── SwingDemo must be created on the event
      }                                  dispatching thread.
    });
  }
}
```

Swing programs are compiled and run in the same way as other Java applications. Thus, to compile this program, you can use this command line:

```
javac SwingDemo1.java
```

To run the program, use this command line:

```
java SwingDemo1
```

When the program is run, it will produce the window shown in Figure 15-1.

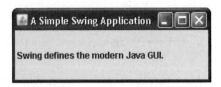

Figure 15-1 The window produced by the **SwingDemo** program

The First Swing Example Line by Line

Because the **SwingDemo** program illustrates several key Swing concepts, we will examine it carefully, line by line. The program begins by importing the following package:

```
import javax.swing.*;
```

This **javax.swing** package contains the components and models defined by Swing. For example, it defines classes that implement labels, buttons, edit controls, and menus. This package will be included in all programs that use Swing.

Next, the program declares the **SwingDemo** class, and a constructor for that class. The constructor is where most of the action of the program occurs. It begins by creating a **JFrame**, using this line of code:

```
JFrame jfrm = new JFrame("A Simple Swing Application.");
```

This creates a container called **jfrm** that defines a rectangular window complete with a title bar; close, minimize, maximize, and restore buttons; and a system menu. Thus, it creates a standard, top-level window. The title of the window is passed to the constructor.

Next, the window is sized using this statement:

```
jfrm.setSize(275, 100);
```

The **setSize( )** method sets the dimensions of the window, which are specified in pixels. Its general form is shown here:

void setSize(int *width*, int *height*)

In this example, the width of the window is set to 275 and the height is set to 100.

By default, when a top-level window is closed (such as when the user clicks the close box), the window is removed from the screen, but the application is not terminated. While this default behavior is useful in some situations, it is not what is needed for most applications. Instead, you will usually want the entire application to terminate when its top-level window is closed. There are a couple of ways to achieve this. The easiest way is to call **setDefaultCloseOperation( )**, as the program does:

```
jfrm.setDefaultCloseOperation(JFrame.EXIT_ON_CLOSE);
```

After this call executes, closing the window causes the entire application to terminate. The general form of **setDefaultCloseOperation( )** is shown here:

void setDefaultCloseOperation(int *what*)

The value passed in *what* determines what happens when the window is closed. There are several other options in addition to **JFrame.EXIT_ON_CLOSE**. They are shown here:

JFrame.DISPOSE_ON_CLOSE

JFrame.HIDE_ON_CLOSE

JFrame.DO_NOTHING_ON_CLOSE

Their names reflect their actions. These constants are declared in **WindowConstants**, which is an interface declared in **javax.swing** that is implemented by **JFrame**.

The next line of code creates a **JLabel** component:

```
JLabel jlab = new JLabel(" Swing defines the modern Java GUI.");
```

JLabel is the easiest-to-use Swing component because it does not accept user input. It simply displays information, which can consist of text, an icon, or a combination of the two. The label created by the program contains only text, which is passed to its constructor.

The next line of code adds the label to the content pane of the frame:

```
jfrm.add(jlab);
```

As explained earlier, all top-level containers have a content pane in which components are stored. Thus, to add a component to a frame, you must add it to the frame's content pane. This is accomplished by calling **add( )** on the **JFrame** reference (**jfrm** in this case). The **add( )** method has several versions. The general form of the one used by the program is shown here:

Component add(Component *comp*)

By default, the content pane associated with a **JFrame** uses a border layout. This version of **add( )** adds the component (in this case, a label) to the center location. Other versions of **add( )** enable you to specify one of the border regions. When a component is added to the center, its size is automatically adjusted to fit the size of the center.

Ask the Expert

Q: I have seen Swing programs that use a method called getContentPane( ) when adding a component to the content pane. What is this method and do I need to use it?

A: This question brings up an important historical point. Prior to JDK 5, when adding a component to the content pane, you could not invoke the **add( )** method directly on a **JFrame** instance. Instead, you needed to explicitly call **add( )** on the content pane of the **JFrame** object. The content pane can be obtained by calling **getContentPane( )** on a **JFrame** instance. The **getContentPane( )** method is shown here:

Container getContentPane( )

It returns a **Container** reference to the content pane. The **add( )** method was then called on that reference to add a component to a content pane. Thus, in the past, you had to use the following statement to add **jlab** to **jfrm**:

```
jfrm.getContentPane().add(jlab); // old-style
```

Here, **getContentPane( )** first obtains a reference to content pane, and then **add( )** adds the component to the container linked to this pane. This same procedure was also required to invoke **remove( )** to remove a component and **setLayout( )** to set the layout manager for the content pane. You will see explicit calls to **getContentPane( )** frequently throughout pre-5.0 code. Today, the use of **getContentPane( )** is no longer necessary. You can simply call **add( )**, **remove( )**, and **setLayout( )** directly on **JFrame** because these methods have been changed so that they automatically operate on the content pane.

The last statement in the **SwingDemo** constructor causes the window to become visible.

```
jfrm.setVisible(true);
```

The **setVisible( )** method has this general form:

void setVisible(boolean *flag*)

If *flag* is **true**, the window will be displayed. Otherwise, it will be hidden. By default, a **JFrame** is invisible, so **setVisible(true)** must be called to show it.

Inside **main( )**, a **SwingDemo** object is created, which causes the window and the label to be displayed. Notice that the **SwingDemo** constructor is invoked using these lines of code:

```
SwingUtilities.invokeLater(new Runnable() {
  public void run() {
    new SwingDemo();
  }
});
```

This sequence causes a **SwingDemo** object to be created on the *event-dispatching thread* rather than on the main thread of the application. Here's why. In general, Swing programs are event-driven. For example, when a user interacts with a component, an event is generated. An event is passed to the application by calling an event handler defined by the application. However, the handler is executed on the event-dispatching thread provided by Swing and not on the main thread of the application. Thus, although event handlers are defined by your program, they are called on a thread that was not created by your program. To avoid problems (such as two different threads trying to update the same component at the same time), all Swing GUI components must be created and updated from the event-dispatching thread, not the main thread of the application. However, **main( )** is executed on the main thread. Thus, it cannot directly instantiate a **SwingDemo** object. Instead, it must create a **Runnable** object that executes on the event-dispatching thread, and have this object create the GUI.

To enable the GUI code to be created on the event-dispatching thread, you must use one of two methods that are defined by the **SwingUtilities** class. These methods are **invokeLater( )** and **invokeAndWait( )**. They are shown here:

static void invokeLater(Runnable *obj*)

static void invokeAndWait(Runnable *obj*)
     throws InterruptedException, InvocationTargetException

Here, *obj* is a **Runnable** object that will have its **run( )** method called by the event-dispatching thread. The difference between the two methods is that **invokeLater( )** returns immediately, but **invokeAndWait( )** waits until **obj.run( )** returns. You can use these methods to call a method that constructs the GUI for your Swing application, or whenever you need to modify the state of the GUI from code not executed by the event-dispatching thread. You will normally want to use **invokeLater( )**, as the preceding program does. However, when constructing the initial GUI for an applet, you will want to use **invokeAndWait( )**. (Creating Swing applets is described in later in this module.)

One more point: The preceding program does not respond to any events, because **JLabel** is a passive component. In other words, a **JLabel** does not generate any events. Therefore, the preceding program does not include any event handlers. However, all other components generate events to which your program must respond, as the subsequent examples in this module show.

Ask the Expert

Q: You state that it is possible to add a component to the other regions of a border layout by using an overloaded version of add( ). Can you explain?

A: As explained, **BorderLayout** implements a layout style that defines five locations to which a component can be added. The first is the center. The other four are the sides (i.e., borders), which are called north, south, east, and west. By default, when you add a component to the content pane, you are adding the component to the center. To specify one of the other locations, use this form of **add( )**:

void add(Component *comp*, Object *loc*)

Here, *comp* is the component to add and *loc* specifies the location to which it is added. The *loc* value must be one of the following:

BorderLayout.CENTER	BorderLayout.EAST	BorderLayout.NORTH
BorderLayout.SOUTH	BorderLayout.WEST	

In general, **BorderLayout** is most useful when you are creating a **JFrame** that contains a centered component (which might be a group of components held within one of Swing's lightweight containers) that has a header and/or footer component associated with it. In other situations, one of Java's other layout managers will be more appropriate.

Progress Check

1. What is **JLabel**?

2. What package must be included in all Swing programs?

3. What is the event-dispatching thread? Why is it important?

---

1. The Swing class that creates a label

2. **javax.swing**

3. The event-dispatching is the thread on which event handlers are invoked. In Swing, all event handlers must be executed on the event-dispatching thread.

Ask the Expert

Q: **I have seen Swing code that does not use either the** invokeLater( ) **or the** invokeAndWait( ) **method. Are they really needed?**

A: In the early days of Swing, it was considered safe to initially display the GUI from within the main application thread. Thus, in the past, Swing applications did not usually call **invokeLater( )** or **invokeAndWait( )** to display the GUI at program startup. However, Sun changed this assessment. Today, Sun states that it is no longer proper to initialize the GUI from within the main thread because it might lead to problems in a small number of cases. Frankly, there are many Swing applications in widespread use that initialize the GUI from within the main thread and operate without problems. (For example, because of its extreme simplicity, the GUI for the first example program could probably be created on the main thread without harm.) However, for new code, the GUI should be created on the event-dispatching thread. Because creating the GUI on the event-dispatching thread is now considered to be best practice, it is the approach followed by all the examples in this book.

CRITICAL SKILL
15.5 Use JButton

One of the most commonly used Swing controls is the push button. A push button is an instance of **JButton**. **JButton** inherits the abstract class **AbstractButton**, which defines the functionality common to all buttons. Swing push buttons can contain text, an image, or both, but this book uses only text-based buttons.

JButton supplies several constructors. The one used here is

JButton(String *msg*)

Here, *msg* specifies the string that will be displayed inside the button.

When a push button is pressed, it generates an **ActionEvent**. **ActionEvent** is defined by the AWT and also used by Swing. **JButton** provides the following methods, which are used to add or remove an action listener:

void addActionListener(ActionListener *al*)

void removeActionListener(ActionListener *al*)

Here, *al* specifies an object that will receive event notifications. This object must be an instance of a class that implements the **ActionListener** interface.

The **ActionListener** interface defines only one method: **actionPerformed( )**. It is shown here:

void actionPerformed(ActionEvent *ae*)

This method is called when a button is pressed. In other words, it is the event handler that is called when a button press event has occurred. Your implementation of **actionPerformed( )** must quickly respond to that event and return. As a general rule, event handlers must not engage in long operations, because doing so will slow down the entire application. If a time-consuming procedure must be performed, then a separate thread should be created for that purpose.

Using the **ActionEvent** object passed to **actionPerformed( )**, you can obtain several useful pieces of information relating to the button-press event. The one used by this module is the *action command* string associated with the button. By default, this is the string displayed inside the button. The action command is obtained by calling **getActionCommand( )** on the event object. It is declared like this:

String getActionCommand( )

The action command identifies the button. Thus, when using two or more buttons within the same application, the action command gives you an easy way to determine which button was pressed.

The following program demonstrates how to create a push button and respond to button-press events. Figure 15-2 shows how the example appears on the screen.

```
// Demonstrate a push button and handle action events.

import java.awt.*;
import java.awt.event.*;
import javax.swing.*;

class ButtonDemo implements ActionListener {

  JLabel jlab;

  ButtonDemo() {

    // Create a new JFrame container.
    JFrame jfrm = new JFrame("A Button Example");

    // Specify FlowLayout for the layout manager.
    jfrm.setLayout(new FlowLayout());

    // Give the frame an initial size.
    jfrm.setSize(220, 90);
```

```
    // Terminate the program when the user closes the application.
    jfrm.setDefaultCloseOperation(JFrame.EXIT_ON_CLOSE);

    // Make two buttons.
    JButton jbtnUp = new JButton("Up");
    JButton jbtnDown = new JButton("Down");

    // Add action listeners.
    jbtnUp.addActionListener(this);
    jbtnDown.addActionListener(this);

    // Add the buttons to the content pane.
    jfrm.add(jbtnUp);
    jfrm.add(jbtnDown);

    // Create a label.
    jlab = new JLabel("Press a button.");

    // Add the label to the frame.
    jfrm.add(jlab);

    // Display the frame.
    jfrm.setVisible(true);
  }

  // Handle button events.
  public void actionPerformed(ActionEvent ae) {
    if(ae.getActionCommand().equals("Up"))
      jlab.setText("You pressed Up.");
    else
      jlab.setText("You pressed down. ");
  }

  public static void main(String args[]) {
    // Create the frame on the event dispatching thread.
    SwingUtilities.invokeLater(new Runnable() {
      public void run() {
        new ButtonDemo();
      }
    });
  }
}
```

Create two push buttons.

Add action listeners for the buttons.

Add the buttons to the content pane.

Handle button events.

Use the action command to determine which button was pressed.

Let's take a close look at the new things in this program. First, notice that the program now imports both the **java.awt** and **java.awt.event** packages. The **java.awt** package is needed because it contains the **FlowLayout** class, which supports the flow layout manager. The

Figure 15-2 Output from the **ButtonDemo** program

java.awt.event package is needed because it defines the **ActionListener** interface and the **ActionEvent** class.

Next, the class **ButtonDemo** is declared. Notice that it implements **ActionListener**. This means that **ButtonDemo** objects can be used to receive action events. Next, a **JLabel** reference is declared. This reference will be used within the **actionPerformed( )** method to display which button has been pressed.

The **ButtonDemo** constructor begins by creating a **JFrame** called **jfrm**. It then sets the layout manager for the content pane of **jfrm** to **FlowLayout**, as shown here:

```
jfrm.setLayout(new FlowLayout());
```

As explained earlier, by default, the content pane uses **BorderLayout** as its layout manager, but for many applications, **FlowLayout** is more convenient. Recall that a flow layout lays out components one row at a time, top to bottom. When one row is full, layout advances to the next row. Although this scheme gives you little control over the placement of components, it is quite simple to use. However, be aware that if you resize the frame, the position of the components will change.

After setting the size and the default close operation, **ButtonDemo( )** creates two buttons, as shown here:

```
JButton jbtnUp = new JButton("Up");
JButton jbtnDown = new JButton("Down");
```

The first button will contain the text "Up", and the second will contain "Down".

Next, the instance of **ButtonDemo** referred to via **this** is added as an action listener for the buttons by these two lines:

```
jbtnUp.addActionListener(this);
jbtnDown.addActionListener(this);
```

This approach means that the object that creates the buttons will also receive notifications when a button is pressed.

Each time a button is pressed, it generates an action event and all registered listeners are notified by calling the **actionPerformed( )** method. The **ActionEvent** object representing the button event is passed as a parameter. In the case of **ButtonDemo**, this event is passed to this implementation of **actionPerformed( )**.

```
// Handle button events.
public void actionPerformed(ActionEvent ae) {
  if(ae.getActionCommand().equals("Up"))
    jlab.setText("You pressed Up.");
  else
    jlab.setText("You pressed down. ");
}
```

The event that occurred is passed via **ae**. Inside the method, the action command associated with the button that generated the event is obtained by calling **getActionCommand( )**. (Recall that, by default, the action command is the same as the text displayed by the button.) Based on the contents of that string, the text in the label is set to show which button was pressed.

One last point: Remember that **actionPerformed( )** is called on the event-dispatching thread as explained earlier. It must return quickly in order to avoid slowing down the application.

Progress Check

1. Show how to construct a push button that displays the string "Emergency Stop".

2. A push button generates what type of event when it is pressed?

3. When using **JButton**, what is the default action command string?

CRITICAL SKILL
15.6 Work with JTextField

Another commonly used control is **JTextField**. It enables the user to enter a line of text. **JTextField** inherits the abstract class **JTextComponent**, which is the superclass of all text components. **JTextField** defines several constructors. The one we will use is shown here:

JTextField(int *cols*)

---

1. **JButton("Emergency Stop");**

2. **ActionEvent**

3. By default, the action command string associated with a **JButton** is the text displayed within the button.

Here, *cols* specifies the width of the text field in columns. It is important to understand that you can enter a string that is longer than the number of columns. It's just that the physical size of the text field on the screen will be *cols* columns wide.

When you press ENTER when inputting into a text field, an **ActionEvent** is generated. Therefore, **JTextField** provides the **addActionListener( )** and **removeActionListener( )** methods. To handle action events, you must implement the **actionPerformed( )** method defined by the **ActionListener** interface. The process is similar to handling action events generated by a button, as described earlier.

Like a **JButton**, a **JTextField** has an action command string associated with it. By default, the action command is the current contents of the text field. However, this default is seldom used. Instead, you will usually set the action command to a fixed value of your own choosing by calling the **setActionCommand( )** method, shown here:

void setActionCommand(String *cmd*)

The string passed in *cmd* becomes the new action command. The text in the text field is unaffected. Once you set the action command string, it remains the same no matter what is entered into the text field. One reason that you might want to explicitly set the action command is to provide a way to recognize the text field as the source of an action event. This is especially important when another control in the same frame also generates action events and you want to use the same event handler to process both events. Setting the action command gives you a way to tell them apart. Also, if you don't set the action command associated with a text field, then by happenstance the contents of the text field might match the action command of another component.

To obtain the string that is currently displayed in the text field, call **getText( )** on the **JTextField** instance. It is declared as shown here:

String getText( )

You can set the text in a **JTextField** by calling **setText( )**, shown next.

void setText(String *text*)

Here, *text* is the string that will be put into the text field.

Ask the Expert

Q: You explained that the action command associated with a text field can be set by calling setActionCommand( ). **Can I use this method to set the action command associated with a push button?**

A: Yes. As explained, by default the action command associated with a push button is the name of the button. To set the action command to a different value, you can use the **setActionCommand( )** method. It works the same for **JButton** as it does for **JTextField**.

The following program demonstrates **JTextField**. It contains one text field, one push button, and two labels. One label prompts the user to enter text into the text field. When the user presses ENTER while focus is within the text field, the contents of the text field are obtained and displayed within a second label. The push button is called Reverse. When pressed, it reverses the contents of the text field. Sample output is shown in Figure 15-3.

```java
// Use a text field.

import java.awt.*;
import java.awt.event.*;
import javax.swing.*;

class TFDemo implements ActionListener {

  JTextField jtf;
  JButton jbtnRev;
  JLabel jlabPrompt, jlabContents;

  TFDemo() {

    // Create a new JFrame container.
    JFrame jfrm = new JFrame("Use a Text Field");

    // Specify FlowLayout for the layout manager.
    jfrm.setLayout(new FlowLayout());

    // Give the frame an initial size.
    jfrm.setSize(240, 120);

    // Terminate the program when the user closes the application.
    jfrm.setDefaultCloseOperation(JFrame.EXIT_ON_CLOSE);

    // Create a text field.
    jtf = new JTextField(10);                    Create a text field that is 10 columns wide.

    // Set the action commands for the text field.
    jtf.setActionCommand("myTF");                Set the action command for the text field.

    // Create the Reverse button.
    JButton jbtnRev = new JButton("Reverse");

    // Add action listeners.
    jtf.addActionListener(this);                 Add action listeners for both the text field
    jbtnRev.addActionListener(this);             and the button.

    // Create the labels.
```

```
    jlabPrompt = new JLabel("Enter text: ");
    jlabContents = new JLabel("");

    // Add the components to the content pane.
    jfrm.add(jlabPrompt);
    jfrm.add(jtf);
    jfrm.add(jbtnRev);
    jfrm.add(jlabContents);

    // Display the frame.
    jfrm.setVisible(true);
  }

  // Handle action events.                              This method handles both
  public void actionPerformed(ActionEvent ae) {  ◄──── button and text field events.

    if(ae.getActionCommand().equals("Reverse")) {  ◄──── Use the action
      // The Reverse button was pressed.                    command to determine
      String orgStr = jtf.getText();                        which component
      String resStr = "";                                   generated the event.

      // Reverse the string in the text field.
      for(int i=orgStr.length()-1; i >=0; i--)
        resStr += orgStr.charAt(i);

      // Store the reversed string in the text field.
      jtf.setText(resStr);
    } else
      // Enter was pressed while focus was in the
      // text field.
      jlabContents.setText("You pressed ENTER. Text is: " +
                              jtf.getText());
  }

  public static void main(String args[]) {
    // Create the frame on the event dispatching thread.
    SwingUtilities.invokeLater(new Runnable() {
      public void run() {
        new TFDemo();
      }
    });
  }
}
```

Much of the program will be familiar, but a few parts warrant special attention. First, notice that the action command associated with the text field is set to "myTF" by the following line:

```
jtf.setActionCommand("myTF");
```

Figure 15-3 Sample output from the **TFDemo** program

After this line executes, the action command string will always be "myTF" no matter what text is currently held in the text field. Therefore, the action command generated by **jtf** will not accidentally conflict with the action command associated with the Reverse push button. The **actionPerformed( )** method makes use of this fact to determine what event has occurred. If the action command string is "Reverse", it can mean only one thing: that the Reverse push button has been pressed. Otherwise, the action command was generated by the user pressing ENTER while the text field had input focus.

Finally, notice this line from within the **actionPerformed( )** method:

```
jlabContents.setText("You pressed ENTER. Text is: " +
                     jtf.getText());
```

As explained, when the user presses ENTER while focus is inside the text field, an **ActionEvent** is generated and sent to all registered action listeners, through the **actionPerformed( )** method. For **TFDemo**, this method simply obtains the text currently held in the text field by calling **getText( )** on **jtf**. It then displays the text through the label referred to by **jlabContents**.

Progress Check

1. **JTextField** generates an **ActionEvent** when the user presses ENTER. True or False?

2. What methods set and obtain the text in a **JTextField**?

3. What method sets the action command in a **JTextField**?

---

1. True

2. **setText( )** and **getText( )**

3. The action command is set by calling **setActionCommand( )**.

Create a JCheckBox

After the push button, perhaps the next most widely used control is the check box. In Swing, a check box is an object of type **JCheckBox**. **JCheckBox** inherits **AbstractButton** and **JToggleButton**. Thus, a check box is, essentially, a special type of button.

    JCheckBox defines several constructors. The one used here is

JCheckBox(String *str*)

It creates a check box that has the text specified by *str* as a label.

    When a check box is selected or deselected (that is, checked or unchecked), an item event is generated. Item events are represented by the **ItemEvent** class. Item events are handled by classes that implement the **ItemListener** interface. This interface specifies only one method: **itemStateChanged( )**, which is shown here:

void itemStateChanged(ItemEvent *ie*)

The item event is received in *ie*.

    To obtain a reference to the item that changed, call **getItem( )** on the **ItemEvent** object. This method is shown here:

Object getItem( )

The reference returned must be cast to the component class being handled, which in this case is **JCheckBox**.

    You can obtain the text associated with a check box by calling **getText( )**. You can set the text after a check box is created by calling **setText( )**. These methods work the same as they do for **JButton**, described earlier.

    The easiest way to determine the state of a check box is to call the **isSelected( )** method. It is shown here:

boolean isSelected( )

It returns true if the check box is selected and false otherwise.

    The following program demonstrates check boxes. It creates three check boxes called Alpha, Beta, and Gamma. Each time the state of a box is changed, the current action is displayed. Also, the list of all currently selected check boxes is displayed. Sample output is shown in Figure 15-4.

```
// Demonstrate check boxes.

import java.awt.*;
import java.awt.event.*;
import javax.swing.*;

class CBDemo implements ItemListener {

  JLabel jlabSelected;
  JLabel jlabChanged;
  JCheckBox jcbAlpha;
  JCheckBox jcbBeta;
  JCheckBox jcbGamma;

  CBDemo() {
    // Create a new JFrame container.
    JFrame jfrm = new JFrame("Demonstrate Check Boxes");

    // Specify FlowLayout for the layout manager.
    jfrm.setLayout(new FlowLayout());

    // Give the frame an initial size.
    jfrm.setSize(280, 120);

    // Terminate the program when the user closes the application.
    jfrm.setDefaultCloseOperation(JFrame.EXIT_ON_CLOSE);

    // Create empty labels.
    jlabSelected = new JLabel("");
    jlabChanged = new JLabel("");

    // Make check boxes.
    jcbAlpha = new JCheckBox("Alpha");
    jcbBeta = new JCheckBox("Beta");
    jcbGamma = new JCheckBox("Gamma");

    // Events generated by the check boxes
    // are handled in common by the itemStateChanged()
    // method implemented by CBDemo.
    jcbAlpha.addItemListener(this);
    jcbBeta.addItemListener(this);
    jcbGamma.addItemListener(this);

    // Add check boxes and labels to the content pane.
    jfrm.add(jcbAlpha);
    jfrm.add(jcbBeta);
```

Create the check boxes.

```
      jfrm.add(jcbGamma);
      jfrm.add(jlabChanged);
      jfrm.add(jlabSelected);

      // Display the frame.
      jfrm.setVisible(true);
    }

    // This is the handler for the check boxes.
    public void itemStateChanged(ItemEvent ie) {        ◄────────── Handle check box
      String str = "";                                              item events.

      // Obtain a reference to the check box that
      // caused the event.                                     Get a reference to the check
      JCheckBox cb = (JCheckBox) ie.getItem();   ◄────────── box that changed.

      // Report what check box changed.
      if(cb.isSelected())   ◄─────────────────────── Determine what happened.
        jlabChanged.setText(cb.getText() + " was just selected.");
      else
        jlabChanged.setText(cb.getText() + " was just cleared.");

      // Report all selected boxes.
      if(jcbAlpha.isSelected()) {
        str += "Alpha ";
      }
      if(jcbBeta.isSelected()) {
        str += "Beta ";
      }
      if(jcbGamma.isSelected()) {
        str += "Gamma";
      }

      jlabSelected.setText("Selected check boxes: " + str);
    }

    public static void main(String args[]) {
      // Create the frame on the event dispatching thread.
      SwingUtilities.invokeLater(new Runnable() {
        public void run() {
          new CBDemo();
        }
      });
    }
  }
```

Figure 15-4 Sample output from the **CBDemo** program

The main point of interest in this program is the item event handler, **itemStateChanged( )**. It performs two functions. First, it reports whether the check box has been selected or cleared. Second, it displays all selected check boxes. It begins by obtaining a reference to the check box that generated the **ItemEvent**, as shown here:

```
JCheckBox cb = (JCheckBox) ie.getItem();
```

The cast to **JCheckBox** is necessary because **getItem( )** returns a reference of type **Object**. Next, **itemStateChanged( )** calls **isSelected( )** on **cb** to determine the current state of the check box. If **isSelected( )** returns true, it means that the user selected the check box. Otherwise, the check box was cleared. It then sets the **jlabChanged** label to reflect what happened.

Finally, **itemStateChanged( )** checks the selected state of each check box, building a string that contains the names of those that are selected. It displays this string in the **jlabSelected** label.

CRITICAL SKILL
15.8 Work with JList

The last component that we will examine is **JList**. This is Swing's basic list class. It supports the selection of one or more items from a list. Although often the list consists of strings, it is possible to create a list of just about any object that can be displayed. **JList** is so widely used in Java that it is highly unlikely that you have not seen one before.

JList provides several constructors. The one used here is

JList(Object[ ] *items*)

This creates a **JList** that contains the items in the array specified by *items*.

Although a **JList** will work properly by itself, most of the time you will wrap a **JList** inside a **JScrollPane**, which is a container that automatically provides scrolling for its contents. Here is the constructor that we will use:

JScrollPane(Component *comp*)

Here, *comp* specifies the component to be scrolled, which in this case will be a **JList**. When you wrap a **JList** in a **JScrollPane**, long lists will automatically be scrollable. This simplifies GUI design. It also makes it easy to change the number of entries in a list without having to change the size of the **JList** component.

A **JList** generates a **ListSelectionEvent** when the user makes or changes a selection. This event is also generated when the user deselects an item. It is handled by implementing **ListSelectionListener**, which is packaged in **javax.swing.event**. This listener specifies only one method, called **valueChanged( )**, which is shown here:

void valueChanged(ListSelectionEvent *le*)

Here, *le* is a reference to the object that generated the event. Although **ListSelectionEvent** does provide some methods of its own, normally you will interrogate the **JList** object itself to determine what has occurred. **ListSelectionEvent** is also packaged in **javax.swing.event**.

By default, a **JList** allows the user to select multiple ranges of items within the list, but you can change this behavior by calling **setSelectionMode( )**, which is defined by **JList**. It is shown here:

void setSelectionMode(int *mode*)

Here, *mode* specifies the selection mode. It must be one of these values defined by the **ListSelectionModel** interface (which is packaged in **javax.swing**):

SINGLE_SELECTION

SINGLE_INTERVAL_SELECTION

MULTIPLE_INTERVAL_SELECTION

The default, multiple-interval selection lets the user select multiple ranges of items within a list. With single-interval selection, the user can select one range of items. With single selection, the user can select only a single item. Of course, a single item can be selected in the other two modes, too. It's just that they also allow a range to be selected.

You can obtain the index of the first item selected, which will also be the index of the only selected item when using single-selection mode, by calling **getSelectedIndex( )**, shown here:

int getSelectedIndex( )

Indexing begins at zero. So, if the first item is selected, this method will return 0. If no item is selected, -1 is returned.

You can obtain an array containing all selected items by calling **getSelectedIndices( )**, shown next:

int[ ] getSelectedIndices( )

In the returned array, the indices are ordered from smallest to largest. If a zero-length array is returned, it means that no items are selected.

The following program demonstrates a simple **JList**, which holds a list of names. Each time a name is selected in the list, a **ListSelectionEvent** is generated, which is handled by the **valueChanged( )** method defined by **ListSelectionListener**. It responds by obtaining the index of the selected item and displaying the corresponding name. Sample output is shown in Figure 15-5.

```java
// Demonstrate a simple JList.

import javax.swing.*;
import javax.swing.event.*;
import java.awt.*;
import java.awt.event.*;

class ListDemo implements ListSelectionListener {

  JList jlst;
  JLabel jlab;
  JScrollPane jscrlp;

  // Create an array of names.
  String names[] = { "Sherry", "Jon", "Rachel",
                     "Sasha", "Josselyn",  "Randy",
                     "Tom", "Mary", "Ken",
                     "Andrew", "Matt", "Todd" };
```

This array will be displayed in a **JList**.

```java
  ListDemo() {
    // Create a new JFrame container.
    JFrame jfrm = new JFrame("JList Demo");

    // Specify a flow Layout.
    jfrm.setLayout(new FlowLayout());

    // Give the frame an initial size.
    jfrm.setSize(200, 160);

    // Terminate the program when the user closes the application.
    jfrm.setDefaultCloseOperation(JFrame.EXIT_ON_CLOSE);

    // Create a JList.
    jlst = new JList(names); // ◄———————— Create the list.
```

Switch to single-selection mode.

```java
    // Set the list selection mode to single-selection.
    jlst.setSelectionMode(ListSelectionModel.SINGLE_SELECTION); // ◄
```

```
  // Add list to a scroll pane.
  jscrlp = new JScrollPane(jlst);   ◄──────── Wrap the list in a scroll pane.

  // Set the preferred size of the scroll pane.
  jscrlp.setPreferredSize(new Dimension(120, 90));

  // Make a label that displays the selection.
  jlab = new JLabel("Please choose a name");

  // Add list selection handler.
  jlst.addListSelectionListener(this);   ◄──────── Listen for list selection events.

  // Add the list and label to the content pane.
  jfrm.add(jscrlp);
  jfrm.add(jlab);

  // Display the frame.
  jfrm.setVisible(true);
}

// Handle list selection events.
public void valueChanged(ListSelectionEvent le) {   ◄─── Handle list selection events.
  // Get the index of the changed item.
  int idx = jlst.getSelectedIndex();   ◄──────── Get the index of the selected/
                                                  deselected item.
  // Display selection, if item was selected.
  if(idx != -1)
    jlab.setText("Current selection: " + names[idx]);
  else // Otherwise, reprompt.
    jlab.setText("Please choose a name");
}

public static void main(String args[]) {
  // Create the frame on the event dispatching thread.
  SwingUtilities.invokeLater(new Runnable() {
    public void run() {
      new ListDemo();
    }
  });
}
}
```

Let's look closely at this program. First, notice the **names** array near the top of the program. It is initialized to a list of strings that contain various names. Inside **ListDemo( )**, a **JList** called **jlst** is constructed using the **names** array. As mentioned, when the array constructor is used (as it is in this case), a **JList** instance is automatically created that contains the contents of the array. Thus, the list will contain the names in **names**.

Figure 15-5 Output from the **ListDemo** program

Next, the selection mode is set to single selection. This means that only one item in this list can be selected at any one time. Then, **jlst** is wrapped inside a **JScrollPane**, and the preferred size of the scroll pane is set to 120 by 90. This makes for a compact, but easy-to-use scroll pane. In Swing, the **setPreferredSize( )** method sets the ideal size of a component. Be aware that some layout managers are free to ignore this request, but most often the preferred size determines the size of the component.

A list selection event occurs whenever the user selects an item or changes the item selected. Inside the **valueChanged( )** event handler, the index of the item selected is obtained by calling **getSelectedIndex( )**. Because the list has been set to single-selection mode, this is also the index of the only item selected. This index is then used to index the **names** array to obtain the selected name. Notice that this index value is tested against –1. Recall that this is the value returned if no item has been selected. This will be the case when the selection event handler is called if the user has deselected an item. Remember: a selection event is generated when the user selects or deselects an item.

Project
15-1

A Swing-Based File Comparison Utility

Project 15-1   A Swing-Based File Comparison Utility

SwingFC.java

Although you know only a small amount about Swing, you can still put it to use to create a practical application. In Project 10-1 you created a console-based file comparison utility. This project creates a Swing-based version of the program. As you will see, giving this application a Swing-based user interface substantially improves its appearance and makes it easier to use. Here is how the Swing version looks:

(continued)

Because Swing streamlines the creation of GUI-based programs, you might be surprised by how easy it is to create this program.

Step by Step

1. Begin by creating a file called **SwingFC.java** and then enter the following comment and **import** statements:

```
/*
    Project 15-1

    A Swing-based file comparison utility.
*/

import java.awt.*;
import java.awt.event.*;
import javax.swing.*;
import java.io.*;
```

2. Next, begin the **SwingFC** class as shown here:

```
class SwingFC implements ActionListener {

  JTextField jtfFirst;  // holds the first file name
  JTextField jtfSecond; // holds the second file name

  JButton jbtnComp; // button to compare the files

  JLabel jlabFirst, jlabSecond; // displays prompts
  JLabel jlabResult; // displays results and error messages
```

The names of the files to compare are entered into the text fields defined by **jtfFirst** and **jtfSecond**. To compare the files, the user presses the **jbtnComp** button. Prompting messages are displayed in **jlabFirst** and **jlabSecond**. The results of the comparison, or any error messages, are displayed in **jlabResult**.

3. Code the **SwingFC** constructor like this:

```
SwingFC() {

  // Create a new JFrame container.
  JFrame jfrm = new JFrame("Compare Files");

  // Specify FlowLayout for the layout manager.
  jfrm.setLayout(new FlowLayout());

  // Give the frame an initial size.
  jfrm.setSize(200, 190);
```

```
// Terminate the program when the user closes the application.
jfrm.setDefaultCloseOperation(JFrame.EXIT_ON_CLOSE);

// Create the text fields for the file names.
jtfFirst = new JTextField(14);
jtfSecond = new JTextField(14);

// Set the action commands for the text fields.
jtfFirst.setActionCommand("fileA");
jtfSecond.setActionCommand("fileB");

// Create the Compare button.
JButton jbtnComp = new JButton("Compare");

// Add action listener for the Compare button.
jbtnComp.addActionListener(this);

// Create the labels.
jlabFirst = new JLabel("First file: ");
jlabSecond = new JLabel("Second file: ");
jlabResult = new JLabel("");

// Add the components to the content pane.
jfrm.add(jlabFirst);
jfrm.add(jtfFirst);
jfrm.add(jlabSecond);
jfrm.add(jtfSecond);
jfrm.add(jbtnComp);
jfrm.add(jlabResult);

// Display the frame.
jfrm.setVisible(true);
}
```

Most of the code in this constructor should be familiar to you. However, notice one thing:
an action listener is added only to the push button **jbtnCompare**. Action listeners are not
added to the text fields. Here's why: the contents of the text fields are needed only when the
Compare button is pushed. At no other time are their contents required. Thus, there is no
reason to respond to any text field events. As you begin to write more Swing programs,
you will find that this is often the case when using a text field.

4. Begin creating the **actionPerformed( )** event handler as shown next. This method is called
   when the Compare button is pressed.

```
// Compare the files when the Compare button is pressed.
public void actionPerformed(ActionEvent ae) {
  int i=0, j=0;
  FileInputStream f1;
```

(continued)

```
FileInputStream f2;

// First, confirm that both file names have
// been entered.
if(jtfFirst.getText().equals("")) {
  jlabResult.setText("First file name missing.");
  return;
}
if(jtfSecond.getText().equals("")) {
  jlabResult.setText("Second file name missing.");
  return;
}
```

The method begins by confirming that the user has entered a filename into each of the text fields. If this is not the case, the missing filename is reported and the handler returns.

5. Add the code that opens the files.

```
// Open first file.
try {
  f1 = new FileInputStream(jtfFirst.getText());
} catch(FileNotFoundException exc) {
  jlabResult.setText("First file not found.");
  return;
}

// Open second file.
try {
  f2 = new FileInputStream(jtfSecond.getText());
} catch(FileNotFoundException exc) {
  jlabResult.setText("Second file not found.");

  // Close the first file if the second file
  // cannot be opened.
  try {
    f1.close();
  } catch(IOException exc2) {
    jlabResult.setText("Cannot close first file.");
  }

  return;
}
```

Notice that if a file is not found, this fact is reported and the handler returns.

6. Now, finish **actionPerformed( )** by adding the code that actually compares the two files.

```
// Compare files.
try {
  do {
```

```
        i = f1.read();
        j = f2.read();
        if(i != j) break;
      } while(i != -1 && j != -1);

      if(i != j)
        jlabResult.setText("Files are not the same.");
      else
        jlabResult.setText("Files compare equal.");
    } catch(IOException exc) {
      jlabResult.setText("File Error");
    }

    try {
      f1.close();
    } catch(IOException exc) {
      jlabResult.setText("Error closing first file.");
    }

    try {
      f2.close();
    } catch(IOException exc) {
      jlabResult.setText("Error closing second file.");
    }

  }
```

7. Finish **SwingFC** by adding the following **main( )** method.

```
  public static void main(String args[]) {
    // Create the frame on the event dispatching thread.
    SwingUtilities.invokeLater(new Runnable() {
      public void run() {
        new SwingFC();
      }
    });
  }
}
```

8. The entire Swing-based file comparison program is shown here:

```
/*
    Project 15-1

    A Swing-based file comparison utility.
*/

import java.awt.*;
import java.awt.event.*;
```

(continued)

```java
import javax.swing.*;
import java.io.*;

class SwingFC implements ActionListener {

  JTextField jtfFirst;  // holds the first file name
  JTextField jtfSecond; // holds the second file name

  JButton jbtnComp; // button to compare the files

  JLabel jlabFirst, jlabSecond; // displays prompts
  JLabel jlabResult; // displays results and error messages

  SwingFC() {

    // Create a new JFrame container.
    JFrame jfrm = new JFrame("Compare Files");

    // Specify FlowLayout for the layout manager.
    jfrm.setLayout(new FlowLayout());

    // Give the frame an initial size.
    jfrm.setSize(200, 190);

    // Terminate the program when the user closes the application.
    jfrm.setDefaultCloseOperation(JFrame.EXIT_ON_CLOSE);

    // Create the text fields for the file names.
    jtfFirst = new JTextField(14);
    jtfSecond = new JTextField(14);

    // Set the action commands for the text fields.
    jtfFirst.setActionCommand("fileA");
    jtfSecond.setActionCommand("fileB");

    // Create the Compare button.
    JButton jbtnComp = new JButton("Compare");

    // Add action listener for the Compare button.
    jbtnComp.addActionListener(this);

    // Create the labels.
    jlabFirst = new JLabel("First file: ");
    jlabSecond = new JLabel("Second file: ");
    jlabResult = new JLabel("");

    // Add the components to the content pane.
```

```
    jfrm.add(jlabFirst);
    jfrm.add(jtfFirst);
    jfrm.add(jlabSecond);
    jfrm.add(jtfSecond);
    jfrm.add(jbtnComp);
    jfrm.add(jlabResult);

    // Display the frame.
    jfrm.setVisible(true);
  }

  // Compare the files when the Compare button is pressed.
  public void actionPerformed(ActionEvent ae) {
    int i=0, j=0;
    FileInputStream f1;
    FileInputStream f2;

    // First, confirm that both file names have
    // been entered.
    if(jtfFirst.getText().equals("")) {
      jlabResult.setText("First file name missing.");
      return;
    }
    if(jtfSecond.getText().equals("")) {
      jlabResult.setText("Second file name missing.");
      return;
    }

    // Open first file.
    try {
      f1 = new FileInputStream(jtfFirst.getText());
    } catch(FileNotFoundException exc) {
      jlabResult.setText("First file not found.");
      return;
    }

    // Open second file.
    try {
      f2 = new FileInputStream(jtfSecond.getText());
    } catch(FileNotFoundException exc) {
      jlabResult.setText("Second file not found.");

      // Close the first file if the second file
      // cannot be opened.
      try {
        f1.close();
      } catch(IOException exc2) {
```

(continued)

```
      jlabResult.setText("Cannot close first file.");
    }

    return;
  }

  // Compare files.
  try {
    do {
      i = f1.read();
      j = f2.read();
      if(i != j) break;
    } while(i != -1 && j != -1);

    if(i != j)
      jlabResult.setText("Files are not the same.");
    else
      jlabResult.setText("Files compare equal.");
  } catch(IOException exc) {
    jlabResult.setText("File Error");
  }

  try {
    f1.close();
  } catch(IOException exc) {
    jlabResult.setText("Error closing first file.");
  }

  try {
    f2.close();
  } catch(IOException exc) {
    jlabResult.setText("Error closing second file.");
  }

}

public static void main(String args[]) {
  // Create the frame on the event dispatching thread.
  SwingUtilities.invokeLater(new Runnable() {
    public void run() {
      new SwingFC();
    }
  });
}
}
```

CRITICAL SKILL
15.9 Use Anonymous Inner Classes
to Handle Events

Up to this point, the programs in this module have used a simple, straightforward approach to handling events in which the main class of the application has implemented the listener interface itself and all events are sent to an instance of that class. While this is perfectly acceptable, it is not the only way to handle events. Two other approaches are commonly used. First, you can implement separate listener classes. Thus, different classes could handle different events and these classes would be separate from the main class of the application. Second, you can implement listeners through the use of *anonymous inner classes*.

Anonymous inner classes are inner classes that don't have a name. Instead, an instance of the class is simply generated "on the fly" as needed. Anonymous inner classes make implementing some types of event handlers much easier. For example, given a **JButton** called **jbtn**, you could implement an action listener for it like this:

```
jbtn.addActionListener(new ActionListener() {
  public void actionPerformed(ActionEvent ae) {
    // Handle action event here.
  }
});
```

Here, an anonymous inner class is created that implements the **ActionListener** interface. Pay special attention to the syntax. The body of the inner class begins after the **{** that follows **new ActionListener( )**. Also notice that the call to **addActionListener( )** ends with a **)** and a **;** just like normal. The same basic syntax and approach is used to create an anonymous inner class for any event handler. Of course, for different events, you specify different event listeners and implement different methods.

One advantage to using an anonymous inner class is that the component that invokes the class' methods is already known. For instance, in the preceding example, there is no need to call **getActionCommand( )** to determine what component generated the event, because this implementation of **actionPerformed( )** will only be called by events generated by **jbtn**. You will see anonymous inner classes at work in the Swing applet shown in the following section.

CRITICAL SKILL
15.10 Create a Swing Applet

The preceding example programs have been Swing-based applications. The second type of program that commonly uses Swing is the applet. Swing-based applets are similar to AWT-based applets described in Module 14, but with an important difference: A Swing applet extends **JApplet** rather than **Applet**. **JApplet** is derived from **Applet**. Thus, **JApplet** includes all of the functionality found in **Applet** and adds support for Swing. **JApplet** is a top-level Swing container. Therefore, it includes the various panes described earlier. As a result, all components are added to **JApplet**'s content pane in the same way that components are added to **JFrame**'s content pane.

Swing applets use the same four lifecycle methods described in Module 14: **init( )**, **start( )**, **stop( )**, and **destroy( )**. Of course, you need override only those methods that are needed by your applet. In general, painting is accomplished differently in Swing than it is in the AWT. Thus, a Swing applet will not usually override the **paint( )** method.

One other point: All interaction with components in a Swing applet must take place on the event-dispatching thread, as described in the preceding section. This threading issue applies to all Swing programs.

Here is an example of a Swing applet. It provides the same functionality as the push-button example shown earlier in this module, but it does so in applet form. It also uses anonymous inner classes to implement the action event handlers. Figure 15-6 shows the program when executed by **appletviewer**.

```
// A simple Swing-based applet

import javax.swing.*;
import java.awt.*;
import java.awt.event.*;

/*
This HTML can be used to launch the applet:

<object code="MySwingApplet" width=200 height=80>
</object>
*/

public class MySwingApplet extends JApplet {        ◄——— Swing applets must extend
  JButton jbtnUp;                                          JApplet.
  JButton jbtnDown;

  JLabel jlab;

  // Initialize the applet.
  public void init() {
    try {
      SwingUtilities.invokeAndWait(new Runnable () {   ◄——— Use invokeAndWait( )
        public void run() {                                   to create the GUI.
          makeGUI(); // initialize the GUI
        }
      });
    } catch(Exception exc) {
```

```
      System.out.println("Can't create because of "+ exc);
    }
  }

  // This applet does not need to override start(), stop(),
  // or destroy().

  // Set up and initialize the GUI.
  private void makeGUI() {
    // Set the applet to use flow layout.
    setLayout(new FlowLayout());

    // Make two buttons.
    jbtnUp = new JButton("Up");
    jbtnDown = new JButton("Down");

    // Add action listener for Up button.
    jbtnUp.addActionListener(new ActionListener() {
      public void actionPerformed(ActionEvent ae) {
        jlab.setText("You pressed Up.");
      }
    });

    // Add action listener for Down button.
    jbtnDown.addActionListener(new ActionListener() {
      public void actionPerformed(ActionEvent ae) {
        jlab.setText("You pressed down.");
      }
    });

    // Add the buttons to the content pane.
    add(jbtnUp);
    add(jbtnDown);

    // Create a text-based label.
    jlab = new JLabel("Press a button.");

    // Add the label to the content pane.
    add(jlab);
  }
}
```

Use anonymous inner classes to handle button events.

There several important things to notice about this applet. First, **MySwingApplet** extends **JApplet**. As explained, all Swing-based applets extend **JApplet** rather than **Applet**. Second, the **init( )** method initializes the Swing components on the event-dispatching thread by setting up a call to **makeGUI( )**. Notice that this is accomplished through the use of **invokeAndWait( )** rather than **invokeLater( )**. Applets must use **invokeAndWait( )** because the **init( )** method

Figure 15-6 Output from the example Swing applet

must not return until the entire initialization process has been completed. In essence, the **start( )** method cannot be called until after initialization, which means that the GUI must be fully constructed.

Inside **makeGUI( )**, the two buttons and label are created, and the action listeners are added to the buttons. Notice that anonymous inner classes are used to implement the action event handlers. You can use these as a model for implementing other event handlers. One of the primary advantages is that the object that causes the event is known because it is the object on which the anonymous inner class is instantiated. Therefore, it is not necessary to obtain the action command to determine which button generated the event. Finally, the components are added to the content pane. Although this example is quite simple, this same general approach must be used when building any Swing GUI that will be used by an applet.

What Next?

Congratulations! If you have read and worked through the preceding 15 modules, then you can call yourself a Java programmer. Of course, there are still many, many things to learn about Java, its libraries, and its subsystems, but you now have a solid foundation upon which you can build your knowledge and expertise.

Here are a few of the topics that you will want to learn more about:

● Swing. Continue exploring Swing. It is an important part of Java programming.

● The AWT, which provides the foundation for Swing.

● Event handling. Although introduced here, there is substantially more to it.

● Java's networking classes.

● Java's utility classes, especially its Collections Framework, which simplifies a number of common programming tasks.

- The Concurrent API, which offers detailed control over high-performance multithreaded applications.

- Java Beans, which supports the creation of software components in Java.

- Creating native methods.

- Servlets. If you will be writing high-powered Web applications, then you will want to learn about servlets. Servlets are to the server side what applets are to the browser.

To continue your study of Java, I recommend my book *Java: The Complete Reference, 7th Edition* (McGraw-Hill/Osborne, 2007). In it you will find comprehensive coverage of the Java language, its key libraries, and hundreds more example programs.

✔

Module 15 Mastery Check

1. In general, AWT components are heavyweight and Swing components are _____.

2. Can the look and feel of a Swing component be changed? If so, what feature enables this?

3. What is the most commonly used top-level container for an application?

4. Top-level containers have several panes. To what pane are components added?

5. Show how to construct a label that contains the message "Select an entry from the list."

6. All interaction with GUI components must take place on what thread?

7. What is the default action command associated with a **JButton**? How can the action command be changed?

8. What event is generated when a push button is pressed?

9. Show how to create a text field that has 32 columns.

10. Can a **JTextField** have its action command set? If so, how?

11. What Swing component creates a check box? What event is generated when a check box is selected or deselected?

12. **JList** displays a list of items from which the user can select. True or False?

13. What event is generated when the user selects or deselects an item in a **JList**?

14. What method sets the selection mode of a **JList**? What method obtains the index of the first selected item?

15. To create a Swing-based applet, what class must you inherit?

16. Usually, Swing-based applets use **invokeAndWait( )** to create the initial GUI. True or False?

17. Add a check box to the file comparer developed in Project 15-1 that has the following text: Show position of mismatch. When this box is checked, have the program display the location of the first point in the files at which a mismatch occurs.

18. Change the **ListDemo** program so that it allows multiple items in the list to be selected.

19. Bonus challenge: Convert the Help class developed in Project 4-1 into a Swing-based GUI program. Display the keywords (**for, while, switch,** and so on) in a **JList**. When the user selects one, display the keyword's syntax. To display multiple lines of text within a label, you can use HTML. When doing so, you must begin the text with the sequence **<html>**. When this is done, the text is automatically formatted as described by the markup. In addition to other benefits, using HTML enables you to create labels that span two or more lines. For example, this creates a label that displays two lines of text, with the string "Top" over the string "Bottom".

```java
JLabel jlabhtml = new JLabel("<html>Top<br>Bottom");
```

No answer is shown for this exercise. You have reached the point where you are ready to apply your Java skills on your own!

20. Continue to learn about Java. A good way to start is by examining Java's standard packages, such as **java.lang**, **java.util**, and **java.net**. Write sample programs that demonstrate their various classes and interfaces. In general, the best way to become a great Java programmer is to write lots of code.

Appendix A

Answers to Mastery Checks

Module 1: Java Fundamentals

1. What is bytecode and why is it important to Java's use for Internet programming?

Bytecode is a highly optimized set of instructions that is executed by the Java run-time interpreter. Bytecode helps Java achieve both portability and security.

2. What are the three main principles of object-oriented programming?

Encapsulation, polymorphism, and inheritance.

3. Where do Java programs begin execution?

Java programs begin execution at **main( )**.

4. What is a variable?

A variable is a named memory location. The contents of a variable can be changed during the execution of a program.

5. Which of the following variable names is invalid?

The invalid variable is **D**. Variable names cannot begin with a digit.

6. How do you create a single-line comment? How do you create a multiline comment?

A single-line comment begins with // and ends at the end of the line. A multiline comment begins with /* and ends with */.

7. Show the general form of the **if** statement. Show the general form of the **for** loop.

The general form of the **if**:

if(*condition*) *statement*;

The general form of the **for**:

for(*initialization*; *condition*; *iteration*) *statement*;

8. How do you create a block of code?

A block of code is started with a { and ended with a }.

9. The moon's gravity is about 17 percent that of the earth's. Write a program that computes your effective weight on the moon.

```
/*
   Compute your weight on the moon.

   Call this file Moon.java.
*/
```

```
class Moon {
  public static void main(String args[]) {
    double earthweight; // weight on earth
    double moonweight; // weight on moon

    earthweight = 165;

    moonweight = earthweight * 0.17;

    System.out.println(earthweight +
                  " earth-pounds is equivalent to " +
                  moonweight + " moon-pounds.");

  }
}
```

10. Adapt Project 1-2 so that it prints a conversion table of inches to meters. Display 12 feet of conversions, inch by inch. Output a blank line every 12 inches. (One meter equals approximately 39.37 inches.)

```
/*
   This program displays a conversion
   table of inches to meters.

   Call this program InchToMeterTable.java.
*/
class InchToMeterTable {
  public static void main(String args[]) {
    double inches, meters;
    int counter;

    counter = 0;
    for(inches = 1; inches <= 144; inches++) {
      meters = inches / 39.37; // convert to meters
      System.out.println(inches + " inches is " +
                      meters + " meters.");

      counter++;
      // every 12th line, print a blank line
      if(counter == 12) {
        System.out.println();
        counter = 0; // reset the line counter
      }
    }
  }
}
```

11. If you make a typing mistake when entering your program, what sort of error will result?

A syntax error.

12. Does it matter where on a line you put a statement?

No, Java is a free-form language.

Module 2: Introducing Data Types and Operators

1. Why does Java strictly specify the range and behavior of its primitive types?

Java strictly specifies the range and behavior of its primitive types to ensure portability across platforms.

2. What is Java's character type, and how does it differ from the character type used by many other programming languages?

Java's character type is **char**. Java characters are Unicode rather than ASCII, which is used by many other computer languages.

3. A **boolean** value can have any value you like because any non-zero value is true. True or False?

False. A boolean value must be either **true** or **false**.

4. Given this output,

```
One
Two
Three
```

use a single string to show the **println( )** statement that produced it.

```
System.out.println("One\nTwo\nThree");
```

5. What is wrong with this fragment?

```
for(i = 0; i < 10; i++) {
  int sum;

  sum = sum + i;
}
System.out.println("Sum is: " + sum);
```

There are two fundamental flaws in the fragment. First, **sum** is created each time the block created by the **for** loop is entered and destroyed on exit. Thus, it will not hold its value between iterations. Attempting to use **sum** to hold a running sum of the iterations is pointless. Second, **sum** will not be known outside of the block in which it is declared. Thus, the reference to it in the **println( )** statement is invalid.

6. Explain the difference between the prefix and postfix forms of the increment operator.

When the increment operator precedes its operand, Java will perform the corresponding operation prior to obtaining the operand's value for use by the rest of the expression. If the operator follows its operand, then Java will obtain the operand's value before incrementing.

7. Show how a short-circuit AND can be used to prevent a divide-by-zero error.

```
if((b != 0) && (val / b)) ...
```

8. In an expression, what type are **byte** and **short** promoted to?

In an expression, **byte** and **short** are promoted to **int**.

9. In general, when is a cast needed?

A cast is needed when converting between incompatible types or when a narrowing conversion is occurring.

10. Write a program that finds all of the prime numbers between 2 and 100.

```java
// Find prime numbers between 2 and 100.
class Prime {
  public static void main(String args[]) {
    int i, j;
    boolean isprime;

    for(i=2; i < 100; i++) {
      isprime = true;

      // see if the number is evenly divisible
      for(j=2; j < i/j; j++)
        // if it is, then it's not prime
        if((i%j) == 0) isprime = false;

      if(isprime)
        System.out.println(i + " is prime.");
    }
  }
}
```

11. Does the use of redundant parentheses affect program performance?

No.

12. Does a block define a scope?

Yes.

Module 3: Program Control Statements

1. Write a program that reads characters from the keyboard until a period is received. Have the program count the number of spaces. Report the total at the end of the program.

```java
// Count spaces.
class Spaces {
  public static void main(String args[])
    throws java.io.IOException {

    char ch;
    int spaces = 0;


    System.out.println("Enter a period to stop.");

    do {
      ch = (char) System.in.read();
      if(ch == ' ') spaces++;
    } while(ch != '.');

    System.out.println("Spaces: " + spaces);
  }
}
```

2. Show the general form of the **if-else-if** ladder.

if(*condition*)
  statement;
else if(*condition*)
  statement;
else if(*condition*)
  statement;
  .
  .
  .
else
  statement;

3. Given

```java
if(x < 10)
  if(y > 100) {
    if(!done) x = z;
    else y = z;
  }
else System.out.println("error"); // what if?
```

to what **if** does the last **else** associate?

The last **else** associates with the outer **if**, which is the nearest **if** at the same level as the **else**.

4. Show the **for** statement for a loop that counts from 1000 to 0 by –2.

```
for(int i = 1000; i >= 0; i -= 2) // ...
```

5. Is the following fragment valid?

```
for(int i = 0; i < num; i++)
  sum += i;

count = i;
```

No; **i** is not known outside of the **for** loop in which it is declared.

6. Explain what **break** does. Be sure to explain both of its forms.

A **break** without a label causes termination of its immediately enclosing loop or switch statement. A **break** with a label causes control to transfer to the end of the labeled block.

7. In the following fragment, after the **break** statement executes, what is displayed?

```
for(i = 0; i < 10; i++) {
  while(running) {
    if(x<y) break;
    // ...
  }
  System.out.println("after while");
}
System.out.println("After for");
```

After **break** executes, "after while" is displayed.

8. What does the following fragment print?

```
for(int i = 0; i<10; i++) {
  System.out.print(i + " ");
  if((i%2) == 0) continue;
  System.out.println();
}
```

Here is the answer:

```
0 1
2 3
4 5
6 7
8 9
```

9. The iteration expression in a **for** loop need not always alter the loop control variable by a fixed amount. Instead, the loop control variable can change in any arbitrary way. Using this concept, write a program that uses a **for** loop to generate and display the progression 1, 2, 4, 8, 16, 32, and so on.

```
/* Use a for loop to generate the progression

   1 2 4 8 16, ...
*/
class Progress {
  public static void main(String args[]) {

    for(int i = 1; i < 100; i += i)
      System.out.print(i + " ");

  }
}
```

10. The ASCII lowercase letters are separated from the uppercase letters by 32. Thus, to convert a lowercase letter to uppercase, subtract 32 from it. Use this information to write a program that reads characters from the keyboard. Have it convert all lowercase letters to uppercase, and all uppercase letters to lowercase, displaying the result. Make no changes to any other character. Have the program stop when the user presses period. At the end, have the program display the number of case changes that have taken place.

```
// Change case.
class CaseChg {
  public static void main(String args[])
    throws java.io.IOException {
    char ch;
    int changes = 0;

    System.out.println("Enter period to stop.");

    do {
      ch = (char) System.in.read();
      if(ch >= 'a' & ch <= 'z') {
        ch -= 32;
        changes++;
        System.out.println(ch);
      }
      else if(ch >= 'A' & ch <= 'Z') {
        ch += 32;
        changes++;
        System.out.println(ch);
      }
```

```
        } while(ch != '.');
        System.out.println("Case changes: " + changes);
    }
}
```

11. What is an infinite loop?

   An infinite loop is a loop that runs indefinitely.

12. When using **break** with a label, must the label be on a block that contains the **break**?

   Yes.

Module 4: Introducing Classes, Objects, and Methods

1. What is the difference between a class and an object?

   A class is a logical abstraction that describes the form and behavior of an object. An object is a physical instance of the class.

2. How is a class defined?

   A class is defined by using the keyword **class**. Inside the **class** statement, you specify the code and data that comprise the class.

3. What does each object have its own copy of?

   Each object of a class has its own copy of the class' instance variables.

4. Using two separate statements, show how to declare an object called **counter** of a class called **MyCounter**.

   ```
   MyCounter counter;
   counter = new MyCounter();
   ```

5. Show how a method called **myMeth( )** is declared if it has a return type of **double** and has two **int** parameters called **a** and **b**.

   ```
   double myMeth(int a, int b) { // ...
   ```

6. How must a method return if it returns a value?

   A method that returns a value must return via the **return** statement, passing back the return value in the process.

7. What name does a constructor have?

   A constructor has the same name as its class.

8. What does **new** do?

The **new** operator allocates memory for an object and initializes it using the object's constructor.

9. What is garbage collection and how does it work? What is **finalize( )**?

Garbage collection is the mechanism that recycles unused objects so that their memory can be reused. An object's **finalize( )** method is called just prior to an object being recycled.

10. What is **this**?

The **this** keyword is a reference to the object on which a method is invoked. It is automatically passed to a method.

11. Can a constructor have one or more parameters?

Yes.

12. If a method returns no value, what must its return type be?

void

Module 5: More Data Types and Operators

1. Show two ways to declare a one-dimensional array of 12 **double**s.

```
double x[] = new double[12];
double[] x = new double[12];
```

2. Show how to initialize a one-dimensional array of integers to the values 1 through 5.

```
int x[] = { 1, 2, 3, 4, 5 };
```

3. Write a program that uses an array to find the average of ten **double** values. Use any ten values you like.

```
// Average 10 double values.
class Avg {
  public static void main(String args[]) {
    double nums[] = { 1.1, 2.2, 3.3, 4.4, 5.5,
                      6.6, 7.7, 8.8, 9.9, 10.1 };
    double sum = 0;

    for(int i=0; i < nums.length; i++)
      sum += nums[i];

    System.out.println("Average: " + sum / nums.length);
  }
}
```

4. Change the sort in Project 5-1 so that it sorts an array of strings. Demonstrate that it works.

```java
// Demonstrate the Bubble sort with strings.
class StrBubble {
  public static void main(String args[]) {
    String strs[] = {
                      "this", "is", "a", "test",
                      "of", "a", "string", "sort"
                    };
    int a, b;
    String t;
    int size;

    size = strs.length; // number of elements to sort

    // display original array
    System.out.print("Original array is:");
    for(int i=0; i < size; i++)
      System.out.print(" " + strs[i]);
    System.out.println();

    // This is the bubble sort for strings.
    for(a=1; a < size; a++)
      for(b=size-1; b >= a; b--) {
        if(strs[b-1].compareTo(strs[b]) > 0) { // if out of order
          // exchange elements
          t = strs[b-1];
          strs[b-1] = strs[b];
          strs[b] = t;
        }
      }

    // display sorted array
    System.out.print("Sorted array is:");
    for(int i=0; i < size; i++)
      System.out.print(" " + strs[i]);
    System.out.println();
  }
}
```

5. What is the difference between the **String** methods **indexOf( )** and **lastIndexOf( )**?

The **indexOf( )** method finds the first occurrence of the specified substring. **lastIndexOf( )** finds the last occurrence.

6. Since all strings are objects of type **String**, show how you can call the **length( )** and **charAt( )** methods on this string literal: "I like Java".

As strange as it may look, this is a valid call to **length( )**:

```
System.out.println("I like Java".length());
```

The output displayed is 11. **charAt( )** is called in a similar fashion.

7. Expanding on the **Encode** cipher class, modify it so that it uses an eight-character string as the key.

```
// An improved XOR cipher.
class Encode {
  public static void main(String args[]) {
    String msg = "This is a test";
    String encmsg = "";
    String decmsg = "";
    String key = "abcdefgi";
    int j;

    System.out.print("Original message: ");
    System.out.println(msg);

    // encode the message
    j = 0;
    for(int i=0; i < msg.length(); i++) {
      encmsg = encmsg + (char) (msg.charAt(i) ^ key.charAt(j));
      j++;
      if(j==8) j = 0;
    }

    System.out.print("Encoded message: ");
    System.out.println(encmsg);

    // decode the message
    j = 0;
    for(int i=0; i < msg.length(); i++) {
      decmsg = decmsg + (char) (encmsg.charAt(i) ^ key.charAt(j));
      j++;
      if(j==8) j = 0;
    }

    System.out.print("Decoded message: ");
    System.out.println(decmsg);

  }
}
```

8. Can the bitwise operators be applied to the **double** type?

No.

9. Show how this sequence can be rewritten using the **?** operator.

```
if(x < 0) y = 10;
else y = 20;
```

Here is the answer:

```
y = x < 0 ? 10 : 20;
```

10. In the following fragment, is the **&** a bitwise or logical operator? Why?

```
boolean a, b;
// ...
if(a & b) ...
```

It is a logical operator because the operands are of type **boolean**.

11. Is it an error to overrun the end of an array?

Yes.

Is it an error to index an array with a negative value?

Yes. All array indexes start at zero.

12. What is the unsigned right-shift operator?

\>>>

13. Rewrite the **MinMax** class shown earlier in this chapter so that it uses a for-each style **for** loop.

```
// Find the minimum and maximum values in an array.
class MinMax {
  public static void main(String args[]) {
    int nums[] = new int[10];
    int min, max;

    nums[0] = 99;
    nums[1] = -10;
    nums[2] = 100123;
    nums[3] = 18;
    nums[4] = -978;
    nums[5] = 5623;
    nums[6] = 463;
    nums[7] = -9;
    nums[8] = 287;
```

```
      nums[9] = 49;

      min = max = nums[0];
      for(int v : nums) {
        if(v < min) min = v;
        if(v > max) max = v;
      }
      System.out.println("min and max: " + min + " " + max);
    }
}
```

14. Can the **for** loops that perform sorting in the **Bubble** class shown in Project 5-1 be converted into for-each style loops? If not, why not?

No, the **for** loops in the **Bubble** class that perform the sort cannot be converted into for-each style loops. In the case of the outer loop, the current value of its loop counter is needed by the inner loop. In the case of the inner loop, out-of-order values must be exchanged, which implies assignments. Assignments to the underlying array cannot take place when using a for-each style loop.

Module 6: A Closer Look at Methods and Classes

1. Given this fragment,

```
class X {
  private int count;
```

is the following fragment correct?

```
class Y {
  public static void main(String args[]) {
    X ob = new X();

    ob.count = 10;
```

No; a **private** member cannot be accessed outside of its class.

2. An access specifier must _____ a member's declaration.

precede

3. The complement of a queue is a stack. It uses first-in, last-out accessing and is often likened to a stack of plates. The first plate put on the table is the last plate used. Create a stack class called **Stack** that can hold characters. Call the methods that access the stack **push( )** and **pop( )**. Allow the user to specify the size of the stack when it is created. Keep all other members of the **Stack** class private. (Hint: You can use the **Queue** class as a model; just change the way that the data is accessed.)

```java
// A stack class for characters.
class Stack {
  private char stck[]; // this array holds the stack
  private int tos;  // top of stack

  // Construct an empty Stack given its size.
  Stack(int size) {
    stck = new char[size]; // allocate memory for stack
    tos = 0;
  }

  // Construct a Stack from a Stack.
  Stack(Stack ob) {
    tos = ob.tos;
    stck = new char[ob.stck.length];

    // copy elements
    for(int i=0; i < tos; i++)
      stck[i] = ob.stck[i];
  }

  // Construct a stack with initial values.
  Stack(char a[]) {
    stck = new char[a.length];

    for(int i = 0; i < a.length; i++) {
      push(a[i]);
    }
  }



  // Push characters onto the stack.
  void push(char ch) {
    if(tos==stck.length) {
      System.out.println(" -- Stack is full.");
      return;
    }

    stck[tos] = ch;
    tos++;
  }

  // Pop a character from the stack.
  char pop() {
    if(tos==0) {
      System.out.println(" -- Stack is empty.");
```

```
      return (char) 0;
    }

    tos--;
    return stck[tos];
  }
}

// Demonstrate the Stack class.
class SDemo {
  public static void main(String args[]) {
    // construct 10-element empty stack
    Stack stk1 = new Stack(10);

    char name[] = {'T', 'o', 'm'};

    // construct stack from array
    Stack stk2 = new Stack(name);

    char ch;
    int i;

    // put some characters into stk1
    for(i=0; i < 10; i++)
      stk1.push((char) ('A' + i));

    // construct stack from another stack
    Stack stk3 = new Stack(stk1);

    //show the stacks.
    System.out.print("Contents of stk1: ");
    for(i=0; i < 10; i++) {
      ch = stk1.pop();
      System.out.print(ch);
    }

    System.out.println("\n");

    System.out.print("Contents of stk2: ");
    for(i=0; i < 3; i++) {
      ch = stk2.pop();
      System.out.print(ch);
    }

    System.out.println("\n");
```

```
    System.out.print("Contents of stk3: ");
    for(i=0; i < 10; i++) {
      ch = stk3.pop();
      System.out.print(ch);
    }
  }
}
```

Here is the output from the program.

```
Contents of stk1: JIHGFEDCBA

Contents of stk2: moT

Contents of stk3: JIHGFEDCBA
```

4. Given this class,

```
class Test {
  int a;
  Test(int i) { a = i; }
}
```

write a method called **swap( )** that exchanges the contents of the objects referred to by two **Test** object references.

```
void swap(Test ob1, Test ob2) {
  int t;

  t = ob1.a;
  ob1.a = ob2.a;
  ob2.a = t;
}
```

5. Is the following fragment correct?

```
class X {
  int meth(int a, int b) { ... }
  String meth(int a, int b) { ... }
}
```

No. Overloaded methods can have different return types, but they do not play a role in overload resolution. Overloaded methods *must* have different parameter lists.

6. Write a recursive method that displays the contents of a string backwards.

```
// Display a string backwards using recursion.
class Backwards {
  String str;

  Backwards(String s) {
```

```
    str = s;
  }

  void backward(int idx) {
    if(idx != str.length()-1) backward(idx+1);

    System.out.print(str.charAt(idx));
  }
}

class BWDemo {
  public static void main(String args[]) {
    Backwards s = new Backwards("This is a test");

    s.backward(0);
  }
}
```

7. If all objects of a class need to share the same variable, how must you declare that variable?

Shared variables are declared as **static**.

8. Why might you need to use a **static** block?

A **static** block is used to perform any initializations related to the class, before any objects are created.

9. What is an inner class?

An inner class is a nonstatic nested class.

10. To make a member accessible by only other members of its class, what access specifier must be used?

private

11. The name of a method plus its parameter list constitutes the method's _____.

signature

12. An **int** argument is passed to a method by using call-by-_____.

value

13. Create a varargs method called **sum( )** that sums the **int** values passed to it. Have it return the result. Demonstrate its use.

There are many ways to craft the solution. Here is one:

```
class SumIt {
  int sum(int ... n) {
    int result = 0;
```

```
        for(int i = 0; i < n.length; i++)
          result += n[i];

        return result;
      }
    }

    class SumDemo {
      public static void main(String args[]) {

        SumIt siObj = new SumIt();

        int total = siObj.sum(1, 2, 3);
        System.out.println("Sum is " + total);

        total = siObj.sum(1, 2, 3, 4, 5);
        System.out.println("Sum is " + total);
      }
    }
```

14. Can a varargs method be overloaded?

Yes.

15. Show an example of an overloaded varargs method that is ambiguous.

Here is one example of an overloaded varargs method that is ambiguous:

```
double myMeth(double ... v ) { // ...
```

```
double myMeth(double d, double ... v) { // ...
```

If you try to call **myMeth( )** with one argument, like this,

```
myMeth(1.1);
```

the compiler can't determine which version of the method to invoke.

Module 7: Inheritance

1. Does a superclass have access to the members of a subclass? Does a subclass have access to the members of a superclass?

No, a superclass has no knowledge of its subclasses. Yes, a subclass has access to all nonprivate members of its superclass.

2. Create a subclass of **TwoDShape** called **Circle**. Include an **area( )** method that computes the area of the circle and a constructor that uses **super** to initialize the **TwoDShape** portion.

```
// A subclass of TwoDShape for circles.
class Circle extends TwoDShape {
  // A default constructor.
  Circle() {
    super();
  }

  // Construct Circle
  Circle(double x) {
    super(x, "circle"); // call superclass constructor
  }

  // Construct an object from an object.
  Circle(Circle ob) {
    super(ob); // pass object to TwoDShape constructor
  }

  double area() {
    return (getWidth() / 2) * (getWidth() / 2) * 3.1416;
  }
}
```

3. How do you prevent a subclass from having access to a member of a superclass?

To prevent a subclass from having access to a superclass member, declare that member as **private**.

4. Describe the purpose and use of both versions of **super**.

The **super** keyword has two forms. The first is used to call a superclass constructor. The general form of this usage is

super(*param-list*);

The second form of **super** is used to access a superclass member. It has this general form:

super.*member*

5. Given the following hierarchy, in what order are the constructors for these classes called when a **Gamma** object is instantiated?

```
class Alpha { ...

class Beta extends Alpha { ...

Class Gamma extends Beta { ...
```

Constructors are always called in order of derivation. Thus, when a **Gamma** object is created, the order is **Alpha**, **Beta**, **Gamma**.

6. A superclass reference can refer to a subclass object. Explain why this is important as it is related to method overriding.

When an overridden method is called through a superclass reference, it is the type of the object being referred to that determines which version of the method is called.

7. What is an abstract class?

An abstract class contains at least one abstract method.

8. How do you prevent a method from being overridden? How do you prevent a class from being inherited?

To prevent a method from being overridden, declare it as **final**. To prevent a class from being inherited, declare it as **final**.

9. Explain how inheritance, method overriding, and abstract classes are used to support polymorphism.

Inheritance, method overriding, and abstract classes support polymorphism by enabling you to create a generalized class structure that can be implemented by a variety of classes. Thus, the abstract class defines a consistent interface which is shared by all implementing classes. This embodies the concept of "one interface, multiple methods."

10. What class is a superclass of every other class?

The **Object** class.

11. A class that contains at least one abstract method must, itself, be declared abstract. True or False?

True.

12. What keyword is used to create a named constant?

final

Module 8: Packages and Interfaces

1. Using the code from Project 8-1, put the **ICharQ** interface and its three implementations into a package called **QPack**. Keeping the queue demonstration class **IQDemo** in the default package, show how to import and use the classes in **QPack**.

To put **ICharQ** and its implementations into the **QPack** package, you must separate each into its own file, make each implementation class **public**, and add this statement to the top of each file.

```
package QPack;
```

Once this has been done, you can use **QPack** by adding this **import** statement to **IQDemo**.

```
import QPack.*;
```

2. What is a namespace? Why is it important that Java allows you to partition the namespace?

A namespace is a declarative region. By partitioning the namespace, you can prevent name collisions.

3. Packages are stored in _____.

directories

4. Explain the difference between **protected** and default access.

A member with **protected** access can be used within its package and by a subclass in any package. A member with default access can be used only within its package.

5. Explain the two ways that the members of a package can be used by other packages.

To use a member of a package, you can either fully qualify its name, or you can import it using **import**.

6. "One interface, multiple methods" is a key tenet of Java. What feature best exemplifies it?

The interface best exemplifies the one interface, multiple methods principle of OOP.

7. How many classes can implement an interface? How many interfaces can a class implement?

An interface can be implemented by an unlimited number of classes. A class can implement as many interfaces as it chooses.

8. Can interfaces be extended?

Yes, interfaces can be extended.

9. Create an interface for the **Vehicle** class from Module 7. Call the interface **IVehicle**.

```
interface IVehicle {

  // Return the range.
  int range();

  // Compute fuel needed for a given distance.
  double fuelneeded(int miles);

  // Access methods for instance variables.
  int getPassengers();
  void setPassengers(int p);
  int getFuelcap();
```

```
    void setFuelcap(int f);
    int getMpg();
    void setMpg(int m);
}
```

10. Variables declared in an interface are implicitly **static** and **final**. What good are they?

Interface variables are valuable as named constants that are shared by all files in a program. They are brought into view by importing their interface.

11. A package is, in essence, a container for classes. True or False?

True.

12. What standard Java package is automatically imported into a program?

java.lang

Module 9: Exception Handling

1. What class is at the top of the exception hierarchy?

Throwable is at the top of the exception hierarchy.

2. Briefly explain how to use **try** and **catch**.

The **try** and **catch** statements work together. Program statements that you want to monitor for exceptions are contained within a **try** block. An exception is caught using **catch**.

3. What is wrong with this fragment?

```
// ...
vals[18] = 10;
catch (ArrayIndexOutOfBoundsException exc) {
  // handle error
}
```

There is no **try** block preceding the **catch** statement.

4. What happens if an exception is not caught?

If an exception is not caught, abnormal program termination results.

5. What is wrong with this fragment?

```
class A extends Exception { ...

class B extends A { ...

// ...
```

```
try {
  // ...
}
catch (A exc) { ... }
catch (B exc) { ... }
```

In the fragment, a superclass **catch** precedes a subclass **catch**. Since the superclass **catch** will catch all subclasses too, unreachable code is created.

6. Can an inner **catch** rethrow an exception to an outer **catch**?

Yes, an exception can be rethrown.

7. The **finally** block is the last bit of code executed before your program ends. True or False? Explain your answer.

False. The **finally** block is the code executed when a **try** block ends.

8. What type of exceptions must be explicitly declared in a **throws** clause of a method?

All exceptions except those of type **RuntimeException** and **Error** must be declared in a **throws** clause.

9. What is wrong with this fragment?

```
class MyClass { // ... }
// ...
throw new MyClass();
```

MyClass does not extend **Throwable**. Only subclasses of **Throwable** can be thrown by **throw**.

10. In question 3 of the Mastery Check in Module 6, you created a **Stack** class. Add custom exceptions to your class that report stack full and stack empty conditions.

```
// An exception for stack-full errors.
class StackFullException extends Exception {
  int size;

  StackFullException(int s) { size = s; }

  public String toString() {
    return "\nStack is full. Maximum size is " +
          size;
  }
}

// An exception for stack-empty errors.
class StackEmptyException extends Exception {

  public String toString() {
    return "\nStack is empty.";
  }
}
```

```
// A stack class for characters.
class Stack {
  private char stck[]; // this array holds the stack
  private int tos;  // top of stack

  // Construct an empty Stack given its size.
  Stack(int size) {
    stck = new char[size]; // allocate memory for stack
    tos = 0;
  }

  // Construct a Stack from a Stack.
  Stack(Stack ob) {
    tos = ob.tos;
    stck = new char[ob.stck.length];

    // copy elements
    for(int i=0; i < tos; i++)
      stck[i] = ob.stck[i];
  }

  // Construct a stack with initial values.
  Stack(char a[]) {
    stck = new char[a.length];

    for(int i = 0; i < a.length; i++) {
      try {
        push(a[i]);
      }
      catch(StackFullException exc) {
        System.out.println(exc);
      }
    }
  }

  // Push characters onto the stack.
  void push(char ch) throws StackFullException {
    if(tos==stck.length)
      throw new StackFullException(stck.length);

    stck[tos] = ch;
    tos++;
  }

  // Pop a character from the stack.
  char pop() throws StackEmptyException {
    if(tos==0)
      throw new StackEmptyException();
```

```
      tos--;
      return stck[tos];
   }
}
```

11. What are the three ways that an exception can be generated?

An exception can be generated by an error in the JVM, an error in your program, or explicitly via a **throw** statement.

12. What are the two direct subclasses of **Throwable**?

Error and **Exception**

Module 10: Using I/O

1. Why does Java define both byte and character streams?

The byte streams are the original streams defined by Java. They are especially useful for binary I/O, and they support random access files. The character streams are optimized for Unicode.

2. Even though console input and output is text-based, why does Java still use byte streams for this purpose?

The predefined streams, **System.in**, **System.out**, and **System.err**, were defined before Java added the character streams.

3. Show how to open a file for reading bytes.

Here is one way to open a file for **byte** input:

```
FileInputStream fin = new FileInputStream("test");
```

4. Show how to open a file for reading characters.

Here is one way to open a file for reading characters:

```
FileReader fr = new FileReader("test");
```

5. Show how to open a file for random access I/O.

Here is one way to open a file for random access:

```
randfile = new RandomAccessFile("test", "rw");
```

6. How do you convert a numeric string such as "123.23" into its binary equivalent?

To convert numeric strings into their binary equivalents, use the parsing methods defined by the type wrappers, such as **Integer** or **Double**.

7. Write a program that copies a text file. In the process, have it convert all spaces into hyphens. Use the byte stream file classes.

```
/* Copy a text file, substituting hyphens for spaces.
```

```
    This version uses byte streams.

    To use this program, specify the name
    of the source file and the destination file.
    For example,

    java Hyphen source target
*/

import java.io.*;

class Hyphen {
  public static void main(String args[])
  {
    int i;
    FileInputStream fin;
    FileOutputStream fout;

    // First make sure that both files have been specified.
    if(args.length !=2 ) {
      System.out.println("Usage: CopyFile From To");
      return;
    }

    // open input file
    try {
      fin = new FileInputStream(args[0]);
    } catch(FileNotFoundException exc) {
      System.out.println("Input File Not Found");
      return;
    }

    // open output file
    try {
      fout = new FileOutputStream(args[1]);
    } catch(FileNotFoundException exc) {
      System.out.println("Error Opening Output File");

      // Close the open input file.
      try {
        fin.close();
      } catch(IOException exc2) {
        System.out.println("Error closing input file.");
      }
      return;
    }

    // Copy File
```

```
        try {
          do {
            i = fin.read();

            // convert space to a hypen
            if((char)i == ' ') i = '-';

            if(i != -1) fout.write(i);
          } while(i != -1);
        } catch(IOException exc) {
          System.out.println("File Error");
        }

        try {
          fin.close();
        } catch(IOException exc) {
          System.out.println("Error closing input file.");
        }

        try {
          fout.close();
        } catch(IOException exc) {
          System.out.println("Error closing output file.");
        }

      }
    }
```

8. Rewrite the program in question 7 so that it uses the character stream classes.

```
/* Copy a text file, substituting hyphens for spaces.

   This version uses character streams.

   To use this program, specify the name
   of the source file and the destination file.
   For example,

   java Hyphen2 source target
*/

import java.io.*;

class Hyphen2 {
  public static void main(String args[])
    throws IOException
  {
    int i;
```

```
FileReader fin;
FileWriter fout;

// First make sure that both files have been specified.
if(args.length !=2 ) {
  System.out.println("Usage: CopyFile From To");
  return;
}

// open input file
try {
  fin = new FileReader(args[0]);
} catch(FileNotFoundException exc) {
  System.out.println("Input File Not Found");
  return;
}

// open output file
try {
  fout = new FileWriter(args[1]);
} catch(IOException exc) {
  System.out.println("Error Opening Output File");

  // Close the open input file.
  try {
    fin.close();
  } catch(IOException exc2) {
    System.out.println("Error closing input file.");
  }

  return;
}

// Copy File
try {
  do {
    i = fin.read();

    // convert space to a hypen
    if((char)i == ' ') i = '-';

    if(i != -1) fout.write(i);
  } while(i != -1);
} catch(IOException exc) {
  System.out.println("File Error");
}

try {
```

```
      fin.close();
    } catch(IOException exc) {
      System.out.println("Error closing input file.");
    }

    try {
      fout.close();
    } catch(IOException exc) {
      System.out.println("Error closing output file.");
    }

  }
}
```

9. What type of stream is **System.in**?

InputStream

10. What does the **read( )** method of **InputStream** return when the end of the stream is reached?

−1

11. What type of stream is used to read binary data?

DataInputStream

12. **Reader** and **Writer** are at the top of the _____ class hierarchies.

character-based I/O

Module 11: Multithreaded Programming

1. Why does Java's multithreading capability enable you to write more efficient programs?

Multithreading allows you to take advantage of the idle time that is present in nearly all programs. The essence of multithreading is that when one thread can't run, another can.

2. Multithreading is supported by the _____ class and the _____ interface.

Multithreading is supported by the **Thread** class and the **Runnable** interface.

3. When creating a runnable object, why might you want to extend **Thread** rather than implement **Runnable**?

You will extend **Thread** when you want to override one or more of **Thread**'s methods other than **run( )**.

4. Show how to use **join( )** to wait for a thread object called **MyThrd** to end.

```
MyThrd.join();
```

5. Show how to set a thread called **MyThrd** to three levels above normal priority.

```
MyThrd.setPriority(Thread.NORM_PRIORITY+3);
```

6. What is the effect of adding the **synchronized** keyword to a method?

Adding **synchronized** to a method allows only one thread at a time to use the method for any given object of its class.

7. The **wait( )** and **notify( )** methods are used to perform _____.

interthread communication

8. Change the **TickTock** class so that it actually keeps time. That is, have each tick take one half second, and each tock take one half second. Thus, each tick-tock will take one second. (Don't worry about the time it takes to switch tasks, etc.)

To make the **TickTock** class actually keep time, simply add calls to **sleep( )**, as shown here.

```java
// Make the TickTock class actually keep time.

class TickTock {

  String state; // contains the state of the clock

  synchronized void tick(boolean running) {
    if(!running) { // stop the clock
      state = "ticked";
      notify(); // notify any waiting threads
      return;
    }

    System.out.print("Tick ");

    // wait 1/2 second
    try {
      Thread.sleep(500);
    } catch(InterruptedException exc) {
      System.out.println("Thread interrupted.");
    }

    state = "ticked"; // set the current state to ticked

    notify(); // let tock() run
    try {
      while(!state.equals("tocked"))
        wait(); // wait for tock() to complete
    }
    catch(InterruptedException exc) {
      System.out.println("Thread interrupted.");
    }
  }
}
```

```
synchronized void tock(boolean running) {
  if(!running) { // stop the clock
    state = "tocked";
    notify(); // notify any waiting threads
    return;
  }

  System.out.println("Tock");

  // wait 1/2 second
  try {
    Thread.sleep(500);
  } catch(InterruptedException exc) {
    System.out.println("Thread interrupted.");
  }

  state = "tocked"; // set the current state to tocked

  notify(); // let tick() run
  try {
    while(!state.equals("ticked"))
      wait(); // wait for tick to complete
  }
  catch(InterruptedException exc) {
    System.out.println("Thread interrupted.");
  }
 }
}
```

9. Why can't you use **suspend( )**, **resume( )**, and **stop( )** for new programs?

   The **suspend( )**, **resume( )**, and **stop( )** methods have been deprecated because they can cause serious run-time problems.

10. What method defined by **Thread** obtains the name of a thread?

    getName( )

11. What does **isAlive( )** return?

    It returns **true** if the invoking thread is still running, and **false** if it has been terminated.

Module 12: Enumerations, Autoboxing, and Static Import

1. Enumeration constants are said to be *self-typed*. What does this mean?

   In the term *self-typed*, the "self" refers to the type of the enumeration in which the constant is defined. Thus, an enumeration constant is an object of the enumeration of which it is a part.

2. What class do all enumerations automatically inherit?

The **Enum** class is automatically inherited by all enumerations.

3. Given the following enumeration, write a program that uses **values( )** to show a list of the constants and their ordinal values.

```
enum Tools {
  SCREWDRIVER, WRENCH, HAMMER, PLIERS
}
```

The solution is:

```
enum Tools {
  SCREWDRIVER, WRENCH, HAMMER, PLIERS
}

class ShowEnum {
  public static void main(String args[]) {
    for(Tools d : Tools.values())
      System.out.print(d + " has ordinal value of " +
                        d.ordinal() + '\n');

  }
}
```

4. The traffic light simulation developed in Project 12-1 can be improved with a few simple changes that take advantage of an enumeration's class features. In the version shown, the duration of each color was controlled by the **TrafficLightSimulator** class by hard-coding these values into the **run( )** method. Change this so that the duration of each color is stored by the constants in the **TrafficLightColor** enumeration. To do this, you will need to add a constructor, a private instance variable, and a method called **getDelay( )**. After making these changes, what improvements do you see? On your own, can you think of other improvements? (Hint: try using ordinal values to switch light colors rather than relying on a **switch** statement.)

The improved version of the traffic light simulation is shown here. There are two major improvements. First, a light's delay is now linked with its enumeration value, which gives more structure to the code. Second, the **run( )** method no longer needs to use a **switch** statement to determine the length of the delay. Instead, **sleep( )** is passed **tlc.getDelay( )**, which causes the delay associated with the current color to be used automatically.

```
// An improved version of the traffic light simulation that
// stores the light delay in TrafficLightColor.

// An enumeration of the colors of a traffic light.
enum TrafficLightColor {
  RED(12000), GREEN(10000), YELLOW(2000);

  private int delay;
```

```
      TrafficLightColor(int d) {
        delay = d;
      }

      int getDelay() { return delay; }
    }

    // A computerized traffic light.
    class TrafficLightSimulator implements Runnable {
      private Thread thrd; // holds the thread that runs the simulation
      private TrafficLightColor tlc; // holds the current traffic light color
      boolean stop = false; // set to true to stop the simulation
      boolean changed = false; // true when the light has changed

      TrafficLightSimulator(TrafficLightColor init) {
        tlc = init;

        thrd = new Thread(this);
        thrd.start();
      }

      TrafficLightSimulator() {
        tlc = TrafficLightColor.RED;

        thrd = new Thread(this);
        thrd.start();
      }

      // Start up the light.
      public void run() {
        while(!stop) {

          // Notice how this code has been simplified!
          try {
            Thread.sleep(tlc.getDelay());
          } catch(InterruptedException exc) {
            System.out.println(exc);
          }

          changeColor();
        }
      }

      // Change color.
      synchronized void changeColor() {
        switch(tlc) {
          case RED:
            tlc = TrafficLightColor.GREEN;
            break;
          case YELLOW:
            tlc = TrafficLightColor.RED;
            break;
          case GREEN:
            tlc = TrafficLightColor.YELLOW;
```

```
      }

      changed = true;
      notify(); // signal that the light has changed
    }

    // Wait until a light change occurs.
    synchronized void waitForChange() {
      try {
        while(!changed)
          wait(); // wait for light to change
        changed = false;
      } catch(InterruptedException exc) {
        System.out.println(exc);
      }
    }

    // Return current color.
    TrafficLightColor getColor() {
      return tlc;
    }

    // Stop the traffic light.
    void cancel() {
      stop = true;
    }
  }

  class TrafficLightDemo {
    public static void main(String args[]) {
      TrafficLightSimulator tl =
        new TrafficLightSimulator(TrafficLightColor.GREEN);

      for(int i=0; i < 9; i++) {
        System.out.println(tl.getColor());
        tl.waitForChange();
      }

      tl.cancel();
    }
  }
```

5. Define boxing and unboxing. How does autoboxing/unboxing affect these actions?

Boxing is the process of storing a primitive value in a type wrapper object. Unboxing is the process of retrieving the primitive value from the type wrapper. Autoboxing automatically boxes a primitive value without having to explicitly construct an object. Auto-unboxing automatically retrieves the primitive value from a type wrapper without having to explicitly call a method, such as **intValue( )**.

6. Change the following fragment so that it uses autoboxing.

```
Short val = new Short(123);
```

The solution is:

```
Short val = 123;
```

7. In your own words, what does static import do?

Static import brings into the global namespace the static members of a class or interface. This means that static members can be used without having to be qualified by their class or interface name.

8. What does this statement do?

```
import static java.lang.Integer.parseInt;
```

The statement brings into the global namespace the **parseInt( )** method of the type wrapper **Integer**.

9. Is static import designed for special-case situations, or is it good practice to bring all static members of all classes into view?

Static import is designed for special cases. Bringing many static members into view will lead to namespace collisions and destructure your code.

10. An annotation is syntactically based on a/an _____ .

interface

11. What is a marker annotation?

A marker annotation is one that does not take arguments.

12. An annotation can be applied only to methods. True or False?

False. Any type of declaration can have an annotation.

Module 13: Generics

1. Generics are an important addition to Java because they enable the creation of code that is

A. Type-safe

B. Reusable

C. Reliable

D. All of the above

D, all of the above.

2. Can a primitive type be used as a type argument?

No, type arguments must be object types.

3. Show how to declare a class called **FlightSched** that takes two generic parameters.

The solution is

```
class FlightSched<T, V> {
```

4. Beginning with your answer to question 3, change **FlightSched**'s second type parameter so that it must extend **Thread**.

The solution is

```
class FlightSched<T, V extends Thread> {
```

5. Now, change **FlightSched** so that its second type parameter must be a subclass of its first type parameter.

The solution is

```
class FlightSched<T, V extends T> {
```

6. As it relates to generics, what is the **?** and what does it do?

The **?** is the wildcard argument. It matches any valid type.

7. Can the wildcard argument be bounded?

Yes, a wildcard can have either an upper or lower bound.

8. A generic method called **MyGen( )** has one type parameter. Furthermore, **MyGen( )** has one parameter whose type is that of the type parameter. It also returns an object of that type parameter. Show how to declare **MyGen( )**.

The solution is

```
<T> T MyGen(T o) { // ...
```

9. Given this generic interface

```
interface IGenIF<T, V extends T> { // ...
```

show the declaration of a class called **MyClass** that implements **IGenIF**.

The solution is

```
class MyClass<T, V extends T> implements IGenIF<T, V> { // ...
```

10. Given a generic class called **Counter<T>**, show how to create an object of its raw type.

To obtain **Counter<T>**'s raw type, simply use its name without any type specification, as shown here:

```
Counter x = new Counter;
```

11. Do type parameters exist at run time?

No. All type parameters are erased during compilation, and appropriate casts are substituted. This process is called erasure.

12. Convert your solution to question 10 of the Mastery Check for Module 9 so that it is generic. In the process, create a stack interface called **IGenStack** that generically defines the operations **push( )** and **pop( )**.

```
// A generic stack.

interface IGenStack<T> {
  void push(T obj) throws StackFullException;
```

```
      T pop() throws StackEmptyException;
    }

    // An exception for stack-full errors.
    class StackFullException extends Exception {
      int size;

      StackFullException(int s) { size = s; }

      public String toString() {
       return "\nStack is full. Maximum size is " +
              size;
      }
    }

    // An exception for stack-empty errors.
    class StackEmptyException extends Exception {

      public String toString() {
       return "\nStack is empty.";
      }
    }

    // A stack class for characters.
    class GenStack<T> implements IGenStack<T> {
      private T stck[]; // this array holds the stack
      private int tos;  // top of stack

      // Construct an empty stack given its size.
      GenStack(T[] stckArray) {
        stck = stckArray;
        tos = 0;
      }

      // Construct a stack from a stack.
      GenStack(T[] stckArray, GenStack<T> ob) {

        tos = ob.tos;
        stck = stckArray;

        try {
          if(stck.length < ob.stck.length)
            throw new StackFullException(stck.length);
        }
        catch(StackFullException exc) {
          System.out.println(exc);
        }
```

```
  // Copy elements.
  for(int i=0; i < tos; i++)
    stck[i] = ob.stck[i];
}

// Construct a stack with initial values.
GenStack(T[] stckArray, T[] a) {
  stck = stckArray;

  for(int i = 0; i < a.length; i++) {
    try {
      push(a[i]);
    }
    catch(StackFullException exc) {
      System.out.println(exc);
    }
  }
}

// Push objects onto the stack.
public void push(T obj) throws StackFullException {
  if(tos==stck.length)
    throw new StackFullException(stck.length);

  stck[tos] = obj;
  tos++;
}

// Pop an object from the stack.
public T pop() throws StackEmptyException {
  if(tos==0)
    throw new StackEmptyException();

  tos--;
  return stck[tos];
}
}

// Demonstrate the GenStack class.
class GenStackDemo {
  public static void main(String args[]) {
    // Construct 10-element empty Integer stack.
    Integer iStore[] = new Integer[10];
    GenStack<Integer> stk1 = new GenStack<Integer>(iStore);

    // Construct stack from array.
    String name[] = {"One", "Two", "Three"};
```

```
String strStore[] = new String[3];
GenStack<String> stk2 =
    new GenStack<String>(strStore, name);

String str;
int n;

try {

  // Put some values into stk1.
  for(int i=0; i < 10; i++)
    stk1.push(i);
} catch(StackFullException exc) {
  System.out.println(exc);
}

// Construct stack from another stack.
String strStore2[] = new String[3];
GenStack<String> stk3 =
    new GenStack<String>(strStore2, stk2);

try {
  // Show the stacks.
  System.out.print("Contents of stk1: ");
  for(int i=0; i < 10; i++) {
    n = stk1.pop();
    System.out.print(n + " ");
  }

  System.out.println("\n");

  System.out.print("Contents of stk2: ");
  for(int i=0; i < 3; i++) {
    str = stk2.pop();
    System.out.print(str + " ");
  }

  System.out.println("\n");

  System.out.print("Contents of stk3: ");
  for(int i=0; i < 3; i++) {
    str = stk3.pop();
    System.out.print(str + " ");
  }

} catch(StackEmptyException exc) {
```

```
      System.out.println(exc);
    }

    System.out.println();
  }
}
```

Module 14: Applets, Events, and Miscellaneous Topics

1. What method is called when an applet first begins running? What method is called when an applet is removed from the system?

When an applet begins, the first method called is **init( )**. When an applet is removed, **destroy( )** is called.

2. Explain why an applet must use multithreading if it needs to run continually.

An applet must use multithreading if it needs to run continually because applets are event-driven programs which must not enter a "mode" of operation. For example, if **start( )** never returns, then **paint( )** will never be called.

3. Enhance Project 14-1 so that it displays the string passed to it as a parameter. Add a second parameter that specifies the time delay (in milliseconds) between each rotation.

```java
/* A simple banner applet that uses parameters.

*/
import java.awt.*;
import java.applet.*;
/*
<applet code="ParamBanner" width=300 height=50>
<param name=message value=" I like Java! ">
<param name=delay value=500>
</applet>
*/

public class ParamBanner extends Applet implements Runnable {
  String msg;
  int delay;
  Thread t;
  boolean stopFlag;

  // Initialize t to null.
  public void init() {
    String temp;

    msg = getParameter("message");
    if(msg == null) msg = " Java Rules the Web ";

    temp = getParameter("delay");
```

```
    try {
      if(temp != null)
        delay = Integer.parseInt(temp);
      else
        delay = 250; // default if not specified
    } catch(NumberFormatException exc) {
        delay = 250 ; // default on error
    }

    t = null;
  }

  // Start thread
  public void start() {
    t = new Thread(this);
    stopFlag = false;
    t.start();
  }

  // Entry point for the thread that runs the banner.
  public void run() {
    char ch;

    // Display banner
    for( ; ; ) {
      try {
        repaint();
        Thread.sleep(delay);
        ch = msg.charAt(0);
        msg = msg.substring(1, msg.length());
        msg += ch;
        if(stopFlag)
          break;
      } catch(InterruptedException exc) {}
    }
  }

  // Pause the banner.
  public void stop() {
    stopFlag = true;
    t = null;
  }

  // Display the banner.
  public void paint(Graphics g) {
    g.drawString(msg, 50, 30);
  }
}
```

4. Extra challenge: Create an applet that displays the current time, updated once per second. To accomplish this, you will need to do a little research. Here is a hint to help you get started: One way to obtain the current time is to use a **Calendar** object, which is part of the **java.util** package. (Remember, Sun provides online documentation for all of Java's standard classes.) You should now be at the point where you can examine the **Calendar** class on your own and use its methods to solve this problem.

```java
// A simple clock applet.

import java.util.*;
import java.awt.*;
import java.applet.*;
/*
<object code="Clock" width=200 height=50>
</object>
*/

public class Clock extends Applet implements Runnable {
  String msg;
  Thread t;
  Calendar clock;

  boolean stopFlag;

  // Initialize
  public void init() {
    t = null;
    msg = "";
  }

  // Start thread
  public void start() {
    t = new Thread(this);
    stopFlag = false;
    t.start();
  }

  // Entry point for the clock.
  public void run() {
    // Display clock
    for( ; ; ) {
      try {
        clock = Calendar.getInstance();
        msg = "Current time is " +
              Integer.toString(clock.get(Calendar.HOUR));
        msg = msg + ":" +
              Integer.toString(clock.get(Calendar.MINUTE));
```

```
        msg = msg + ":" +
               Integer.toString(clock.get(Calendar.SECOND));
        repaint();
        Thread.sleep(1000);
        if(stopFlag)
          break;
      } catch(InterruptedException exc) {}
    }
  }

  // Pause the clock.
  public void stop() {
    stopFlag = true;
    t = null;
  }

  // Display the clock.
  public void paint(Graphics g) {
    g.drawString(msg, 30, 30);
  }
}
```

5. Briefly explain Java's delegation event model.

In the delegation event model, a *source* generates an event and sends it to one or more *listeners*. A listener simply waits until it receives an event. Once received, the listener processes the event and then returns.

6. Must an event listener register itself with a source?

Yes; a listener must register with a source to receive events.

7. Extra challenge: Another of Java's display methods is **drawLine( )**. It draws a line in the currently selected color between two points. It is part of the **Graphics** class. Using **drawLine( )**, write a program that tracks mouse movement. If the button is pressed, have the program draw a continuous line until the mouse button is released.

```
/* Track mouse motion by drawing a line
   when a mouse button is pressed. */

import java.awt.*;
import java.awt.event.*;
import java.applet.*;
/*
  <applet code="TrackM" width=300 height=100>
  </applet>
*/

public class TrackM extends Applet
```

```java
implements MouseListener, MouseMotionListener {

int curX = 0, curY = 0; // current coordinates
int oldX = 0, oldY = 0; // previous coordinates
boolean draw;

public void init() {
   addMouseListener(this);
   addMouseMotionListener(this);
   draw = false;
}

/* The next three methods are not used, but must
   be null-implemented because they are defined
   by MouseListener. */

// Handle mouse entered.
public void mouseEntered(MouseEvent me) {
}

// Handle mouse exited.
public void mouseExited(MouseEvent me) {
}

// Handle mouse click.
public void mouseClicked(MouseEvent me) {
}

// Handle button pressed.
public void mousePressed(MouseEvent me) {
  // save coordinates
  oldX = me.getX();
  oldY = me.getY();
  draw = true;
}

// Handle button released.
public void mouseReleased(MouseEvent me) {
  draw = false;
}

// Handle mouse dragged.
public void mouseDragged(MouseEvent me) {
  // save coordinates
  curX = me.getX();
  curY = me.getY();
  repaint();
}
```

```
// Handle mouse moved.
public void mouseMoved(MouseEvent me) {
  // show status
  showStatus("Moving mouse at " + me.getX() + ", " + me.getY());
}

// Display line in applet window.
public void paint(Graphics g) {
  if(draw)
    g.drawLine(oldX, oldY, curX, curY);
}
}
```

8. Briefly describe the **assert** keyword.

The **assert** keyword creates an assertion, which is a condition that should be true during program execution. If the assertion is false, an **AssertionError** is thrown.

9. Give one reason why a native method might be useful to some types of programs.

A native method is useful when interfacing to routines written in languages other than Java, or when optimizing code for a specific run-time environment.

Module 15: Introducing Swing

1. In general, AWT components are heavyweight and Swing components are *lightweight*.

2. Can the look and feel of a Swing component be changed? If so, what feature enables this?

Yes. Swing's pluggable look and feel is the feature that enables this.

3. What is the most commonly used top-level container for an application?

JFrame

4. Top-level containers have several panes. To what pane are components added?

Content pane

5. Show how to construct a label that contains the message "Select an entry from the list."

JLabel("Select an entry from the list")

6. All interaction with GUI components must take place on what thread?

event-dispatching thread

7. What is the default action command associated with a **JButton**? How can the action command be changed?

The default action command string is the text shown inside the button. It can be changed by calling **setActionCommand( )**.

8. What event is generated when a push button is pressed?

ActionEvent

9. Show how to create a text field that has 32 columns.

```
JTextField(32)
```

10. Can a **JTextField** have its action command set? If so, how?

Yes, by calling **setActionCommand( )**.

11. What Swing component creates a check box? What event is generated when a check box is selected or deselected?

JCheckBox creates a check box. An **ItemEvent** is generated when a check box is selected or deselected.

12. **JList** displays a list of items from which the user can select. True or False?

True

13. What event is generated when the user selects or deselects an item in a **JList**?

ListSelectionEvent

14. What method sets the selection mode of a **JList**? What method obtains the index of the first selected item?

setSelectionMode( ) sets the selection mode. **getSelectedIndex( )** obtains the index of the first selected item.

15. To create a Swing-based applet, what class must you inherit?

JApplet

16. Usually, Swing-based applets use **invokeAndWait( )** to create the initial GUI. True or False?

True

17. Add a check box to the file comparer developed in Project 15-1 that has the following text: Show position of mismatch. When this box is checked, have the program display the location of the first point in the files at which a mismatch occurs.

```
/*
     Project 15-1

     A Swing-based file comparison utility.

     This version has a check box that causes the
     location of the first mismatch to be shown.
*/

import java.awt.*;
import java.awt.event.*;
import javax.swing.*;
```

```java
import java.io.*;

class SwingFC implements ActionListener {

  JTextField jtfFirst;  // holds the first file name
  JTextField jtfSecond; // holds the second file name

  JButton jbtnComp; // button to compare the files

  JLabel jlabFirst, jlabSecond; // displays prompts
  JLabel jlabResult; // displays results and error messages

  JCheckBox jcbLoc; // check to display location of mismatch

  SwingFC() {

    // Create a new JFrame container.
    JFrame jfrm = new JFrame("Compare Files");

    // Specify FlowLayout for the layout manager.
    jfrm.setLayout(new FlowLayout());

    // Give the frame an initial size.
    jfrm.setSize(200, 220);

    // Terminate the program when the user closes the application.
    jfrm.setDefaultCloseOperation(JFrame.EXIT_ON_CLOSE);

    // Create the text fields for the file names.
    jtfFirst = new JTextField(14);
    jtfSecond = new JTextField(14);

    // Set the action commands for the text fields.
    jtfFirst.setActionCommand("fileA");
    jtfSecond.setActionCommand("fileB");

    // Create the Compare button.
    JButton jbtnComp = new JButton("Compare");

    // Add action listener for the Compare button.
    jbtnComp.addActionListener(this);

    // Create the labels.
    jlabFirst = new JLabel("First file: ");
    jlabSecond = new JLabel("Second file: ");
    jlabResult = new JLabel("");

    // Create check box.
```

```
    jcbLoc = new JCheckBox("Show position of mismatch");

    // Add the components to the content pane.
    jfrm.add(jlabFirst);
    jfrm.add(jtfFirst);
    jfrm.add(jlabSecond);
    jfrm.add(jtfSecond);
    jfrm.add(jcbLoc);
    jfrm.add(jbtnComp);
    jfrm.add(jlabResult);

    // Display the frame.
    jfrm.setVisible(true);
  }

  // Compare the files when the Compare button is pressed.
  public void actionPerformed(ActionEvent ae) {
    int i=0, j=0;
    int count = 0;
    FileInputStream f1;
    FileInputStream f2;

    // First, confirm that both file names have
    // been entered.
    if(jtfFirst.getText().equals("")) {
      jlabResult.setText("First file name missing.");
      return;
    }
    if(jtfSecond.getText().equals("")) {
      jlabResult.setText("Second file name missing.");
      return;
    }

    // Open first file.
    try {
      f1 = new FileInputStream(jtfFirst.getText());
    } catch(FileNotFoundException exc) {
      jlabResult.setText("First file not found.");
      return;
    }

    // Open second file.
    try {
      f2 = new FileInputStream(jtfSecond.getText());
    } catch(FileNotFoundException exc) {
      jlabResult.setText("Second file not found.");

      // Close the first file if the second file
```

```
      // cannot be opened.
      try {
        f1.close();
      } catch(IOException exc2) {
        jlabResult.setText("Cannot close first file.");
      }

      return;
    }

    // Compare files.
    try {
      do {
        i = f1.read();
        j = f2.read();
        if(i != j) break;
        count++;
      } while(i != -1 && j != -1);

      if(i != j) {
        if(jcbLoc.isSelected())
          jlabResult.setText("Files differ at location " + count);
        else
          jlabResult.setText("Files are not the same.");
      }
      else
        jlabResult.setText("Files compare equal.");

    } catch(IOException exc) {
      jlabResult.setText("File Error");
    }

    try {
      f1.close();
    } catch(IOException exc) {
      jlabResult.setText("Error closing first file.");
    }

    try {
      f2.close();
    } catch(IOException exc) {
      jlabResult.setText("Error closing second file.");
    }

  }

  public static void main(String args[]) {
    // Create the frame on the event dispatching thread.
```

A

Answers to Mastery Checks

```
      SwingUtilities.invokeLater(new Runnable() {
        public void run() {
          new SwingFC();
        }
      });
    }
}
```

18. Change the **ListDemo** program so that it allows multiple items in the list to be selected.

```
// Demonstrate multiple selection in a JList.

import javax.swing.*;
import javax.swing.event.*;
import java.awt.*;
import java.awt.event.*;

class ListDemo implements ListSelectionListener {

  JList jlst;
  JLabel jlab;
  JScrollPane jscrlp;

  // Create an array of names.
  String names[] = { "Sherry", "Jon", "Rachel",
                     "Sasha", "Josselyn",  "Randy",
                     "Tom", "Mary", "Ken",
                     "Andrew", "Matt", "Todd" };

  ListDemo() {
    // Create a new JFrame container.
    JFrame jfrm = new JFrame("JList Demo");

    // Specify a flow Layout.
    jfrm.setLayout(new FlowLayout());

    // Give the frame an initial size.
    jfrm.setSize(200, 160);

    // Terminate the program when the user closes the application.
    jfrm.setDefaultCloseOperation(JFrame.EXIT_ON_CLOSE);

    // Create a JList.
    jlst = new JList(names);

    // By removing the following line, multiple selection (which
    // is the default behavior of a JList) will be used.
//    jlst.setSelectionMode(ListSelectionModel.SINGLE_SELECTION);

    // Add list to a scroll pane.
```

```
      jscrlp = new JScrollPane(jlst);

      // Set the preferred size of the scroll pane.
      jscrlp.setPreferredSize(new Dimension(120, 90));

      // Make a label that displays the selection.
      jlab = new JLabel("Please choose a name");

      // Add list selection handler.
      jlst.addListSelectionListener(this);

      // Add the list and label to the content pane.
      jfrm.add(jscrlp);
      jfrm.add(jlab);

      // Display the frame.
      jfrm.setVisible(true);
    }

    // Handle list selection events.
    public void valueChanged(ListSelectionEvent le) {
      // Get the indices of the changed item.
      int indices[] = jlst.getSelectedIndices();

      // Display the selections, if one or more items
      // was selected.
      if(indices.length != 0) {
        String who = "";

        // Construct a string of the names.
        for(int i : indices)
          who += names[i] + " ";

        jlab.setText("Current selections: " + who);
      }
      else // Otherwise, reprompt.
        jlab.setText("Please choose a name");
    }

    public static void main(String args[]) {
      // Create the frame on the event dispatching thread.
      SwingUtilities.invokeLater(new Runnable() {
        public void run() {
          new ListDemo();
        }
      });
    }
  }
```

Appendix B

Using Java's Documentation Comments

A s explained in Module 1, Java supports three types of comments. The first two are the // and the /* */. The third type is called a *documentation comment*. It begins with the character sequence /**. It ends with */. Documentation comments allow you to embed information about your program into the program itself. You can then use the **javadoc** utility program (supplied with the JDK) to extract the information and put it into an HTML file. Documentation comments make it convenient to document your programs. You have almost certainly seen documentation generated with **javadoc**, because that is the way the Java API library was documented by Sun.

The javadoc Tags

The **javadoc** utility recognizes the following tags:

Tag	Meaning
@author	Identifies the author of a class.
{@code}	Displays information as-is, without processing HTML styles, in code font.
@deprecated	Specifies that a class or member is deprecated.
{@docRoot}	Specifies the path to the root directory of the current documentation.
@exception	Identifies an exception thrown by a method.
{@inheritDoc}	Inherits a comment from the immediate superclass.
{@link}	Inserts an in-line link to another topic.
{@linkplain}	Inserts an in-line link to another topic, but the link is displayed in a plain-text font.
{@literal}	Displays information as-is, without processing HTML styles.
@param	Documents a method's parameter.
@return	Documents a method's return value.
@see	Specifies a link to another topic.
@serial	Documents a default serializable field.
@serialData	Documents the data written by the **writeObject( )** or **writeExternal( )** methods.
@serialField	Documents an **ObjectStreamField** component.
@since	States the release when a specific change was introduced.
@throws	Same as **@exception**.
{@value}	Displays the value of a constant, which must be a **static** field.
@version	Specifies the version of a class.

Document tags that begin with an "at" sign (@) are called *stand-alone* tags, and they must be used on their own line. Tags that begin with a brace, such as {**@code**}, are called *in-line* tags, and they can be used within a larger description. You may also use other, standard HTML tags in a documentation comment. However, some tags such as headings should not be used, because they disrupt the look of the HTML file produced by **javadoc**.

You can use documentation comments to document classes, interfaces, fields, constructors, and methods. In all cases, the documentation comment must immediately precede the item being documented. When you are documenting a variable, the documentation tags you can use are **@see**, **@serial**, **@serialField**, {**@value**}, and **@deprecated**. For classes and interfaces, you can use **@see**, **@author**, **@deprecated**, **@param**, and **@version**. Methods can be documented with **@see**, **@return**, **@param**, **@deprecated**, **@throws**, **@serialData**, {**@inheritDoc**}, and **@exception**. A {**@link**}, {**@docRoot**}, {**@code**}, {**@literal**}, **@since**, or {**@linkplain**} tag can be used anywhere. Each tag is examined next.

@author

The **@author** tag documents the author of a class or interface. It has the following syntax:

@author *description*

Here, *description* will usually be the name of the author. You will need to specify the **-author** option when executing **javadoc** in order for the **@author** field to be included in the HTML documentation.

{@code}

The {**@code**} tag enables you to embed text, such as a snippet of code, into a comment. That text is then displayed as-is in code font, without any further processing such as HTML rendering. It has the following syntax:

{@code *code-snippet*}

@deprecated

The **@deprecated** tag specifies that a class, interface, or member is deprecated. It is recommended that you include **@see** or {**@link**} tags to inform the programmer about available alternatives. The syntax is the following:

@deprecated *description*

Here, *description* is the message that describes the deprecation. The **@deprecated** tag can be used in documentation for variables, methods, classes, and interfaces.

{@docRoot}

{**@docRoot**} specifies the path to the root directory of the current documentation.

@exception

The **@exception** tag describes an exception to a method. It has the following syntax:

@exception *exception-name explanation*

Here, the fully qualified name of the exception is specified by *exception-name,* and *explanation* is a string that describes how the exception can occur. The **@exception** tag can only be used in documentation for a method.

{@inheritDoc}

This tag inherits a comment from the immediate superclass.

{@link}

The {**@link**} tag provides an in-line link to additional information. It has the following syntax:

{@link *pkg.class#member text*}

Here, *pkg.class#member* specifies the name of a class or method to which a link is added, and *text* is the string that is displayed.

{@linkplain}

The {**@linkplain**} tag inserts an in-line link to another topic. The link is displayed in plain-text font. Otherwise, it is similar to {**@link**}.

{@literal}

The {**@literal**} tag enables you to embed text into a comment. That text is then displayed as-is, without any further processing such as HTML rendering. It has the following syntax:

{@literal *description*}

Here, *description* is the text that is embedded.

@param

The **@param** tag documents a parameter to a method or a type parameter to a class or interface. It has the following syntax:

@param *parameter-name explanation*

Here, *parameter-name* specifies the name of a parameter. The meaning of that parameter is described by *explanation*. The **@param** tag can be used only in documentation for a method, a constructor, or a generic class or interface.

@return

The **@return** tag describes the return value of a method. It has the following syntax:

@return *explanation*

Here, *explanation* describes the type and meaning of the value returned by a method. The **@return** tag can be used only in documentation for a method.

@see

The **@see** tag provides a reference to additional information. Its most commonly used forms are shown here:

@see *anchor*

@see *pkg.class#member text*

In the first form, *anchor* is a link to an absolute or relative URL. In the second form, *pkg.class#member* specifies the name of the item, and *text* is the text displayed for that item. The text parameter is optional, and if not used, then the item specified by *pkg.class#member* is displayed. The member name, too, is optional. Thus, you can specify a reference to a package, class, or interface in addition to a reference to a specific method or field. The name can be fully qualified or partially qualified. However, the dot that precedes the member name (if it exists) must be replaced by a hash character.

@serial

The **@serial** tag defines the comment for a default serializable field. It has the following syntax:

@serial *description*

Here, *description* is the comment for that field.

@serialData

The **@serialData** tag documents the data written by the **writeObject( )** and **writeExternal( )** methods. It has the following syntax:

@serialData *description*

Here, *description* is the comment for that data.

@serialField

For a class that implements **Serializable**, the **@serialField** tag provides comments for an **ObjectStreamField** component. It has the following syntax:

@serialField *name type description*

Here, *name* is the name of the field, *type* is its type, and *description* is the comment for that field.

@since

The **@since** tag states that a class or member was introduced in a specific release. It has the following syntax:

@since *release*

Here, *release* is a string that designates the release or version in which this feature became available.

@throws

The **@throws** tag has the same meaning as the **@exception** tag.

{@value}

{@value} has two forms. The first displays the value of the constant that it precedes, which must be a **static** field. It has this form:

{@value}

The second form displays the value of a specified **static** field. It has this form:

{@value *pkg.class#field*}

Here, *pkg.class#field* specifies the name of the **static** field.

@version

The **@version** tag specifies the version of a class. It has the following syntax:

@version *info*

Here, *info* is a string that contains version information, typically a version number, such as 2.2. You will need to specify the **-version** option when executing **javadoc** in order for the **@version** field to be included in the HTML documentation.

The General Form of a Documentation Comment

After the beginning /**, the first line or lines become the main description of your class, variable, or method. After that, you can include one or more of the various @ tags. Each @ tag must start at the beginning of a new line or follow one or more asterisks (*) that are at the start of a line. Multiple tags of the same type should be grouped together. For example, if you have three **@see** tags, put them one after the other. In-line tags (those that begin with a brace) can be used within any description.

Here is an example of a documentation comment for a class:

```
/**
 * This class draws a bar chart.
 * @author Herbert Schildt
 * @version 3.2
 */
```

What javadoc Outputs

The **javadoc** program takes as input your Java program's source file and outputs several HTML files that contain the program's documentation. Information about each class will be in its own HTML file. **javadoc** will also output an index and a hierarchy tree. Other HTML files can be generated.

An Example that Uses Documentation Comments

Following is a sample program that uses documentation comments. Notice the way each comment immediately precedes the item that it describes. After being processed by **javadoc**, the documentation about the **SquareNum** class will be found in **SquareNum.html**.

```java
import java.io.*;

/**
 * This class demonstrates documentation comments.
 * @author Herbert Schildt
 * @version 1.2
 */
public class SquareNum {
  /**
   * This method returns the square of num.
   * This is a multiline description.  You can use
   * as many lines as you like.
   * @param num The value to be squared.
   * @return num squared.
   */
  public double square(double num) {
    return num * num;
  }

  /**
   * This method inputs a number from the user.
   * @return The value input as a double.
   * @exception IOException On input error.
   * @see IOException
   */
  public double getNumber() throws IOException {
    // create a BufferedReader using System.in
    InputStreamReader isr = new InputStreamReader(System.in);
    BufferedReader inData = new BufferedReader(isr);
    String str;

    str = inData.readLine();
    return (new Double(str)).doubleValue();
  }

  /**
   * This method demonstrates square().
```

```
 * @param args Unused.
 * @exception IOException On input error.
 * @see IOException
 */
public static void main(String args[])
  throws IOException
{

  SquareNum ob = new SquareNum();
  double val;

  System.out.println("Enter value to be squared: ");
  val = ob.getNumber();
  val = ob.square(val);

  System.out.println("Squared value is " + val);
  }
}
```

Index